America Now

Short Readings from Recent Periodicals

America Now

Short Readings from Recent Periodicals
Fifth Edition

Edited by

ROBERT ATWAN
Series Editor, *The Best American Essays*
Director, The Blue Hills Writing Institute at Curry College

Exercises prepared with the assistance of

Jennifer Ivers
Boston University

Kathleen O'Brien
Boston University

Bedford / St. Martin's   Boston ◆ New York

For Bedford / St. Martin's

Developmental Editor: Ellen Thibault
Production Editor: Kendra LeFleur
Production Manager: Pat Ollague
Marketing Manager: Brian Wheel
Editorial Assistant: Christine Turnier-Vallecillo
Production Assistant: Tina Lai
Copyeditor: Lisa Wehrle
Text Design: Jean Hammond
Cover Design: Hannus Design Associates
Cover Digital Photography: Lightstream
Composition: Pine Tree Composition, Inc.
Printing and Binding: Haddon Craftsman, Inc.

President: Joan E. Feinberg
Editorial Director: Denise B. Wydra
Editor in Chief: Karen S. Henry
Director of Marketing: Karen Melton
Director of Editing, Design, and Production: Marcia Cohen
Managing Editor: Elizabeth M. Schaaf

Library of Congress Control Number: 2002112254

For information, write: Bedford / St. Martin's, 75 Arlington Street, Boston, MA 02116 (617-399-4000)

ISBN: 0–312–40174–4

Acknowledgments

Ad Council National Campaign Against Youth Violence (advertisement). "Kalie Was My Baby Sister." Reprinted courtesy of the Ad Council and The National Crime Prevention Council.

The Advocate (cover image). "Mark Bingham, Person of the Year." *The Advocate,* January 22, 2002. ©2002 by Liberation Publications, Inc.

Preface for Instructors

People write for many reasons, but one of the most compelling is to express their views on matters of current public interest. Browse any newsstand, library magazine rack, or Web portal home page and you'll find an abundance of articles and opinion pieces responding to current issues and events. The fifth edition of *America Now* retains its generous sampling of this timely and provocative material.

America Now is designed to immerse introductory writing students in the give-and-take of public dialogue and to stimulate thinking, discussion, and composition. Its overriding instructional principle — which informs everything from the choice of readings and topics to the design of questions — is that participation in informed discussion will help generate and enrich student writing. The book systematically encourages its users to view reading, thinking, discussion, and writing as closely interrelated activities. It assumes that (1) attentive reading and reflection will lead to informed discussion; (2) participation in open and informed discussion will result in a broadening of viewpoints; (3) an awareness of different viewpoints will stimulate further reflection and renewed discussion; and (4) this process in turn will lead to thoughtful papers. The book's general introduction, "The Empowered Writer," briefly takes the student through the process and offers some useful guidelines for engaging in productive discussion. Instructors may also find helpful my essay "Writing and the Art of Discussion," which can be found in the Instructor's Edition and online at the *America Now* Web site.

New to This Edition

Eighty-three selections — all new and *very* current. Drawn from fifty recent periodicals, including twenty-two online student newspapers, every essay is not only new to the book but — perhaps more important — has appeared within a year or two of the book's publication. Over half the selections were published in 2002. *America Now* is the most up-to-date short essay reader available.

Eight new issues of current interest. Eight of the fifteen thematic chapters have been changed in this edition to reflect the changing interests of students over the past two years and to stimulate discussion and writing. Among these topics are sexism and language, animal rights, cloning, and reparations for slavery.

A greater focus on argumentation. The **Opposing Views** throughout the book now include both students and professionals debating animal rights, and the connections between toy guns and violence. New **Student Forums** feature a broad diversity of opinion on such controversial issues as God and the Constitution and reparations for slavery.

A greater number and variety of visual elements. Among the book's twenty-three black-and-white images are nine new opinion or advocacy advertisements ("Op-Ads") on issues such as racial profiling, the separation of church and state, gun control, and animal rights. Other images include a magazine cover and several photographs, comic strips, and cartoons. The all-new first chapter, with its visual focus, shows students how a memorable 9/11 photograph of three firefighters at the World Trade Center led to a heated debate about history and public memorials.

New **"America Then"** selections, such as an 1847 runaway slave poster and a 1944 ad for bodybuilding, provide students with historical contexts for today's issues. These images introduce an entirely new visual feature to the book and appear in seven of the fifteen chapters.

New annotated Web links — titled *Read It Now, See It Now,* or *Hear It Now* — appear in each chapter and point students to specific essays, interviews, photos, music, and speeches that relate to the topic at hand. These links build a new guided research component into the book to help students extend their reading, thinking, and writing about the issues in *America Now.*

New companion Web site (bedfordstmartins.com/americanow) provides students with access to the latest essays on topics covered in the book. Links to **New Readings** will be periodically updated and added to, and the front page of the site will indicate what's new and where you can find it. In addition to the readings, the site will offer research resources for each chapter, easy access to the links in the book, and electronically scored *ESL and Developmental Quizzes* for each unit.

Using America Now

Professional and Student Writing from a Wide Variety of Sources

The book's thirty-two selections from professional writers are drawn from twenty-eight recent periodicals, ranging from professional journals such as *The Black Scholar* to influential general magazines such as *The Atlantic Monthly* and *Harper's*. As would be expected in a collection that focuses heavily on social trends and current events, *America Now* features a wide variety of newspapers and news-oriented magazines: the *Boston Globe*, the *New York Times*, the *San Francisco Chronicle*, the *Wall Street Journal, Time, Newsweek*, and both the *New York Times Magazine* and the *Washington Post Magazine*. With its additional emphasis on public discourse, this collection also draws on some of America's leading political magazines: *The Nation, The Progressive, Mother Jones, The National Review*. Magazines appealing primarily to specialized audiences such as *Brain, Child; Columbia Journalism Review;* and the *Chronicle of Higher Education* are also represented along with two popular online periodicals, *Africana.com* and *Salon.com*. In general, the selections illustrate the variety of personal, informative, and persuasive writing read daily by millions of Americans. In addition to their range and interest, the selections are short (many under three pages, and some no longer than a page) to keep student interest and to serve as models for the student's own writing, generally assigned to be about the same length.

America Now also features twenty-nine published student selections — essays, ads, and cartoons — almost all of which appeared in college newspapers across the country that are available on the Internet. These recent works reveal student writers confronting in a public forum the same topics and issues that challenge some of our leading social critics and commentators and show how student writers can enter into and influence public discussion. In this way, *America Now* encourages students to view the act of writing as a form of personal and public empowerment. Too frequently, students see the writing they do in a composition class as having little connection with real-world problems and issues.

The student selections in the book prove that writing can make a difference, and since they clearly display what students write about on their own outside of class, the student selections are sure to spark lively, interesting discussion inside the classroom.

Opposing Views on Timely Topics
for Discussion and Debate

Student essays not only make up a large percentage of this edition, they also shape the volume's contents. As we monitored the broad spectrum of college newspapers available on the Internet — and reviewed several hundred student essays — we gradually found the most commonly discussed campus issues and topics. Certain issues, such as reparations for slavery, racial profiling, the legacy of 9/11, animal rights, and the renewed meaning of patriotism, have provoked so much recent student response that they could have resulted in several single-topic collections. Many college papers do not restrict themselves to news items and editorial opinion but make room for personal essays as well. Some popular student topics were gender, group identity, heroes and role models, and body image, all of which are reflected in the book's table of contents.

To facilitate group discussion and in-class work, *America Now* features fourteen bite-sized units and one longer, in-depth chapter. These tightly focused chapters permit instructors to cover a broad range of themes and issues in a single semester. Each unit can be conveniently handled in one or two class periods. In general, the chapters move from accessible, personal topics (for example, body image, identity, and gender) to more public issues (guns, animal rights, cloning), thus accommodating instructors who prefer to start with personal writing and gradually progress to exposition, analysis, and argument.

Since composition courses naturally emphasize issues revolving around language and the construction of meaning, *America Now* also includes several chapters designed to encourage students to examine the powerful influence of words and symbols. Language issues also surface in many selections throughout the book.

For instructors who want to concentrate on developing argumentation skills, the book arranges several controversial topics into **Opposing Views** and **Student Forums.** Opposing Views feature both students and professionals debating race in America, ethics, the separation of church and state, and violence, and in Student Forums students express a range of opinion on issues relating to government, law, and civil liberties. In addition, one longer chapter (on reparations for slavery) provides instructors with an opportunity to cover a controversial issue in depth.

The Role of the Internet

Nearly all of the student pieces were located on the Internet. *America Now* was the first composition reader to draw heavily on this rapidly expanding resource for readers, writers, and anyone interested in discussion of current political and cultural affairs. As Web pages, chat rooms, online forums, and other discussion sites proliferate, students will find a wide-open environment for sharing information, opinions, and concerns. All kinds of public forums are quickly growing more convenient and accessible; most periodicals, for example, now welcome e-mail responses, and today student writers can enter the public sphere as never before. In addition to student essays from Internet sources, *America Now* includes selections from several online magazines.

Because nearly all college campuses offer students electronic resources, the book's issues and topics can be examined in greater detail by means of Web links that appear in each chapter. *Read It Now, See It Now*, and *Hear It Now* features allow students to explore individual topics more extensively. The recommended Web sites are all easily accessible and cost nothing. For the most part, these sites will continually update information and thus help keep the *Now* in *America Now*.

The Visual Focus of Public Discussion Today

America Now encourages students to pay close attention to the persuasive power of language and images. Reflecting the growing presence of advertising in public discussion, among the book's twenty-two images are nine carefully selected advertisements designed by various groups and organizations to initiate public change. The ads — on issues such as racial profiling, the separation of church and state, gun control, and animal rights — are distributed throughout the book; students are encouraged to uncover the visual and verbal strategies of recent "opinion advertising" employed by various advocacy groups and intended to influence the consciousness and ideology of large audiences.

Along with the advertisements, the book features several visual texts aimed at demonstrating the persuasive combination of word and image. The first unit, for example, is intended to show students how a memorable photograph of firefighters at the World Trade Center on 9/11 led eventually to a heated controversy over the relation between historical accuracy and multicultural values. The photograph is followed by essays (one by the photographer himself) and student responses offering a range of opinion on whether a document should be in any way altered to honor diversity and promote inclusive values. The unit offers instructors the opportunity to discuss with students some of the ways the media can influence public opinion through photography and the construction of memorials.

Other visual texts include a magazine cover and several photographs, cartoons and comic strips — including a cartoon that asks us to consider the cultural significance of the burka and the bikini and a comic strip that uses humor to point out some societal attitudes toward guns. An assortment of visual selections — titled "America Then" — provides students with historical perspectives to "America Now." These images demonstrate that many of the current issues we're dealing with have roots in the past. They include a 1915 handgun ad in the toy guns and violence chapter; two World War II propaganda posters in the patriotism chapter along with a famous World War II photograph in the chapter on how 9/11 will be remembered in American history; an 1890s photograph that depicts runaway boys in the unit on gender; and a 1970s sci-fi film poster in the cloning chapter. Each of these historical images is accompanied by introductory notes that will help students make the connection between issues concerning America "then" and "now."

The Instructional Apparatus:
Before, During, and After Reading

The apparatus of *America Now* supports both discussion-based instruction and more individualized approaches to reading and writing. Taking into account the increasing diversity of students (especially the growing number of nonnative speakers) in today's writing programs, the apparatus offers extensive help with college-level vocabulary and features a "Words to Learn" list preceding each selection. This vocabulary list with brief definitions will allow students to spot ahead of time some of the words they may find difficult; encountering the word later in context will help lock it in memory. It's unrealistic, however, to think students will acquire a fluent knowledge of new words by memorizing a list. Therefore, the apparatus following each selection includes additional exercises under the headings "Vocabulary/Using a Dictionary" and "Responding to Words in Context." These sets of questions introduce students to prefixes, suffixes, connotations, denotations, tone, and etymology.

To help promote reflection and discussion, the book includes a prereading assignment for each main selection. The questions in "Before You Read" provide students with the opportunity to explore a few of the avenues that lead to fruitful discussion and interesting papers. A full description of the advantages gained by linking reading, writing, and classroom discussion can be found in my introduction to the instructor's manual.

Along with the discussion of vocabulary, incrementally structured questions follow individual selections. Picking up on the vocabulary lists preceding each selection, another question set, "Responding to Words in Context," supplements the existing "Vocabulary/Using a Dictionary" questions and asks students to use what they have learned from the dictionary exercises and vocabulary lists. Following the vocabulary questions, the "Discussing Main Point and Meaning" and "Examining Sentences, Paragraphs, and Organization" questions help to guide students step by step through the reading process, culminating in the set of "Thinking Critically" questions. As instructors well know, beginning students can sometimes be too trusting of what they see in print, especially in textbooks. Therefore, the "Thinking Critically" questions invite students to take a more skeptical attitude toward their reading and to form the habit of challenging a selection from both analytical and experiential points of view. The selection apparatus concludes with "In-Class Writing Activities," which emphasize freewriting exercises and collaborative projects.

In addition to the selection apparatus, *America Now* also contains end-of-chapter questions designed to stimulate further discussion and writing. The chapter apparatus approaches the reading material from topical and thematic angles with an emphasis on group discussion. The introductory comments to each chapter highlight the main discussion points and the way selections are linked together. These points and linkages are then reintroduced at the end of the chapter through three sets of interlocking study questions and tasks: (1) a suggested topic for discussion, (2) questions and ideas to help students prepare for class discussion, and (3) several writing assignments that ask students to move from discussion to composition — that is, to develop papers out of the ideas and opinions expressed in class discussion and debate. Instructors with highly diverse writing classes may find "Topics for Cross-Cultural Discussion" a convenient way to encourage an exchange of perspectives and experiences that could also generate ideas for writing. Located at the book's Web site are *ESL and Developmental Quizzes* that test vocabulary and comprehension skills. Electronic scoring, which can be monitored by instructors, offers immediate feedback.

The Instructor's Edition

Jennifer Ivers and Kathleen O'Brien, both of Boston University, prepared the instructor's manual (which is found in the Instructor's Edition of this book), bringing to the task not only a familiarity with the text but years of classroom experience at all levels of composition instruction. The manual contains an essay for each unit, offering suggestions for teaching the selections together and separately; and suggested answers and possible discussion topics based on every question posed in the text. Anyone using *America Now* should be sure to consult the manual before designing a syllabus, framing a discussion topic, or even assigning individual selections. Liz deBeer of Rutgers University also contributed a helpful essay on designing student panels ("Forming Forums") and advice on using the book's apparatus in both developmental and mainstream composition classes.

Acknowledgments

While putting together the fifth edition of *America Now* I was fortunate to receive the assistance of many talented individuals. In addition to their work on the instructor's manual, Jennifer Ivers and Kathleen O'Brien offered many useful suggestions for the book's instructional apparatus.

To revise a text is to entertain numerous questions: What kind of selections work best in class? What types of questions are most helpful? How can reading, writing, and discussion be most effectively intertwined? This edition profited immensely from the following instructors who generously took the time to respond to the last edition: Joan Blankmann, Northern Virginia Community College; Mikel Cole, University of Houston–Downtown; Kim Halpern, Pulaski Technical College; Sherry Manis, Foothill College; and Melody Nightingale, Santa Monica College. I'd also like to acknowledge instructors who reviewed the previous edition and whose ideas and suggestions have informed this fifth edition: Kim M. Baker, Roger Williams University; Diane Bosco, Suffolk County Community College; Steven Florzcyk, the State University of New York, New Paltz; Patricia W. Julius, Michigan State University; Jessica Heather Lourey, Alexandria Technical College; Michael Orlando, Bergen Community College; Hubert C. Pulley, Georgia Southern University; Andrea D. Shanklin, Howard Community College; Linda Weiner, the University of Akron; and Martha Anne Yeager-Tobar, Cerritos College.

Other people helped in various ways. I'm indebted to Barbara Gross of Rutgers University, Newark, for her excellent work in preparing the instructor's manual for the first edition. Two good friends, Charles O'Neill and Jack Roberts, both of St. Thomas Aquinas College, went over my early plans for the book and offered many useful suggestions.

As always, it was a pleasure to work with the superb staff at Bedford/St. Martin's. Jane Betz, my editor on the first edition, shaped the book in lasting ways and helped with the planning of the revision. Of all the people acknowledged, I owe the most gratitude to this edition's developmental editor, Ellen Thibault. Her insightful suggestions, remarkable good sense, and uncanny ability to keep track of so many minute details made this collection a pleasure to work on from start to finish. Christine Turnier-Vallecillo, this edition's editorial assistant, worked energetically on the instructor's edition and the book's Web site, and managed and cleared permissions for the many images in the book. Jason Reblando researched author headnotes and cleared text permissions under a tight schedule. Kendra LeFleur guided the book through production with patience and care, staying on top of many details, and Elizabeth Schaaf managed the production process with her usual attentiveness. I was fortunate to receive the careful copyediting of Lisa Wehrle. In the advertising and promotion department, Tom Macy, Hope Tompkins, and Jill Chmelko deserve warm thanks for their work.

I am grateful to Charles H. Christensen, the recently retired president of Bedford/St. Martin's, for his generous help and thoughtful suggestions throughout the life of this book. Finally, I especially want to thank Bedford's new president, Joan E. Feinberg, who conceived the idea for *America Now* and who continues to follow it closely through its various editions, for her deep and abiding interest in college composition. It is a great pleasure and privilege to work with her.

R. A.

Contents

1   How Will We Remember 9/11?   1

How should the tragic events of 9/11 be remembered? In years to come, will there be a public monument or memorial? Shortly after the attacks some New Yorkers decided to construct an enormous bronze sculpture to honor the city's heroic firefighters. It would be modeled after the famous photograph of three firefighters raising the American flag amidst the wreckage of Ground Zero. The only problem with this idea was that the proposed statue would revise the photograph by altering the identities of the firefighters. In place of the three white firefighters who raised the flag, there would be three different firefighters — one white, one African American, and one Hispanic. Was that political correctness run amuck? Would the proposed statue honor diversity or distort history?

Writing for one of the nation's most influential journalism reviews, the photojournalist who shot the famous Ground Zero picture argues that like "history itself, the photo should not be changed, even for the best of intentions".... A teen newsmagazine asks its readers whether the proposed statue was a "fitting tribute to the diversity of New York's heroes" and receives a spectrum of answers from students all over the nation.... A newspaper columnist thinks that the plan to doctor the photographs is "a perfect example of the mush the multiculturalists are making of our society."... How does another famous flag-raising photo snapped a half-century ago affect our response to the World Trade Center firefighter image?

2 Who Is a Hero — and Why?   25

For centuries, the word *hero* signified a brave and courageous
individual, but is the term's meaning changing in our time,
when it is commonly applied to comic book characters, movie
stars, and sports personalities? After the terrorist attacks of
9/11, do we now use the term differently, or does the word still
refer to the older virtues? Looking at Mark Bingham, one of the
passengers who most likely helped bring down one of the hijacked jetliners on 9/11, a *New York Times* reporter reflects on
the distinction the media was making between a "gay hero" and
a "hero who was gay." . . . That distinction made many of Mark
Bingham's friends uneasy, claims the nation's most influential
gay magazine in a profile of the brawny rugby player it named
"person of the year." . . . A Boston University student argues
that "real super heroes" may be found closer to home than you
may imagine. . . . A photographer succinctly shows us how
America selected and celebrated its heroes at a Halloween parade. . . . "What happens when we put every victim of tragedy

on a pedestal?" asks a newspaper correspondent who believes that the events of 9/11 resulted in "hero inflation."

3 Our Body Image: Is It a Serious Issue?   58

Opinion polls regularly show that most Americans are discontented with their appearance. Usually, women want to shed pounds and men want to gain muscle in the hope of achieving their "ideal" body image. Yet how attainable are these goals? And how does our body image affect our self-esteem? A newspaper editorial wonders whether women in bikinis may be as culturally restrained as women in burkas.... Though the garment may look wholly repressive to us, a syndicated cartoonist reveals some advantages of wearing a burka.... A Seattle University student finds the media images of the beauty "ideal" to be not only unhealthy but absurd.... A prominent cultural reporter argues that the Barbie Doll was not so innocent.... A 1944 bodybuilding ad sponsored by "The World's Most Perfectly Developed Man" promises transformation. How does it connect with the "ideal" male body of today?

4   Can We Choose Our Personal Identities?   83

Do you ever see yourself as a representative of an ethnic or racial group? How important is it to your sense of identity to belong to this particular group? How do you identify yourself if, like so many Americans, you belong to more than one ethnic or racial group? A literature professor and activist feels "blessed to inhabit" two different worlds. . . . "My father is an Asian . . . and my mother is Caucasian, so where does that leave me?" asks an entering college freshman. . . . A Yale junior warns Americans that it's insensitive to turn a deeply respected cultural or religious symbol into an exotic fashion statement.

5   What Is America? Who Are Americans?   102

We live in a period of growing ethnic and cultural diversity. Is this trend pulling America apart into fragmented groups, or is it a sign of our national vitality? Responding to the most recent U.S. census, a Native American anthropologist wonders whether

we can choose a race, or does race choose us?... A prominent Hispanic author and radio commentator believes that the
"trouble with today's ethnic and racial and sexual identifications
is that they threaten to become evasions of more general citizenship." ... "What is our concept of assimilation?" asks a Muslim
Arab American from Florida State University.... An advertisement suggests that assimilation and integration are threatened
because our government does not declare English as our national
language and as a result too many immigrants fail to learn it.

6   Can Gender Equality Truly Exist?   126

Do males and females behave as though they come from different planets? Can gender differences be overcome so that a true
equality between the sexes is possible? Who gets short-changed
more by our society — boys or girls? A noted humorist proposes
a few tests that will "scientifically" determine whether you are
male or female.... "Are American boys in far worse shape than
girls?" An organization called Supporting Our Sons seems to
think so. ... If a widening war on terror requires the reinstate-
ment of the military draft, asks a California Polytechnic student,
will women continue to remain excluded? ... "Going toe to toe
with men is a feminist act; going drink for drink with them
isn't," says the headline to a *Time* magazine column.

7 **Sexism and Language:
Do Pronouns Make a Difference?**   **155**

When writing, is it necessary to avoid the all-purpose masculine
pronoun in favor of more inclusive constructions? Or is one
simply being trivial or politically correct in insisting on a gender-
neutral grammar? What differences does it make whether we
use masculine pronouns or not? A major weekly news magazine
reports on a new, "gender-neutral" translation of the Bible....
A University of Nebraska student defends the new translation
as a step in the right direction.... Masculine pronouns have
nothing to do with a person's sex but derive instead from "the
unique demands of English grammar," argues the opinion editor of Western Michigan University's school paper.

8 **Can Words Be Dangerous?**   **173**

Do the words we use make any difference? Can they create hos-
tile environments? Can they have awesome political conse-
quences? What personal or social risks do some words carry?
A prominent African American Web site wonders why the
N-word is acceptable for blacks to use but not for whites....
"What's wrong with cursing and vulgar language?" asks a

9   God and the Constitution: How Separate Must They Be?   196

When our founders agreed on a First Amendment that prohibited Congress from establishing a national religion or from denying anyone religious freedom, how far did they intend their restrictions to go? Did they want to prohibit all forms of religious expression and public display? Six students respond to a University of Arizona newspaper editorial that asks if the motto "In God We Trust" can legally be placed in public schools.... The Anti-Defamation League urges Americans to maintain a strong "wall separating church and state".... A federal judge rules in a highly controversial decision that the present text of the Pledge of Allegiance is unconstitutional.... "Does this country really want to reach the point where every mention of religion needs to be eliminated in the name of constitutional purity?" asks a San Francisco newspaper.

10   What Does Patriotism Mean?   223

Patriotism: what does the word mean to you? Does it conjure
up images of national pride and honor? Or does it suggest conformity and fanaticism? An African American editorial writer
celebrates today's "spacious, postmodern patriotism." . . . What
does my country want me to do, wonders a noted essayist and
humorist, simply go out and shop? . . . A World War II poster
depicts the meaning of sacrifice. . . . Let's make sure the love of
our country doesn't lead to the rejection of its principles, warns
a University of Virginia newspaper editor.

11   Guns and Violence: Is There a Connection?   247

Gun control and firearm regulation have been divisive issues in America for many years. As violent crime increases, do people believe they need guns for protection? Or does the availability of guns create the violent crime? A parent's magazine sponsors a debate over toy guns for children — are they harmless, or do they contribute to violent behavior?... What happens when a student writes an anti-gun poem? One cartoonist considers the consequences.... The National Crime Prevention Council takes out an ad warning parents to lock up their guns. . . . The National Rifle Association places an ad promoting "the right to bear arms." ... A Georgetown University student wonders why cuddly teddy bears receive more federal safety regulations than firearms.... A 1915 gun ad taps into the fear of "drug fiends" to promote a revolver. Would such an ad appear today?

12   Can We Prevent Racial Profiling?   274

What exactly does *racial profiling* mean? Do you think identifying potential criminals by means of race, ethnicity, or other observable features is a necessary part of law enforcement? Or do you believe that any such selection represents racial discrimination? America's leading financial paper argues that our national safety should take precedence over an individual's inconvenience.... Profiling "provokes unnecessary fear and fuels further discrimination and segregation," says a Northern Arizona University student.... A celebrated public figure is more likely to be stopped by police than a convicted mass murderer, a stark advertisement contends.... What do "racial profiling" and "affirmative action" have in common? asks a noted African American law professor.

13 Do Animals Possess Rights?   297

Do you think animal experimentation is necessary for medical progress that will save countless human lives, or do you think it is cruel and unnecessary? Should we take a more compassionate and ethical view towards animals, or should we proceed even further and grant them legal rights that would hold up in a court of law? An internationally prominent expert on apes describes the "fuzzy" distinction between us and them.... On college campuses, two leading activist organizations use advertising to oppose primate experimentation.... Primate research is "absolutely essential" if we want to eliminate many diseases that plague our society, claims an ad in support of animal experimentation.... A University of Utah student finds it hard to believe that some would deny a "small child life because it may be at the expense of

14   Should Human Cloning Be Allowed?   318

If human cloning is a real scientific possibility, what should our position be? Does it offer us a remarkable medical opportunity that will save countless lives through tissue and organ transplants? Or will it lead to a moral nightmare that will destroy human nature as we know it? A prominent libertarian author defends scientific progress, while two conservative critics of cloning point out the "post-human" horrors that lay ahead if scientists proceed unrestrained. . . . Human cloning "is just about impossible," claims a San Francisco State biology professor in his response to the debate. . . . No sooner was a theory of cloning scientifically advanced in the early 1970's than a science fiction film proclaimed its dangers. . . . A University of Oregon student finds that the sci-fi horrors of cloning can't match the real-life horrors of patients dying needlessly from the serious shortage of donated organs. . . . A college cartoonist pictures the biotechnological future.

15   Should Reparations Be Paid for Slavery?   343

Should African Americans receive reparations as payment for
centuries of slavery? A new movement is now emerging that believes reparations would be a just way to compensate black
Americans for the physical suffering and economic misery inflicted on their ancestors. But resistance to reparations is also
strong, and many questions persist: should all African American
individuals receive a government check? Or should the money go
to social and educational programs to benefit the most economi-
cally distressed communities? Why would anyone whose ancestors came to the United States after slavery was abolished be expected to pay anything? The author of the best-seller *The Debt*
explains why the time has come for reparations. . . . One of the
nation's leading African American legislators describes why Congress must "undertake an official study of the impact of slavery
on the social, political and economic life of our nation." . . . An
historic ad vividly demonstrates the bitter reality of slavery. . . .
Three African American scholars respond to an antireparations
ad that provoked heated campus controversy across the na-

tion. . . . When "you trade on the past victimization of your own people, you trade honor for dollars," argues a noted black essayist. . . . Student opinion on reparations is widely divided as is evidenced by college writers from the University of Michigan, the University of Minnesota, the University of Wisconsin-Madison, Purdue University, and the University of Louisville.

Introduction:
The Empowered Writer

It is not possible to extricate yourself from the question in which your age is involved.

–Ralph Waldo Emerson

What Is America Now?

America Now collects very recent essays and articles that have been carefully selected to encourage reading, provoke discussion, and stimulate writing. The philosophy behind the book is that interesting, effective writing originates in public dialogue. The book's primary purpose is to help students proceed from class discussions of reading assignments to the production of complete essays that reflect an engaged participation in those discussions.

The selections in *America Now* come from two main sources — from popular, mainstream periodicals and from college newspapers available on the Internet. Written by journalists and columnists, public figures and activists as well as by professors and students from all over the country, the selections illustrate the types of material read by millions of Americans every day. In addition to magazine and newspaper writing, the book also features a number of recent opinion advertisements (what I call "Op-Ads" for short). These familiar forms of "social marketing" are often sponsored by corporations or nonprofit organizations and advocacy groups to promote policies, programs, and ideas such as gun control, family planning, literacy, civil rights, or conservation. Such advertising texts allow one to pinpoint and discuss specific techniques of verbal and visual persuasion that are critical in the formation of public opinion.

The selections are gathered into fifteen units that cover today's most widely discussed issues and topics: racial profiling, cloning, reparations, the aftermath of 9/11, violence, gender inequalities, the separation of church and state, and so on. As you respond to the readings in discussion, debate, and writing, you will be actively taking part in the major controversies of our time.

Although I have tried in this new edition of *America Now* to represent as many viewpoints as possible on a variety of controversial topics, it's not of course possible in a collection of this scope to include under each topic either a full spectrum of opinion or a universally satisfying balance of opposing opinions. For some featured topics, an entire book would be required to represent the full spectrum of opinion; for others, a rigid pro-con, either-or format could distort the issue and perhaps overly polarize student responses to it. Selections within a unit will usually illustrate the most commonly held opinions on a topic so that readers will get a reasonably good sense of how the issue has been framed and the public discourse and debate it has generated. But if a single opinion isn't immediately or explicitly balanced by an opposite opinion, or if a view seems unusually idiosyncratic, that in no way implies that it is somehow editorially favored or endorsed. Be assured that questions following *every* selection will encourage you to analyze and critically challenge whatever opinion or perspective is expressed in that selection.

Participation is the key to this collection. I encourage you to view reading and writing as a form of participation. I hope you will read the selections attentively, think about them carefully, be willing to discuss them in class, and use what you've learned from your reading and discussion as the basis for your papers. If you do these things, you will develop three skills necessary for successful college work and beyond: the ability to read critically, to discuss topics intelligently, and to write persuasively.

America Now invites you to see reading, discussion, and writing as closely related activities. As you read a selection, imagine that you have entered into a discussion with the author. Take notes as you read. Question the selection. Challenge its point of view or its evidence. Compare your experience with the author's. Consider how different economic classes or other groups are likely to respond. Remember, just because something appears in a newspaper or book doesn't make it true or accurate. Form the habit of challenging what you read. Don't be persuaded by an opinion simply because it appears in print or because you believe you should accept it. Trust your own observations and experiences. Though logicians never say so, personal experiences and keen observations often provide the basis of our most convincing arguments.

When your class discusses a selection, be especially attentive to what others think of it. It's always surprising how two people can read the same article and reach two entirely different interpretations. Observe the range of opinion. Try to understand why and how people arrive at different conclusions. Do some seem to be missing the point? Do some distort the author's ideas? Have someone's comments forced you to rethink the selection? Keep a record of the discussion in your notebook. Then, when you begin to draft your paper, consider your essay as an extension of both your imaginary conversation with the author and the actual class discussion. If you've taken detailed notes of your own and the class's responses to the selection, you should have more than enough information to get started.

Participating in Class Discussion: Six Basic Rules

Discussion is a learned activity. It requires a variety of essential academic skills: speaking, listening, thinking, and preparing. The following six basic rules are vital to healthy and productive discussion.

1. *Take an active speaking role.* Good discussion demands that everyone participates, not (as so often happens) just a vocal few. Many students remain detached from discussion because they are afraid to speak in a group. This fear is quite common — so common that psychological surveys show that speaking in front of a group is generally one of our worst fears. A leading communication consultant suggests that people choke up because they are more worried about how others will respond than about what they themselves have to say. It helps to remember that most people will be more interested in *what* you say than in how you say it. Once you get over the initial fear of speaking in public, your speech skills will improve with practice.

2. *Listen attentively.* No one can participate in group discussion who doesn't listen attentively. This may sound obvious, but just think of how many senseless arguments you've had because either you or the person with whom you were talking completely misunderstood what was said. A good listener not only hears what someone is saying but understands *why* he or she is saying it. One of the most important things about listening is that it leads to one element that lively discussion depends on: good questions. When the interesting questions begin to emerge, you know good discussion has truly begun.

3. *Examine all sides of an issue.*   Good discussion requires that we be patient with complexity. Difficult problems rarely have obvious and simple solutions, nor can they be easily summarized in popular slogans. Complex issues demand to be turned over in our minds so that we can see them from a variety of angles. Group discussion will broaden our perspective and deepen our insight into difficult issues and ideas.

4. *Suspend judgment.*   Class discussion is best conducted in an open-minded and tolerant spirit. To fully explore ideas and issues, you will need to be receptive to the opinions of others even when they contradict your own. Remember, discussion is not the same as debate. Its primary purpose is communication, not competition. In discussion you are not necessarily trying to win everyone over to your point of view. The goal of group discussion should be to open up a topic so that everyone in the group will be exposed to a spectrum of attitudes. Suspending judgment does not mean you shouldn't hold a strong belief or opinion about an issue; it means that you should be willing to take into account rival beliefs or opinions. An opinion formed without an awareness of other points of view—one that has not been tested against contrary ideas—is not a strong opinion but merely a stubborn one.

5. *Avoid abusive or insulting language.*   Free and open discussion can only occur if we respect the beliefs and opinions of others. If we speak in ways that fail to show respect for differing viewpoints— if we resort to name-calling or use demeaning and malicious expressions, for example—we not only embarrass ourselves but we close off the possibility for an intelligent and productive exchange of ideas. Contrary to what you might gather from some popular radio and television talk shows, shouting insults and engaging in hate-speech are signs of verbal and intellectual bankruptcy. They are usually the last resort of someone who has nothing to say.

6. *Come prepared.*   Discussion is not merely random conversation. It demands a certain degree of preparation and focus. To participate in class discussion, you must consider assigned topics beforehand and read whatever is required. You should develop the habit of reading with pen in hand, underlining key points and jotting down questions, impressions, and ideas in your notebook. The notes you bring to class will be an invaluable aid in group discussion.

Group Discussion as a Source of Ideas

Group discussion can stimulate and enhance your writing in several important ways. First, it supplies you with ideas. Let's say that you are participating in a discussion about how we express personal identity (see Unit 4). One of your classmates mentions some of the problems a mixed ethnic background can cause. But suppose you also come from a mixed background, and, when you think about it, you believe that your mixed heritage has given you more advantages than disadvantages. Hearing her viewpoint may inspire you to express your differing perspective on the issue. Your perspective could lead to an interesting personal essay.

Suppose you now start writing that essay. You don't need to start from scratch and stare at a blank piece of paper or computer screen for hours. Discussion has already given you a few good leads. First, you have your classmate's opinions and attitudes to quote or summarize. You can begin your paper by explaining that some people view a divided ethnic identity as a psychological burden. You might expand on your classmate's opinion by bringing in additional information from other student comments or from your reading to show how people often focus on only the negative side of mixed identities. You can then explain your own perspective on this topic. Of course, you will need to give several examples showing *why* a mixed background has been an advantage for you. The end result can be a first-rate essay, one that takes other opinions into account and demonstrates a clearly established point of view. It is personal, and yet it takes a position that goes beyond one individual's experiences.

Whatever the topic, your writing will benefit from reading and discussion, activities that will give your essays a clear purpose or goal. In that way, your papers will resemble the selections found in this book: They will be a *response* to the opinions, attitudes, experiences, issues, ideas, and proposals that inform current public discourse. This is why most writers write; this is what most newspapers and magazines publish; this is what most people read. *America Now* consists entirely of such writing. I hope you will read the selections with enjoyment, discuss the issues with an open mind, and write about the topics with purpose and enthusiasm.

The Practice of Writing

Suppose you wanted to learn to play the guitar. What would you do first? Would you run to the library and read a lot of books on music? Would you then read some instructional books on guitar playing? Might you try to memorize all the chord positions? Then would you get sheet music for songs you liked and memorize them? After all that, if someone handed you an electric guitar, would you immediately be able to play like Jimi Hendrix or Eric Clapton?

I don't think you would begin that way. You would probably start out by strumming the guitar, getting the feel of it, trying to pick out something familiar. You would probably want to take lessons from someone who knows how to play. And you would practice, practice, practice. Every now and then your instruction book would come in handy. It would give you basic information on frets, notes, and chord positions, for example. You might need to refer to that information constantly in the beginning. But knowing the chords is not the same as knowing how to manipulate your fingers correctly to produce the right sounds. You need to be able to *play* the chords, not just know them.

Learning to read and write well is not that much different. Though instructional books can give you a great deal of advice and information, the only way anyone really learns to read and write is through constant practice. The only problem, of course, is that nobody likes practice. If we did, we would all be good at just about everything. Most of us, however, want to acquire a skill quickly and easily. We don't want to take lesson after lesson. We want to pick up the instrument and sound like a professional in ten minutes.

Wouldn't it be a wonderful world if that could happen? Wouldn't it be great to be born with a gigantic vocabulary so we instantly knew the meaning of every word we saw or heard? We would never have to go through the slow process of consulting a dictionary whenever we stumbled across an unfamiliar word. But, unfortunately, life is not so easy. To succeed at anything worthwhile requires patience and dedication. Watch a young figure skater trying to perfect her skills and you will see patience and dedication at work; or watch an accident victim learning how to maneuver a wheelchair so he can begin again an independent existence; or observe a new American struggling to learn English. None of these skills is quickly and easily acquired. Like building a vocabulary, they all take time and effort. They all require practice. And they require something even more important: the willingness to make mistakes. Can someone learn to skate without taking a spill? Or learn a new language without mispronouncing a word?

Writing as a Public Activity

Many people have the wrong idea about writing. They view writing as a very private act. They picture the writer sitting all alone and staring into space waiting for ideas to come. They think that ideas come from "deep" within and only reach expression after they have been fully articulated inside the writer's head.

These images are part of a myth about creative writing and, like most myths, are sometimes true. A few poets, novelists, and essayists do write in total isolation and search deep inside themselves for thoughts and stories. But most writers have far more contact with public life. This is especially true of people who write regularly for magazines, newspapers, and professional journals. These writers work within a lively social atmosphere in which issues and ideas are often intensely discussed and debated. Nearly all the selections in this book illustrate this type of writing.

As you work on your own papers, remember that writing is very much a public activity. It is rarely performed alone in an "ivory tower." Writers don't always have the time, the desire, the opportunity, or the luxury to be all alone. They may be writing in a newsroom with clacking keyboards and noise all around them; they may be writing at a kitchen table, trying to feed several children at the same time; they may be writing on subways or buses. The great English novelist D. H. Lawrence grew up in a small impoverished coal miner's cottage with no place for privacy. It proved to be an enabling experience. Throughout his life he could write wherever he happened to be; it didn't matter how many people or how much commotion surrounded him.

There are more important ways in which writing is a public activity. Much writing is often a response to public events. Most of the articles you encounter every day in newspapers and magazines respond directly to timely or important issues and ideas, topics that people are currently talking about. Writers report on these topics, supply information about them, discuss and debate the differing viewpoints. The units in this book all represent topics now regularly discussed on college campuses and in the national media. In fact, all of the topics were chosen because they emerged so frequently in college newspapers.

When a columnist decides to write on a topic like reparations for slavery, she willingly enters an ongoing public discussion about the issue. She didn't just make up the topic. She knows that it is a serious issue, and she is aware that a wide variety of opinions have been expressed about it. She has not read everything on the subject but usually knows enough about the different arguments to state her own position or attitude persuasively. In fact, what helps make her writing persuasive is that she takes into account the opinions of others. Her own essay, then, becomes a part of the continuing debate and discussion, one that you in turn may want to join.

Such issues are not only matters for formal and impersonal debate. They also invite us to share our *personal* experiences. Many of the selections in this book show how writers participate in the discussion of issues by drawing on their experiences. For example, the short essay by Brent Staples, "The Meaning of That Star-Spangled Hard Hat," is based largely on the author's personal observations and experience, though the topic—patriotic respect for the American flag — is one widely discussed and debated by countless Americans, especially since the attacks of September 11, 2001. Nearly every unit of *America Now* contains a selection that illustrates how you can use your personal experiences to discuss and debate a public issue.

Writing is public in yet another way. Practically all published writing is reviewed, edited, and re-edited by different people before it goes to press. The author of a magazine article has most likely discussed the topic at length with colleagues and publishing professionals and may have asked friends or experts in the field to look it over. By the time you see the article in a magazine, it has gone through numerous readings and probably quite a few revisions. Though the article is credited to a particular author, it was no doubt read and worked on by others who helped with suggestions and improvements. As a beginning writer, it's important to remember that most of what you read in newspapers, magazines, and books has gone through a writing process that involves the collective efforts of several people besides the author. Students usually don't have that advantage and should not feel discouraged when their own writing doesn't measure up to the professionally edited materials they are reading for a course.

What Is "Correct English"?

One part of the writing process may seem more difficult than others—correct English. Yes, nearly all of what you read will be written in relatively correct English. Or it's probably more accurate to say "corrected" English, since most published writing is revised or "corrected" several times before it appears in print. Even skilled professional writers make mistakes that require correction.

Most native speakers don't actually *talk* in "correct" English. There are numerous regional patterns and dialects. As the Chinese American novelist Amy Tan says, there are "many Englishes." What we usually consider correct English is a set of guidelines developed over time to help standardize written expression. This standardization—like any agreed-upon standards such as weights and measures—is a matter of use and convenience. Suppose you went to a vegetable stand and asked for a pound of peppers and the storekeeper gave you a half pound but charged you for a full one. When you complained, he said, "But that's what *I* call a pound." What if you next bought a new compact disc you've been waiting for, and when you tried to play it you discovered it wouldn't fit your CD player. Life would be very frustrating if everyone had a different set of standards: Imagine what would happen if some towns used a red light to signal "go" and a green one for "stop." Languages are not that different. In all cultures, languages—especially written languages—have gradually developed certain general rules and principles to make communication as clear and efficient as possible.

You probably already have a guidebook or handbook that systematically sets out certain rules of English grammar, punctuation, and spelling. Like our guitar instruction book, these handbooks serve a very practical purpose. Most writers—even experienced authors—need to consult them periodically. Beginning writers may need to rely on them far more regularly. But just as we don't learn how to play chords by merely memorizing finger positions, we don't learn how to write by memorizing the rules of grammar or punctuation.

Writing is an activity, a process. Learning how to do it — like learning to ride a bike or prepare a tasty stew—requires *doing* it. Correct English is not something that comes first. We don't need to know the rules perfectly before we can begin to write. As in any activity, corrections are part of the learning process. You fall off the bike and get on again, trying to "correct" your balance this time. You sample the stew and "correct" the seasoning. You draft a paper about the neighborhood you live in and as you (or a classmate or instructor) read it over, you notice that certain words and expressions could stand some improvement. And step by step, sentence by sentence, you begin to write better.

Writing as Empowerment

Writing is one of the most powerful means of producing social and political change. Through their four widely disseminated gospels, the first-century evangelists helped propagate Christianity throughout the world; the writings of Adam Smith and Karl Marx determined the economic systems of many nations for well over a century; Thomas Jefferson's Declaration of Independence became a model for countless colonial liberationists; the carefully crafted speeches of Martin Luther King Jr. and the books and essays of numerous feminists have altered twentieth-century consciousness. In the long run, many believe, "the pen is mightier than the sword."

Empowerment does not mean instant success. It does not mean that your opinion or point of view will suddenly prevail. It does mean, however, that you have made your voice heard, that you have given your opinions wider circulation, that you have made yourself and your position a little more visible. And sometimes you get results: a newspaper prints your letter; a university committee adopts your suggestion; people visit your Web site. Throughout this collection you will encounter writing specifically intended to inform and influence a wide community.

Such influence is not restricted to professional authors and political experts. This collection features a large number of student writers who are actively involved with the same current topics and issues that engage the attention of professionals—reparations, group identity, gun control, gender differences, cloning, and so on. The student selections, all of them previously published and written for a variety of reasons, are meant to be an integral part of each unit, to be read in conjunction with the professional essays, and to be criticized and analyzed on an equal footing. The student writing stands up.

America Now urges you to voice your ideas and opinions—in your notebooks, in your papers, in your classrooms, and, most important, on your campus and in your communities. Reading, discussing, and writing will force you to clarify your observations, attitudes, and values, and as you do you will discover more about yourself and the world. These are exciting times. Don't sit on the sidelines of controversy. Don't retreat into invisibility and silence. Jump in and confront the ideas and issues currently shaping America.

America Now

Short Readings from Recent Periodicals

1

How Will We Remember 9/11?

Every so often a controversy arises that touches on so many different issues that it helps define and clarify our underlying national tensions. At first, the plan appeared wholly appropriate: to construct a suitable monument to honor the firefighters who died during the terrorist attack on the World Trade Center. Yet once the plan was publicly disclosed, it ignited a heated controversy that provoked responses throughout the nation. The monument's designer had decided to model a 19-foot bronze statue after the now-famous photograph depicting three New York City firefighters raising the U.S. flag above a small mountain of debris at Ground Zero (see p. 3). But in the interests of honoring the diversity of the city's firefighters, the memorial's planners deviated from the photograph so that instead of three white firemen the statue would depict a white, an African American, and a Latino. The immediate public response was so negative — even the three firefighters opposed the monument — that the design for the memorial was abandoned. Though that particular monument will not be built, the controversy continues and the issues it raises will become an inseparable part of all future memorials.

In "The After-Life of a Photo That Touched a Nation," Thomas Franklin, the photojournalist who snapped the photograph that became a symbol of American patriotism after the terrorist attacks, describes how the photo — from the very moment it was first published — has "taken on a life of its own." Despite the good intentions of the proposed monument, Franklin argues, to alter the photograph would be to distort history. This topic is picked up by Debbie Nevins in

1

"The Colors of Courage." In covering the issue for *Teen Newsweek*, Nevins invites her student readers to consider a question: "Was the proposed statue a fitting tribute to the diversity of New York's heroes? Or did it alter the truth for the sake of political good intentions?" The responses she received from students throughout the nation show how opinions vary depending on the way one views the purposes of a memorial and the importance of multiculturalism. One especially strong opinion on the matter is voiced by columnist Steve Tefft in an essay with a title that makes his position crystal clear, "A Monument to Multicultural Mush."

In the final selection we look at a similar photograph taken over fifty years ago during one of the fiercest battles of World War II. This photo also took on a life of its own, being widely copied in various media from Hollywood movies to U.S. postage stamps. Tom Franklin's World Trade Center photograph may make us wonder how much the power of his image depends on the public's recognition of Joe Rosenthal's now-classic photo of the flag raising at Iwo Jima, a photo that also has provoked a good deal of controversy about historical authenticity and patriotic sentiment.

How will 9/11 live in memory? The first anniversary commemorations did not perhaps offer a reliable guide to what that day will mean ten or twenty years from now, since the ongoing news coverage of the event has been incessant and has hardly allowed the events to fade from memory. Still, psychologists studying the effects of 9/11 memories have already noted some false recollections. For example, nearly 75% of Americans polled nationally confidently claim to have seen on television that morning the two hijacked jetliners crash into the twin towers of the World Trade Center, despite the fact that there was no available video that day of the first crash. As the research progresses, psychologists believe they will find more and more inaccuracies, as the events take on mythic proportions. Over time, psychological studies will no doubt also investigate what effect these distorted memories have on the planning and construction of a fitting memorial.

Web **Read It and See It Now:** "America Remembers 9/11," **bedfordstmartins.com/ americanow,** Chapter 1. Hosted by CNN, this retrospective site offers hundreds of documents, images, and the texts and videos of memorial services.

Web **Read It, See It, Hear It Now:** "9/11 Digital Archive," **bedfordstmatrins.com/ americanow,** Chapter 1. Maintained by George Mason University and the City University of New York, this archive of interviews, images, and audio recordings preserves 9/11 histories.

Web **Read It Now:** "After September 11th: An Online Reader for Writers," **bedford stmartins.com/americanow**, Chapter 1. This page, hosted by Bedford / St. Martin's, provides educational resources and coverage of 9/11 memorials.

Web **See It Now:** "Images from Ground Zero," **bedfordstmartins.com/americanow**, Chapter 1. This exhibit presents select images by Joel Meyerowitz, the only photographer allowed unrestricted access to Ground Zero.

THOMAS E. FRANKLIN

The After-Life of a Photo That Touched a Nation

[COLUMBIA JOURNALISM REVIEW / March–April 2002]

Before You Read

How important are photographs in journalism? How important are they to the historical record? What about memorials? When memorials refer to historical events, should they represent actual moments with strict accuracy — or can they also present emotions or memories stirred by the event?

Words to Learn

Ground Zero (para. 1): military term that usually refers to the exact location (the coordinates) of a bomb or explosion (n.)

unceremonious (para. 2): informal; abrupt (adj.)

sentiment (para. 6): expression of tender emotion (n.)

accolades (para. 6): praise; approval (n.)

memorial (para. 7): monument or holiday designed to establish re-membrance of a person or event (adj., n.)

propaganda (para. 7): material distributed to support a cause or doctrine; often used negatively (n.)

ironic (para. 9): having the opposite of an intended effect (adj.)

credibility (para. 11): worthiness of belief; trustworthiness (n.)

chronicler (para. 11): one who records, in order, the events of history (n.)

THOMAS E. FRANKLIN *(b. 1953) has been a staff photographer for the* Bergen Record *in New Jersey since 1993. He received Photo of the Year Awards from* Editor & Publisher Magazine *and the* Associated Press Managing Editors.

Much of what happened to me on September 11 is a blur, but   1
this moment I clearly remember: It was 4:45 P.M., and all the firemen
and rescue workers were evacuating Ground Zero after word came
that a third building — WTC 7 — was ready to fall. I had only a few
frames left, and an entire day's worth of pictures to develop, so I prepared to head back to New Jersey.

Before leaving, I took one last look at Ground Zero. Three fire-   2
fighters were attaching an American flag to a slanted pole while
standing on top of a pile of rubble about fifteen feet high. I was about
thirty yards away, and I zoomed in and fired off a few frames with
my digital camera. The flag-raising itself was spontaneous and unceremonious. It took only a few minutes, and I don't think the firemen
had any idea they were being watched. One firefighter hoisted the
flag up as the other two looked on. I shot a burst of frames as it went
up, then ran to where they were. But before I could shoot any more
they disappeared into the crowd leaving the area.

It was over like that, or so I thought.   3

This photograph of three New York City firemen raising the flag   4
has become to many the symbol of that horrific day. From the very
moment it was first published in *The Record*, it has taken on a life of
its own, and has lodged in the public consciousness like no other
photograph since the flag-raising on Iwo Jima.

I have received thousands of letters, e-mails, and phone calls.   5
Many just wanted to tell me how much this image meant to them, how
it lifted them and gave them hope at a time of deep despair. Others
called it a symbol of strength and courage, a reminder that Americans
were united and strong. Former New York Mayor Rudolph Giuliani
called it "one of the most important photographs I have ever seen."

The outpouring of sentiment touched me, yet at times saddened   6
me as well. A fellow photographer in New England e-mailed to say
how awesome he thought the photo was, then told me about his dad,
who was among the missing. His story and countless others haunt
me. The pain of that day still hovers over this picture, a ghostly reminder that, behind all the attention and accolades, so many important lives were lost.

My photograph has been used in ways I never could have imag-   7
ined. Christmas tree ornaments, pumpkin carvings, figurines, coins,
jewelry, T-shirts, and plaques — all without authorization. It was
reenacted at the World Series and the Super Bowl, and reproduced on
country barns and people's lawns. It was at the core of a heated debate over a memorial statue, and was scattered across Afghanistan by

the U.S. military, part of its propaganda campaign. I have driven past 30-foot murals of it painted on the sides of buildings, and seen it staring back at me from bumper stickers in traffic jams.

While covering the World Series in October, I had the strange experience of having an unwitting storeowner try to sell me the photograph on decals. A colleague, Dave Adornato, and I were shopping for FDNY hats outside Yankee Stadium before the game, when Dave saw the decals for sale. "Hey Tom, there's your photo," he said. The man with the decals held one up and studied it, then studied my face. "Doesn't look like you," he said. Dave told him that I was the photographer. "Oh," he said. "In that case, special price for you."

8

> *When you change the elements of a news photograph, it diminishes the credibility of photojournalists as chroniclers of history.*

The recent flap over the firefighter memorial statue, which was to be modeled after my photo, was unfortunate, yet so ironic. The three firemen in the photo are white, but the statue was to depict a white, a Latino, and an African American [see **See It Now**, p. 13]. After an outcry, the memorial's planners went back to the drawing board. I am disappointed that the photograph — the source of so much unity and pride — became the subject of such division.

9

On September 11, it was difficult to pack my emotions away and focus on my job. I was scared. I wanted to be home with my wife and family. I thought about my older brother, Stephen, who works in lower Manhattan and takes the train through the World Trade Center each morning. But everything I saw was so worthy of photographing. The huge, smoldering mound of metal beams and concrete and cables. Firemen searching for survivors. Rescue workers shuffling back and forth, while others stood around in shock. I recorded it all. I understood how important my job was; that images like mine would be looked at throughout history.

10

I support the idea of a memorial representing diversity, but when you change the elements of a news photograph, or in this case the statue of that photograph, it diminishes the credibility of photojournalists as chroniclers of history. The picture I took on September 11 captures an important moment. Like history itself, the photo should not be changed, even for the best of intentions.

11

The fact that countless people have told me that my work has given them hope in a difficult time gives me great satisfaction. It's my hope that this picture can continue to unite us.

12

Vocabulary/Using a Dictionary

1. What does the term *Ground Zero* (para. 1) mean in reference to the 9/11 tragedy?

2. What words does *memorial* (para. 7) resemble?

3. Given the definition of *chroniclers* (para. 11), what do you think *chronological* means? How about *synchronous*?

Responding to Words in Context

1. In paragraph 2, Franklin speaks of "[shooting] a burst of frames." Examine his word choice and use of imagery here. Do you think he chose these words on purpose?

2. Franklin says that his photograph has come to be a "symbol" of 9/11 to many people (para. 4). What is a symbol, given this statement? What other famous American symbols can you think of?

3. Franklin writes that the U.S. military used the photographs as "part of its propaganda campaign" (para. 7). What are the different meanings of the word *propaganda*? Why might Franklin have chosen this word?

Discussing Main Point and Meaning

1. Examine Franklin's photograph. Describe what you see to be the meaning of the firefighters' gesture. How do you feel about it personally? What is the most prominent element of the photograph: the firefighters, the wreckage, or the flag?

2. What is Franklin's main purpose in writing this essay? Can you identify any passages where you think he is trying to argue rather than merely describe?

3. Why does Franklin list the many uses to which his photograph has been put in paragraphs 7 and 8 before discussing the planned memorial in paragraph 9?

4. Reread paragraph 11. Why does Franklin think that the memorial should not alter the image in his photograph? How is the "credibility of photojournalists" related to the historical record? How would changing Franklin's photograph be like or unlike changing the many other reproductions: stickers, Christmas tree ornaments, T-shirts, and so on?

Examining Sentences, Paragraphs, and Organization

1. In the first sentence of this piece Franklin writes that seeing the three firefighters raise the flag brought clarity to what was otherwise a "blur" of memories. Does this transition from blurriness to clarity seem an appropriate starting point to you? Why or why not?

2. Paragraph 3 is but one sentence: "It was over like that, or so I thought." Describe both the content and form of this paragraph, and how the surrounding paragraphs relate to each other.

3. Why does Franklin include the anecdote of the decal salesman in paragraph 8? Why does he include the man's comment, "special price for you"?

Thinking Critically

1. Do you think that Franklin — as the photographer of the famous picture — has a unique perspective on this issue? Are you more or less inclined to agree with him because he took the photograph? Explain your answer.

2. In paragraph 10, Franklin discusses his experience on September 11, when he felt that everything he saw was "worthy of photographing." What does this mean? Is this perspective reflected in any other 9/11 images that you've seen that were taken by other photographers?

In-Class Writing Activities

1. Weigh in on this controversy by writing an essay about what you think an appropriate memorial to the 9/11 firefighters would be. Would it involve Franklin's photo at all? Would the accuracy of the moment matter as much as the general truth and feelings the memorial evokes? Sketch out the appearance of your memorial if you need to, but be sure to describe the main features in some detail.

2. Franklin's essay begins with a description of a moment on 9/11 that he remembers very clearly. Think of a moment on that day that you remember very clearly — whether it was watching televised coverage of the events, listening to the radio, or trying to reach loved ones on the phone. How is that moment symbolic of the event for you? Why does it stand out in your mind?

DEBBIE NEVINS

The Colors of Courage: Did a Proposed 9/11 Statue Distort History or Honor Diversity?

[TEEN NEWSWEEK / February 4, 2002]

Before You Read

What is the relationship between the concerns and politics of today and the recordings of history? Should inclusiveness or political correctness be allowed to affect or distort the way we represent important events? Are memorials obligated to portray facts?

Words to Learn

hoist (para. 1): erect; heave (v.)
evoke (para. 1): call to mind (v.)
GI (para. 1): general infantry soldier (n.)

solidarity (para. 1): unity; camaraderie (n.)
furor (para. 5): uproar; disturbance (n.)

You know the image. Probably everyone in the country has seen   1
the picture. Three firefighters hoist a battered American flag over the
ruins of the World Trade Center. Their pose hauntingly evokes an
earlier photo of World War II GIs raising the flag in Iwo Jima.
Thomas Franklin's now-famous photograph is one of the most powerful images from September 11. In it we see the intense horror of the

---

DEBBIE NEVINS (b. 1953) is a former high school teacher and newspaper reporter. She is currently the managing editor of Teen Newsweek. *Nevin has been recognized with awards from the* New England Press Association *and the* Educational Press Association of America.

wreckage. But we also see the patriotism and solidarity of New York's many heroes — qualities that inspired the nation.

When a New York businessman decided to erect a memorial to the 343 firefighters killed that day, Franklin's image seemed to be the perfect choice to serve as a model.   2

The 19-foot-high, $180,000 bronze statue was to go outside Fire Department Headquarters in Brooklyn.   3

The statue looked just like the photo, but there was one difference. In the photo, the three firefighters are white. In the statue, the men were portrayed as a white, an African American, and a Hispanic.   4

The proposed statue set off a furor. By changing the races of the firefighters, critics charged, the artist was distorting history. After days of heated public debate last month, Fire Commissioner Nicholas Scoppetta canceled the controversial statue. He said he "will consider new options" for a memorial.   5

Was the proposed statue a fitting tribute to the diversity of New York's heroes? Or did it alter the truth for the sake of political good intentions?   6

Honor for All!

The monument was never meant to portray the event literally, supporters say. As art, the statue was an interpretation of a larger reality. The figures in the statue were to be symbols of all firefighters, not just portraits of three actual men, they say. As such, the figures were to honor the diversity of the firefighters killed in the attack and that of the city itself.   7

> By changing the race of the firefighters, critics charged, the artist was distorting history.

Of the 343 firefighters who died that day, 12 were black and another 12 were Hispanic.   8

"Given that those who died were of all races and all ethnicities, and that the statue was to be symbolic of those sacrifices, ultimately a decision was made to honor no one in particular, but everyone who made the supreme sacrifice," Fire Department spokesman Frank Gribbon said.   9

Don't Rewrite History!

Carlo Casoria, who lost his firefighter son, Thomas, said, "They're rewriting history in order to achieve political correctness." (Being "politically correct" means going to unnecessary lengths to avoid causing offense, usually in matters of race, ethnicity or gender.)   10

Firefighter Tony Marden of Ladder 165 in Queens, New York, 11
called the decision "an insult to those three guys to put imaginary
faces on that statue. It's not a racial thing. That shouldn't even be an
issue."

The three firefighters in the photograph — George Johnson, Dan 12
McWilliams, and Bill Eisengrein — are themselves opposed to any
rendering of the scene that does not depict them.

A memorial honoring heroes of all races is fine, many critics say. 13
Just don't alter the historic truth to achieve it.

What Do You Think?

Was the statue as planned the right tribute to New York's fire- 14
fighters?

Let us know at Letters@teennewsweek.com. 15

[For a sampling of responses, see the next section. The letters are
reprinted as they appeared in *Teen Newsweek*.]

Responses to "The Colors of Courage," by Debbie Nevins

Dear Teen Newsweek,

I am writing in regards to the article titled "The Colors of 1
Courage" (issue 17). I was shocked when I read that race is still a big
argument at a time when our country needs unity.

My father has been a firefighter for twenty-three years and I have 2
just started my career as a firefighter as well. It did not take me long
to discover the brotherhood of all firefighters. No matter what race
or sex, a firefighter will always help his brother firefighter. The [N.Y.
firefighters] have said the three guys that raised the flag were not just
symbolizing white firefighters but it was a symbol of ALL New York
firefighters. To my father and me, when you wear the badge you are
no longer a race of some sort but you are now a firefighter and it is
your duty to help others and your fellow firefighters no matter what
race or gender.

— *Coolville, OH*

I think the way they changed the statue is not right at all. It wasn't 3
a black, white, and Hispanic who hoisted the flag on that fateful day —
it was three white Americans. If you would like to make a cultural

diversity memorial, think of another creative way to do it. Those three men should not have any part of that memory taken from them.

— *Emmett, ID*

I think making the statue with diversity is a very good thing. It   4
represents all those who died helping others on September 11. The only thing that the statue is missing, if it wants to represent everyone accurately, is a woman. . . .

— *Portland, TN*

The [memorial] should be something that not only represents   5
[the losses of] 9/11 but the fact that it was indeed a wake-up call. It helped people come together, it made us all stronger, and helped to appreciate the very thing that we take for granted everyday . . . LIFE!

— *Belpre, OH*

I believe that the proposed statue was not the right tribute to the   6
New York firefighters. I also think that in worrying so much about being politically correct we are dividing the country into racial groups. When do we, as a people, decide to get past the ethnic groups, unite as a country, and see ourselves as Americans?

— *Toledo, OH*

We believe instead of making the three people portrayed in the   7
statue different races they should remain faceless and genderless because this statue should immortalize ALL men and women of different races who gave their lives to save countless others.

— *Louisville, KY*

What the sculptor did was a lie. The sculptor didn't need to   8
change the men's faces for they already represented our county as a whole.

— *Portland, TN*

. . . In my opinion, the statue honored diversity. It's not fair if it   9
seems only the white men are being honored, so I think it was a wise decision to make the statue the way the artist did.

— *West Milwaukee, WI*

. . . the last thing that New York needs right now is another conflict.   10

— *Holland, PA*

... I think that it doesn't really matter what the statue looks like 11
as long as we're all safe in our world and nation.

— *Walsenburg, CO*

Web **See It Now:** Flag Raising at Ground Zero, bedfordstmartins.com/americanow,
Chapter 1. Take a look at a clay model of the proposed firefighter memorial
statue. The image accompanies a *Newsday* editorial about the statue and the
goals of art and journalism.

Web **Read It Now:** "Ground Zero Statue Criticized," bedfordstmartins.com/
americanow, Chapter 1. This CNN article provides perspectives on the controversial statue — from firefighters, attorneys, and the newspaper that holds
the copyright of the image it was based on. Also included are links to articles
about other 9/11 memorials.

Web **Read and See It Now:** "Ideas for Memorials," bedfordstmartins.com/
americanow, Chapter 1. This page, hosted by the *Gotham Gazette*, provides
links to numerous proposals (and accompanying images) for a World Trade
Center memorial, with links to the latest news on the topic.

Vocabulary/Using a Dictionary

1. How is the word *evoke* (para. 1) similar to the word *provoke*?
   What do you think their shared root (*vocāre*) means?

2. What words does the word *furor* (para. 5) remind you of?

3. Nevins defines *political correctness* in paragraph 10. Is her definition consistent with what you would have guessed the expression to mean? Would you alter or add to her definition in any
   way?

Responding to Words in Context

1. Nevins describes the proposed memorial as a "19-foot-high,
   $180,000 bronze statue" (para. 3). Why do you think she
   chooses to highlight the size and cost of the planned sculpture?

2. Nevins quotes a Fire Department spokesperson who calls the
   deaths of the firefighters on 9/11 a "supreme sacrifice" (para. 9).

What is the definition of *supreme*? How does it relate to the actions of the firefighters?

Discussing Main Point and Meaning

1. Does Nevins have a point of view on this issue, or do you think she stays neutral throughout the article? Cite evidence from the text to support your answer.

2. Describe the similarities you find in the photograph of the firefighters on 9/11 and the photo of soliders in Iwo Jima during World War II (p. 21). Are there any differences?

3. Nevins gives the exact number of the black and Hispanic firefighters who died on 9/11 (para. 8). Why does she do this? Does it affect your position on the proposed memorial at all?

4. The three firefighters in the famous photograph are said to be opposed to altering the original image of them in any way. Why does their opinion matter in the context of the debate? Should they have the right to decide whether the photo is changed? Why or why not?

5. In the written responses to Nevins's piece, several students seem to express no overt opinion on whether to change the image of the firefighters. Do these nonpositions in effect present another kind of position? If so, what?

Examining Sentences, Paragraphs, and Organization

1. "You know the image" is the opening line of this article. What kind of tone does this sentence set?

2. There are several section headings in this article: "Honor for All!" "Don't Rewrite History!" and "What Do You Think?" Why do you think the author breaks up this essay in such a manner?

3. Do the letters responding to Nevins represent a diversity of opinions? Are those opinions organized in any specific structure? If so, what effect do you think the sequence of letters is meant to have?

Thinking Critically

1. Critics of the proposed memorial charge that "the artist was distorting history" (para. 5). What responsibility, if any, does an

artist have to history? Does history take priority over artistic vision? Explain your answer.

2. Why do many people respond emotionally to the sight of the flag being raised in the aftermath of destruction? Would a different image — of a firefighter ascending the stairs of one of the burning towers or carrying someone from the wreckage — be a more fitting tribute? Are Americans too impressed by symbolism?

In-Class Writing Activities

1. Using Nevins's article as well as the written responses to it, write your own essay about the proposed monument. Acknowledge (perhaps by quoting or paraphrasing) other perspectives while arguing for your own.

2. The photograph discussed here has been frequently compared to the famous World War II photograph of the soldiers at Iwo Jima (and the monument recreating the photo in Washington, D.C.). Describe another monument you are familiar with — for example, the Vietnam War memorial, the Martin Luther King Jr. memorial, the Lincoln memorial — what do you think a memorial is primarily meant to do? How do the best memorials achieve their purpose?

STEVE TEFFT

A Monument to Multicultural Mush

[THE BARNSTABLE PATRIOT / January 25, 2002]

Before You Read

What is multiculturalism and why does it arouse such strong opinions? How can we hold our diversity as a value without letting it drown out other values?

Words to Learn

heart-rending (para. 2): poignant; tear-jerking (adj.)

commissars (para. 3): officials in charge of political indoctrination (n.)

addled (para. 3): confused; spoiled (adj.)

akin (para. 5): similar; of the same kind (adj.)

noxious (para. 6): poisonous; harmful (adj.)

effrontery (para. 7): nerve; impudence (n.)

posterity (para. 9): future generations (n.)

hackles (para. 10): willingness to fight; hairs or feathers at the back of the neck (n.)

Two quick questions: who are Dan McWilliams, George Johnson, and Billy Eisengrein, and what race are they?   1

The first question matters. Williams, Johnson, and Eisengrein are   2
the three New York City firemen caught on film at an unforgettable moment. They raised the American flag over the wreckage of the World Trade Center on last September 12. The photo of their proud and heart-rending act has elicited comparisons to Joe Rosenthal's famous picture of the Marines raising the flag at Mount Suribachi. It adorns office walls and computer screens everywhere.

STEVE TEFFT *(b. 1958) is a freelance columnist and newswriter/producer for WCVB-TV in Boston. He has also worked as a radio newscaster.*

The second question should not matter, and indeed probably *did* not matter to most Americans until very recently. Williams, Johnson, and Eisengrein happen to be white. Big deal? Not to anyone but America's culture commissars, who apparently see the image as an affront to their diversity-addled sensibilities.

The firemen photo was chosen as the model for a statue that was to be built in honor of the brave Fire Department of New York members, many of whom gave their lives during the horrors of September 11. Unfortunately, the pinheads who planned the monument found it necessary to change the races of two of the firemen. Sculptor Forest Ratner, with the unaccountable blessing of the FDNY hierarchy, created a mock sculpture to show one white, one black and one Hispanic fireman raising the flag. The point was to represent the "diversity" of those who died in the disaster. To the politically correct crowd, the firemen's heroic and symbolic actions were secondary to their skin pigmentations.

They were heroes whose color didn't matter, but whose actions did.

As Rich Lowry of the *National Review* pointed out, changing the races of the firemen was akin to "Stalinist Russia airbrush(ing) out officials from a photograph once they became politically inconvenient."

Until the controversy arose, it's fairly certain that most people didn't give a damn about the race of the firemen. They weren't "white firemen," they were simply firemen doing their jobs. They were heroes, *American* heroes whose color didn't matter, but whose actions did. Now, thanks to the noxious efforts of the multicultural Left, we are forced to acknowledge the men's race ahead of their hearts.

Besides the moral effrontery of the matter, the PC statue was simply dishonest. It depicted a photograph that was never taken. It recalls the ill-fated John F. Kennedy/John F. Kennedy Junior monument proposed a few years ago for the Hyannis JFK museum. That piece of "art" would have depicted President Kennedy at 46 (his age at death) walking next to a 39-year-old John-John (his age at death). The scene never happened. It never *could* have happened. It was downright creepy, bizarre, and factually false. The New York monument design is all that and more.

Black and Hispanic firefighters were certainly among those who died in the crush of World Trade Center debris. They are heroes whose actions we can never fully appreciate. But none of them was photographed raising the flag; and to use those who *were* photographed as political pawns is downright sickening.

This episode is a perfect example of the mush the multicultural-   9
ists are making of our society. In their eyes, who we are is not as important as *what* we are. Our thoughts matter less than our skin color
or sexual orientation. We are not individuals, but members of racial
and ethnic groups to be categorized as if we were different types of
dog food. Certain groups are undeniably preferable to others; to wit,
if the firemen photographed had been all black or Hispanic, would
their races have been changed for posterity? It's highly doubtful.

Fortunately, the statue affair got enough press and raised enough   10
hackles that the planned monument has been scrapped. The FDNY
higher-ups say they'll consider "alternative options" for a statue. Unfortunately, what we'll probably get is an ultra-safe, let's-offend-no-
one statue, no statue at all.

But we'll know forever that Dan Williams, George Johnson, and   11
Billy Eisengrein are white. Just what the multicultural bean-counters
wanted.

Vocabulary/Using a Dictionary

1. Why does Tefft use the term *pigmentations* (para. 4) instead of
   colors to describe skin differences attributable to race?

2. *Pawns* are pieces in a chess game. Why does Tefft describe the
   firefighters in the photo as *political pawns* (para. 8)?

3. What do you guess the phrase *bean-counters* means (para. 11)?

Responding to Words in Context

1. The word *commissars* (para. 3) originated in the Soviet Union
   where a group of officials were put in charge of changing or forcing people's political beliefs. Why does Tefft invoke a communist
   term to describe multicultural proponents?

2. A common use of the word *addled* (para. 3) is to describe a drug
   user's brain (that is, *drug-addled*). Why does Tefft use the phrase
   diversity-addled sensibilities, in reference to proponents of multiculturalism (para. 3)?

Discussing Main Point and Meaning

1. Paragraph 7 compares the proposed 9/11 memorial to a proposed memorial of John F. Kennedy and John F. Kennedy Jr.

Tefft argues that something that "never *could* have happened" should not be memorialized. Analyze the logic of this argument. Should the facts of a moment override an artistic or sociopolitical purpose?

2. In paragraph 9, Tefft presents the view that "who we are is not as important as *what* we are." What does this mean? Do you agree with the statement? Do you agree with Tefft's characterization that this is the multiculturalist position?

3. Tefft says that multiculturalism treats members of ethnic groups like "different types of dog food" (para. 9). Is this accurate? Is it fair?

4. Tefft's general tone could be characterized as frustrated and sarcastic. Is this the most appropriate tone Tefft could use for his purpose? Why or why not?

Examining Sentences, Paragraphs, and Organization

1. Where does the introduction to this essay end? How do you know where the body of the argument begins? Is there an identifiable thesis statement?

2. This article begins and ends with the naming of the three firefighters in the famous 9/11 photograph. Why do you think Tefft does this? What effect does this "framing" device have?

3. Towards the end of his piece, Tefft wonders, "if the firemen photographed had been all black or Hispanic, would their races have been changed for posterity?" (para. 9). Why do you think this question is reserved for the end of the argument? Would it have had a different effect at the beginning?

Thinking Critically

1. What do you think of Tefft's view that multiculturalists value firefighters' skin color more than their heroism? Does this strike you as an exaggeration? Why or why not? Is it possible to honor all of the firefighters of 9/11 — regardless of race — while at the same time putting forward a multicultural agenda? Or does the latter necessarily degrade the former?

2. Tefft describes the flag raising of 9/11 as a "heroic and symbolic" action (para. 4). Do you agree with his description? How does

this flag raising compare with the flag raising at Iwo Jima? (See **America Then,** below.)

3. Think about Tefft's argument that if the firefighters were black or Hispanic their races would not have been altered for a memorial. Is this a fair hypothetical example if the vast majority of firefighters have always been white?

In-Class Writing Activities

1. Rewrite this essay without the sarcasm or emotion of Tefft's prose. Make the same basic argument with a tone of understanding and compassion for the opposition. Does this make a more or less persuasive argument? Explain why.

2. Write a rebuttal letter from a multiculturalist to Tefft, responding to all of the main points in the article. Quote Tefft's article as necessary.

AMERICA THEN . . . 1945

JOE ROSENTHAL

Flag Raising at Iwo Jima

[February 23, 1945]

On Sunday, February 25, 1945, a war-weary nation found on the front page of its morning papers a photograph that would become one of the most famous pictures ever taken and the most reproduced photograph of all time. The Pulitzer Prize–winning picture, shot by combat photographer Joe Rosenthal, showed five men raising the U.S. flag atop an extinct volcanic mountain on the Pacific island of Iwo Jima, which was the site of some of the heaviest casualties of World War II (after thirty-six days of battle, nearly seven thousand U.S. soldiers, most of them Marines, had died). Though it depicts a single incident from a particular battle, the photograph served as the

model for the Marine Corps War Memorial in Washington, D.C., a monument intended to honor all Marines who died for their country since 1775. The photo was widely copied in other media, and an engraving of it appeared on a 1945 U.S. postage stamp.

Rosenthal's inspirational photograph has stirred up quite a bit of controversy over the years. Though allegations that it was deliberately "staged" or "posed" for patriotic effect have not held up, it is true that the photograph does not depict the first flag raising on Iwo Jima. Earlier on the morning of February 23, a group of Marines while still under fire hoisted the Stars and Stripes as a sign the mountain had been taken. But Marine commanders thought the first flag was too small and ordered a second larger and more visible flag to be hoisted at the site. A few hours later, after the terrain was completely free of resistance, the larger flag was raised by five Marines and a Navy corpsman. Rosenthal missed the first flag raising, but his camera immortalized the second. Over the years Rosenthal has main-

tained that he never staged the photo for effect and his case has been amply confirmed. But one could argue that even though no one deliberately posed for Rosenthal's photo, the Marine Corps command did stage a second flag raising when it saw that the first smaller flag was not making the proper impact.

Three of the men who raised the second flag survived Iwo Jima and they would later pose for the sculptor who designed the Marine Corps War Memorial (the others were modeled from photos and physical descriptions). Rosenthal's picture does not focus on the faces of the men, and a large part of the photograph's symbolic power appears to be in the anonymity of the figures. But the monument, which was erected in 1954, strove for greater realism. Although he altered the photograph to reveal the faces of the six men, the sculptor retained their precise ground positions. The figure furthest from the flag, whose right hand seems raised as though he were still trying desperately to hold it, was Marine Pfc. Ira Hayes, a Pima Indian from Arizona (1923–1955) who found little glory on his return to the States and whose life was the subject of a ballad popularized by Bob Dylan (1970).

Web **See It Now:** The Marine Corps War Memorial, **bedfordstmartins.com/ americanow**, Chapter 1. This image is accompanied by information about the battle of Iwo Jima, Joe Rosenthal's photograph, and the national memorial.

Web **Hear It Now:** The Ballad of Ira Hayes, sung by Bob Dylan, **bedfordstmartins .com/americanow**, Chapter 1. This page also includes song lyrics, biographical information on Ira Hayes, and background information on Joe Rosenthal's photograph.

Discussing the Unit

Suggested Topic for Discussion

What are American values? How can they be symbolized or memorialized by a single image or statue? Many believe that Thomas E. Franklin's photo is a perfect symbol of American identity, while others think it leaves out the crucial element of racial and ethnic diversity and our tolerance for difference. What do you think? Do you agree with Steve Tefft's view that a racially diverse version of Franklin's image would be "multicultural mush?" Or do you think, like some of Debbie Nevins's readers, that a memorial should honor the diversity of our nation? Do you think the photograph of the flag-raising on Iwo Jima (p. 21) succeeds in honoring diversity?

Preparing for Class Discussion

1. Examine the tone and point of view in each of the selections in this chapter. Tone is the emotional quality of a writer's voice, and point of view represents the author's particular vantage point or perspective. Who is the most neutral of the three authors? Who is the least neutral? How does the level of neutrality contribute to your response to each of the selections?

2. How do you think Franklin would respond to the articles by Nevins and Tefft? How would he respond to the letters Nevins received? Would he be heartened by some and disappointed by others, or do you think he would wish for the controversy to disappear completely?

From Discussion to Writing

1. Reexamine the letters Nevins received in response to her piece. How do you think some of these teenagers would respond to Franklin and Tefft? Write a letter from one of the letter writers to either Franklin or Tefft explaining a different perspective on the issue. Try to persuade the reader that the youth of the nation ought to be taken more seriously with regard to some of these important issues.

2. When Maya Lin won a design competition for the Vietnam War memorial, there was a huge debate over whether it was appropriate for an Asian American to design the memorial, since the Vietcong had been the enemy of the United States during the war. Veterans of the war were especially angry about the decision. In the end, Lin designed what has proven to be one of the most moving and profound memorials in America, and many Vietnam veterans changed their minds on the controversy as a result. Write an essay describing the similarities and differences between the two controversies: their subjects, purposes, and outcomes.

3. After carefully considering both the Franklin and Rosenthal flag-raising photographs, write an essay in which you compare and

contrast them. What major similarities do you find? In what important ways do you think the photographs differ? Why do you think so many who saw the Franklin photograph were reminded of the Iwo Jima picture? Is the similarity only based on the flag-raising activity? To what extent do you think Franklin, a professional photojournalist, had the Rosenthal photo in the back of his mind when he captured the firefighters at the World Trade Center? Also consider the controversy surrounding the Iwo Jima photograph as summarized in the chapter. In what ways does it pertain to the question of whether a monument must be historically authentic?

Topics for Cross-Cultural Discussion

1. How important are race and ethnicity in other countries? How do you think other countries might react to a similar controversy — where racial diversity was placed before historical accuracy for a public monument?

2. How significant is the flag in other countries, in terms of national identity? What general attitudes do citizens have toward their national flag? How does this attitude compare to that of U.S. citizens toward the U.S. flag? If there are differences, what do you attribute them to?

2

Who Is a Hero — and Why?

Young people everywhere possess a deep need for heroes or role models — individuals whose talents they admire and whose careers they hope to emulate. Some find their heroes on baseball fields or basketball courts; others look for them in comic books or movies; and still others locate them in classrooms, courtrooms, boardrooms, or books.

But what exactly do we mean by a hero? Are heroes simply famous people? Or is a hero necessarily a brave and courageous individual? Must a hero also serve as a role model? In "Mark Bingham: Gay Hero or Hero Who Was Gay?" Evelyn Nieves examines how the media and the gay community responded after learning that Mark Bingham, a Flight 93 passenger who most likely helped to thwart hijackers on 9/11, was homosexual. At issue is the relevance of Bingham's sexual orientation: Should he be "seen as an American who acted heroically and who happened to be gay" or should he be "honored as an example of a gay man who became a hero?" That issue also runs through a more extensive portrait of Bingham that appeared in the nation's most prominent gay magazine, *The Advocate*, which also portrayed Bingham on its cover as "Person of the Year." In "This Is Mark Bingham," Jon Barrett reveals a complex, brawny, gregarious giant of a human being whom friends remember as "a larger-than-life figure" and as a superb athlete who believed he had a "chance to be [a] role [model] for other gay folks who wanted to play sports but never felt good enough or strong enough."

As the actions of Mark Bingham on United Airlines Flight 93 demonstrate, the tragic events of 9/11 brought out many heroes.

According to Boston University student Dan Levin they also helped create a new spectrum of role models: firefighters, police officers, and soldiers. "They should make posters out of these people," Levin writes in "Real Superheroes." Just how thoroughly such real heroes had captured America's attention is dramatically seen in James Estrin's photograph of a Halloween parade the month following the terrorist attacks. But did America after 9/11 go a little over the top when it came to identifying heroes? Although the victims of the attacks "deserve tremendous sympathy," Nicholas Thompson argues in "Hero Inflation," "not all died in a way that people have previously described as heroic." Changing "the definition of hero," he adds, "to accommodate tragic victims may actually weaken us by diminishing the idea of role models who perform truly extraordinary acts."

EVELYN NIEVES

Mark Bingham: Gay Hero or Hero Who Was Gay?

[THE NEW YORK TIMES / January 16, 2002]

Before You Read

Do you recall names or stories of any passengers on United Airlines Flight 93 who rushed the cockpit to stop the terrorists on September 11, 2001? One such passenger, Mark Bingham, was homosexual. What is the difference between calling him a gay hero or a hero who was gay?

EVELYN NIEVES *has been the San Francisco bureau chief of the* New York Times *since 1990. Her countless articles in the* Times *earned her the 2001 Media Alliance Award.*

Words to Learn

brawny (para. 1): having strong muscles (adj.)

commandeering (para. 2): to take possession of by force (v.)

icon (para. 4): an emblem, symbol, or object of uncritical devotion (idol) (n.)

eulogize (para. 4): to speak in praise of some person or thing (v.)

advocate (para. 4): one who argues or pleads for a cause or proposal (n.)

transformative (para. 5): something that changes in structure, appearance, or character (adj.)

impetus (para. 11): a driving force; incentive (n.)

stereotype (para. 14): something agreeing with a pattern; especially an idea that many people have of a thing or a group that may often be untrue or only partially true (n.)

ambivalence (para. 18): simultaneous attraction toward and repulsion from a person, object, or action (n.)

Mark Bingham was one of those people who pop up all over the high school yearbook, a popular, brawny, 6-foot-5 rugby player who could have played any sport, just as he could have talked his way into any room.

When the story of the passengers on United Airlines Flight 93 who fought their hijackers on September 11 became public, everyone who knew Mr. Bingham was sure he was one of the leaders. The hijackers commandeering the cockpit had to be right in front of Mr. Bingham as he sat in seat 4D in first class. Those who remembered him fighting off an armed mugger knew he was a man of action, never one to back away from a dangerous confrontation.

In the weeks and months since September 11, Mr. Bingham, a thirty-one-year-old public relations executive who played rugby for the University of California, has become one of the most celebrated heroes of that horrible day.

He has also become an icon among gays. The man tearfully eulogized by Senator John McCain of Arizona is also the subject of a cover story and Person of the Year in *The Advocate,* the national gay and lesbian biweekly news magazine. He has inspired a Web site, markbingham.org, and plans for a permanent memorial in his honor in the Castro, San Francisco's famous gay neighborhood.

That he was gay might seem irrelevant to any discussion about his role in Flight 93, many gay rights advocates say. September 11, they agree, was a transformative day for the nation, when what was

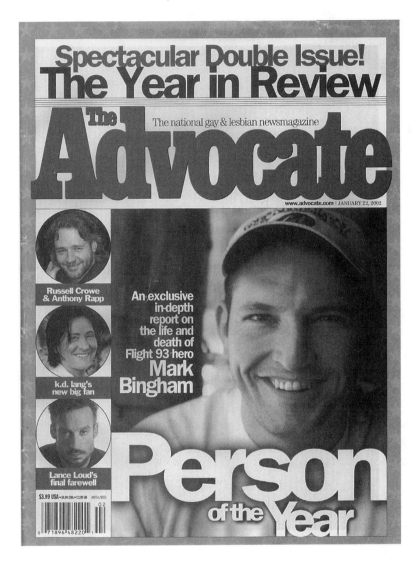

notable about this country of diverse groups is how everyone united in grief and outrage. But the sexual orientation of September 11 heroes is not really irrelevant, gay civil rights groups add, at a time when openly gay men and lesbian women are barred from the military and when gay couples do not have the same rights as heterosexual ones.

"When you ask what difference does it make if the heroes were   6
gay, I say I agree with you," said Judy Wieder, editor in chief of *The
Advocate,* which devoted its October 23 issue to "the gay heroes of
the terrorist tragedy."

"That's precisely our point," Ms. Wieder said. "They were just   7
like everybody else. So we ask, why is it that when they died, they
were equal to everyone, but had they lived, they would not have the
same equality as heterosexuals?"

The importance of identifying gay heroes became especially im-   8
portant, gay advocates say, after the Reverend Jerry Falwell and the
Reverend Pat Robertson asserted, just two days after the attacks, that
an angry God had allowed the terrorists to succeed because the
United States had become a nation of abortion, homosexuality, secular schools and courts, and the American Civil Liberties Union.

*Part of Mr.
Bingham's appeal
as a gay hero is
that he was not a
stereotype.*

"Maybe because of the lack of visible heroes   9
for us, there's a greater significance in finding heroes," said Joan M. Garry, executive director of
the Gay and Lesbian Alliance Against Defamation
(GLAAD), which has been critical of news organizations that did not mention Mr. Bingham's sexual orientation. Later profiles were more forthright, Ms. Garry said, in part because GLAAD was
urging the news media to tell the full stories.

Mr. Bingham's sexual orientation was not his full story, his   10
friends and mother, Alice Hoglan, say. "Mark was a fully alive person," said Ms. Hoglan, a flight attendant for United Airlines who
raised her son as a single mother. "I don't mind at all that he is being
identified as a gay hero, though that was just one aspect of him. He
was proud of being gay, just as he was proud of being a Republican,
and proud of playing rugby, and proud of his friends."

Daniel Chu, a Chi Psi fraternity brother of Mr. Bingham in the   11
early 1990s, who registered and maintains the markbingham.org
Web site, said his friend's sexual orientation was not the impetus for
the site.

"Most of us in the fraternity didn't know about Mark's sexual   12
orientation," he said, "and we didn't find out about it until a week
before he graduated. School was not really Mark's No. 1 priority.
Mark was always about people. Always."

The Web site has become a sprawling tribute, with testimonials   13
from friends gay and straight. "I don't think he would have asked for
this," Mr. Chu said. "But I'm sure he's cracking up to see a big deal

made of something he did every day. If a friend needed help, he was always there. If a friend needed someone to talk to, he was always there. That's the way Mark was. He loved life and lived it to its fullest."

To gay advocates, part of Mr. Bingham's appeal as a gay hero, or   14
a hero who was gay, is that he was not a stereotype. For Michelangelo Signorile, a gay journalist, what was notable about the early coverage of the September 11 heroes is not that it omitted Mr. Bingham's sexual orientation but that it seemed to overlook Mr. Bingham entirely.

In many of the early reports, he said, most of the attention was   15
focused on Mr. Bingham's seatmate on the plane, Todd Beamer, who is believed to have uttered the now-famous "Let's roll" comment as the passengers sought to overcome the hijackers.

"I feel that in general the average American doesn't have any idea   16
who Mark Bingham is," Mr. Signorile said. "Everyone knows Todd Beamer because he had a wife, he was heterosexual, he had a story, the great American family. But we just didn't hear that much about Mark Bingham."

For many gays and lesbians, Mr. Signorile said, there has been a   17
real tension between two ways of looking at the issue of whether Mark Bingham should be seen as an American who acted heroically and who happened to be gay, or whether he should be honored as an example of a gay man who became a hero.

"I think in the gay community you see both of these strains, an   18
ambivalence because many have both of these feelings. On the one hand they say: 'Why focus on it?' And, on the other hand, they say, 'We want people to know.'"

Web **Read It Now:** Mark Bingham.org, **bedfordstmartins.com/americanow,** Chapter 1. This is a tribute site dedicated to Mark Bingham.

Web **Read It Now:** Eulogy for Mark Bingham, **bedfordstmartins.com/americanow,** Chapter 1. Read the text of the eulogy given by Senator John McCain, September 22, 2001.

Vocabulary/Using a Dictionary

1. How is *commandeer* (para. 2) related to the verb *command*?

2. *Impetus* (para. 11) comes from the same Latin origin as the word *impetuous.* Look up *impetuous* in the dictionary to find its Latin origin.

Responding to Words in Context

1. Why does Nieves choose the word *brawny* (para. 1) to describe Mark Bingham? How does this word challenge stereotypes of gay men? How does it feed into the image of a hero?

2. How is the word *icon* (para. 4) different from just an image or even a role model? Why is *icon* the most appropriate term for the way the gay community views Bingham?

3. Bingham was named Person of the Year in *The Advocate* (para. 4). How does the meaning of the word *advocate* explain the mission of the magazine and editor in chief Judy Wieder's assertion in paragraphs 6 and 7 that Bingham is a gay hero?

Discussing Main Point and Meaning

1. What is the difference between a gay hero and a hero who is gay?

2. What reasons do gay rights advocates give for viewing Bingham as a gay hero?

3. How do family and friends describe Bingham? Is he a gay hero or a hero who is gay for them? Explain using evidence from the text.

Examining Sentences, Paragraphs, and Organization

1. What kind of image does Nieves create of Bingham in the first three paragraphs? Why do you think she leaves out of this description any mention of Bingham's sexual orientation?

2. Nieves organizes the article by describing Bingham (para. 1–3), explaining gay rights advocates' view of him (para. 4–9), depicting remembrances of family and friends (para. 10–13), and finally conveying the ambivalent views of members of the gay community (14–18). Explain the logic behind this structure. Does this structure suggest Nieves favors one view of Bingham over another? Explain your answer.

3. In response to the journalist's question implying Bingham's sexual orientation does not matter, Wieder agrees (para. 6). Then she goes on to say, "That's precisely our point" (para. 7). Look at the rest of her response in paragraph 7. How does Wieder use agreement to actually challenge the question? How persuasive is this strategy?

Thinking Critically

1. Why do you think gay rights activists view Bingham as a gay hero whereas family and friends do not?

2. Journalist Michelangelo Signorile theorizes Americans are more familiar with Todd Beamer than Mark Bingham because passenger Beamer was heterosexual (paras. 14 and 15). Is Signorile's theory sound? Is it an argument for or against Bingham as a gay hero?

3. Look at the excerpt from Senator John McCain's eulogy for Mark Bingham. (See **Read It Now**, p. 30). Does anything in this excerpt identify Bingham as a gay hero?

In-Class Writing Activities

1. If you were to write a eulogy for Bingham, would you entitle it "Eulogy for a Gay Hero" or "Eulogy for an American Hero"? Respond in a brief essay explaining the reasons for and implications of your choice.

2. One could read the argument for seeing Bingham as a gay hero in terms of identity politics, an ideology based on shared characteristics. One application of this ideology is the belief that positive representatives of groups traditionally lacking powerful positions (such as gays, minorities, and women) help to empower others of the same category. What are the benefits of such an approach? What are potential drawbacks? Apply these questions to various choices we make in a democracy, such as voting, hiring practices, and finding heroic role models. Discuss these questions as a group and draft a response that reflects your varying perspectives.

JON BARRETT

This Is Mark Bingham

[THE ADVOCATE / January 22, 2002]

Before You Read

The Advocate, the magazine from which this essay comes, is a bi-weekly publication for members of the gay and lesbian communities. *The Advocate* devoted its October 23 issue to the gay heroes arising out of the September 11 tragedy. Judy Wieder, the editor-in-chief for *The Advocate,* argues for the importance of identifying gay heroes in promoting gay rights. Not surprisingly, *The Advocate* named one September 11 hero, Mark Bingham, as its Person of the Year. Based on this information, what do you expect from this article's description of Bingham? In particular, how much emphasis do you think the author will give to Bingham's sexual orientation?

Words to Learn

muster (para. 1): to convene, assemble (v.)

wake (para. 4): a track left behind (n.)

heralded (para. 5): hailed, greeted, publicized (v.)

moniker (para. 6): a name, a nickname (slang, n.)

nadir (para. 14): the lowest point (n.)

cliques (para. 15): small, exclusive groups of people (n.)

cantankerous (para. 17): ill natured, quarrelsome (adj.)

gregarious (para. 21): social, companionable (adj.)

placate (para. 36): to soothe, especially by concessions; appease (v.)

anathema (para. 40): a person or thing accursed; one intensely disliked (n.)

mayhem (para. 46): needless or willful damage (n.)

satellite: (para. 51): subsidiary, ancillary (n.)

JON BARRETT (b. 1968) is the senior news editor for The Advocate *in Los Angeles. He has also written for* Teen People, Paper, *and* Cosmopolitan. *His book,* Hero of Flight 93: Mark Bingham, *will be published in the fall of 2002.*

It took a while for Alice Hoglan to muster the courage — not to   1
mention the technological know-how — to check the messages on her
son's mobile phone. Mark Bingham had had the phone with him
when he boarded United Airlines Flight 93 nearly two months earlier.
So, of course, it was destroyed along with everything else on board
when the plane crashed in a field in Somerset County, Pa. But like
some sort of space-age time capsule that captured the terror and the
confusion that has become known as September 11, Bingham's voice
messages sat on an AT&T Wireless computer waiting to be retrieved.

Hoglan knew there were at least two messages because she had   2
left them herself. Mark woke her up at 6:44 A.M. Pacific time with an
air phone call to tell her that his flight had been hijacked. However, it
wasn't until after the call was disconnected and Hoglan turned on the
TV that she realized the hijackers' probable plan for her son's plane.

"Mark, this is your mom," she said in her first message. "It's   3
9:54 A.M. [Eastern time]. It's a suicide mission, and the hijackers are
planning to use your plane as a target." Today, she corrects herself
when she repeats the message: "Of course I meant to say 'weapon.'"

Her messages were two of the forty-four left on Mark's phone in   4
the wake of the hijacking. One was from Mark's father, Jerry Bingham, in Florida. "I'm looking at this big wreck and I'm hoping you're
nowhere near it," he said, according to Hoglan. Others were from
rugby teammates, fraternity brothers, business associates, and
boyfriends. And at least one was from his roommate in New York
City, Amanda Mark. "Mark, call me!" she pleaded.

Mounting evidence suggests Mark had access to the information   5
his mother was trying to get to him. Cockpit recordings support the
theory that he and the others on board took amazing measures in attempting to overcome the hijackers. The victims of Flight 93 have been
heralded as citizen soldiers who, when faced with then-unimaginable
circumstances, gave their own lives to save thousands of others. Mark,
meanwhile, has been singled out by the media as the "gay hero."

It's a distinction that makes many of those who were close to him   6
uneasy. Not that they were uncomfortable with Mark's sexual orientation. Most of them don't hesitate to mention his nickname, "Bear
Trap." He liked his men big and hairy, they say. It's just that the
moniker "gay hero" says so little about a man who was as varied as
the forty-four unheard voice messages his mother found on his
phone.

The word *giant* better represents Mark Bingham, his friends   7
might say. But even then they wouldn't be talking about his 6-foot-4,

220-pound frame. They would be describing the life they watched him lead.

One of Alice Hoglan's most vivid memories is from the summer 8 of 1970, when she split from her husband and moved from Phoenix — the town in which Mark was born on May 22 of that year — to Miami. "I ran to the airport with him stuck like a football under my arm," she says.

Mark — who at the time was called Jerry, after his father — 9 knew that day only through the stories his mom told him. But it was nevertheless one of the most significant in his life in that it marked the start of his partnership with his mother.

"We were always a team, and I depended on him way too 10 much," Hoglan says. "It was too much emotional strain for a little boy to have a single mom thrashing about for support."

After eight years in Miami, where Mark and his mother lived on a 11 house-boat in the shadow of the Orange Bowl — hence Mark's lifelong obsession with the Miami Dolphins — the pair moved to California.

Soon after her divorce, Hoglan decided to take the *K* from her 12 son's middle name, Kendall, and call him Kerry — a name she says he hated because "it sounded like a girl's." So when her son was ten and about to start a new school in Redlands, California, she gave him an opportunity few people ever have. "I said, 'Kerry, you've been complaining about your name, and now's the time to change it, because people here don't know you yet.'" After thinking about his mom's proposition for just a minute, he responded, "OK, I'll be Mark."

"It was a brave and very definite thing. He just chose it," Hoglan 13 remembers. "And when we got to the classroom and the teacher said 'This is Mark Bingham,' I heard a kid say, in a whining voice, 'Another Mark!'"

The two of them didn't stay anywhere long those first few years 14 in California. In addition to Redlands, they were in Riverside, before being inspired by one of Hoglan's favorite authors — John Steinbeck — and moving to Monterey. There they lived in the back of a pickup for a few weeks while Hoglan looked for work and, more than a couple of times, depended on the fish Mark could catch at the wharf for supper. "I look back on it now and say, 'Wow, that was a really cool, character-building experience,'" Hoglan says. "But it was pretty grim. There was never a lot of money, and that may have been the nadir of our existence."

Mark was a sophomore at Los Gatos High School in Los Gatos, 15 California — where he and his mom had moved a few years earlier —

when he met Todd Sarner. "I think what brought us together origi-nally is that we didn't fit into any of the cliques," says Sarner, also a sophomore at Los Gatos at the time. "We weren't really jocks, and we weren't really the nerdy, brainy kids."

Sixteen years later their relationship was so strong that Mark had been the best man at Sarner's wedding, and Sarner was the one who dropped Mark off at the San Francisco airport in late August for what turned out to be his last flight out of the city. But Sarner is the first to tell you that their friendship didn't start out that way.   16

"We kind of had a cantankerous relationship at the beginning," he says. "Back then a lot of the fights were about what heavy metal band was the best. Mark was really into a band called Queensryche, and I was into a Japanese metal band called Loudness."   17

Sometimes Mark, Sarner, and other friends would collaborate on music videos — complete with big hair, makeup, and air guitar — that they would videotape at Mark's house, usually when Hoglan, who is a flight attendant for United Airlines, was away on a trip. "They would get made up in these outrageous Metallica and Iron Maiden getups, using my makeup," Hoglan says.   18

Mark and Sarner also collaborated on the rugby field. And though the sport didn't exactly suit Sarner, it was perfect for Mark. As physical a sport as rugby is, it no doubt helped cultivate the sense of fearlessness in Mark that Sarner later addressed in his eulogy on Sep-tember 22 in Berkeley, California. "I tend to believe that the truth is that Mark did have fear," he said, "but that he took action anyway."   19

Mark traveled overseas with his high school rugby club — breaking several of his bones along the way — and was recruited to play for the University of California, Berkeley, where he helped the school win two national championships. But when nineteen-year-old Mark met thirty-eight-year-old Mark Wilhelm, his athletic accomplish-ments must have paled next to the seemingly insurmountable task of keeping his sexual orientation a secret.   20

Wilhelm had placed a personal ad in a San Jose, California, newspaper, and Mark was one of the men who responded. His letter reflected a tug-of-war between the gregarious, confident young man everybody knew — the guy who could roll over any foe on the field while winning the friendship of any face in the crowd — and a private life he was only beginning to accept himself. "I've got no idea what I want to do with my life, but I know I'll be a success at something," he wrote Wilhelm. "I'm naïve but smart, funny but shy. I've lots of friends, but I'm lonely for a buddy that can share my secret."   21

Mark, who Wilhelm said was in the physical shape "few of us ever   22
see past nineteen," shared more about himself after the two of them
met in person. He told Wilhelm that he had known he was gay since he
was twelve. He also said, while probably adding a dramatic bent to
what was undoubtedly a very real fear, "If my family or friends ever
found out, I'd have to kill myself." Wilhelm adds, "Mark was very
closeted, but it was almost as if he was leaning against the door."

In fact, it was less than two years afterward that Mark came out   23
to Sarner, who laughs now when he remembers his initial reaction:
"When did *that* happen?" And only months after that, Mark came
out to his mother when they were driving around California's
Sonoma County.

"I was just loving being with my son that day," Hoglan says,   24
pulling her long hair back with one hand. "Then he said, 'Mom, I
have something to tell you, and I've promised myself that I was going
to tell you before the sun went down.' And when he said that, the sun
was streaming into our faces — it was setting.

"I was really astounded [when he told me]. I hadn't any idea that   25
my son was gay, and up until that time I had been vaguely antigay,"
Hoglan says. "So with those words, I began a journey."

Mark was on a journey as well. His best friend and mother knew   26
he was gay, but to most people Mark was still the outstanding rugby
player, the Chi Psi fraternity president, and the guy who would get so
blasted on vodka and orange juice at Cal football games that he
sometimes dashed onto the field in often-successful attempts to tackle
the opposing team's mascot. His softer side was no less remarkable.
Friends say he had a Clintonian[1] ability to bring people out of their
shells, to make them feel like no one else was more important. He
made a concerted effort to be both the life and the lifeblood of all his
social circles.

He was also a mama's boy who, along with some college friends,   27
parked in front of his mom's house a car that was painted from front
fender to back bumper with the words ALICE HOGLAN IS A GODDESS. "I
don't know where he got that," Hoglan says, still blushing, with a
mixture of embarrassment and pride. "I never told him that I was a
goddess!"

Mark was fresh out of college and in classic form when in De-   28
cember 1993 he met Paul Holm at a Christmas party. "I noticed him

---

[1] *Clintonian:* A reference to the social skills of former U.S. President, Bill Clinton.

standing at this table, where he proceeded to eat a whole bowl of shrimp," Holm says. Mark noticed Holm too and walked over, stuck out his hand, and with a big grin said, "Hi, I'm Mark Bingham. Who are you?" The two of them spent the rest of the party talking about a number of things, not the least among them Cal Berkeley, where Holm had also gone to school.

At 7 o'clock the next morning a telephone call and Mark's voice on the answering machine woke Holm up. "I don't know if you re-member me," the voice said. "It's Mark from last night, and I wanted to see if you wanted to get together today." The two of them were to-gether for the next six years.   29

"We had a very intense and wonderful relationship," says Holm, who shared with Mark his home in San Francisco's Castro district for five of the years they were together. "We did everything from sitting in front of the TV watching football to traveling to France once or twice a year."   30

The couple also had a fondness for feasting on fine food and wine while chewing on each other's hopes for the future. It was during one such meal that Mark first mapped out an ambition to start his own public relations firm. "We spent hours and hours talking about everything, including business," says Holm, who started his own firm, the Holm Group, when he and Mark were together. "When I was going through some memorabilia, I found an old menu where, on the back, we had written the potential names for our companies. And there was THE BING-HAM GROUP in big letters among all the others."   31

> *Mark was very proud of being a gay man, but it wasn't the first thing he would define himself as.*

Upon graduating from Cal in 1993 with a degree in social sci-ences, with an emphasis in international relations, Mark went to work for high-tech PR powerhouse Alexander Communications (now Alexander Ogilvy) and later took a job with 3Com. High-tech PR, like rugby before it, was a perfect fit for Mark, who as a teenager knew his Commodore 64 inside and out. And there was no better place to ride the rising high-tech wave of success than San Francisco in the mid 1990s.   32

Soon the going got so good that Mark decided to realize the dream he first outlined on the back of a restaurant menu. The Bing-ham Group officially opened for business in 1999 in a loft space Mark shared with a friend's Web-design firm. By focusing on what he knew best — high-tech PR — Mark was able to secure a number of   33 clients, hire several employees, and, in May 2000, open his own office on San Francisco's Lafayette Street.

"At the office-warming party there were probably two hundred people, and it took me twenty minutes to get in the door and another fifteen minutes to get a spot inside," Hoglan says. "But by that time in my life I had become much more accustomed to having Mark be a larger-than-life figure. He wasn't famous, exactly, but he was extremely popular, and I kind of basked in his reflection." 34

Derrick Mickle was playing in a flag football game at San Francisco's Dolores Park when he first ran head-on into Mark. "Here was this huge guy who was just tearing people up," he says. "And it was kind of frustrating because I had played a lot of pickup football growing up and there was always an unspoken rule that you didn't showboat." 35

Mickle soon learned that Mark wasn't showing off but that he just "never dumbed down his game to placate anyone." It wasn't long before Mickle, who played rugby at Vassar College, tossed the idea of a gay rugby team Mark's way. When the idea was no more than a "what if," Mark was enthusiastic, he says. But when Mickle got serious, Mark became "dead against" the prospect. "He said, 'You'll never get accepted by the [rugby] union'; 'The guys out there will tear you up'; and 'You won't ever find enough players.'" 36

Mickle went ahead without Mark's blessing, and just two months after he first fielded a "rag-trap of rugby players" for the San Francisco Fog's first practice in October 2000, Mark had a change of heart. "He came out for a practice and proceeded to act the same way as when I met him. He just plowed through the field, leaving a sea of bodies," Mickle says, adding that after the team's initial response of "What the hell is this guy doing?" Mark's intensity eventually helped raise the level of everyone's game. 37

And after practice, "Mark's great, nurturing spirit came through," says Bryce Eberhart, who was among those Mark ran over on the field that first practice. "He went up to everyone and patted them on the back and told them they were doing a great job." 38

Once again Mark had fallen in step with a program that was just right for that point in his life. And in the summer of 2001, when the Fog was accepted as a permanent member of the Northern California Rugby Football Union, he didn't hesitate to share his enthusiasm in an e-mail to his teammates: 39

"When I started playing rugby at the age of sixteen, I always thought that my interest in other guys would be anathema," he wrote. "I loved the game but knew I would need to keep my sexuality 40 a secret forever. As we worked and sweated and ran and talked together this year, I finally felt accepted as a gay man and a rugby player. My two irreconcilable worlds came together.

"We have the chance to be role models for other gay folks who   41
wanted to play sports but never felt good enough or strong enough," he continued. "More importantly, we have the chance to show the other teams in the league that we are as good as they are. Good rugby players. Good partyers. Good sports. Good men."

Despite the tone of his e-mail, Mark never considered himself a   42
gay activist. In fact, he thought of himself more as a man of action than a man of example. He supported John McCain's 2000 presidential bid, for instance, despite the Arizona senator's stand on gay issues — he opposes hate-crimes legislation and the Employment Non-Discrimination Act. McCain, who spoke at Mark's September 22 memorial service and calls him "an American hero," tells *The Advocate* he won Mark's support in the campaign because "I was straightforward and not your typical politician."

Says Holm: "Mark was very proud of being a gay man, [but] it   43
wasn't the first thing he would define himself as."

But whether Mark intended it to be or not, 2001 was turning out   44
to be a transitional year for him in many ways, including the way in which he integrated his sexual orientation with the rest of his life.

"The two things in his life that he thought would never come to-   45
gether did," Mickle says, referring to Mark's e-mail to the team. "When they fused, it was like a lightbulb going off in his head."

After his six-year relationship with Holm ended in 1999, Mark   46
was for the first time socializing as a single and openly gay man. And, along with Eberhart and other new friends from the Fog, he liked to mix it up while going out on the town — maybe stopping by a straight club before hitting a gay bar, such as the Lone Star Saloon, which uses the slogan "Bears, Bikers, and Mayhem!"

"If we were going to do some sort of nasty shot in a bar and no   47
one wanted to do it, Mark was always the first one to give it a try," Eberhart says. "He would be the one to eat the worm."

Mickle says Mark was not "straight-*acting*," as some people   48
have suggested since September 11. "He was just acting like Mark. Sure, your gaydar would hit 0 every time [you saw him], but you would be so wrong."

Things were changing at work as well. Business was so good   49
when Mark opened his firm that he was basically able to pick and choose what clients he wanted to work with, says Peer-Olaf Richter, an account executive who started working for Mark in January 2001.

But by that summer the bottom had fallen out of the technology market, and the Bingham Group's roster had fallen from six full-time clients to two. That was incredibly hard for Mark.

"I learned very early on that he was really good at making immediate contact, chitchat, and building bridges between people," Richter says. "Then, when the industry turned sour and it got to be much more about hard facts, I don't think he really enjoyed the profession. Essentially, everything he had built up in that short amount of time had basically crumbled and fallen to pieces." 50

Mark, a man who friends say hated to lose at anything, started to spend less time at his San Francisco office. He also was considering relocating full-time to New York City, where he already was living part-time and had opened a satellite office in the Chelsea apartment he shared with Amanda Mark. 51

And, Richter says, while he and his colleagues were in the office worrying about the loss of clients and the shrinking budgets, Mark was checking in from Hawaii, Las Vegas, Monaco, or Pamplona, Spain — where he took his now-infamous run with the bulls. "At the time, we were sitting in the office saying to ourselves, 'What is that man doing?'" Richter says. 52

Hoglan acknowledges that her son was a "wild and unpredictable boss" at times. She also concedes that there were times that as a mother she wanted to urge him to settle down. "He spent a lot of money, goofed off with his friends, worked like a dog, and lived the life that I have always dreamed of," she says. "And now I'm just really glad that he did." 53

Mark spent Monday night, September 10, at Matt Hall's home in Denville, N.J., where the two men ate ice cream, watched *Monday Night Football,* and then chatted while Mark trimmed his goatee in front of the bathroom mirror. 54

The two met on America Online in June, and after several dates they spent a week together in early September at the Southern Decadence festival in New Orleans. A shy guy who says he "never made the first move," Hall was amazed with the confidence Mark exuded. "He took me by the hand in front of the Phoenix bar and said, 'Let's go meet people,'" Hall says. "Then he started going up to people and saying, 'Hi, I'm Mark Bingham from California. This is Matt from New Jersey.'" 55

Their time together had been romantic, but Hall says they had an understanding that they were to be "just friends." Nevertheless, that Monday night in Denville, Mark turned to Hall and asked, "When do we talk about making this relationship more exclusive?" 56

"I just looked at him and said, 'You need to be on this coast full-   57
time,'" Hall says, admitting that even though Mark's question took
him by surprise, he was excited about the possibility of a more serious relationship with him.

The tension from Mark's question hung over the men well into   58
the next morning, and by 7 A.M., when they were racing toward
Newark airport, it was heightened by the stressful possibility that
Mark was going to miss his flight home to San Francisco. He ended
up being the last to board the plane, getting to his seat so late that he
had only enough time to make a quick mobile phone call to Hall before turning off "all electronic devices," as the flight attendants were
instructing.

"He called me at 7:49 A.M. and said, 'Hi, thanks for driving so   59
crazy to get me here. I've made the plane, I'm sitting in first class, and
I'm drinking a glass of orange juice,'" Hall says. "I said, 'OK, have a
good trip. Give me a call when you get there.' I never told him how
much I loved him," Hall adds. "With Mark, you were always going
to see him again. You were always going to talk with him again."

Nobody knows for sure what Mark did those two hours after he   60
hung up with Matt Hall. One can imagine that he ate a first-class
breakfast, rummaged through the newspaper for the latest on the Dolphins, who were scheduled to play the Buffalo Bills that weekend, and
reached across the aisle to introduce himself to his fellow passengers.

We do know that at 9:44 A.M. Eastern time, he called his mom.   61
"Hi, Mom, this is Mark Bingham," he said when she picked up the
phone. "I just wanted to say that I love you. I am on a flight from
Newark to San Francisco, and there are three guys on board who've
taken over the plane, and they say they have a bomb." It's the minutes after that call to his mother, those between when the hijackers
took control of the plane and when it crashed in Pennsylvania, that
have everyone really guessing.

Todd Sarner says that one of the most frustrating things he's ex-   62
perienced since September 11 has been knowing "more than anything
I've known in my life" that Mark was involved in taking the plane
down — but then not knowing how to adequately explain how he
knows.

"I keep having this image from watching Mark play rugby a cou-   63
ple of years ago," he adds. "His team had just kicked the ball, and
there were probably fifteen people between Mark and the guy who
caught it. And I just remember watching Mark do something I've

seen him do a thousand times — duck down his head and go through the crowd fearlessly, like he wasn't even there, and then tackle that guy."

Did Mark Bingham help tackle the terrorists on September 11?   64
Investigators will be combing through the wreckage of Flight 93 and listening to the cockpit voice recorder for months and maybe years to find out. But the people who knew Mark and watched him live his life say they have all the proof they need.

Vocabulary/Using a Dictionary

1. Look up the Latin origin of the word *muster* (para. 1). How does the Latin origin help explain the connotation of the word?

2. Look up the definition of *heraldry* in the dictionary. How does the definition of *heraldry* explain the connotation of *heralded* (para. 5)?

3. List at least three synonyms for *cultivate* (para. 19).

Responding to Words in Context

1. Bingham's friends say the word *giant* best describes him (para. 7). What are different meanings of the word that apply here?

2. Bingham uses the word *anathema* (para. 40) to describe how his rugby teammates would view his interest in other guys. What does this word suggest about the way Bingham views his sexual orientation?

3. Look at the word *gaydar* in paragraph 48. Based on its context in the paragraph, come up with your own definition of this slang term.

Discussing Main Point and Meaning

1. Define Bingham's personality based on Barrett's portrait. How big of a role does the writer assign Bingham's homosexuality?

2. Think back to your response to the question in the Before You Read section (on page 26). Did this essay fulfill or challenge your expectations?

3. Does this essay portray Bingham as a gay hero? Use evidence from the text to support your answer.

Examining Sentences, Paragraphs, and Organization

1. Explain the organizational structure of the essay by dividing the article into different sections, identifying the purpose or topic of each section. How does the organization shape the way you view Bingham?

2. What do you see as the purpose of paragraphs 4 through 7? How do they portray Mark Bingham?

3. In paragraph 19, Todd Sarner comments on his friend's sense of fearlessness but then ponders his state of mind on September 11, concluding, "'I tend to believe that the truth is Mark did have fear . . . but that he took action anyway.'" Why do you think Barrett includes this detail in his article? Does it make Bingham seem more or less heroic to you?

4. At the end of paragraph 22, Bingham's friend Mark Wilhelm says of Bingham's sexuality, "'Mark was very closeted, but it was almost as if he was leaning against the door.'" Look at this sentence in connection to the rest of the paragraph. What do you think it means? Why do you think Barrett chose to include this point in his portrait of Bingham?

Thinking Critically

1. Look at Barrett's claim that Bingham had been "singled out by the media as the 'gay hero'" (para. 5). "It's a distinction that makes many of those who were close to him uneasy" (para. 6). Do these sentences neutrally report information or suggest a certain position? Also, consider the intended audience for this article. How do you think readers of *The Advocate* would react to this claim?

2. Looking at paragraphs 40 and 41 of the essay, to what degree do you think Bingham would identify himself as a gay man? How do you think Bingham would react to the label "gay hero?"

3. Look at paragraph 42, in which Barrett discusses Bingham's involvement with John McCain's presidential campaign. Does this paragraph solidify or challenge your answer to the previous paragraph? Explain.

In-Class Writing Activities

1. Write an essay in which you use Barrett's brief biography of Bingham to identify personal qualities that might make an individual prone to acts of heroism. Based on this analysis, explore to what extent personality traits versus the situation individuals find themselves in contribute to the making of a hero.

2. Working in small groups, detail how Barrett's profile of Bingham defies stereotypes of gay men.

DAN LEVIN

Real Superheroes

[THE DAILY FREE PRESS, BOSTON UNIVERSITY / January 15, 2002]

Before You Read

What was your view of firefighters, police officers, and soldiers before September 11? What was your view of these public servants shortly after September 11? What is your image of them now?

Words to Learn

perpetual (para 1): lasting for an indefinitely long duration (adj.)

peril (para. 3): a condition of imminent danger; exposure to the risk of harm or loss (n.)

grunt (para. 6): one who performs routine or mundane tasks; infantrymen in the U.S. military, especially the Vietnam War (slang, n.)

scrutiny (para. 6): a close, careful examination or study (n.)

proverbial (para. 7): widely referred to as if the subject of a proverb; famous (adj.)

DAN LEVIN *(b. 1982) is a junior at Boston University. He wrote this article for* The Daily Free Press *at Boston University as a way of "honoring those who have died to save others."*

Spider-Man is my hero. Before you start snickering, let me explain. He was a perpetual dork, who amazingly received superpowers and managed to score a supermodel as a wife. Yet, all kidding aside, the truth is that we can find our heroes everywhere, even though some of us may choose to escape the harsh reality of the everyday world and embrace comic book characters or sports celebrities. The basketball star Charles Barkley once defended his brash behavior by claiming "I am not a role model." Well Chuck, you're right.

The real role models are certain people on the street. They're your next-door neighbor, your best friend's parents. You see them at grocery stores, during the holidays, and at county fairs. They should make posters out of these people that we can tape to our walls. They get paid squat, but they do what they do because they love what they do. They're our firefighters, police officers, and soldiers.

> *The real role models are certain people on the street. They're our firefighters, police officers, and soldiers.*

I think our generation as a whole has taken too much for granted. Firemen save cats from trees, police officers stop people from making it to work on time, and soldiers march in straight lines and salute. In the wake of September 11, I think it's time to set some things straight. Firefighters save lives. On an hourly basis, they are out there, making sure that people survive the most horrifying experience of being trapped in burning buildings. As we saw during the World Trade Center disaster, they are wholly prepared to sacrifice their own lives to help others in peril. And it's sad that the majority of us never even thought twice when we passed a station house and saw them laughing and enjoying their morning coffee. Many of those New York firefighters will never savor that morning coffee again.

Police officers are no different. College students gripe because they only think of the police as people who have nothing better to do than break up parties. Be glad. They could have worse things to do. Things that may make you wet the bed. They get into fire-fights with bank robbers. They see the aftermath of murders, gang shoot outs, brutal rapes, vicious assaults, and drunk driving accidents. They get killed. They work long hours for less pay than you or I would ever accept for putting our life on the line each day. And they do it gladly.

Only in the aftermath of that terrible tragedy did we finally recognize what these heroic men and women did to serve their communities. Only afterwards did the money pour in to help the families of those who died trying to help others. It shouldn't have taken that kind of a tragedy to do it, but it did. You should be supporting them every chance you get, because who knows when they'll have to save your life.

As for the underappreciated, no one is more so than the American soldier. The grunt. The guy in the field. You want to talk about stuff that wakes you up in a cold sweat, calling for Mommy? Imagine being in a tank fight, with massive explosions taking place all around you. Imagine being pinned down, calling for backup while the enemy keeps advancing. Imagine having to shoot someone ten yards away because it's either him or you. And what do we give these honorable men and women who serve our country? Scrutiny.

Let's not blame soldiers for what they do. They defend our liberty, our freedom, and our rights as human beings. The rest of the world doesn't enjoy the liberties we do, and we take that for granted as well. We shouldn't. September 11 altered our way of thinking forever. Let's not scrutinize our soldiers for how this war, or any other before or after, was or will be fought. Wars aren't won by tiptoeing around proverbial land mines. Our military has a job to do — to protect us from enemies, both domestic and foreign. Few of us are experts on military strategy, so let's not second-guess our armed forces. Let them do their job, and congratulate them when they come home. They do a job that most of us could never do. All these people do jobs that most of us could never do. Let's admire them for that.

Vocabulary/Using a Dictionary

1. *Scrutiny* (para. 6) comes from Latin words meaning "to search" (*scrutar*) and also, "trash" (*scruta*). What does the origin of the word imply about the meaning of *scrutiny*?

2. The root of the word *proverbial* (para. 7) is *verbum*. Look up other words with *verb* in them. Think about what these words have in common to come up with a definition for the root *verbum*.

Responding to Words in Context

1. Levin uses slang throughout the essay, including *dork* (para. 1), *squat* (para. 2), and *grunt* (para. 6.) What is the effect of these words?

2. Why does Levin refer to "the basketball star Charles Barkley" only to call him "Chuck" in the next sentence? What tone does such word choice create?

Discussing Main Point and Meaning

1. Why do you think Levin titles his essay "Real Superheroes"? Who does he consider the real superheroes?

2. What image of firefighters, police officers, and soldiers does Levin assume his audience holds? How does Levin attempt to change his readers' views? What does Levin want his readers to do as a result of reading his essay?

Examining Sentences, Paragraphs, and Organization

1. Why does the author begin by establishing Spider-Man as his hero? How does the introduction set up both the argument and tone of the essay?

2. In paragraph 4, Levin describes "Things that may make you wet the bed." Later, he writes of "stuff that wakes you up in a cold sweat, calling for Mommy" (para. 6). Why does Levin address the reader in this way? How do these sentences shape his argument and tone?

3. In paragraph 6, Levin's sentence structure repeats "Imagine . . ." several times. How does such repetition of the command to imagine convey Levin's point?

Thinking Critically

1. In paragraph 5, Levin bemoans the fact that it takes a tragedy for us to give to charities supporting families of slain firefighters and police officers. He encourages readers to give money "every chance you get." How sound is Levin's advice? Is it an effective solution to the problem of taking these public servants for granted?

2. In the conclusion, the essay asks the audience to neither scrutinize nor blame soldiers' actions during war because we aren't military strategists. How valid is the logic of such a claim? What are the implications of Levin's reasoning?

In-Class Writing Activities

1. Write your own brief essay entitled "Real Superheroes" in which you describe your own perspective on heroes. What is your definition of a superhero?

2. In small groups, describe the appearance, actions, personality, and lifestyle of a fictional superhero such as Batman, Wonder Woman, or Xena, Warrior Princess. How does this superhero reflect the values of his or her society?

NICHOLAS THOMPSON

Hero Inflation

[THE BOSTON GLOBE / January 13, 2002]

Before You Read

After September 11, 2001, many Americans hailed New York City emergency personnel, passengers on United Airlines Flight 93, and even victims of the terrorist attack as heroes. Before you read, make a list of characteristics you believe define a hero. Compare your list to Thompson's in the following selection.

Words to Learn

acclaim (para. 1): enthusiastic applause or approval (n.)

ingenuity (para. 7): inventive skill or imagination; cleverness (n.)

adversity (para. 10): a state of hardship or affliction; misfortune (n.)

grist for the mill (para. 10): something that can be turned to one's advantage (idiom, n.)

eclipse (para. 11): to surpass, outshine (v.)

pantheon (para. 11): a temple dedicated to all gods (n.)

NICHOLAS THOMPSON *(b. 1975) is a Markle Fellow with the New America Foundation and was previously an editor of the* Washington Monthly. *His work has also appeared in the* Boston Globe, *the* Chicago Tribune, *the* New York Times, Slate, *and the* Washington Post, *among other publications. He is a Phi Beta Kappa graduate of Stanford University where he earned degrees in earth systems, political science, and economics.*

incorrigibly (para. 15): incapable of being corrected or reformed (adv.)

paragon (para. 15): a model or pattern of excellence or perfection of a kind; a peerless example (n.)

inflation (para. 16): the act of raising or expanding abnormally (n.)

salve (para. 17): something that soothes or heals; balm (n.)

Since September 11, America has become a nation of heroes. Paul McCartney, Willie Nelson, and Bruce Springsteen played a "tribute to heroes" that raised $150 million for victims of the attacks. Firefighters and rescue workers have earned acclaim for heroism, but so has nearly everyone who directly suffered on that horrible morning.

"The fatalities of that day are all heroes and deserve to be honored as such," said Thomas Davis, a Republican congressman from Virginia, while successfully working to obtain a full burial plot in Arlington National Cemetery for the former National Guardsman who piloted the plane that crashed into the Pentagon.

The victims of the terrorist attacks deserve tremendous sympathy. They died tragically and often horrifically. But not all died in a way that people have previously described as heroic. And even the heroism attributed to the rescue workers stems as much from the country's needs in responding to the disaster as from what actually happened in the collapsing buildings.

It is long overdue that Americans appreciate their public servants. It is also necessary to honor those who died simply for being in America. But changing the definition of hero to accommodate tragic victims may actually weaken us by diminishing the idea of role models who perform truly extraordinary acts.

To the ancient Greeks, "heroes," such as Hercules or Odysseus, performed great deeds, frequently challenged the gods, and were immortalized after death. Heroes lived in times and realms halfway between gods and men and often were deemed to have brought prosperity to the people who praised them.

That definition gradually evolved in this country as Americans adapted it to the people most respected here. Heroes won that standing by courageously transforming the world — Martin Luther King Jr. or Mother Teresa for example. Or heroes could earn that title simply for incredible acts of bravery several steps above the call of duty — Oskar Schindler,[1] a young girl who plunges into a dangerous

---

[1] *Oskar Schindler:* A German industrialist (1908–1974) born in Austria-Hungary who hired Jewish workers during the Holocaust, saving them from Nazi death camps.

icy river and saves a stranger's life, or maybe someone from battle such as Henry Johnson who fought off twenty Germans with a knife and a couple of hand grenades in World War I.

Roughly speaking, American heroes first needed bravery. But 7 bravery is not sufficient because evil people can be brave, too. So, the second trait in American historical lore is nobility. Heroes must work toward goals that we approve of. Heroes must show ingenuity. Lastly, they should be successful. Rosa Parks wouldn't have been nearly as much of a hero if she hadn't sparked a boycott that then sparked a movement. Charles Lindbergh wouldn't have been nearly as heroized if the *Spirit of St. Louis* had crashed into the Atlantic, or if scores of other people had made the flight before.

Recently though, a fourth trait — victimhood — seems to have 8 become as important as anything else in determining heroic status. Today heroes don't have to do anything; they just need to be noble victims.

For example, if J. Joseph Moakley was known at all nationally, it 9 was as a hard-working Massachusetts congressman who almost always followed the Democratic Party line. But when he was stricken with leukemia, he became a national hero, earning praise from the president and seemingly everyone else in Washington. He was cited from the balcony, traditionally the spot reserved for heroes, by President Bush during the State of the Union message. (This paper [the *Boston Globe*] even wrote about a letter received at his house addressed simply to "Joe Moakley, Hero.") His death earned almost as much newspaper coverage as the death this year of the ninety-eight-year-old Mike Mansfield, a giant of the U.S. Senate who served as majority leader longer than anyone in history and initiated the Senate Watergate Committee.

> *Victimhood seems to have become important in determining heroic status.*

But that shouldn't surprise us. Books about overcoming adversity 10 clog the bestseller lists, and perseverance during illness — any illness — is grist for the heroic mill. If John F. Kennedy wanted to run for president today, he might constantly mention his struggle against Addison's disease [2] as opposed to emphasizing his exploits on his PT boat in the Pacific.

Of course, victimhood hasn't completely eclipsed action in our 11 national selection of heroes. The biggest heroes have many of the

[2] *Addison's disease:* A rare endocrine or hormonal disorder characterized by weight loss, muscle weakness, fatigue, low blood pressure, and sometimes darkening of the skin.

virtues of traditional heroes but also are victims — for example, the 350 firefighters who died in the World Trade Center and who now stand atop our national pantheon. These men have been honored everywhere from the current cover of *Sports Illustrated* to a recent best-selling comic book that makes them into superheroes. They even inspired thousands of Halloween costumes. [See photo on p. 53.]

But although the firemen who died in the Trade Center bravely   12 fought the flames and led the evacuation, they did so as workers doing the best they could in their jobs — people trained by the city to rush into buildings and save others. Firefighters choose a very worthy line of work, but to die while doing it isn't completely different from, say, the computer programmers who stayed in the Trade Center and perished while desperately trying to preserve the data backing people's financial portfolios. Just after Christmas, a New Bedford policeman carried a woman out of a burning building. "I'm not a hero," he said upon emerging outside. "I'm just a worker."

There were no doubt some unconditional individual heroes on   13 September 11, including some of the people on United Flight 93 who fought the hijackers and individual firefighters and police who went well beyond the requirements of the job, but most of the other people who died in the attacks were simply victims, much like the tens of thousands of innocent people killed in home fires, or on highways, every year.

They deserve our grief and their families and communities merit   14 great sympathy. But it's time for a little more perspective when Congress almost unanimously passes a bill called the "True American Heroes Act" awarding Congressional Gold Medals — the highest honor that body can give — to every government official who died in the attacks, including Port Authority employees who were killed in their World Trade Center offices.

Of course, some of the hero-making is born of necessity. In the af-   15 termath of the attacks, we needed to turn the narrative away from the horror of the images on television and our clear vulnerability. As soon as the buildings came down, we needed to build the victims up. It also helped to reclassify everyone on the opposing side as incorrigibly demonic and everyone on our side as paragons of virtue. After the 11th, the first part was easy and the second part took a little bit of work.

That wasn't of course a wholly bad thing. The inflation of the   16 heroism of September 11 surely helped the nation recover and pull together. Moreover, America probably didn't have enough heroes.

James Estrin/The New York Times

In the Spirit of the Day

Max Greenberg, 1, at a Halloween parade in Lower Manhattan. This year, even adults donned heroic and patriotic costumes.

An August *U.S. News & World Report* poll revealed that more than half of all Americans didn't consider a single public figure heroic. Right before the attacks, Anheuser Busch planned an ad campaign titled "Real American Heroes" that, among other things, saluted the inventor of the foot-long hot dog.

But just because the sometimes false focus on heroism helped the nation salve its wounds doesn't make such attitudes wholly good either. Heroes often end up as role models, a task not well suited for

17

JAMES ESTRIN (b. 1957) whose image "In the Spirit of the Day" is reprinted above, is a staff photographer for the New York Times. *As a freelance photographer he has contributed to* Life, Time, Newsweek, Forbes, U.S. News & World Report, *and* People.

victims. Moreover, by lowering the bar for heroism, we cheapen the word and, in some ways, the exploits of people who have earned the right to be called that in the past.

Finally, when people earn classification as heroes, those acting in   18
their names often try to take it a step too far. Last month, for example, the federal government announced plans to disburse about as much money this year to families of attack victims as the entire international aid community has slated to give to Afghanistan over the next decade — and that money will come in addition to incredible amounts of charitable aid also already raised. Nevertheless, a spokesman for a victims' lobby group immediately dissented, demanding more. "We are exploring our legal options and lining up attorneys," he said. Almost no criticism could be found in response.

Emerson once wrote that "every hero becomes a bore at last."   19
Well, at least their lawyers and lobbyists do.

Vocabulary/Using a Dictionary

1. Look up *grist* and *mill* in the dictionary. Based on these definitions, how do you think the idiom "grist for the mill" came about?

2. What other definitions of *pantheon* (para. 11) than "a temple dedicated to all gods" apply to Thompson's use of the term?

3. Based on the definition of *inflation* (para. 16), explain what you think the relation is to the economic use of the term.

Responding to Words in Context

1. Look up *victimhood* (para. 8) in the dictionary. If you cannot find it, try to develop a definition by examining its use in this essay, by looking up related words, or by thinking about other *hoods* with which you are familiar.

2. What does Thompson want to suggest by using the word *clog* (para. 10)?

3. Why do you think Thompson uses the word *narrative* (para. 15)?

Discussing Main Point and Meaning

1. What does Thompson mean by his title? How does it reflect the main point of his essay?

2. How does the *New York Times* photo "In the Spirit of the Day" (p. 53) relate to Thompson's argument?

3. What examples does Thompson offer of true heroes? How do they fit his criteria for heroism? How effective do you find his examples?

4. What examples does the essay provide of inflated heroism based on victimhood? Why, according to the essay, have we changed our standards of heroism? What does Thompson see as the consequences of our shift in definition?

Examining Sentences, Paragraphs, and Organization

1. Look at the way Thompson begins paragraphs 3, 4, 5, 7 and 12–18. What is the purpose of these sentences and clauses?

2. Why does Thompson begin his definition of heroism with the examples of the ancient Greeks (para. 5)? How effective is this strategy?

3. Thompson devotes paragraph 9 to a discussion of Congressman J. Joseph Moakley, a figure unrelated to the September 11 tragedy. How useful is this example? What purpose does it serve?

4. How does Thompson's conclusion respond to the entire argument?

Thinking Critically

1. Is Thompson's inclusion of the 350 firefighters who died in the World Trade Center (paras. 11 and 12) reasonable? How sound are his comparisons of firefighters to computer programmers (para. 12) and September 11 victims to innocent people who have died in fires and automobile accidents (para. 13)?

2. Thompson concludes building victims into heroes "helped to reclassify everyone on the opposing side as incorrigibly demonic and everyone on our side as paragons of virtue" (para. 15). How is this conclusion connected to Thompson's observations that "the federal government announced plans to disburse about as much money this year to families of attack victims as the entire international aid community has slated to give to Afghanistan over the next decade — and that money will come in addition to incredible amounts of charitable aid already raised" (para. 18)? What argument is Thompson making here and how legitimate do you find it?

In-Class Writing Activities

1. Suppose you must choose a Halloween costume that reflects your image of a hero. Freewrite about what costume you would choose and why.

2. In small groups, make a list of criteria to define a hero. Then make a list of people who fit the definition. How do your lists reflect the values, needs, or both of society?

Discussing the Unit

Suggested Topic for Discussion

The selections in this unit all address our conceptions of heroism after September 11, 2001. Think about how your own ideas of heroism changed in relation to the tragedy. Before September 11, whom did you find heroic? After September 11, did your ideas or examples of heroism change? Was September 11 a hero-building event for a nation sometimes considered to be devoid of heroes? Are we more likely to call victims *heroes* because they died in a national tragedy? Has your view of firefighters and police changed as a result of September 11? Should we seek out heroes in this tragedy who reflect the diversity of the U.S. population?

Preparing for Class Discussion

1. Bring to class two or three current nonfiction best-seller lists. You can find these online or in Sunday editions of the *New York Times* or your local newspaper. Looking at the titles and description of the books, if available, form a generalization of the qualities of subjects or personalities that emerge. Discuss what interests or values the list reflects. Does the list confirm Nicholas Thompson's argument that Americans value tales of overcoming adversity? Do you see in it any of the respect for authority that Dan Levin calls for? Can you define any characteristics of an American hero based on the lists?

2. Compare Levin's view of firefighters to Thompson's. How do they differ? Whose depiction of firefighters do you find to be the most accurate and why?

3. Compare the view of Mark Bingham in both Evelyn Nieves's and Jon Barrett's pieces on him. How do family and friends view Bingham in each essay? How do gay rights activists see him in both texts?

4. Look at the essays by Nieves, Barrett, Levin, and Thompson. How does each piece depict how the concept of heroism reflects the needs of a nation or a specific group of people?

From Discussion to Writing

1. Write an essay in which you argue whether Bingham is a gay hero or a hero who is gay. You should use the texts by Nieves and Barrett to fairly represent an opposing view and provide support for your position.

2. Write an essay in which you evaluate the tone of the essays by Nieves, Barrett, Levin, and Thompson. How do the tones compare to each other? How does tone relate to the audience and argument? Which tone do you find the most effective and why?

3. Write an essay entitled "Living after September 11, 2001 — A Nation in Need of Heroes." Using your responses to Preparing for Class Discussion question 4, your essay should analyze how each article reflects heroism as a concept that answers the needs of a nation or group of people. You should also offer your own definition of heroism, analyzing how it responds to the needs of Americans or a group of people after September 11.

Topics for Cross-Cultural Discussion

1. Describe a typical hero from another country. How does this hero reflect the country's values? Do you notice any similar characteristics to an American hero like Rosa Parks or Mark Bingham?

2. Describe the status of a firefighter, police officer, or soldier in another country. Look at such factors as pay and social status. How much does the country seem to value these occupations compared to America?

Our Body Image:
Is It a Serious Issue?

Are you content with the way you look? Opinion polls show most Americans are not and that, in general, women are less content with their appearances than men. As individual self-esteem grows increasingly dependent on physical attractiveness, many Americans every year go to extreme measures to alter their looks through drugs, radical diets, or cosmetic surgery.

Our media's obsession with sexual attractiveness has produced hostile reaction in many foreign cultures where women are prohibited from appearing in public uncovered. Is our "uncovering" of the female body, however, a sign of our freedom and lack of oppression? In "The Burka and the Bikini" Joan Jacobs Brumberg and Jacquelyn Jackson examine both extremes of female apparel, and though they don't approve of such restrictive practices as the Taliban's, they do believe that "American girls and women have been stripped bare by a sexually expressive culture whose beauty dictates have exerted a major toll on their physical and emotional health." This women's issue is also taken up by syndicated cartoonist Joel Pett, who humorously suggests a few advantages that wearing a burka might offer a contemporary woman.

A large part of women's struggle with self-image comes from their daily exposure to the impossible physical ideals displayed throughout the popular media. As Seattle University student Rachel

Drevno writes in "Pop Culture Is Destroying True Beauty": "I find it absurd that we live in a society that supposedly prides itself on 'individuality' and 'uniqueness' but then turns around and promotes a popular culture that relies heavily on uniformity and a set of ideal standards." How does such "a set of ideal standards" come about in the first place? How might young girls begin forming such ideal images? Though the accounts are many and complex, one common narrative begins in 1959 with the birth of a small plastic fashion doll. In "Thank Barbie for Britney," Kay Hymowitz looks into the origins of the influential and infamous Barbie Doll. "Between her sexy look and her TV appearances," she claims, Barbie "marked a big turning point in American childhood."

It's not only women, however, who often appear concerned and anxious about their physical appearance. As one of the most famous Charles Atlas ads from the 1940s reveals, the self-esteem of American males has for generations been linked to muscular development and physical strength.

JOAN JACOBS BRUMBERG
AND JACQUELYN JACKSON

The Burka and the Bikini

[THE BOSTON GLOBE / November 23, 2001]

Before You Read

Have you ever seen images of Afghan women in burkas? What is your reaction to the all-enveloping dress that covers a woman from head to toe, even veiling her face? Do you see the burka as a sign of repression? Now imagine a woman in a very revealing bikini. Is this form of dress a sign of women's liberation, an example of the freedom denied Afghan women? Think about media images of women in bikinis. What do their bodies usually look like? Do they create an impossible standard of slimness for other women to achieve? Is this image unhealthy?

Words to Learn

burka (para. 1): a long enveloping garment worn in public places by Muslim women to screen them from the view of men and strangers (n.)

subtext (para. 1): an underlying theme (n.)

locus (para. 2): place, locality (n.)

cursory (para. 4): rapidly and often superficially done (adj.)

osteoporosis (para. 4): a condition affecting especially older women and characterized by fragile and porous bones (n.)

anthrax (para. 8): an infectious and usually fatal bacterial disease of warm-blooded animals (as cattle and sheep) that is transmissible to humans; a bacterium causing anthrax (n.)

JOAN JACOBS BRUMBERG *is the Stephen H. Weiss Presidential Fellow and Professor at Cornell University where she has been teaching history, human development, and women's studies for twenty years. She is the author of* The Body Project: An Intimate History of American Girls *(1997).* JACQUELYN JACKSON *is a women's health advocate and was the executive producer of the documentary* The Body Project.

purdah (para. 10): a curtain, especially one serving to screen women from the sight of men and strangers (n.)

anorexia nervosa (para. 10): a serious disorder of eating behavior marked especially by a pathological fear of gaining weight leading to faulty eating patterns, malnutrition, and usually excessive weight loss (n.)

psyche (para. 10): soul, self, mind (n.)

The Female Body — covered in a burka or uncovered in a bikini — is a subtle subtext in the war against terrorism. The United States did not engage in this war to avenge women's rights in Afghanistan. However, our war against the Taliban, a regime that does not allow a woman to go to school, walk alone on a city street, or show her face in public, highlights the need to more fully understand the ways in which our own cultural "uncovering" of the female body impacts the lives of girls and women everywhere.   1

Taliban rule has dictated that women be fully covered whenever they enter the public realm, while a recent U.S. television commercial for *Temptation Island 2* features near naked women. Although we seem to be winning the war against the Taliban, it is important to gain a better understanding of the Taliban's hatred of American culture and how women's behavior in our society is a particular locus of this hatred. The irony is that the images of sleek, bare women in our popular media that offend the Taliban also represent a major offensive against the health of American women and girls.   2

During the twentieth century, American culture has dictated a nearly complete uncovering of the female form. In Victorian America, good works were a measure of female character, while today good looks reign supreme. From the hair removal products that hit the marketplace in the 1920s to today's diet control measures that seek to eliminate even healthy fat from the female form, American girls and women have been stripped bare by a sexually expressive culture whose beauty dictates have exerted a major toll on their physical and emotional health.   3

The unrealistic body images that we see and admire every day in the media are literally eating away at the female backbone of our nation. A cursory look at women's magazines, popular movies and television programs reveal a wide range of images modeling behaviors that directly assault the human skeleton. The ultra-thin woman pictured in a magazine sipping a martini or smoking a cigarette is a prime candidate for osteoporosis later in life.   4

In fact, many behaviors made attractive by the popular media, in-   5
cluding eating disorders, teen smoking, drinking, and the depression
and anxiety disorders that can occur when one does not measure up
are taking a major toll on female health and well-being. The American Medical Association last year acknowledged a link between violent images on the screen and violent behavior among children. In a
world where eight-year-olds are on diets, adult women spend $300
million a year to slice and laser their bodies and legal pornography is
a $56 billion industry, it is time to note the dangers of unhealthy
body images for girls and women.

Now that the Taliban's horrific treatment of women is common   6
knowledge, dieting and working out to wear a string bikini might
seem to be a patriotic act. The war on terrorism has certainly raised
our awareness of the ways in which women's bodies are controlled
by a repressive regime in a far away land, but what about the con-
straints on women's bodies here at home, right
here in America?

It is time to note   In the name of good looks (and also corporate   7
the dangers of   profits — the Westernized image of the perfect
unhealthy body   body is one of our most successful exports) con-
images for girls   temporary American women continue to engage in
and women.   behaviors that have created major public health
concerns.

Although these problems may seem small in   8
the face of the threat of anthrax and other forms of bioterrorism,
there is still a need to better understand how American culture developed to the point that it now threatens the health of its bikini-clad
daughters and their mothers.

Covered or uncovered, the homefront choice is not about moral-   9
ity but the physical and emotional health of future generations.

Whether it's the dark, sad eyes of a woman in purdah or the anx-   10
ious darkly circled eyes of a girl with anorexia nervosa, the woman
trapped inside needs to be liberated from cultural confines in whatever form they take. The burka and the bikini represent opposite ends
of the political spectrum but each can exert a noose-like grip on the
psyche and physical health of girls and women.

Web **Hear It Now:** An Interview with Joan Jacobs Brumberg and Jacquelyn Jackson, **bedfordstmartins.com/americanow**, Chapter 3. The authors of "The
Burka and the Bikini" discuss their views on the psyches and physical health
of American girls and women.

Web **Read It Now:** The American Medical Association on the Impact of the Media, bedfordstmartins.com/americanow, Chapter 3. This statement of the AMA (referred to by Brumberg and Jackson) provides the organization's position on media violence and discusses its impact on children.

Web **Read It Now:** Taliban Restrictions on Women, **bedfordstmartins.com/ americanow**, Chapter 3. This list of restrictions on women and their bodies was compiled by RAWA, the Revolutionary Association of the Women of Afghanistan, a human rights organization established in Kabul in 1977.

Vocabulary/Using a Dictionary

1. Look up *suppressive* and *oppressive* in the dictionary. How do their meanings compare to *repressive* (para. 6)? Are there any significant differences?

2. Look up *terrorism* and *biological warfare* in the dictionary to form your own definition of *bioterrorism* (para. 8). Offer an example of *bioterrorism* from the essay.

3. *Confines* (para. 10) functions as both a noun and a verb. Look up the definition of both the verb and noun *confines* in the dictionary to explain their relation to one another. Does the essay use *confines* as a noun or verb?

Responding to Words in Context

1. In paragraph 2, Jacobs Brumberg and Jackson write "Taliban rule has *dictated* that women be fully covered" and in paragraph 3 they repeat the use of the word *dictate* to explain "American girls and women have been stripped bare by a sexually expressive culture whose beauty *dictates* have exerted a major toll on their physical and emotional health." How does the word *dictated* function in paragraph 2 compared to the word *dictates* in paragraph 3? Why do you think the authors repeat the use of *dictate* in paragraph 3 to discuss American standards of beauty?

2. In paragraph 2 the authors assert that the "bare women in our popular media that *offend* the Taliban also represent a major *offensive* against the health of American women and girls." What

does the word *offensive* mean in this context? Why do you think Jacobs Brumberg and Jackson chose to use this word?

3. The essay employs the use of the term *homefront* in paragraph 9. What does *homefront* mean, and what meaning do the writers convey by using this word?

4. What two meanings of the word *backbone* apply to the sentence "media are literally eating away at the female *backbone* of our nation" (para. 4)? What point do the authors want to make?

Discussing Main Point and Meaning

1. Why do the authors compare a burka to a bikini? What argument do they make?

2. Find as many references to war as you can in the essay. In addition to the word *war*, read carefully for words we usually use in describing actions or territory in a war. Why do you think the authors use images of war to describe body image in America?

3. What evidence do the authors provide to support their claim that body images in the American media present a health threat to American women? How convincing is the evidence?

Examining Sentences, Paragraphs, and Organization

1. Explain the meaning of the first sentence in the essay. How does this sentence reflect the argument the essay makes?

2. Why is it ironic "that the images of sleek, bare women in our popular media that offend the Taliban also represent a major health offensive against the health of American women and girls" (para. 2)? What does *ironic* mean, and how does it apply to this sentence?

3. In paragraph 6, the authors declare, "Now that the Taliban's horrific treatment of women is common knowledge, dieting and working out to wear a string bikini might seem to be a patriotic act." What point do the writers want to make, and how does it reflect the scope of their larger argument?

4. Look at paragraph 9, in which Jacobs Brumberg and Jackson conclude that "the homefront choice is not about morality but the physical and emotional health of future generations." Why do the writers reject a moral argument? How does their emphasis instead on the health of women compare to the Taliban's reasons

for requiring women to wear the burka? How does the authors' description of their argument reflect the evidence they use?

Thinking Critically

1. How legitimate do you find the essay's comparison of the burka to the bikini? More specifically, how does the Taliban's power over women in Afghanistan compare to the power of the American media to define body image? What assumptions do the authors make about women in relation to the American media? How valid do you find their assumptions?

2. Why do the writers use evidence from the American Medical Association regarding the link between on-screen violence and the violent behavior of children in paragraph 5? How does this evidence connect to the point the writers want to make? Does this evidence sufficiently prove their point? Is there other evidence you would find more convincing?

In-Class Writing Activities

1. "The Burka and the Bikini" relies on a comparison between the power of the Taliban government and the power of the American media to shape its argument. In small groups, draft a response describing the Taliban's treatment of women in Afghanistan. Next, offer a list of examples that illustrate the power of the American media. (The examples should include but do not need to be limited to the issue of body image.) You may also choose to refute the claim of media influence.

2. In a parenthetical aside, the essay offers the idea that "the Westernized image of the perfect body is one of our most successful exports" (para. 7). Freewrite a response explaining how an image can be an export, what the implications of such an idea are, and how Islamic nations might view such an export.

JOEL PETT

So Why Do They Wear the Burkas
If They Don't *Have* To?

[LEXINGTON HERALD-LEADER / December 15, 2001]

Before You Read

Even after the fall of the Taliban government in Afghanistan, many women choose to wear burkas, the all-enveloping garment of Afghan women, even though the law no longer requires it. Why do you think this is?

JOEL PETT (b. 1953), winner of the 2000 Pulitzer Prize in editorial cartooning, has been the editorial cartoonist at the Lexington Herald-Leader, *in Kentucky, since 1984. His cartoons have appeared in hundreds of papers and magazines nationwide, including the* New York Times, *the* Washington Post, *the* Los Angeles Times, *the* Philadelphia Daily News, *the* Boston Globe, *the* Atlanta Journal-Constitution, USA Today, Newsweek, George, Business Week, Ms., *and* Discover.

Web **See It Now:** More Political Cartoons, by Joel Pett, **bedfordstmartins.com/ americanow**, Chapter 3. This archive includes Pett's work to date and a brief biography.

Discussing Main Point and Meaning

1. What is the daughter referring to in her question? What point does her mother make in response?

2. Is there an argument to this editorial cartoon? If so, what is it?

Examining Details, Imagery, and Design

1. What is your reaction to the image of the woman in the burka on the newspaper cover? What do you notice about the details of the breakfast table? What meaning do you get from both of these images?

2. How are the age, gender, and nationality of each character reflective of the content of their speech and concerns?

3. How would you classify the tone of the cartoon? Is it purely humorous? Is there a serious message? Do you find the tone mixed? Explain your answers.

Thinking Critically

1. Look at the list of reasons in the mother's response to her daughter. Which ones are personal? Which ones seem political? Rank her reasons in order of what you believe to be the most significant to the least. What does your order reveal about your own concerns?

2. How do the daughter's question and the mother's response reflect a Western perspective?

In-Class Writing Activities

1. Draw your own version of the cartoon in which you add two characters who respond to the daughter and mother. One character should represent the Taliban's perspective and the other the perspective of an American feminist.

2. Write a brief essay in which you respond to the daughter's question. Your response can take different forms. Perhaps you will

want to explain the cultural, political, and personal reasons for why many Afghan women choose to wear the burka even after the overthrow of the Taliban. Or maybe you'd prefer to answer the question from a perspective similar to the mother's in which you address the sources of pressure American women face when confronting ideal body image.

RACHEL DREVNO

Pop Culture Is Destroying True Beauty

[THE SPECTATOR ONLINE, SEATTLE UNIVERSITY / October 11, 2001]

Before You Read

How would you define beauty? Consider popular culture's images of beauty for both women and men. How would you describe the standard of beauty for women and men? How does this standard compare to your own definition of true beauty?

Words to Learn

vulnerability (para. 1): something that leaves one open to attack (n.)

emaciated (para. 2.): having the appearance of being very thin (adj.)

newfangled (para. 2): of the newest style (adj.)

inundated (para. 2): flooded; overwhelmed (v.)

commodities (para. 3): objects of commerce; products or qualities that are useful or valued (n.)

atrocity (para. 4): a savagely brutal, cruel, or wicked act or object (n.)

RACHEL DREVNO *(b. 1983) is a sophomore studying psychology and English at Seattle University. Her ultimate goal is to become a child psychologist. Drevno, who wrote this piece during her freshman year, feels that "every woman in the United States has to deal with society telling her how she is supposed to look." She hopes that one day women will be able to embrace who they are, without the approval of the media.*

scantily (para. 6): barely sufficient (adv.)

objectified (para 6): made into an object (v.)

provocatively (para. 6): serving to provoke or excite (adv.)

Our society affects us every day. In simple ways, it makes us aware of new products or calls our attention to new movies. Or it can affect us more deeply by suggesting we aren't good enough because we don't look a certain way. Billboards, magazine ads, and TV commercials portray ideal images of people as skinny, beautiful, and sexy, frequently playing on the general public's vulnerability about their bodies. These messages generally go unnoticed until people reach a point where they dislike everything about themselves. 1

Everywhere you look you will find images of women and men who typify what our society considers "beautiful." More often than not the women have visible ribs, hipbones that jut out, and emaciated faces. Men are portrayed as sculptures chiseled out of granite, with rockhard abs and broad shoulders. Rarely do advertisers use someone with a little meat on their bones to sell their product, unless of course they are pitching some newfangled weight-loss product. Open a magazine, closely watch a movie or TV show, and you can't help but be inundated with images of "perfect people." 2

> You can't help but be inundated with images of "perfect people."

In countless movies, characters who at first appear quiet, nerdy, or unfashionably dressed are overlooked until they receive a makeover and then suddenly to our surprise they become hot commodities. But such rapid makeovers (usually set to lively music) do not yield the same results in real life. Every year men and women spend absurd amounts of money on products that promise to make them beautiful, skinny, or physically enhanced in some way. Slap a pretty face on a box, add a so-called "guarantee," and people will flock to buy it. 3

I have friends who starve themselves, or throw up everything they eat, because pop culture tells them they aren't worthy unless they look perfect. Somewhere along the way, movies, magazines, TV shows, and music videos have persuaded women to believe that they must be skinny to be accepted. Our popular culture has led women to hate their un-ideal bodies. It's an atrocity that our society continues to sanction such images, especially when it is quite evident that they damage the self-esteem of millions. 4

On occasion someone's self-hatred can be fatal. A good friend of   5
mine lost a cousin to anorexia. Her cousin was 18 years old and she
had a heart attack. How can we sit back and watch things like this
happen? We need to live in a world where it is acceptable to be thin
and equally acceptable not to be thin.

I am tired of reading magazines and seeing ads that display scant-   6
ily clad, objectified women to sell products. I don't need to see a
woman wearing a bra and underwear and a pair of wings, posing
provocatively. That image certainly doesn't encourage me to run out
and buy a bra. Instead it causes me to question my appearance.

I find it absurd that we live in a society that supposedly prides it-   7
self on "individuality" and "uniqueness" but then turns around and
promotes a popular culture that relies heavily on uniformity and a set
of ideal standards. I don't pretend to assume that one day people will
be accepted for exactly who they are and not what society thinks they
should be. I would, however, like to imagine that one day people
won't feel so ashamed of who they are because they don't look like
Brad Pitt or Julia Roberts. It should not be up to the movie industry,
or any other industry for that matter, to decide for us what is beautiful and what is not. Beauty is different for everyone. There should be
no standards to follow. If we continue to see beauty as a carbon copy
of our cultural ideal, the true meaning of beauty will die.

Web **Read It Now:** Facts about Eating Disorders, **bedfordstmartins.com/
americanow**, Chapter 3. This report from the National Institute of Mental
Health is a document provided by the National Library of Medicine. For
more articles and reports, see the Eating Disorders page at MEDLINEplus.

Vocabulary/Using a Dictionary

1. Look up *scant* in the dictionary to find a few synonyms. Turn
   each one into an adverb. Which one best applies to the adverb
   scantily (para. 6)?

2. Look up *provoke* in the dictionary and list several synonyms.
   Which of those synonyms apply to the adjective *provocatively*
   (para. 6)?

Responding to Words in Context

1. *Commodities* (para. 3) is an economic term. More specifically, *commodity* also means "an article of commerce." How does this term contribute to Drevno's argument? What other economic terms does she include in her essay, and to what effect?

2. *Atrocity* (para. 4) is a particularly strong word to used to describe popular culture's production of a standard of beauty. Do you think Drevno's use of the word is justified considering the content of paragraph 4? Explain your answer.

3. What does *objectified* (para. 6) mean? In what ways does Drevno feel women are *objectified*?

Discussing Main Point and Meaning

1. Look at the title of the essay in relation to the argument. What does the author mean by "pop culture" and "true beauty?" How does Drevno suggest that pop culture destroys true beauty?

2. List the words in the essay around which Drevno puts quotation marks. Why does she use quotation marks around these words? How does this use of punctuation convey the article's meaning?

3. What different examples does the essay give of popular culture's influences? How do these examples reflect the scope of the problem according to Drevno?

Examining Sentences, Paragraphs, and Organization

1. Look at the first example Drevno offers of how society affects us. Why do you think she begins with this example?

2. What kind of evidence does Drevno offer in paragraphs 4 and 5? How effective is her use of evidence in terms of both logical and emotional appeals?

3. In paragraph 6 the author concludes, "That image certainly doesn't encourage me to run out and buy a bra. Instead it causes me to question my appearance." What point is Drevno making here, and how does it relate to her larger argument?

4. The final sentences of the essay declare, "If we continue to see beauty as a carbon copy of our cultural ideal, the true meaning of beauty will die." What is a *carbon copy*? Why does the author think a carbon copy will destroy true beauty?

Thinking Critically

1. In one sentence, summarize the problem Drevno defines in the essay. Does the essay offer any solutions to the problem? If so, what are they? If not, should the essay provide a solution? Explain your answers.

2. Look very carefully at the subjects of Drevno's sentences that explain who or what is defining beauty. Make a list of the things or people Drevno identifies as the sources of the problem. Do you think Drevno accurately identifies the responsible parties? What kind of cause and effect relationship does the list suggest, if any?

3. Drevno identifies the absurdity of a world that supposedly values individuality and uniqueness only to produce popular culture that requires uniformity (para. 7). Apply this statement to American culture. What evidence do you see that Americans value individuality? Where do you think this value comes from? Would you define popular culture in the same way Drevno does? Why or why not? If you do believe Americans value both individuality and conformity at the same time, can you explain this inconsistency?

In-Class Writing Activities

1. At the end of her essay, Drevno concludes, "There should be no standards to follow" (para. 7). Of course, she is referring to standards of beauty. Write several sentences in which you replace beauty with another quality, such as intelligence, athletic performance, academic progress, or conduct in a specific situation. How would the meaning of Drevno's statement change? Are standards in general a problem, or only when applied to certain qualities? Who defines different standards? How is beauty different than other qualities? Respond to these questions in a freewrite.

2. In a small group, address the problem of uniform standards of beauty. Who or what is the source of the problem? What are potential solutions to the problem? Who is responsible for solving the problem?

3. Drevno's essay addresses several ways in which popular culture influences us. Choose an example from the essay that you believe has not been the subject of much discussion and write an essay

offering evidence of this influence as well as an analysis of its consequences.

KAY HYMOWITZ

Thank Barbie for Britney

[NATIONAL REVIEW ONLINE / May 3, 2002]

Before You Read

Does Barbie play a role in the sexualization of childhood? Do toy manufacturers exploit children by advertising to them?

Words to Learn

epidemic (para. 1): widespread outbreak of a disease (n.)

bulimia (para. 1): a serious eating disorder chiefly of females that is characterized by compulsive overeating usually followed by self-induced vomiting or laxative or diuretic abuse (n.)

perturbed (para. 3): disturbed; thrown into confusion; upset (v.)

collagen-enhanced (para. 4): cosmetically altered through a substance injected into the lips to make them appear fuller (adj.)

phenomenal (para. 5): an extraordinary person or thing (adj.)

prevailing (para. 6): successful; dominating (adj.)

subordination (para. 6): condition of being lower in rank or class (n.)

hormonal (para. 6): relating to or affected by the hormones (adj.)

KAY HYMOWITZ *is a senior fellow at the Manhattan Institute, a contributing editor at* City Journal *(New York City), and an affiliate scholar at the Institute for American Values. She is the author of* Ready or Not: Why Treating Our Children as Small Adults Endangers Their Future and Ours *(2000).*

Ruth Handler, legendary founder of Mattel Toys and creator of   1
Barbie, the company's most successful product, died last week, thereby
prompting the most urgent cultural debate since Botox[1] made the
headlines. Was Barbie, as feminists said, poisonous for young girls'
self-image and the cause of an epidemic of anorexia and bulimia? Or
was she — as conservatives insisted, taking the view that "the enemy
of my feminist enemy is my friend" — simply good childhood fun?

Actually, both sides are wrong. Barbie may not have prompted a   2
national crisis in female self-esteem, but she's no innocent either. The
vampy fashion doll helped to bring about the sexualization of childhood, evidence of which is everywhere today. In truth, Barbie is the
not-so-spiritual godmother of Britney Spears.

To understand this point, you need to consider Barbie's origins. Up   3
until 1959, the year of Barbie's birth, little girls spent a lot of their time
burping and feeding the pudgy baby dolls that were a mainstay of the
toy market. But sometime in the late 1950's, during a European trip with
her daughter, Ruth Handler stumbled across "Lilli,"
a popular German doll. A hard-nosed business-
woman, Handler was not especially troubled that
Lilli was modeled on — and I'm not making this
up — a cartoon prostitute. Nor was she evidently
perturbed by the fact that Lilli was sold in bars and
tobacco shops to grown-up men who evidently were
taken with her tight (removable) sweater and short (removable) skirt.

Was Barbie poisonous for young girls' self-image?

But even without knowing the doll's scandalous past, many par-   4
ents were less than thrilled once Barbie hit American stores. In fact,
marketing researchers found that mothers *hated* Barbie. They thought
she was too grown up for their four- to twelve-year-old daughters, the
doll's target market. Before being redesigned with a sunnier California
look, Barbie was sold in a sultry leopard-skin bathing suit, sunglasses,
and with what looked like collagen-enhanced lips. Mothers had good
reason to suspect she was meant to be a swinger — a kind of Playboy
for little girls. After all, she had her own Playboy Mansion, called
"Barbie's Dream House." She had a flashy car and a sexy wardrobe.
God knows what she was doing on those make believe dates their
daughters quickly began arranging for her.

Still, Mattel wasn't overly worried about *what* mothers thought,   5
because the company had just developed a brilliant new advertising
strategy that all but bypassed parents. Previously, toy manufacturers,

[1] *Botox:* A form of a bacterial toxin that paralyzes facial muscles for cosmetic purposes.

who rarely advertised anyway, never hawked their wares directly to kids. But in the late 1950's, Ruth and Eliot Handler gambled their company's entire net worth on an advertising slot during *The Mickey Mouse Club.* The risk paid off big time: The first product to be given its own TV ad, the "Burp Gun" (don't ask), was a phenomenal success. Barbie came next; little girls immediately grasped her faintly forbidden allure and went on a "Buy me!" rampage.

Between her sexy look and her TV appearances, Barbie, then, 6
marked a big turning point in American childhood. It's not that no one had ever tried to make a buck off kids before. But up until Barbie, manufacturers and advertisers generally respected the prevailing cultural view about both the vulnerability of children and their subordination to their parents. Ruth Handler helped to change all that. As those disapproving mothers well understood, Barbie invited girls to identify not with mom but with their hormonal and independent older teenaged sisters. Television further fueled the fantasy of teen sophistication and independence by speaking directly to kids, and sometimes trying to sell them things their parents might disapprove of. It didn't happen right away, but over time children's television increasingly hyped the teenager as the childhood ideal: Think of *Teenage Mutant Ninja Turtles, Blossom,* and *Sesame Street*'s rock-and-rolling muppets. By the 1980s, bewildered parents began to see the emergence of the tween — eight- to twelve-year-olds who look (and in some cases act) like teenagers. Today's eight-year-old girls want their MTV, and demand their belly shirts and lip gloss. Even six-year-olds are Britney wannabes.

This herstory makes moot the question of whether or not you 7
should let your girls play with Barbie. When they were little, my own daughters had so many dolls that my living-room floor often looked like an Omaha Beach of half-naked Barbies (and Barbie heads and arms). But that phase doesn't last very long. The irony for Mattel is that, today, no self-respecting seven-year-old would be caught dead playing with a Barbie. Who needs a doll when you can play the teen vamp yourself?

Web **Read It Now:** Advertising to Children, **bedfordstmartins.com/americanow,** Chapter 3. This brief chapter from the *Toy Industry Factbook,* published by the Toy Industry Association, Inc., provides the history of television advertising to children and information about how it is monitored.

Web **Read It Now:** Guidelines for Children's Advertising, **bedfordstmartins.com/americanow,** Chapter 3. This document, published by the Children's Advertising Review Unit, which is operated by the Better Business Bureau for the advertising industry, is intended to promote responsible advertising practices.

Web **See It Now:** A Barbie doll showcase, **bedfordstmartins.com/americanow,** Chapter 3. Hosted by **Barbiecollectibles.com,** this site features hundreds of images and brief histories of collectible Barbies from 1959 to the present. You can also search the site by Barbie theme for such incarnations as Fairy of the Forest Barbie and Harley Davidson Barbie.

Vocabulary/Using a Dictionary

1. Look up the noun *vamp* in the dictionary. Based on this definition, what does Hymowitz imply about Barbie in using the adjective *vampy* (para. 2) to describe her?

2. Look up the definition of *hawk* as a verb. Considering the literal definition, what figurative connotation does "*hawked* their wares directly to kids" (para. 5) carry?

3. What are two different definitions of the adjective *moot* (para. 7)? Which definition applies to the writer's conclusion, "This herstory makes *moot* the question of whether or not you should let your girls play with Barbie" (para. 7)? Explain your answer.

Responding to Words in Context

1. Hymowitz holds Barbie responsible for the "*sexualization* of childhood" (para. 2). Come up with your own definition of *sexualization*. It may help to think about other *-ations* you know about, such as *commercialization* and *exploitation.*

2. The writer uses the coined term *tween* (para. 6). How does she define this term? Why is it necessary or unnecessary to coin a new term to describe this age range?

3. Hymowitz describes what she has written about Barbie as *herstory* (para. 7). Considering the context of her discussion, come up with a definition for *herstory.*

Discussing Main Point and Meaning

1. The author rejects both the feminist and conservative view of Barbie. What are their respective views of Barbie, and how is Hymowitz's argument different?

2. How is the history of Barbie's origin a key point in the larger argument of the essay?

3. Why did mothers object to Barbie?

4. What change did Barbie bring about in advertising and childhood?

Examining Sentences, Paragraphs, and Organization

1. Hymowitz begins the essay by declaring the death of Barbie's creator set off "the most urgent cultural debate since Botox made the headlines" (para. 1). How would you describe the author's tone? How does this sentence establish the tone for the rest of the essay?

2. The second paragraph ends by establishing Barbie as "the not-so-spiritual godmother of Britney Spears." What does this sentence mean? How does it reflect the essay's argument?

3. The essay concludes, "The irony for Mattel is that, today, no self-respecting seven-year-old would be caught dead playing with a Barbie" (para. 7). Do you agree? Explain the irony that Hymowitz points out.

Thinking Critically

1. The writer puts great significance on Barbie's role in changing childhood. In particular, she argues Barbie caused young girls to emulate older teens rather than their mothers (para. 6), thereby leading to the sexualization of childhood. Does Hymowitz convince you Barbie plays a key role in changing childhood? Why or why not? How do you think childhood has changed from the introduction of Barbie in the late 1950s? If you believe children have lost their innocence in the late twentieth century, what other factors do you see at work?

2. A key point in the argument is the effect of advertising in targeting children. How valid is the writer's claim that this strategy fails to recognize the vulnerability of children and undermines parents' authority (para. 6)? How pervasive do you think ads targeting children are? What effect do you think these advertisements have?

3. The writer dismisses both the feminist and conservative perception of Barbie (para. 1). Nevertheless, can you classify Hymowitz's argument as either feminist or conservative? Why or why not? How would you categorize the argument?

In-Class Writing Activities

1. Working in small groups, design a toy for children and develop a marketing strategy for selling the toy. Draft a rationale for toy design and marketing decisions. Your rationale should not only consider the potential success of the product and marketing technique, but also the ethical questions Hymowitz's essay introduces.

2. Write a brief essay in which you analyze the cultural impact of a children's toy. Hymowitz's essay serves as a model of the type of argument you'll want to write. You may choose to write about Barbie, but if you do, come up with your own argument rather than merely paraphrasing Hymowitz's. Other options might include G.I. Joe, a toy gun, or a violent video game.

3. In a freewrite, list the many cultural influences that shape childhood. Consider a broad range of factors, not just the media.

AMERICA THEN . . . 1944

CHARLES ATLAS

Fame Instead of Shame

Body building is a relatively recent phenomenon. For centuries, workers developed muscles while on the job — farming, lifting, hauling, etc. The blacksmith, for example, was often the strongest person in American villages. It was only after the rapid expansion of clerical and sales jobs in the twentieth century that people stopped developing their muscles through work and instead began developing them through working out. In other words, muscles became symbolically important when they were no longer physically required. One of the first people to profit from this modern cultural trend was Charles Atlas (1893–1972), who not only invented one of the earliest types of isometric workouts but — more significantly — designed a marketing strategy that has lasted for years (as shown by the exercise equipment continually promoted on TV "infomercials"). Ads for Charles Atlas's "Dynamic Tension" began appearing in the 1920s. One of the most famous of these ads appeared in the mid 1940s: "How Joe's Body Brought Him Fame Instead of Shame."

Web **See It Now:** Charles Atlas Advertisement, **bedfordstmartins.com/ americanow,** Chapter 3. This full-page advertisement is from the December 1923 issue of *Physical Culture,* two years after winning the "World's Most Perfect Man" competition sponsored by the magazine.

Web **Read It Now:** A Synopsis on Charles Atlas, **bedfordstmartins.com/ americanow,** Chapter 3.

Discussing the Unit

Suggested Topic for Discussion

Many of us are familiar with the argument that media-produced body images can lead to eating disorders in females. This unit provides a new twist to that familiar argument by asking readers to compare American media and American female dress to the Taliban and the burka Afghan women wear in "The Burka and the Bikini" and the editorial cartoon by Joel Pett. In addition, Rachel Drevno's student essay draws our attention to the way popular culture's standards of ideal body image affect both women and men. Kay Hymowitz — in analyzing the influence of Barbie — rejects the body image argument altogether and instead contends that Barbie helped to promote the sexualization of childhood. Finally, the "America Then" selection, an ad featuring Charles Atlas, provides an example of the media's representation of a man's body in the mid 1940s. How does the power of the American media in shaping our conceptions of ideal female beauty compare to the Taliban's rigid enforcement of proper female behavior? How does this comparison influence your perspective of media and body image? How does the media-produced ideal body image affect men compared to its effect on women? How does today's representation by the media of men's bodies compare to that of the past, as illustrated by the 1940s Charles Atlas ad? What other consequences can media advertising produce?

Preparing for Class Discussion

1. Many of these pieces assume the media plays a powerful role in shaping our conceptions of body image. What are other factors besides the media that affect the way you view your own body?

Does the media also influence these factors? Who or what do you think causes the media to promote a certain standard of beauty?

2. Bring to class several advertisements from both men's and women's magazines (including both fitness and fashion magazines) or describe television ads dealing with weight loss and exercise. How many of the ads seem to promote healthy versus unhealthy lifestyle practices? Explain your conclusions.

3. Explore key differences and similarities between the arguments of Jacobs Brumberg and Jackson, Drevno, and Hymowitz.

From Discussion to Writing

1. For some Afghan women, wearing a burka is a sign of religious commitment; for others, it is a sign of political oppression. For some American women, a bikini is a sign of sexual liberation; for others, it is a symbol of media oppression. Write an essay in which you discuss the personal and political significance of an article of clothing. You may choose to write about a burka or bikini or some other form of dress, such as a Grateful Dead T-shirt, a tie with the pattern of an American flag, a pair of designer jeans, or a military uniform. The article of clothing may belong to you or someone else. Why do you think the wearer chose this article of clothing? What does it suggest about the wearer's personality? What kind of statement does the clothing make? Use your own observations and the texts to develop your ideas.

2. In the *Boston Globe* cartoon by Joel Pett, the daughter asks, "Why do they wear the burkas if they don't *have* to?" Replace the word *burka* with *bikini* and write a dialogue in which Jacobs Brumberg and Jackson, Drevno, and Hymowitz answer the question. The dialogue should reflect each essay's argument.

3. Assume you are the president of an advertising agency and Jacobs Brumberg and Jackson, Drevno, and Hymowitz have all come to you asking you to design an ad. Jacobs Brumberg and Jackson want the ad to reflect positive body image. Drevno wants the ad to promote "true beauty." Hymowitz wants the ad to sell a children's toy. Draw or describe an ad you would create for each client. Write an essay defending your advertisements, explaining how each meets the needs of your clients. Do you think the Charles Atlas ad would serve as a useful model for your advertisement?

Topics for Cross-Cultural Discussion

1. How does female or male dress in another country compare to America? How do the differences or similarities reflect different or shared values?

2. How influential do you think the American standard of beauty is for other cultures in the world? Do you see American body image as a successful export? Do you see any resistance to this export? Explain using specific examples of your own as well as support from the texts in this unit.

3. Describe a children's toy that is popular in a country other than the U.S. What effect, if any, does the toy have on children?

4

Can We Choose
Our Personal Identities?

How important is ethnic heritage to our sense of personal identity? Aren't we all separate individuals first — with our own complicated histories — and members of groups second? And if we belong to more than one racial or ethnic group — if our identities are "mixed" — is it necessary to choose one as more authentic than the others? Is it possible to select out of a mixture of identities one dominant identity without disrespecting the others? Or do most people who represent multiple categories choose whatever identity is most advantageous at the moment?

This unit features three personal essays that show the risks and rewards of a "hyphenated existence" in a nation that prides itself on cultural diversity. In "Muslims in the Mosaic," Eisa Nefertari Ulen describes what it feels like to be both American Muslim and African American after the terrorist attacks of 9/11. Finding strength in her two identities, she believes it is again time "for Black America to act as the moral conscience of this nation." Although he, too, possesses two identities, Aka Lauenstein Denjongpa discovers in "The Color of Aka" that money may create as many barriers between people as their racial or ethnic differences. He recalls his first day at prep school where everything "was race- and money-segregated, and there I was with my two bags and a trunk, leaning on my parents' old red van, my blond, white mom on one side and my Asian father with his long black hair on the other." Describing herself as a "patchwork of different cultures," Sunita Puri was shocked to discover that many acquaintances regard the sacred Hindu symbol she wears between her eyebrows "as a fashion statement rather than a statement of cultural belonging." "Assigning new cultural meanings to symbols with very old traditions or deep personal significance," she warns Americans, "is inappropriate and insensitive."

EISA NEFERTARI ULEN

Muslims in the Mosaic

[ESSENCE / January 2002]

Before You Read

How difficult is it to be religious in a predominantly secular world? How does being an African American Muslim in America pose specific identity-related conflicts? What can be done to address those conflicts?

Words to Learn

mosaic (title): design made with various small, colored pieces of tile (n.)

activism (para. 1): theory or practice based on aggressive or militant action (n.)

secular (para. 2): of or pertaining to a nonreligious body or system (adj.)

kufi (para. 3): usually knitted or crocheted cap, worn by African American Muslims, named for an African word for "crown" (n.)

sanctuary (para. 4): place of refuge or asylum (n.)

defile (para. 4): to make filthy; to violate (v.)

sanctity (para. 5): sacredness (n.)

acquiesce (para. 5): consent passively (v.)

Eisa Nefertari Ulen (b. 1968) teaches English at Hunter College of the City University of New York. She has contributed articles and reviews to the Quarterly Black Review of Books, *the* Washington Post, Ms., Vibe, Shade, Heart and Soul, Emerge, Source, City Sun, *and* Black Issues Book Review.

I am an American Muslim, a woman who freely chose Islam, the second largest religion in the world, as my personal path to spiritual power. I am also African American, instilled with a legacy of activism since childhood.

I am blessed to inhabit what many people think of as two different worlds — live in the secular, democratic United States, where many religions are practiced, and I also devoutly follow Islam. As a woman I can attest that these worlds are essentially parallel. Among all people there is good — and evil. I bear witness to the Christian woman beaten by her lover in the street outside my Brooklyn apartment and the Muslim woman tied to a whipping post in Nigeria. I bear witness to the woman forced to work in strip clubs to survive in Atlanta and the woman forced to cover herself from head to toe to survive in Afghanistan. In both worlds I bear witness to sisters constrained by man's convenient misinterpretations of law.

> *Yet no one profiled scrubbed-faced White men in button-down collars.*

I also bear witness to my brothers — Black men in sleek cars — who are profiled by the police. Now, since the terrorist attacks, it's my Muslim brothers — men in knitted *kufis* — who are profiled by their neighbors. And there are my American Muslim sisters who, because they wear the *hijab* (veil), now hesitate to leave their homes. Yet no one profiled scrubbed-faced White men in button-down collars after Timothy McVeigh bombed the Oklahoma City federal building.

We must acknowledge and reject this double standard in America's popular response to evil. When we are tempted to blame last September's terrorist attacks on Islam, we should consider that the Ku Klux Klan burned crosses and set fire to Black churches, lighting symbols of Christian redemption and sanctuary with the fires of hatred. Madness is wrought when terrorists twist faith — any faith — to justify horror, as they did on September 11, 2001. With my sisters and brothers of every faith, I wept as fire twisted steel, bodies fell from a hundred stories in the sky and thousands of lives were destroyed. The mass murder of innocents defiles the very meaning of Islam, which promotes love, unity, and justice.

I chose Islam because I insist on justice and because I love Allah. I think Allah chose me because I write, teach, and demonstrate. Black life has often been held in opposition to American life. But since September 11, as a Muslim, I've felt my life held in opposition yet again. With more than 1 billion Muslims, Islam represents about 20 percent of the world's diverse people. The United States, too, is a mosaic of cultures, and Islam — with up to 6 million American Muslims, approximately 30 percent of them African American — belongs in that mosaic. At congregational *Jummah* prayer at the mosque, I sit with my many-hued Muslim sisters. I celebrate the sanctity of difference in Islam. But as we Americans rightfully insist on justice and legal retribution for the attacks, we African Americans must remember our history. If we forget our shared experience as people of color in America, if we shrink and cower from one another because some of us don't know or understand Islam, we simply acquiesce to more death, more war.

African Americans' social consciousness has consistently shaped a better America. How many immigrants have been able to find peace and enjoy democracy in this country as a result of Black people's efforts to ensure that we *all* have a place at the front of the bus? It is time, yet again, for Black America to act as the moral conscience of this nation. We sisters, Black women of all faiths, must unite and protect the ideal of American freedom, standing up for any sister in this country who feels vulnerable to taunts and threats because she is veiled. We must do this because we understand that beneath her hijab, that sister is one of us.

Web **Read It Now:** *Muslims:* Introduction, **bedfordstmartins.com/americanow**, Chapter 4. This document provides an overview of the essays, images, and interviews featured in *Muslims,* a Frontline program on PBS (the Public Broadcasting System). Resources include a list of the basic beliefs of Muslims.

Web **See It and Hear It Now:** *Muslims:* Portraits of Ordinary Muslims, **bedford stmartins.com/americanow**, Chapter 4. These images and videos of interviews with diverse Muslims from around the world are from *Muslims,* a Frontline program on PBS.

Vocabulary/Using a Dictionary

1. *Mosaic* (title) shares a root (*musaicum*) with *museum.* How is a museum like a mosaic?

2. *Sanctuary* (para. 4), like *sanctity* (para. 5), comes from the root *sanctus,* meaning "holy." What do you think it means to be *sanctimonious?* What do you think it means to *sanction* something?

3. Nefertari Ulen says that "if we shrink and cower from one another because some of us don't know or understand Islam, we simply acquiesce to more death, more war" (para. 5). The word *acquiesce* means to "consent passively." How does the author's point here relate to her earlier reference to *activism* (para. 1)?

Responding to Words in Context

1. In paragraph 1, Nefertari Ulen announces that she has chosen Islam as her "path to spiritual power." What do you think she means by "spiritual power?" How does it compare to the political activism she also discusses in this paragraph?

2. "In both worlds I bear witness to sisters constrained by man's convenient misinterpretations of law" (para. 2). Do you think the author is making a gender distinction with the word *man's* or does she mean to include men and women in her criticism?

3. What does Nefertari Ulen refer to when she speaks of black men being "profiled" by the police (para. 3)?

Discussing Main Point and Meaning

1. Why does the author compare a Christian woman to a Muslim woman, and a stripper to a veiled Afghan woman in paragraph 2?

2. What is the "double standard" the author refers to in paragraph 4?

3. What "mosaic" is it that Muslims are a part of, according to this article?

4. Paraphrase the author's main argument in this essay. Is it primarily about religion, race, or gender?

Examining Sentences, Paragraphs, and Organization

1. In paragraph 2, what phrase is repeated several times? What is the effect of this repetition?

2. In paragraph 1, Nefertari Ulen refers to Islam as the "second largest religion in the world"; in paragraph 5, she says Muslims represent twenty percent of the world's population. Do these figures reveal anything to you about religion in general?

3. The final paragraph begins with a general appeal to African Americans or black America, but the paragraph ends with a call to action directed at black women specifically. Why the shift?

Thinking Critically

1. "Yet no one profiled scrubbed-faced White men in button-down collars after Timothy McVeigh bombed the Oklahoma City federal building" (para. 3). What is Nefertari Ulen criticizing in this sentence? Is her comparison appropriate? Why or why not?

2. In paragraph 6, the author argues that African Americans have shaped American "social consciousness" and enabled peace and democracy for immigrants. Do you agree? Explain.

In-Class Writing Activities

1. How does your understanding of Islam compare to Nefertari Ulen's description of it as promoting "love, unity, and justice" (para. 4)? Were you surprised by that definition? Write a short essay about your general impression of Islam both before and after reading this piece.

2. This is an essay largely about the relationship between race and religion. What is your experience with that intersection? Describe the way these two influences do or do not interact in your own life.

AKA LAUENSTEIN DENJONGPA

The Color of Aka

[RUMINATOR REVIEW, MACALESTER COLLEGE / Fall 2001]

Before You Read

Who do you hang out with at school? Does your racial background or your economic status play a role in who your friends are? Is identity inherited? Does it change over time?

Words to Learn

Himalayan (para. 1): of or from the Himalayas mountain range in South Central Asia (adj.)

Tibet (para. 3): country in southern China; formerly a theocratic state governed by Buddhism (n.)

shrine (para. 4): space or site containing sacred objects, generally used for prayer and spiritual offerings (n.)

My father is Asian, from the Himalayan kingdom of   1
Sikkim, and my mother is Caucasian, so where does that leave me? My father is a short man, with very proud posture and a protruding potbelly. He has coarse black hair that would make a prize stallion jealous. My mother has dirty-blond hair with a skin tone that looks like stirred-up milk — no matter how much you stir, it is still white. Then there is me, with a tan skin color, coarse brown hair, golden-hued eyes, tall and built, proud and yet also very lost.

I had two names growing up. My parents needed to put a   2
name on the birth certificate in order to take me home from the

AKA LAUENSTEIN DENJONGPA was born and raised in Massachusetts. He wrote this piece as a freshman at Rollins College in Winter Park, Florida, and expects to graduate in 2005.

hospital in Danvers, Massachusetts. My father liked Jefferson, as in Thomas Jefferson, and my mother liked Nathaniel, as in Nathaniel Bowditch, the great navigator from Salem. My father, an immigrant, wanted a powerful American name. He thought an American name would give me an advantage over others like himself who were foreign and often considered to be inferior. In the end I got named Nathaniel. I never liked that name, though. I could never spell it, and I also hated the sound of it.

Shortly after I was born, I received another name, one that I have assumed. The name was given to me by my father's Buddhist teacher, Lama Jigtse. He died before I was old enough to have any clear memories of him, but I have heard stories about him since I was very young — stories about his capture by Chinese Muslims in his home region of Golok, Tibet; about the vision telling him to leave Tibet; how he came to the United States and diverted a storm from hitting Rhode Island.

When I was a baby, my parents drove me down to Providence to meet Lama. I am told we were both impressed with each other. I was mesmerized by the bubbling Christmas lights on his shrine and the many Buddhist books wrapped in cloth. Lama allowed me to walk over the books, something I would normally have been spanked for. Walking over, on, or putting your feet in the direction of anything holy is very disrespectful in Buddhism, but Lama protected me, never letting me get scolded or spanked. He even let me explore his face with my hands and feet. He was impressed with what he saw in me, an ability that only Lamas or great Buddhist practitioners have. He saw his own teacher, Akiterton, a great leader in eastern Tibet.

The name he gave me was Aka.

My schooling started at Saint Mary's, the brick elementary school right up the hill from where my family lives in Beverly, Massachusetts. Saint Mary's was an all-white Catholic school that did not exactly fit my race or religion (I was — and am — a Buddhist), but the funny thing about my experience at Saint Mary's was that I never felt different or alone, no matter what religion, race, or financial situation I dealt with.

Then, I graduated from the eighth grade at Saint Mary's and was sent off to the wilderness of western Massachusetts to a boarding school. Berkshire School was a minefield, filled with lost souls about to explode. I could not find a place where I belonged, and it seemed the harder I looked the more separated I became.

The first thing I felt arriving at Berkshire was a strong sense of 8
insecurity. I saw the rich kids, mostly white, hanging together, pulling
up in Mercedeses, BMWs, and Lexuses. The black kids stuck together
as well, wearing hats, bandanas, jeans, and Timberland boots. I saw
Asians, dressed in Versace, Gucci, and Armani. They wore those
clothes just like it was a regular day. (Not even my Sunday best was
in the Versace category.) Everything was race- and money-segregated,
and there I was with my two bags and a trunk, leaning on my parents' old red van, my blond, white mom on one side and my Asian father with his long black hair on the other.

I made a connection with minorities, even while I was trying to 9
understand whether I was a minority or even what a minority was.
The black kids refused to believe I was anything but a minority. The
white kids refused to believe I was anything but white. And the Asian
kids were just confused by my distant attitude toward them.

I soon discovered that the difference between me and most of the 10
kids at Berkshire was money. One of my friends at school crashed his
new Jeep, but it was replaced a week later by a
new and better Audi. An Asian friend came home
with me one weekend and spent more than a
grand on a shopping spree at stores like Versace,
Armani, and some Middle Eastern suit store you
had to get buzzed into.

I was trying to understand whether I was a minority.

I began to wish and even pretend that I had 11
that kind of money, too. I felt as if even the poor
kids had more than I did. Money and materials became a competition. Trying not to compete over money left me feeling alone and
scared. For some people, identity was as simple as looking in the mirror, but for me it took a little more soul-searching.

The question I was most often asked was, "Why not hang out 12
with Asians, if you feel so strongly about race?" I thought about this
a lot. I couldn't just answer off the top of my head. I noticed that the
values I believed in were not usually shared by the other Asians at my
school — values like not wasting money, not wanting too much, sharing, and offering food to others before serving yourself. I wasn't
blaming them because it wasn't their fault, and it wasn't mine either.
It was a barrier that stood between us.

During my four years at Berkshire I spent time amongst them all: 13
whites, blacks, Asians, the rich, and the poor. I sat with them, played
sports and video games with them, and even hung out with them after
school had ended for vacation — things you only do with your friends,

no matter how diverse their colors or personalities. Maybe I shouldn't be thinking about race at all. After all, I am the difference between a cup of stirred-up milk and a stallion with a long black mane.

Around the age of eleven I began to wonder what my name, Aka, 14 meant, and what my destiny as Aka was. Before this my father had always said, "Just be a compassionate person," but I wanted more than that.

"Aka means a lot," he said. 15

"Well, I got time, but you're running out." 16

"Okay, okay. The first thing you must understand is that 'Ah' is 17 the first vowel in the Tibetan alphabet, and 'Khaa' is the first consonant. The second part is harder to understand. Are you sure you want me to tell you now?"

"Of course, I want to know." 18

"You really are the incarnate Akiterton, you know that?" 19

I stared at my dad. He had a way of asking these questions (truth- 20 seeking but unanswerable). I wondered if he knew how overwhelming his questions were. My dad continued without my answering.

"'Ah' is the first sound of the universe. It comes from 'Khaa,' the 21 space. It is easier understood like this: 'Khaa' is the space and the creator. 'Ah' is the sound and the creation that came from 'Khaa.' I told you it was difficult."

"So which one am I?" 22

"That is the hardest part, Aka. You are both." 23

Web **Read It Now:** Buddhism, **bedfordstmartins.com/americanow**, Chapter 4. This short essay from *The Columbia Encyclopedia* at Bartleby.com covers the basic beliefs, practices, and history of Buddhism.

Vocabulary/Using a Dictionary

1. Lauenstein Denjongpa says he "assumed" the name Aka (para. 3). What does *assume* mean in this context? How is the word more commonly used? How are the meanings related?

2. When Lauenstein Denjongpa says he is "the difference between a cup of stirred-up milk and a stallion with a long black mane" (para. 13), what does he mean? Does he refer to a kind of mathematical "difference" (for example, the difference between 5 and 8 is 3) or a more substantive "difference" (for example, the

difference between a chair and a table is that one gives you a place to sit and one gives you a place to set objects)? Why do you think he uses the word *difference* rather than *combination* or *mixture*?

Responding to Words in Context

1. Lauenstein Denjongpa refers to his father as an "Asian, from the Himalayan kingdom of Sikkim," and his mother as simply "Caucasian" (para. 1). Are *Asian* and *Caucasian* complementary terms? Why does the author expand on his father's background but refer to his mother only with a racial term?

2. The name Nathaniel means "gift of God." Why is this meaning ironic?

3. In paragraphs 8 and 10, Lauenstein Denjongpa refers to many specific brand names. Why?

Discussing Main Point and Meaning

1. Is Lauenstein Denjongpa's argument about race, money, destiny, or some combination of the three? Can you paraphrase his main point?

2. Why do you think Lauenstein Denjongpa "never felt different or alone, no matter what religion, race, or financial situation [he] dealt with" at St. Mary's (para. 6)?

3. Why doesn't Lauenstein Denjongpa spend as much time with the Asians at his high school as with other friends?

4. For what purpose does the writer include the conversation with his father about his name in the last several paragraphs?

Examining Sentences, Paragraphs, and Organization

1. Examine the following sentence: "My mother has dirty-blond hair with a skin tone that looks like stirred-up milk — no matter how much you stir, it is still white" (para. 1). Why do you think Lauenstein Denjongpa uses the image of "stirred-up milk" to describe his mother?

2. Lauenstein Denjongpa's essay is a first-person account of his experiences with race and identity. How would this essay change if

it were a more general account of the issue written in the third person?

3. This essay concludes with: "That is the hardest part, Aka. You are both." Does this conclusion resolve to any degree the issues the author has raised? Or does it raise additional questions?

Thinking Critically

1. Lauenstein Denjongpa clearly chooses his Asian heritage as his primary identity, and yet he shies away from other Asian students at his high school. At the end of this essay, where do you think Lauenstein Denjongpa's Asian identity stands? Is he more or less comfortable with who he is?

2. Lauenstein Denjongpa says very little about his mother and her background, other than describing her skin and hair color. Is this a weakness of the essay, or is his mother's ethnic identity irrelevant?

In-Class Writing Activities

1. Describe a story from your childhood that emphasizes your ethnic or racial identity in some way, like the story Lauenstein Denjongpa tells of receiving the name Aka. Does the story still have meaning for you, or have you outgrown the identity it illustrates?

2. Describe the cliques at your high school. Is there some logic to explain the way students at your school segregate themselves? What differences is that logic based on? Where did you fit in?

SUNITA PURI

Cultural Identity vs. Ethnic Fashions

[THE YALE HERALD ONLINE, YALE UNIVERSITY / February 2, 2001]

Before You Read

Is wearing the symbols of another culture an insult or a compliment? Under what circumstances is it appropriate to adopt or stylize the cultural or religious articles of a traditional heritage and turn them into "fashion statements?"

Words to Learn

Punjabi (para. 1): of or from the Punjab state in northwest India (adj.)

kudiya (para. 1): one of the many languages of India; from the Kerala district (n.)

sari (para. 2): traditional outer garment worn by many Indian and Pakistani women (n.)

imperialism (para. 3): practice of extending a nation's authority over other nations, usually by way of politics or economics (n.)

appropriating (para. 3): taking possession of for one's own exclusive use (v.)

I live a hyphenated existence. South Asian-American. Indian-American. Punjabi-American. Physically, I am also a patchwork of different cultures: I wear jeans and T-shirts, I braid my hair in Punjabi *kudiya* style, have a nose ring, and wear a *bindi*, a small colored dot worn in between the eyebrows by South-

1

A junior at Yale University when she wrote this essay, SUNITA PURI (b. 1979) graduated in 2002 with a degree in social and cultural anthropology. She is a Rhodes Scholar at Oxford University for 2002–2003 studying race relations and the status of minorities in Britian. Puri's service work and academic research have centered largely on issues of domestic violence, eating disorders, and mental health in South Asian and Asian American immigrant communities.

Asian women. Depending on who you talk to, though, I can be seen as an Indian trying to be "fashionably ethnic" in superficially "multi-cultural" American surroundings. While my extended family sympathizes with my efforts to reconcile my sense of belonging to both India and America, I do not meet with such understanding from those surrounding me who interpret my wearing *bindis* as a fashion statement rather than a statement of cultural belonging.

I recently had a conversation with an acquaintance who believed that I wear *bindis* because, in his words, "It's a, you know, convenient way to sort of like assert an identity. Like, you're making a statement, but it's not offensive or anything. It's actually fashionable." I was shocked, especially at his claim that many others agreed with him. I wear my *bindis* to demonstrate my adherence to and respect for my culture and religion and the large roles they occupy in my identity and everyday life — not to imitate a pop icon. My acquaintance then pulled out a picture of Destiny's Child, taken at a recent awards program. Not only were the women clad in outfits made from sari material, but they all sported matching, colorfully flashy *bindis*. 2

> *I wear my* bindis *to demonstrate my respect for my culture and religion.*

This is cultural imperialism at its worst. Pop icons like Madonna perpetuate a faulty understanding of Indian culture by selecting exotic images from India, such as the *bindi,* taking them completely out of cultural context and popularizing them in the West. What people like Madonna don't realize, however, is that appropriating the *bindi* in such a way has devastating effects on the symbol's meaning in South Asia. For example, while in Delhi over the summer, I was hard pressed to find plain red *bindis,* finding instead very flashy, so-called "export quality" *bindis,* replete with sparkles and a variety of colors. The *bindi* is no longer what it once was — a symbol of being Hindu and of having a symbolic union with God. Now, it is not only a fashionable item to wear, but is also mass-produced specifically for export to other countries. The Madonnas and Gwen Stefanis of the world — along with those who have blindly followed their example — have successfully changed the meaning of the *bindi* in South Asia, for the worse. 3

And this new meaning obviously extends to South Asian-Americans, among them young women such as myself who are labeled as consumers of teenybopper culture rather than as heirs to the cultural legacy represented in small part by *bindis*. My stomach turns when I 4 see non-South Asians wearing *bindis* to proms, social events, or simply "as part of their outfits." Without realizing it, they are transforming the meaning of the *bindi* from an inherently sacred entity to an accessory whose popularity will undoubtedly fade, as all trends do. And the popularization of this trend may suggest to our peers that those of us who wear *bindis* to bridge our hyphenated existences do so only to assert cultural identity in an acceptable, Americanized way.

While I do not mean to imply that all Americans think this way, even knowing a handful that do is insulting, both to me personally and to South Asian culture. How am I, for example, supposed to react when I enter a bookstore and see *The Bindi Kit* lying on the shelf marked "International Books"? Am I supposed to be happy that *bindis* are now being sold along with body paint in kits that encourage girls to wear *bindis* as exotic belly button ring substitutes surrounded by colorful paint?   5

One could argue that the *bindi* phenomenon is a good thing because it could motivate interested Americans to examine diverse South Asian cultures and histories more closely. Even though this might be true, I resent the fact that a culture should be considered worthy of study or attention because of the fashion appeal of its symbols or traditions.   6

Assigning new cultural meanings to symbols with very old traditions or deep personal significance is inappropriate and insensitive. It reduces the complexities of South Asian culture to mere physical items, rather than the continual process that culture is.   7

So please — don't wear *bindis,* and don't think of my homeland simply as the origin of yoga, incense, and exoticism if you are going to ignore the context and meanings of these cultural components as well as the reasons why we "ethnic folk" appreciate, treasure, and cling to them.   8

Web **Read It Now:** "India Fashion: Traditions and Customs," **bedfordstmartins.com/ americanow,** Chapter 4. This brief article provides an overview of the significance of the bindi, sindoor, nose ring, and bangles; from IndiaExpress.com.

Vocabulary/Using a Dictionary

1. *Imperialism* (para. 3) comes from the Latin word *imperium* for "command." In what way are Destiny's Child's saris and bindis *commanding*?

2. As a verb, *appropriate* (para. 3) means to take possession of something for one's own exclusive use. As an adjective, *appropriate* means suitable for a purpose. Do you see any correlations between these two meanings?

Responding to Words in Context

1. What do you think the phrase "fashionably ethnic" (para. 1) means? Can you give any examples of this phrase in addition to Puri's bindis, braids, and nose ring? How does the phrase compare to the popular saying "fashionably late?"

2. Puri calls Madonna a "pop icon" (para. 3). What does this phrase mean?

3. In paragraph 4, the author writes: "And the popularization of this trend may suggest to our peers that those of us who wear *bindis* to bridge our hyphenated existences do so only to assert cultural identity in an acceptable, Americanized way." What does Puri mean by the term *Americanized* here? Who or what is responsible for the process of *Americanization*?

Discussing Main Point and Meaning

1. How does Puri define or describe her "hyphenated existence" (paras. 1 and 4)?

2. Why do the sparkly, multicolored bindis signify a loss of meaning to Puri (para. 3)?

3. What is Puri's problem with "*The Bindi Kit*" (para. 5)?

4. Puri writes: "I resent the fact that a culture should be considered worthy of study or attention because of the fashion appeal of its symbols or traditions" (para. 6). Why does "fashion appeal" have such a negative affect on culture in Puri's mind?

Examining Sentences, Paragraphs, and Organization

1. Puri's introduction is largely about herself, though her main point is really not a merely personal one. Why would she spend so much time describing her personal experience in the first paragraph?

2. In paragraph 2, Puri presents a quote from and paraphrases a conversation with an acquaintance who finds her bindis "fash-

ionable." What does Puri want this anecdote to illustrate? How does the anecdote rate as evidence of her point?

3. Puri appeals to her audience in the conclusion: "So please — don't wear *bindis*" (para. 8). Who, specifically, do you think this appeal is directed at? Is the entire essay directed toward the same specific audience? Or are different parts directed at different readers?

Thinking Critically

1. Puri writes in paragraph 6: "One could argue that the *bindi* phenomenon is a good thing because it could motivate interested Americans to examine diverse South Asian cultures and histories more closely." She dismisses this argument because the interest would be based on "fashion appeal." Do you think her dismissal is logical? Is it possible that a superficial interest could lead to a deeper, more complex one?

2. What do you make of Puri's "jeans and T-shirts" style (para. 1)? Does it signify a merely superficial interest in American culture? Puri describes her style as "a patchwork of different cultures" (para. 1). Why does she consider the mixing of cultural fashion acceptable for herself, but not for Americans who are not South Asian?

In-Class Writing Activities

1. Describe your own "hyphenated existence." What cultures do you recognize as having an influence on your identity? What pieces of tradition have you incorporated into your personal appearance? Which influences were you born with and which ones did you adopt voluntarily?

2. Write a short essay comparing and contrasting bindis to another ethnic fashion statements or ethnic trends adopted by Americans (for example, dreadlocks, devotion statues of the Buddah, salsa music, sushi, and so on). Use your example to support or challenge Puri's argument that these kinds of trends are insults.

Discussing the Unit

Suggested Topic for Discussion

What is the deepest essence of who you are? Do you, like Aka Lauenstein Denjongpa, identify more with one parent than the other? Have there been circumstances that have challenged your sense of identity, such as the fashion trends Sunita Puri describes? Have you — like Eisa Nefertari Ulen — had experiences that have made you want to reinforce your identity?

Preparing for Class Discussion

1. Can stories like these three authors present be produced only in the United States? Is the struggle to be many things at once an inherently American struggle? How do you think the authors in this unit would respond to these questions?

2. In some way or other, each of these authors *chooses* a mode of identifying her- or himself ethnically. Do we all have choices like this? Can some choose more easily than others? Explain.

From Discussion to Writing

1. Objects that identify ethnicity play a role in each of these essays. Examine and compare the *kufis* and *hijabs* Nefertari Ulen alludes to, the *bindis* Puri discusses, and the cars and clothing Lauenstein Denjongpa names. How do these objects play the same roles? How do they play different roles?

2. These selections deal not only with an ethnic identity but also with a religious component to that identity. How are religion and ethnicity part of identity? How are they two completely different issues? Write a short essay describing your position, using the three selections here as evidence where you can.

Topics for Cross-Cultural Discussion

1. What comes first in other cultures: race, ethnicity, religion, gender? Is the need to identify one's identity based on one or some combination of these categories important in other countries?

2. Nefertari Ulen identifies herself as an African American Muslim, Puri is a Punjabi American, and Lauenstein Denjongpa is an Asian American of Himalayan descent. Do you relate to any one of these perspectives more than another? Explain your answer.

5

What Is America?
Who Are Americans?

In the preceding unit we heard three personal stories of hyphenated identity. In this unit we examine the issues of ethnic and racial
identity from a larger perspective, one that takes into account the
most recent U.S. census and some significant demographic and immigration trends. The story here is not so much about individuals but
rather our society and culture as a whole.

In "What the Census Doesn't Count," Russell Thornton, a Native American anthropology professor, continues the topic raised in
Unit 4, where individuals explored the options of choosing their
racial or ethnic identity. Pointing out that the 2000 census for the
first time officially allowed Americans to choose their race, Thornton
nevertheless asks an unsettling question: "Is race really something we
can choose, or is it chosen for us?" Results of the 2000 census also
led the U.S. Census Bureau to predict that Hispanics would "replace"
African Americans as "America's largest minority." This fact disturbs
one of the nation's most prominent Hispanic essayists and commentators, Richard Rodriguez, who argues in "Black and Tan Fantasy"
that the census bureau's claim "manages both to trivialize the significance of Hispanics in our national life, as well as to insult African
Americans by describing Hispanics as replacing blacks." Although
Hadia Mubarak, an Arab American student at Florida State University, begins with a personal anecdote, her essay takes on one of the

major issues resulting from the enormous increase in U.S. immigration over the past decade: assimilation. "What is our concept of assimilation?" she asks. As she explores the blurred boundaries of assimilation, she concludes that if the "presence of diversity threatens our sense of identity as a culture, then we have no identity worth preserving." A group promoting English as the official language of the United States takes out an advertisement to show how it is "fighting to prevent America from being divided by language."

RUSSELL THORNTON

What the Census Doesn't Count

[THE NEW YORK TIMES / March 23, 2001]

Before You Read

What is the value of knowing how many of us are one race and how many are another? Why do we need to know who is of mixed race? Does the census really tell us who we are as a people?

Words to Learn

census (title): poll, survey; in the United States, the official count of citizens made every ten years (n.)
mulatto (para. 5): a person having one Caucasian and one African parent; related to those of mixed Caucasian and African ancestry (n., adj.)
demographic (para. 7): pertaining to the study of populations (adj.)

RUSSELL THORNTON *(b. 1942) grew up in various locations in eastern Oklahoma. He has taught anthropology at the University of California, Los Angeles; the University of California, Berkeley; Dartmouth College; the University of Minnesota; and the University of Pennsylvania. Thornton is the author of* American Indian Holocaust and Survival: A Population History Since 1492 *(1987) and* The Cherokees: A Population History *(1992).*

The 2000 census was the first in which Americans could choose to identify themselves as having more than one race, and some 6.8 million people, about 2.4 percent of the population, did so. What does this identification mean for these Americans? Do others accept it? Is race really something we can choose, or is it chosen for us?

Race, we now know, is a social notion, not a biological reality. Physical appearances used to construct races — particularly skin color — are all but meaningless as indicators of important biological differences. Nevertheless, the races society has created are real to many people and have important psychological and social implications for individuals. According to the 2000 census, three of every ten Americans are members of one of four defined minority groups — African Americans, Asian Americans, Native Americans, and Latinos. Some seven of every ten Americans consider themselves white.

The 2000 census remains silent on whether the people around a given person consider him or her to be white, Asian American, or something else altogether. And that relative suspension of social judgment is the 2000 census's greatest innovation; it recognizes who you think you are as an important piece of information.

Since the census began, the government has attempted to enumerate citizens in terms of the important categories of the period. The first census, in 1790, was primarily concerned with counting landholding white males. Subsequent censuses became more inclusive. In 1890, for example, all Native Americans were first counted as part of the United States population; eighty years later the census included a question about Latinos.

All censuses through 1990 classified each American as being of only one of the designated races — except for the "mulatto" category common through the nineteenth century, which mainly concerned people who appeared to census enumerators to be somewhere between black and white. The mulatto category was the ancestor of today's mixture option, with the difference that today it is up to the individual rather than the census enumerator to name and describe the mixture.

Race, as we now know, is a social notion, not a biological reality.

The mulatto concept lived on somewhat quietly from 1900 to 1960 in the practice of having census workers split the differences themselves, so to speak, in problematic cases of mixture, or classify people in the category "all other races."

In particularly difficult cases, the enumerators were to ask members of a person's community about what race that person was thought to be. This practice shows that in those years the important question was what society thought you were—not your own thoughts on who you were.

The 2000 census finally acknowledged the private reality of racially mixed citizens, capping the trend toward self-reporting begun with the 1960 census. But racial mixture in our country, of course, dates back centuries, despite the many state laws prohibiting marriages between whites and nonwhites. Among Native Americans, the story has long been—and it is not a very amusing story—that the first Indian-white child in North America was born nine months after the first white man arrived. Similarly, the mulatto census category accounted for significant percentages of the population in some states. It was not merely a demographic footnote.

The Native American case is in many ways an extreme one. In the 2000 census, 2.6 million Americans reported they were Native American. Some 1.5 million others reported that they were Native American and another race, typically white. This ratio—37 percent of a group reporting themselves as racially mixed—far exceeds percentages for other groups. For example, only about 5 percent of African Americans reported mixed ancestry.

A high percentage of racially mixed Native Americans is not surprising for those familiar with Native American history. The Native American population of what is now the United States declined from more than 5 million around 1492 to as few as 250,000 by 1900. It then began to increase, in part because of intermarriage, especially with whites; indeed, given the small numbers, it could hardly have increased without intermarriage. This situation created identity struggles for children of these marriages as they sought to define who they were and have others accept it. Children of Native American and African American intermarriages, for example, typically could not get others to accept their "Indianness" and almost always were defined as African American.

In such cases, we can see a variety of choices being made. Individuals may choose one identity for themselves, but others in society may make another choice for them. The black-Indian child may think of himself as Indian, but if no one around him does, then he has run up against the limit of his own power to choose a racial identity. And this constriction of choice extends backward in our history as it is verified by the terms we use: the racial categories themselves, black, white, and so on, were not necessarily "chosen" in the past, any more than we are completely free to choose them today.

We might imagine race as something that shifts unstably between individual freedom of choice (as in the new census) and a group's complete lack of freedom to choose. The reality of American life and our past exists between these twin poles, and the choices involved in it can perhaps never be entirely free.

A man who looks African American is typically going to be treated as an African American. That the man may also be Native American, Asian American, and/or white, and may have designated himself accordingly in the 2000 census, may be of no importance to anyone other than himself.

Americans are now relatively free to decide who they are, in racial terms, when filling out a census. But that is one of the few times when they are free to do so. Race is a social, not private, reality. And the census should not be misused to make racial policies, which have much more to do with how we act toward each other than what we think about ourselves.

Web **See It and Read It Now:** Population Change and Distribution: Census 2000 Brief, **bedfordstmartins.com/americanow,** Chapter 5. This brief report, published by the U.S. Census Bureau, includes the major findings of the latest census, with detailed charts, tables, and a map.

Vocabulary/Using a Dictionary

1. What do you think the word *enumerator* (para. 5) means? Look it up in your dictionary if you aren't sure. What other words share its root meaning?

2. Did you know the word *mulatto* before reading this article? It comes from the Spanish word for "mule." What do you think a mule has to do with race? Can you speculate about the application of this term to people?

3. Thornton discusses the "mulatto census category" as being "not merely a demographic footnote" (para. 7). What does *demographic* mean? Why do you think that demographic information would usually have been placed in a footnote?

4. Do you know the meaning of *constriction* (para. 10)? What are some synonyms and antonyms for it?

Responding to Words in Context

1. What does the author mean in paragraph 3 when he refers to the "suspension of social judgment?" What things besides judgment can be *suspended*?

2. When the author insists that race is a "social" notion or reality (paras. 2 and 13), what does he mean by the term *social*?

3. Examine the way the word *designate* is used in paragraphs 5 and 12. Can you guess what this word means based on these two applications? How do you think the word is related to *design*?

Discussing Main Point and Meaning

1. Summarize how the U.S. census has changed from 1790 to 2000. What do you perceive to be the biggest change?

2. What does Thornton refer to as "twin poles" in paragraph 11?

3. "[T]he census should not be misused to make racial policies, which have much more to do with how we act toward each other than what we think about ourselves" (para. 13). What kinds of policies do you think Thornton is concerned about here? Do you share his concern?

4. Thornton emphasizes that race is a "social" rather than a "private" reality. How do you think this social reality is different for people who identify with one race and people who consider themselves to be of mixed origins? Is social reality more powerful than private reality or vice versa?

Examining Sentences, Paragraphs, and Organization

1. A rhetorical question is a question asked for stylistic effect with no expectation of an answer from the audience. Examine the four rhetorical questions in paragraph 1 and describe the stylistic effect they have on the introduction to this article.

2. Identify the thesis statement or main idea somewhere in the first three paragraphs.

3. "Among Native Americans, the story has long been — and it is not a very amusing story — that the first Indian-white child in North America was born nine months after the first white man arrived" (para. 7). Why does Thornton insert the appositive "and

it is not a very amusing story" in the middle of this sentence? What does he mean to convey to the reader here?

4.   There are many numbers and statistics used throughout this article. Identify and discuss the one that surprises you the most.

Thinking Critically

1.   Why do you think race is such an important factor in the U.S. census? Why do you think it is such a problematic one? Can you think of any arguments for a "color-blind" census?

2.   Because Thornton is Native American, he speaks about Native American history from an "insider's" perspective. Do you think that his critique applies equally to the Latino, African, or Asian American perspectives? How about the Caucasian perspective?

In-Class Writing Activities

1.   In small groups, develop a mock census for your college or university. What categories should be identified and for what purposes? Do you know anything about the demographics at your school? Do you think the administration and faculty are sensitive to those demographics?

2.   "According to the 2000 census, three of every ten Americans are members of one of four defined minority groups — African Americans, Asian Americans, Native Americans, and Latinos. Some seven of every ten Americans consider themselves white" (para. 2). Do these numbers surprise you, or are they what you would expect? Do you think they will change by the time of the next census in 2010? Why or why not? Write a short essay describing how you think the 2010 census might change — in either its questions or its results.

RICHARD RODRIGUEZ

Black and Tan Fantasy

[SALON.COM / May 30, 2001]

Before You Read

Are we too simplistic in our thinking about race? What does it mean to be Hispanic or Asian or African American?

Words to Learn

Hispanic (para. 1): Spanish speaking (adj.)

Latinos (para. 2): from Latin America (South America, Central America, and the West Indies) (n.)

Civil Service (para. 2): government-related public service employment (nonlegal and nonmilitary) (n.)

white noise (para. 2): electronic background noise (as from a TV or radio) (n.)

ascendancy (para. 2): dominance (n.)

malice (para. 3): hatred; cruelty (n.)

demographers (para. 3): those who study the characteristics of populations (n.)

Cinco de Mayo (para. 7): the Fifth of May; commemoration of the victory of the Mexican Army over the French at the Battle of Puebla in 1862 (n.)

bureaucratic (para. 9): related to an excessively complex system of administration based on rules, hierarchy, and authority (adj.)

pretense (para. 12): deceit; sham; facade (n.)

Appalachian (para. 13): from the mostly rural Appalachian mountain region in eastern North America, the heart of which is generally thought to be in West Virginia (adj.)

RICHARD RODRIGUEZ (b. 1944) has been a writer for over twenty years. He has worked as a journalist and essayist for the MacNeil-Lehrer News-Hour, an editor for the Pacific News Service, and contributing editor for Harper's Magazine, U.S. News & World Report, *and the Sunday Opinion section of the* Los Angeles Times. *He recently published* Brown: The Last Discovery of America *(2002).*

A dark little secret — the divide at the heart of America's racial and ethnic politics — has been exposed by the contest for mayor of Los Angeles. In America's largest Hispanic city, a majority of African American voters are expected to side with the white candidate, against the Hispanic candidate.

All is not well along the spectrum of America's rainbow, despite the tendency of some on the political left to describe "blacks and Latinos" in one breath. From Miami to Dallas to Compton, blacks and Latinos are engaged in a terrible competition for the meanest jobs; for the security of Civil Service positions; for political office; for white noise. It is no exaggeration to say that African Americans have paid the price of Hispanic numerical ascendancy. In Los Angeles, for example, the famous "black neighborhoods" have suddenly become Hispanic — immigrant, Spanish-speaking.

The U.S. Census Bureau is candid, but makes matters worse. Out of malice or stupidity, federal demographers have taken to predicting that Hispanics are destined to "replace" African Americans as "America's largest minority." This year, the bureau estimates Hispanic numbers to be nearly equal to those of blacks. But Hispanics are poised to take the lead. The bureau manages both to trivialize the significance of Hispanics in our national life, as well as to insult African Americans by describing Hispanics as replacing blacks. But to date, the nation's Hispanic political leadership has remained largely silent about the Census Bureau's grammar.

If I were an African American, I would not be so silent. What does it mean, I would ask, that Hispanics are becoming America's largest minority? The notion of African Americans as a minority is one born of a distinct and terrible history of exclusion — the sin of slavery, decades of segregation, and every conceivable humiliation against a people, lasting through generations.

To say, today, that Hispanics are becoming America's largest minority mocks this entire history. It dilutes the noun "minority" until it means little more than a population segment.

This is exactly what Hispanics have become — a population segment, an advertiser's target audience, or a market share. Not coincidentally, it was an advertising agency that got the point of Hispanic totals as early as the 1980s. It was then that the Coors beer company erected billboards throughout the Southwest celebrating "The Decade of the Hispanic."

Nowadays, on television and in newspapers, you will notice Hispanic actors, a growing Hispanic population in the American South and Midwest, Ricky Martin's views on God and the world, and multimillion-dollar baseball stars with Spanish surnames and unreliable swings. Nowadays, white politicians of both parties happily mangle Spanish phrases in their speeches, and President Bush celebrates Cinco de Mayo on the White House lawn.

If I were African American, I would tire of the cha-cha-cha, the salsa, and all those happy adjectives that cluster around Hispanic, the noun. I would resent the blast of Latino numbers. I would resent the politicians — whatever their color — who insist on lumping blacks and Hispanics together.   8

I would remember how, not so many generations ago, Hispanics, particularly Mexicans and Cubans, routinely resisted the label "minority." In a black-and-white America, Hispanics tended to side with white, or at least tended to keep their distance from black. But then came the success of the black civil rights movement in the South. And when that movement moved north, African Americans gained bureaucratic notice and remedies from Washington.   9

What does it mean, I would ask, that Hispanics are becoming America's largest minority?

Suddenly, all sorts of Americans who would never have thought to compare themselves to African Americans wanted to compare themselves to blacks. White, middle-class feminists claimed the black analogy. And so did gays.   10

There were even sweet grandmothers who took to naming themselves "Gray Panthers" in imitation of Huey P. Newton. And, of course, Hispanics claimed the black analogy. The problem, all these years after, is that we Hispanics have had to lie about ourselves to claim the black analogy. We have had to pretend to be other than we are. We have had to impersonate a new black race in the world.   11

In truth, despite our pretense, Hispanics do not constitute a racial group. Members of every race in the world can claim to be Hispanics. As Hispanics — the blond Cuban, the black Dominican, the mestizo Mexican — we assert a cultural tie.   12

The notion of Hispanicity might thus be revolutionary in a nation that has always identified its citizens according to blood. But, to date, Hispanics have largely failed to tell the truth about ourselves, and thus have limited our significance to the nation. Hispanics end up today proposing embarrassing absurdities. The white Hispanic with blue eyes applies to college as a "minority." Meanwhile, the   13

Appalachian white with blue eyes cannot apply to college as a minority, because she is "only" white.

By telling you these things, I do not mean to betray "my people,"   14
though I tend to think of the nation entire — all Americans — as my
people. Yes, I call myself Hispanic, but I also see myself within the
history of African Americans and Irish Catholics and American Jews
and the Chinese in California.

And more.   15

I believe there are useful purposes in having citizens who feel ex-   16
cluded from the mainstream organize themselves — to lobby, to petition, to attract the interests of government and employers. But when
Americans organize into subgroups, it should be with an eye at merging into the whole, not remaining separate. What was the point of the
black civil rights movement of the early twentieth century if not
integration?

The trouble with today's ethnic and racial and sexual identifica-   17
tions is that they threaten to become evasions of more general citizenship. Soon groups beget subgroups: Last week there was a meeting in
Atlanta of Colombian Americans, their first convention. Almost in
parody of Hispanics nationally, Colombian Americans announced
themselves to be "America's fastest growing minority."

On the other hand, if you are looking for reasons to feel opti-   18
mistic about our shared American future, you might talk with those
kids one meets in Oakland, California, today who have outgrown the
Census Bureau's labels. I mean the kids who call themselves "Blaxicans." These children exist in some future tense, well ahead of the
politicians and the rest of us who live in a nation that divides and divides again, by sex or color or accent or grievance.

The Blaxican will describe our national life, long after the politics   19
of the moment have faded to gray.

Web   **See It and Read It Now:** The Hispanic Population: Census 2000 Brief, **bedford**
stmartins.com/americanow, Chapter 5. This brief document, published by
the U.S. Census Bureau, outlines the changes in the Hispanic population and
includes detailed charts, tables, and a map.

Vocabulary/Using a Dictionary

1. Why is Rodriguez so troubled by the term *Hispanic* (para. 1)?
    How is it different from *Latino* or *Mexican*?

2. If you break down the Greek root parts of *demographer* (para. 3) you get "the people" (*demos*), and "write" (*graphos*). How does this translate into the work a *demographer* does?

Responding to Words in Context

1. Rodriguez describes blacks and Latinos as competing for the "meanest jobs" (para. 2). What imagery does the word *meanest* conjure up for the reader in terms of working conditions?
2. "But to date, the nation's Hispanic political leadership has remained largely silent about the Census Bureau's grammar" (para. 3), Rodriguez writes. What does he mean by *grammar*? How does this use depart from our typical use of the word? How is it related to that typical use?
3. "If I were African American, I would tire of the cha-cha-cha, the salsa, and all those happy adjectives that cluster around Hispanic, the noun" (para. 8). Why does this statement apply only to the noun form of *Hispanic*? Why not the adjective form?
4. Why does the author object to the claim by Colombian Americans to be "America's fastest growing minority" (para. 17)?

Discussing Main Point and Meaning

1. How does Rodriguez describe his own ethnic identity? Does his description surprise you?
2. Describe Rodriguez's perspective on African American and Hispanic relations.
3. Why do you think Rodriguez brings up college application procedures (para. 13)? How do his comments relate to your own experience?
4. Why is Rodriguez encouraged by the Oakland teenagers who call themselves "Blaxicans" (paras. 18 and 19)?

Examining Sentences, Paragraphs, and Organization

1. Why does Rodriguez open his essay with an allusion to a mayoral race in Los Angeles?
2. Examine and describe the transition from paragraph 3 to paragraph 4.

3. Find the repetition in paragraphs 10 and 11. Does it seem intended or accidental? What effect does this repetition have?

Thinking Critically

1. Rodriguez is a highly acclaimed writer and television commentator. Do you think his success informs his position on ethnic politics? If he were poor and unknown, do you think he would have a different perspective on minority status?

2. Do you think that Hispanics should be represented as a race on the U.S. census? Should Hispanics be granted minority status when it comes to college admissions, government grants, or corporate hiring practices? Do the same questions apply to Asians? What about Native Americans? And aren't some "African Americans" from the West Indies, South America, and the Middle East? Is there any such thing as race, biologically speaking?

3. Rodriguez criticizes groups who have "claimed the black analogy" (paras. 10 and 11), but then he argues for "merging into the whole, not remaining separate" (para. 16). Is there a contradiction here?

In-Class Writing Activities

1. Make up a word like *Blaxican* that describes the combination of influences on your ethnic identity. Include nonfamily influences with which you feel a significant affinity. Maybe you have learned to speak a foreign language fluently, or perhaps many of your friends are from a country you've never been to but feel familiar with. Write a short essay in which you name and explain the word you've come up with.

2. Write a letter to the U.S. Census Bureau either supporting or criticizing their classification of Hispanics, depending on your personal opinion. Quote Rodriguez's essay as necessary.

3. Pretend that you are Rodriguez and have been assigned to write an article about the race relations and politics at your school. Who sits with whom in the dining halls? What ethnic "fashion statements" are people making these days? How easy is it to tell what race or ethnicity the students at your school are? Are there groups that are more politically influential on campus than others?

HADIA MUBARAK

Blurring the Lines between Faith and Culture

[FSVIEW & FLORIDA FLAMBEAU, FLORIDA STATE UNIVERSITY / March 4, 2002]

Before You Read

Do you wear symbols of faith on your body? Do you think religion should be or is immune to cultural influence? What does it mean to assimilate in American culture?

Words to Learn

assimilate (para. 1): incorporate; integrate; absorb (v.)
omnipresent (para. 3): existing everywhere; ubiquitous (adj.)
pinnacle (para. 8): height; peak (n.)

Walking into an airport at Mobile, Alabama, eyes follow me as   1
if I am the object of examination under the scrutinizing lens of a microscope. Accustomed to the curious stares, I disregard them and walk up to the ticket counter, speaking to the agent in perfect English. Perhaps the surprised eyes that glance up are asking the same question that the lady asked on Oprah's October 5 "Islam 101" talk show. "Why have you failed to assimilate?" she asked the Muslim women sitting in the audience, their hair covered beneath a scarf, their bodies hidden beneath long-sleeve shirts, long dresses, skirts, or pants. "Everyone in this country has assimilated," the lady in the audience continued, "except for the Muslims."

There is an inherent difference between religion and culture, the   2
lines of which are often blurred. Hijab, the covering of a woman's

---

Hadia Mubarak *grew up in Panama City, Florida. She is studying international affairs and English at Florida State University and expects to graduate in 2003.*

hair and body, has nothing to do with culture; it is a mark of faith. Faith is not derived from culture or the city in which one was born. Faith is a product of one's life experiences, fears, hopes, and inability to predict or control the future. It is a submission to God, to fate, and to one's humanity. Faith breaks down barriers; it does not create them.

An expression of my belief and commitment to God, the hijab I wear does not conflict with my American culture whose language, food, and customs I absorbed like a baby groping for words. I wear this hijab for God, not for a culture that dictates the way I live from miles abroad. Culture does not define God, because God is omnipresent. How does one assimilate a faith, an act of worship to God, which transcends all boundaries?

> *People didn't even see me when they looked at me, but rather saw an image they had formulated.*

Had this been cultural, perhaps I would not have been the only girl in my summer school in Jordan to cover her hair. Perhaps scores of immigrant Muslim women would not be covering their hair after coming to America, inclined to fulfill commandments of God they never bothered to practice back home. The story of my Egyptian friend, who dragged her husband to fabric stores to buy cloth for headscarves after coming to America, is a case that can be multiplied 100 times over.

As my hijab is misleadingly viewed as a failure to assimilate, I am reminded of the obstacles that lie ahead as I struggle to validate my roots as a Muslim Arab American and mold the missing piece of a puzzle that can bridge those worlds. The bubble in which I lived my childhood years suddenly burst when I reached adolescence, awakening to the encroaching reality of a biased world. I began to realize that people didn't even see me when they looked at me, but rather saw an image they had formulated in their minds from glimpses of Hollywood movies showing Arab fanatics hijacking a plane or from a *Dateline* documentary about female honor killings or some book they read about a Saudi Arabian princess escaping the oppression of a male-dominated society. Before they've even learned my name, heard my laughter or witnessed my tears, before they've seen me kick a soccer ball or debate an argument, they have judged me and think they know who I am.

I relish in the freedom the hijab gives me, the freedom from having my body exposed as a sex object or from being judged on a scale of one-ten by strange men who have no right to know what my body or hair look like. For Muslim women, the hijab is a form of modesty, security, and protection, shifting the focus of attention from a woman's physical attraction, or lack thereof, to the personality that lies beneath. By forcing people to look beyond her physical realm, a woman is valued for her mind and personality.

The word "assimilation" is like a mound of clay that bounces from one pair of hands to another. It is shaped by the hands in which it sits, with no defining boundaries. 7

What is our concept of assimilation? Is it the cultural genocide endured by Native Americans, torn from their families and forced to replace one language with another, their culture shattered into pieces they would struggle to fit together for a lifetime to come? If the presence of diversity threatens our sense of identity as a culture, then we have no identity worth preserving. Fortunately for us, American culture is the pinnacle of diversity, marked by the conglomeration of Chinese food, Japanese animations, Latino music, French twists, Greek gyros, and yes, women with veils. 8

Vocabulary/Using a Dictionary

1. *Assimilate* (para. 1) shares origins with *assemble, resemble, similar,* and *simultaneous.* What do you think the Latin root origin — *similes* — means?

2. What do you think the prefix *omni-* in *omnipresent* (para. 3) means? Do you know any other words with the same prefix?

Responding to Words in Context

1. In parking garages, we sometimes have to get parking tickets *validated*; in academic writing, an argument's *validity* is determined by the quality of its logic; under the law, one's ownership of a house requires possession of a *valid* title. Compare these uses to Mubarak's desire to *validate* her "roots as a Muslim Arab American" (para. 5).

2. What does Mubarak mean when she says "I relish the freedom the hijab gives me" (para. 6)? Use the word *relish* in a sentence of your own.

Discussing Main Point and Meaning

1. Why does the author make a distinction between "religion and culture" (para. 2)? She also states that the lines between the two are "often blurred" (para. 2). Who is doing the blurring? Do you think that by writing this article the author wants to redraw the lines or bring appreciation to the ways that religion and culture overlap?

2. In paragraph 4, Mubarak alludes to women who would not have worn the hijab at home but do so in America. How do their actions support her main argument?

3. Mubarak argues that the hijab "has nothing to do with culture; it is a mark of faith" (para. 2). She also argues in paragraph 6 that the hijab is "a form of modesty, security, and protection, shifting the focus of attention from a woman's physical attraction, or lack thereof, to the personality that lies beneath." How do you think faith and freedom from superficiality discussed here are related? Why do you think the author sees "modesty, security, and protection" as related to faith more than culture?

4. "If the presence of diversity threatens our sense of identity as a culture, then we have no identity worth preserving" (para. 8). Try to paraphrase, or put into your own words, the concept in this statement.

Examining Sentences, Paragraphs, and Organization

1. Reread paragraph 3. What is the main point of the paragraph? How does the paragraph follow from and set up for the paragraphs preceding and succeeding it? Can you identify explicit transitions between the paragraphs?

2. "Before they've even learned my name, heard my laughter or witnessed my tears, before they've seen me kick a soccer ball or debate an argument, they have judged me and think they know who I am" (para. 5). What are the strengths of this sentence? Describe those elements that make this sentence so effective.

3. Examine the list of things that concludes this essay: "Chinese food, Japanese animations, Latino music, French twists, Greek gyros, and yes, women with veils" (para. 8). Do you think these items make sense as a list? Are there any that stand out more than others? Explain your answer.

Thinking Critically

1. Does Mubarak make her understanding of the differences between religion and culture clear enough? Isn't clothing usually a function of culture (for example, Scottish kilts, Indian saris, African dashikis, Japanese kimonos)? Does clothing play such a large role in any other religions besides Islam?

2. Is there also a gender issue here? Why should women have to be more modest than men? If a Muslim woman feels more "security and protection" (para. 6) because of her garments, isn't there an underlying problem in male behavior that should be addressed? Do you think Mubarak overlooks this element intentionally or accidentally?

In-Class Writing Activities

1. Describe an article of clothing you wear (including jewelry, holiday costumes, or even makeup) that is an expression of either your religion or your culture (even if it's North American culture). Compare your feelings about this article to Mubarak's feelings about the hijab.

2. Before the war in Afghanistan began in October 2001 and the fundamentalist Muslim Taliban regime was toppled, Afghan women were required by law to wear burkas, heavy garments that cover even their faces, unlike a standard hijab, which generally exposes the face. They were also barred from going out in public without a male family member as an escort, and forbidden to pursue careers or choose their own mates. What do you think Mubarak would have to say about burkas? By exposing her face, playing soccer, and writing a newspaper article, she differentiates herself significantly from Afghan women under the Taliban. Write a short essay as if from Mubarak's point of view on the subject of the burka. (You might also want to review the essay in Unit 3, "The Burka and the Bikini," p. 60.)

U.S. ENGLISH

I Pledge Allegiance . . .

[NATIONAL REVIEW / September 25, 2000]

Before You Read

Should the United States have an official or legal language? How much help should immigrants receive from the government in their own languages? Is it every U.S. resident's responsibility to learn English?

Words to Learn

bandera (graphic): Spanish for "flag" (n.)
los Estados Unidos (graphic): Spanish for "United States" (n.)
Amerika (graphic): German spelling of "America" (n.)
Republik (graphic): German spelling of "Republic" (n.)

I pledge allegiance to the bandera de los Estados Unidos de Amerika und der Republik...

Sounds like a recent political convention.

It used to be that our political parties believed that becoming an American meant learning English. Now, the Republicans feature an address at their convention *entirely* in a foreign language. Then in August, President Clinton issued an executive order expanding multilingual services by the government. And through all of this "Compassionate" politicians remain silent. Instead of encouraging assimilation, they play ethnic politics that actually slows down an immigrant's integration into the American mainstream.

With over 1.4 million members, we're fighting to prevent America from being divided by language. Declaring English our national language, and expecting immigrants to learn it would be a good place to start.

We're not suggesting that America speak "English Only." But go to any major city, and you'll begin to question whether many will ever speak English at all. Today over 329 languages are spoken in America. Should government provide services in all of them? Doesn't it make more sense to teach English–our common language–to all immigrants.

Do Something Today. Join Us. We must stop this attempt to divide our country. Become a member of US ENGLISH today. Together we can standup to the politicians and special interests.

To Join Call 1-800-U.S.ENGLISH.

1747 Pennsylvania Avenue, NW, Suite 1100
Washington, DC 20006
http://www.us-english.org

Vocabulary/Using a Dictionary

At the end of paragraph 1, the words *assimilation* and *integration* are used synonymously. Are these words synonyms? Why do you think U.S. English uses them interchangeably?

Responding to Words in Context

The word *immigrant* is used three times in this ad (paras. 1–3) to describe those who need to learn to speak English. Do only *immigrants* speak other languages? Why do you think this word is used exclusively? Why are the terms *nonnative speakers, non-English speakers,* or *foreigners* not used?

Discussing Main Point and Meaning

1. Is U.S. English worried only about language-based divisions, or do they have a political position as well?
2. What do you think this ad means by "ethnic politics" (para. 1)?
3. Should the government teach immigrants English? Should immigrants receive government services in their native languages?

Examining Details, Imagery, and Design

1. In the graphic, the Pledge of Allegiance is represented in three different languages. What is un-American about this image? How is this image, in fact, quintessentially American? Consider the style and grammar of the English used in the ad. Do you detect any errors or awkwardness? Would you punctuate any sentences differently?
2. The ad states, "Today over 329 languages are spoken in America" (para. 3). What purpose is served in adding the word *over* before the very precise number of "329"?

Thinking Critically

1. Some demographers predict that eventually Spanish will outpace English as the most common first language in America. What do you think U.S. English would want to do about that? What do you think about it? Is there anything wrong with allowing people

to use their language of choice, or must the U.S. have an official policy on what language citizens should use?

2. Look at another example of "difference" that gets accommodated by the government: disability. Millions of buildings have been retrofitted for wheelchair ramps, many important government documents are available in Braille, and the mentally retarded are often provided with subsidies for assisted living. Why is language so different?

In-Class Writing Assignments

1. Using the same graphic, write an ad that argues *for* a multilingual population. Follow the general format of the U.S. English ad and address similar issues (the role of politics, provision of government services, language instruction policies, and so on).

2. What is your own language history? Do you have a primary language that is not English? If English is your first language, do you speak another? Do you like hearing foreign languages around you, or would you prefer it if everyone spoke in the same language? Write a short personal essay on these topics.

Discussing the Unit

Suggested Topic for Discussion

How would you answer the questions in the title of this unit: What is America? Who are Americans? What are the responsibilities of citizenship? What are the responsibilities of government? Should a government keep tabs on all of the intricate differences of its citizens? Do citizens have the right to use their differences as bargaining chips? This unit brings many of these issues to the surface, though it provides few simple solutions.

Preparing for Class Discussion

1. In each of the essays in this unit, the author refers to people from ethnic groups outside his or her own. Russell Thornton, a Native American, refers to African Americans, Asian Americans, and

Latinos. Richard Rodriguez, a Mexican American, discusses African Americans especially, but also various other groups. Hadia Mubarak, a Muslim Arab American, alludes to Chinese, Japanese, Latinos, French, and Greeks at the end of her essay. Compare the way these authors compare their own experiences to those of other ethnic groups in America. Do they all have the same purpose?

2. How does the topic of assimilation figure into each of these selections (including the ad from U.S. English)? Do any of the selections present the same view on assimilation? Or are the perspectives all entirely distinct?

3. Now that you've read all of the selections in this unit, do you think you have a better understanding of what racial and ethnic identity are? Is there a specific author who articulates the way you see your own ethnic identity?

From Discussion to Writing

1. In small groups, create a round-table discussion among Thornton, Rodriguez, Mubarak, and a representative from U.S. English on one of the following topics: "gangsta rappers" who are not African American, racial profiling by police, immigration quotas (limits), or the debate over making English the official national language. Write a short script for the round-table and prepare to present it to the class.

2. Mubarak is the only student represented in this discussion, and hers is the youngest voice in the unit. Write a short essay describing what you perceive to be the generational differences in perspective on racial and ethnic issues in the United States. Where are these issues headed in the future? How do you think the next generation will feel about racial categories?

Topics for Cross-Cultural Discussion

1. Rodriguez complains about "the Census Bureau's labels." Are there more words for mixed identity in languages other than English? What are they? How do they compare to *race, ethnicity,* or *minority*?

2. How do other countries keep track of the race and language of its citizens? Are there linguistic requirements or a national language? Must one specify a particular race for census data? Are governments more or less interested in the differences of its citizens than the United States government is in its citizens?

6

Can Gender Equality Truly Exist?

It's commonly observed that girls and boys display different types of behavior from early childhood on. At play, for example, boys tend to be more aggressive and competitive, while girls are generally more social and accommodating. What psychologists are deeply interested in finding out, however, is whether these differences are mostly biological and genetic — are boys "wired" to be more aggressive than girls? — or are primarily a result of cultural conditioning. If our society expects boys to be more aggressive, one argument goes, they will automatically become so. In this chapter several writers address the issue of gender difference and equality as these arise in various situations.

In "Punch and Judy," one of the nation's most popular humorists, Dave Barry, offers readers a "scientific quiz" that will help determine whether they are "male or female." Lampooning scientific studies in general, especially those that appear only to confirm the obvious, he suggests several important "gender-based syndromes that the psychology community might want to look into," such as the "laundry refolding" and "inflatable pool toy" syndromes. But not everyone takes gender differences so lightly: two advertisements for a national, nonprofit organization called "Supporting Our Sons" warns Americans that their boys may be in far worse psychological shape than their girls. (That boys might experience more troubled lives than girls is also a point made by nineteenth century reformer Jacob Riis in his photograph "Homeless Boys".)

In what ways has the feminist movement's decades-long dedication to gender equality affected today's social roles and behavior? To what extent will women be routinely doing what men have traditionally done? In "The Draft: Debating War and Gender Equality," Jana Larsen, a student at California Polytechnic State University, wonders whether women will and should be conscripted if our "war on terror" expands to the point that the military draft will need to be reinstated. As of today, she says, "The Department of Defense's policy does not assign women to positions involving close combat, there is no military need to draft women, and there are congressional concerns about the societal impact." But given our current climate of equality between the sexes, should women continue to be excluded from the draft? In the unit's final selection, "Libation as Liberation?" a celebrated essayist looks at the role equality plays with respect to a different "draft" — the kind that comes out of beer kegs. Examining the growing trend of binge drinking among women on college campuses, Barbara Ehrenreich concludes that "gender equality wouldn't be worth fighting for if all it meant was the opportunity to be as stupid and self-destructive as men can be."

DAVE BARRY

Punch and Judy

[THE WASHINGTON POST MAGAZINE / July 9, 2000]

Before You Read

Have you ever noticed the way boys and girls play together in groups? Have you observed the way women communicate with each other compared to men? Do you notice any significant differences? Do you think men and women respond to conflicts differently? If so, to what do you attribute the differences?

Words to Learn

deadlock (para. 2): a stoppage of action because neither party in a struggle will give in (n.)

syndrome (para. 5): a group of signs and symptoms that occur together and characterize a particular abnormality (n.)

subatomic (para. 7): of or relating to the inside of an atom or to particles smaller than an atom (adj.)

Are you a male, or a female? To find out, take this scientific quiz:

1. Your department is on a tight deadline for developing a big sales proposal, but you've hit a snag on a key point. You want to go one way; a co-worker named Bob strongly disagrees. To break the deadlock, you:

a. Present your position, listen to the other side, then fashion a workable compromise.

b. Punch Bob.

2. Your favorite team is about to win the championship, but at the last second the victory is stolen away by a terrible referee's call. You:

DAVE BARRY *(b. 1947) is a longtime humor columnist and author of* Dave Barry Is Not Taking This Sitting Down! *(2000). Barry won the Pulitzer Prize for commentary in 1988.*

a. Remind yourself that it's just a game, and that there are far more important things in your life.

b. Punch Bob again.

How to score: If you answered "b" to both questions, then you   4
are a male. I base this statement on a recent article in the *New York Times* about the way animals, including humans, respond to stress. According to the article, a group of psychology researchers have made the breakthrough discovery that — prepare to be astounded — males and females are different.

The researchers discovered this by studying both humans and   5
rats, which are very similar to humans except that they are not stupid enough to purchase lottery tickets. The studies show that when males are under stress, they respond by either fighting or running away (the so-called "fight or flight" syndrome); whereas females males respond by nurturing others and making friends (the so-called "tend and befriend" syndrome).

> *Prepare to be astounded — males and females are different.*

This finding is big news in the psychology   6
community, which apparently is located on a distant planet. Here on Earth, we have been aware for some time that males and females respond differently to stress. We know that if two males bump into each other, they will respond like this:

FIRST MALE: Hey, watch it!

SECOND MALE: No, *you* watch it!

FIRST MALE: Oh yeah?

(They deliberately bump into each other again.)

Two females, in the identical situation, will respond like this:

FIRST FEMALE: I'm sorry!

SECOND FEMALE: No, it's my fault!

FIRST FEMALE: Say, those are cute shoes!

(They go shopping.)

If the psychology community needs further proof of the differ-   7
ence between genders, I invite it to attend the party held in my neighborhood each Halloween. This party is attended by several hundred small children, who are experiencing stress because their bloodstreams — as a result of the so-called "trick or treat" syndrome — contain roughly the same sugar content as Cuba. Here's how the various genders respond:

— The females, 97 percent of whom are dressed as either a ballerina or a princess, sit in little social groups and exchange candy.

— The males, 97 percent of whom are dressed as either Batman or a Power Ranger, run around making martial-arts noises and bouncing violently off one another like crazed subatomic particles.

Here are some other gender-based syndromes that the psychology community might want to look into: 8

— The "laundry refolding" syndrome: This has been widely noted by both me and a friend of mine named Jeff. What happens is, the male will attempt to fold a piece of laundry, and when he is done, the female, with a look of disapproval, will immediately pick it up and refold it so that it is much neater and smaller. "My wife can make an entire bed-sheet virtually disappear," reports Jeff.

— The "inflatable pool toy" syndrome: From the dawn of human civilization, the task of inflating the inflatable pool toy has always fallen to the male. It is often the female who comes home with an inflatable pool toy the size of the Hindenburg,[1] causing the youngsters to become very excited. But it is inevitably the male who spends two hours blowing the toy up, after which he keels over with skin the color of a Smurf,[2] while the kids, who have been helping out by whining impatiently, leap joyfully onto the toy, puncturing it immediately.

I think psychology researchers should find out if these syndromes   9 exist in other species. They could put some rats into a cage with tiny pool toys and miniature pieces of laundry, then watch to see what happens. My guess is that there would be fighting. Among the male researchers, I mean. It's a shame, this male tendency toward aggression, which has caused so many horrible problems, such as war and ice hockey. It frankly makes me ashamed of my gender. I'm going to punch Bob.

Vocabulary/Using a Dictionary

1. Look up the origin of *deadlock* (para. 1) in the dictionary. You will want to find its literal definition and may need to use the *Oxford English Dictionary* to help you find the answer.

2. Look up *fashion* (para. 2) as a verb. What are appropriate synonyms? Why do you think Barry chose *fashion* instead of other synonyms?

---

[1]*Hindenberg:* An 804-foot long airship of conventional Zeppelin design.
[2]*Smurf:* A small blue dwarf with a white hat that served as a hugely popular animated television character and toy in the early 1980s.

Responding to Words in Context

1. Barry labels his quiz *scientific* (para. 1). What expectations does this term set up? Is the quiz scientific? How does Barry's use of the adjective *scientific* foreshadow the tone and point of the rest of the essay?

2. Barry prepares readers to be "*astounded*" by a "*breakthrough discovery*" (para. 4). What do these words lead you to expect? Do the results of the study meet your expectations? How would you describe Barry's tone here? What point does Barry make through word choice and tone in this paragraph?

3. In paragraphs 6–8 Barry uses the terms *male* and *female* to describe a conversation, children at a Halloween party, the "'laundry refolding' syndrome," and the "'inflatable pool toy' syndrome." How does *male/female* differ from *men/women*? Why do you think Barry chose to use *male/female* rather than *men/women*?

Discussing Main Point and Meaning

1. Barry has two arguments here: one about sex and gender and the other about the value of psychological research. Explain Barry's two arguments.

2. What does the title "Punch and Judy" allude to? How does the title capture the meaning of the argument?

3. List the various syndromes Barry describes in the essay. How do these syndromes reflect Barry's view of psychological research?

Examining Sentences, Paragraphs, and Organization

1. This essay is obviously full of humor. Pick out one sentence in the essay that you find particularly amusing and explain how the humor works.

2. Barry starts the essay with a quiz. How effective is the quiz as an introductory paragraph?

3. In paragraph 6, Barry uses a conversation to demonstrate how men and women react differently to stressful situations. How accurate do you find Barry's characterization of men and women? How is paragraph 6 a response to the study Barry discusses in paragraph 4?

4. In paragraph 7, Barry offers exact percentages of the number of children in certain Halloween costumes. Why do you think Barry is so specific here when earlier in the paragraph he vaguely mentions "several hundred small children?"

Thinking Critically

1. The research study Barry alludes to in paragraphs 3 and 4 uses humans and animals to test the reaction to stress, concluding that males and females in all species respond differently. What reasonable conclusions can the researchers make about male and female differences in humans considering they have used animals in their study?

2. While the writer never mentions the term, his humorous essay takes up the classic nature versus nurture debate, which asks how much inborn traits and social environment govern human behavior. Look through the essay's examples. Which ones seem to fall under nature (or inborn traits)? Which ones belong to nurture (or social environment)? Of course, you may also argue that you cannot determine which category the example falls under or you may assert that the example exhibits features of both nature and nurture. Regardless of your response, explain your reasoning.

In-Class Writing Activities

1. Working in groups, design a quiz to determine if males and females respond differently in a given situation. Your quiz should have three questions with three multiple-choice options for each answer. You'll need to create different scenarios for each question. You may want to follow Barry's model of a stressful situation or any other situation in which you think males and females would make different choices. For the answer portion of the quiz, design three responses, one of which should reflect what you deem to be typically male behavior, the other female, and one gender neutral. You may choose to make your quiz humorous like Barry's or take it seriously. After you design your quiz, have your classmates take it, asking them only to identify their sex at the top of the page. Score each quiz using a code for male, female, and gender neutral responses. Evaluate to what degree the responses fall along typical gender lines.

2. Freewrite a response in which you discuss your observations of children at play or adults in conflict situations, paying particular attention to sex. Do your own observations match Barry's?

3. Brainstorm a list of stereotypical gender differences between males and females that are not based on physical features. Your list can include a variety of factors — including dress, behavior, communication skills, personality traits, occupations, emotions, beliefs, treatment of others, and so on. After you make the list, point out which differences seem to be more relevant than others. How do you think these differences relate to societal expectations?

SUPPORTING OUR SONS

Are Boys in Trouble?

[BRAIN, CHILD / Summer 2001]

Before You Read

We often hear about girls' issues with self-esteem and declining academic performance in math and science when they enter middle school. But what about boys? What kind of emotional and academic difficulties do you think boys encounter?

Web **Read It Now:** "More Statistics about Boys and Boyhood," at the Supporting Our Sons Web site **bedfordstmartins.com/americanow**, Chapter 6. This article features research on boys and their relationships to school, discipline, violence, and more. "Your Son: Nature vs. Nurture," is a brief article on theories of development.

Web **Read It Now:** "Lost Boys," by Amy Benfer, at *Salon.com,* **bedfordstmartins. com/americanow**, Chapter 6. Benfer considers the idea of empowerment in relation to why girls are surging ahead while boys lag behind in academics.

Vocabulary/Using a Dictionary

1. How would you define *self-esteem*? What synonyms would you use?

2. The ad asks "Are boys in trouble?" and "Are boys in crisis?" Use a dictionary to look up the words *trouble* and *crisis*. How are they different in meaning?

Responding to Words in Context

1. What does the word *typical* suggest? Is it the same as *average* or *normal*? Why do you think the ad sponsors chose not to use other terms?

2. What is *special education*? What is the effect of choosing this phrase? What other phrases might have been used in its place?

Discussing Main Point and Meaning

1. How do both ads answer the questions they pose?

2. Categorize the problems boys face according to both advertisements.

3. The second ad asks, "Are boys in crisis?" Does Dr. Pollack's statement provide evidence that boys are in crisis according to its definition?

4. Supporting Our Sons, the sponsor of the advertisements, is an "organization dedicated to the development of the *whole boy.*" What do you think the sponsor means by *whole boy*? Look at the description of problems boys face to construct your answer.

Examining Details, Imagery, and Design

1. Notice the type size and design in the advertisements. How do they work to capture the reader's attention?
2. What do you notice about the images of the child in each advertisement? What meaning does each image convey?
3. Analyze the writing style of the texts in each ad. How does the first ad, "Are Boys in Trouble?" use repetition of sentence structure to create a certain effect? How does the second ad, "Are Boys in Crisis?" use adverbs to create meaning?

Thinking Critically

1. What would you ask the Supporting Our Sons organization about the statistics they use in their advertisement to determine their credibility?
2. Both ads compare boys' performance and emotional life to that of girls. What image of girls do you get from these ads? How accurate do you think that image is? How do you think the problems girls face compare to that of boys?
3. What factors do you think contribute to the problems boys face according to the advertisements?

In-Class Writing Activities

1. Working in small groups, create an advertisement about the problems girls face. Identify the problems in your text, consider whether to compare boys to girls, and describe images that would effectively convey your meaning. Draft a response explaining your choices.
2. In explaining the reasons behind many of the problems these advertisements identify, Daniel Kindlon and Michael Thompson, in chapter 1 of their best-selling book *Raising Cain: Protecting the Emotional Life of Boys* (1999), argue:

    > Stereotypical notions of masculine toughness deny a boy his emotions and rob him of the chance to develop the full range of emotional resources. We call this process, by which a boy is steered away from his inner world, the emotional *mis*education of boys. It is a training away from healthful attachment and emotional understanding and expression, and it affects even the youngest boy,

who learns quickly, for instance, that he must hide his feelings and silence his fears. A boy is left to manage conflict, adversity, and change in his life with a limited emotional repertoire.

Write a brief essay in which you offer examples of the "emotional *mis*education" of boys and explain how this miseducation relates to some of the problems boys face according to Supporting Our Sons.

3. Assume the role of a parent or teacher. Brainstorm solutions to the problems the advertisements identify.

AMERICA THEN . . . 1890

JACOB RIIS

Homeless Boys

Toward the end of the nineteenth century, a noted reformer and photographer, Jacob Riis, undertook a dramatic investigation of urban poverty. His now-famous book, How the Other Half Lives *(1890), portrayed the world of the New York City slums with an unprecedented realism that shocked and disturbed readers throughout the nation. Many of the photographs, such as "Homeless Boys, New York City," show raggedly dressed boys living on the edge, with little family or social support. Of these boys, Riis wrote:*

"Whence this army of homeless boys? is a question often asked. The answer is supplied by the procession of mothers that go out and in at Police Headquarters the year round, inquiring for missing boys, often not until they have been gone for weeks and months, and then sometimes rather as a matter of decent form than from any real interest in the lad's fate. The stereotyped promise of the clerks who fail to find his name on the books among the arrests, that he 'will come back when he gets hungry,' does not always come true. More likely he went away because he was hungry. Some are orphans, actually or in effect, thrown upon the world when their parents were 'sent up' to

the island or to Sing Sing, and somehow overlooked by the 'Society,' which thenceforth became the enemy to be shunned until growth and dirt and the hardships of the street, that make old early, offer some hope of successfully floating the lie that they are 'sixteen.' A drunken father explains the matter in other cases, as in that of John and Willie, aged ten and eight, picked up by the police. They 'didn't live nowhere,' never went to school, could neither read nor write. Their twelve-year-old sister kept house for the father, who turned the boys out to beg, or steal, or starve. Grinding poverty and hard work beyond the years of the lad; blows and curses for breakfast, dinner, and supper; all these are recruiting agents for the homeless army. Sickness in the house, too many mouths to feed."

JANA LARSEN

The Draft: Debating War and Gender Equality

[MUSTANG DAILY, CALIFORNIA POLYTECHNIC STATE UNIVERSITY /
October 16, 2001]

Before You Read

Given the recent war on terrorism, have you heard any talk about re-instating the draft? What is your attitude toward the draft in general? Do you think both men and women should sign up for Selective Service once they turn eighteen? Does women's increased presence in the military influence your stance on drafting women?

Words to Learn

conscription (para. 2): enrollment by compulsion into military or naval service (n.)

re-instituting (para. 3): initiating again (v.)

reinstated (para. 7): restored to a former position, condition, or capacity (v.)

activated (para. 7): called to active duty; to have formally assembled a military unit (v.)

postponement (para. 7): the act of putting off for a later time (n.)

deferment: (para. 7): the act of delaying, especially official post-ponement of military service (n.)

inductees (para. 7): those enrolled for military training or service (n.)

artillery (para. 17): a branch of the military armed with mounted firearms (n.)

JANA LARSEN (b. 1963) received her B.S. degree in public relations and journalism from California Polytechnic State University in March 2002. She wrote this essay as a senior, following the announcement of the U.S. war on terrorism.

Everyone's talking about it. No one has had to do it yet, but it might happen. It would take an act of Congress to make it happen. If it does happen, then who goes first, how would they find out, and when would they go?

What is it that everyone is talking about? The draft. Or, in other words: conscription, call of duty, selective service, or involuntary recruiting. Whatever you call it, many are concerned about its return since America went to war with terrorism.

As of right now, no one is being drafted, and, "at this point in time Congress is not considering re-instituting the draft," according to Stacie Paxton, Rep. Lois Capps' spokesperson.

On September 25 [, 2001] at a Pentagon news conference, Secretary of Defense Donald Rumsfeld said, "(The draft)...is not something that we've addressed and is not something that is immediately before us."

Therefore, the Selective Service System remains in a standby, caretaker status. An official statement posted on September 25, stated that, "While no heightened measures have been undertaken to bring the nation closer to the reestablishment of conscription, young men are reminded that they are required by federal law to register within 30 days of the 18th birthday."

This brings to mind what sequence of events would have to happen for the draft to be reinstated? And with the equality movement that has occurred over the past thirty years, would women be drafted?

First, for the draft to be reinstated, Congress and the president would have to authorize a draft. This occurs when more troops are required in a crisis than the volunteer military can supply. Second, a lottery based on birthdays determines the order in which registered men are called up by the Selective Service. The first to be called will be men whose twentieth birthday falls during that year, followed by those ages twenty-one to twenty-five. Men that are age eighteen and those turning nineteen would probably not be drafted. Third, all parts of Selective Service are activated. Next if a man is found fit for military service, he is given 10 days to claim an exemption, postponement, or deferment. At that point, he has 10 days to report to a local military station. Lastly, 193 days from the onset of the crisis, the Selective Service must deliver the first inductees to the military.

That is what can be expected for a young man; the draft is looked at differently concerning women. The Department of Defense's policy does not assign women to positions involving close combat, there is no military need to draft women, and there are congressional concerns about the societal impact.

The exclusion of women from the draft has been challenged in   9 the courts and reevaluated by the Department of Defense during the past twenty years. In May 1994, President Clinton asked the Secretary of Defense to review the arguments for

Drafting women would simply be a logical consequence of equality.

and against the exclusion of women "now that they can be assigned to combat roles other than ground combat." The Department of Defense's position remained unchanged about drafting women; however, it recognized the vastly increasing role being played by women in each of the Armed Services, which includes more than 16 percent of recruits.

Master Sgt. Greg Slane, of the Provost Marshall Office at Camp   10 Roberts, is a thirty-year veteran of the Marine Corps, with the last twenty years being served in the National Guard. He is currently serving as a military police officer at Camp Roberts. Slane reflected the opinion of not drafting women, but recognizes their talents and abilities.

"I've seen a lot of women and men in the service, and I have a lot   11 of regard for the women," he said. "I don't think that they should be drafted, though. I do believe that if they do want to serve in the military that there is a place for them. I think that women can serve as well as men can but why should we put women through that? I don't want to take away from their abilities; I am sure that they can serve in combat just as well as men can."

On the other side of the battle over whether women should be   12 drafted and their role in the military, Mary Armstrong, director of Women's Studies at California Polytechnic gave her opinion.

"Currently, the military assigns women a 'limited' or 'adjusted'   13 role, that is, women in the military do not do all the same things as men in the military. Thus, drafting women 'the same as men' into an organization that does not treat them 'the same as men' seems logically flawed to me.

"Equally important, however, is the fact that many women and   14 men feel strongly that the opportunities and the dangers of the military should be open across the board, and that drafting women would simply be a logical consequence of equality.

"But it is hard to successfully argue that women should be drafted   15 in the name of full equality when the organization of the military does not offer them a fully equal role," she said in an e-mail interview.

While it is true that the military doesn't offer a fully equal role to women, more opportunities are opening to women in combat and non-combat branches. There are now more women starting a career in the military.   16

"I am looking forward to the opportunities that are opening to females," said Chrissy Gritzke, California Polytechnic ROTC cadet. "I am looking at a career in engineering or air defense artillery. I have a female friend that graduated in June and is at her officer basic training course. She is training for long-range air defense artillery."   17

According to the U.S. Department of Labor Web site on women in the military, between 1987 and 1991, women accounted for almost 11 percent of persons in the military. At the last report in 1999, they accounted for 14 percent. Unlike the male veteran population, which is projected to decline by about 28 percent between 1990 and 2010, the female veteran population is projected to increase by 17 percent, from 1,094,000 to 1,281,000 during that period. It also stated on the site that women veterans are younger than their male counterparts, more educated, and more likely to have graduated from high school and attended college.   18

Web **Read It Now:** Women and the Draft in America, **bedfordstmartins.com/americanow,** Chapter 6. This report from the Selective Service System traces the history of women and the draft. Other resources at this site include an overview of what would happen if the draft policy were reinstated and who would be drafted or exempted.

Vocabulary/Using a Dictionary

1. What are four synonyms for *conscription* (para. 2)? Which synonym best fits the meaning of *conscription* as Larsen uses it?

2. Look up two definitions of *caretaker* (para. 5). Which definition best fits its use in paragraph 5?

3. Look up two definitions of *authorize* (para. 7). Which definition best fits its use in paragraph 7?

Responding to Words in Context

1. Paragraph 2 offers four synonyms for the draft: *conscription, call of duty, selective service,* and *involuntary recruiting.* Do all these terms carry the same connotation? Explain.

2. In describing the draft process, Larsen mentions a man fit for service has the options to claim *exemption, postponement,* or *deferment* (para. 7). What is the difference between these three terms?

Discussing Main Point and Meaning

1. Is Larsen's essay an objective report on the debate of whether women should be drafted, or does she advocate one position over another? Explain your answer.

2. What are the Department of Defense's reasons for not requiring women to register for Selective Service?

3. What argument does Mary Armstrong give both for and against drafting women (paras. 12–15)? Does Armstrong seem to favor one argument over the other?

Examining Sentences, Paragraphs, and Organization

1. What is the effect of the vague pronoun reference in the first paragraph's introduction?

2. What purpose do the statistics serve in paragraph 18's conclusion?

3. Briefly describe the organizational structure of the essay. How does the organization shape the writer's argument?

Thinking Critically

1. What argument does Master Sgt. Greg Slane give in paragraphs 10 and 11 for opposing the drafting of women? How substantial and logical is his argument?

2. Evaluate the logic of Armstrong's analysis in paragraphs 12–15 of why women should and should not be drafted. How sound is her deductive reasoning?

3. Larsen claims, "There are now more women starting a career in the military" (para 16). What does this point have to do with drafting women? Is this a good enough reason to draft women? Why or why not?

In-Class Writing Activities

1. Brainstorm a list of cultural assumptions about women and their social roles that have kept them from being drafted into the armed forces. Which of these assumptions have changed over

time? Should these changes warrant requiring women to sign up for the draft? Why or why not?

2. Assume that the United States has reinstated the draft to fight the war on terrorism. In addition, they now require women to sign up for the draft. Write two short responses to this decision, one from a personal, emotional perspective, the other that evaluates the soundness of this public policy decision. As you write your personal response, assume this means you or a close female friend or relative will need to join the armed forces. Compare your responses. How different are they? Would you assign more value to one response over the other? Explain.

3. There are many ways someone can avoid the draft. In the past, those who were mentally or physically impaired, enrolled in college, or proved conscientious objector status could all avoid military service. In a freewrite, compare gender to these other factors for being excused from military service during a time of war.

4. In all previous drafts, only men were conscripted. If the government orders another draft, do you think a larger percentage of women should be drafted to make up for past inequities that placed the burden of involuntary military service entirely on men? Express your opinion in an informal paragraph or two.

BARBARA EHRENREICH

Libation as Liberation?

[TIME / April 2002]

Before You Read

Is binge drinking a problem on your campus? What gender do you associate with binge drinking? Why do you think people binge drink?

Words to Learn

libation (title): an act of pouring a liquid as a sacrifice (as to a god); also, the liquid poured; drink (n.)

liberation (title): freedom from bondage and restraint; equal rights and status (n.)

addled (para. 2): confused, muddled (adj.)

amphoras (para. 2): ancient Greek jars or vases that are oval shaped and have two handles (n.)

self-assertion (para. 3): insistence on a recognition of one's own rights and claims (n.)

suffrage (para. 3): the right to vote (n.)

temperance (para. 3): habitual moderation in the indulgence of the appetites or abstinence from the use of intoxicating drink (n.)

puritanical (para. 5): marked by moral strictness and purity (adj.)

redoubts (para. 6): defended positions; protective barriers; small, usually temporary fortifications (n.)

nihilistic (para. 6): characterized by a viewpoint that traditional values and beliefs are unfounded and that existence is senseless and useless (adj.)

crypto- (para. 7): hidden, concealed, secret (prefix)

ennui (para. 7): boredom (from French) (n.)

appropriate (para. 7): to take possession of (v.)

BARBARA EHRENREICH is a contributing editor of Harper's, *a columnist for* The Progressive, *and a writer for* Time. *Her widely published social and political criticism has covered diverse topics including the history of women healers and the origins of war.*

So women finally are nearing equality in yet another area of so-   1
cial endeavor — the hotly contested field of binge drinking. Mullah
Omar[1] must be smirking in his safe house as he reads the Harvard
School of Public Health study showing that college women are now
drinking as fast and barfing as hard as the guys. It's exactly what the
Taliban would have predicted: that alcohol abuse blends perfectly
with women's liberation.

The ancient Greeks had the same suspicion. The fifth century B.C.   2
playwright Euripides portrayed the oppressed and frustrated women
of Thebes, egged on by the wine god Dionysus, abandoning their babies in the cradle and their weaving on the loom to run off into the
hills for nights of wild drinking and dancing, further enlivened by the
women's enthusiastic dismemberment of any living creatures they
came upon. At one point the queen mother, in her wine-addled
frenzy, rips apart her own son, the king, leaving the audience with
one clear lesson: keep the women indoors and those wine-filled amphoras tightly sealed.

But the foremothers of American feminism would have been   3
scandalized by the idea of drinking as a form of female self-assertion.
A little over a century ago, the suffrage movement and the temperance crusade were largely one and the same. Many temperance activists wanted the vote, if only to enact prohibition; and suffragists
applauded the temperance movement's attacks on taverns, in which
axes were deployed to smash open kegs and let the beer drain away
on the floor. The connection between the causes seemed obvious at
the time: drunken men frittered away the family's paycheck and then
went home to abuse their wives. The idea that women might have
drinking problems would have seemed as outrageous, in about 1870,
as the concept of a chocolate martini would a hundred years later.

Today, of course, we have both chocolate martinis and women's   4
suffrage, "grrrl power" and a variety of tasty wine coolers for the
kids. Not many women see getting falling-down drunk as a feminist
statement, but plenty find drinking a good way to get along with the
guys. In a corporate culture in which deals are often closed over multiple martinis or glasses of Merlot, the lone sipper of club soda risks
looking like a latter-day Carrie Nation.[2] And while the feminist foremothers aimed to make men more like women — nicer, that is, and

---

[1]*Mullah Mohammed Omar* (1959–): Leader of the Taliban.
[2]*Carrie Nation* (1846–1911): Born Carry Amelia Moore, Nation was one of the leaders of a U.S. movement to ban the sale and consumption of alcohol that often used violent means.

sober — today's alpha gals aspire to resemble the men, warts and hangovers included.

Among the younger, binge-prone set, feminism may have added — however indirectly — to women's recent achievements in the alcohol-consumption department. Second-wave feminists, meaning those who forged the movement in the 1970s, were, as third wavers never tire of pointing out, just a wee bit on the puritanical side — washing down their tofu with Celestial Seasonings and constantly harping on the danger of date rape. So if you're seventeen and want to express your grrrl-ish toughness, while simultaneously kicking sand in Mom's face, what better way than to go out and get "roofed" on a pint of cranberry vodka? Just as the daughters of suffragists became the cigarette-smoking flappers of the 1920s, the rebellious daughters of second-wave feminists may help account for the recent rise of binge drinking at some of the historically feminist-leaning women's colleges.

> Today's alpha gals aspire to resemble the men, warts and hangovers included.

But the theory linking feminism to female drunkenness gets into trouble when you discover where the hard-drinking women can be found on most campuses — not in the women's center, as Mullah Omar might imagine, but in the sorority houses. A 1996 study that appeared in the student personnel administrators' *Journal [of American College Health]* found that 80 percent of Greek women in colleges were binge drinkers, compared with 35 percent of non-Greek women. Now sororities are no longer training grounds for Stepford wives,[3] but neither are they redoubts of militant feminism. Within them, bingeing seems to be more of a nihilistic escape than a rebellion of any kind. As a sorority member on spring break explained to me, she and her friends binge because otherwise they would be "totally bored."

Whatever is behind female bingeing — conformity, crypto-feminism, ennui — it's hardly a feminist act. Gender equality wouldn't be worth fighting for if all it meant was the opportunity to be as stupid and self-destructive as men can be. Not that twenty-first century feminism is likely to revert to nineteenth century prohibitionism. Women no longer seek to eliminate all the dangerous and exciting things that men have historically tried to keep for themselves. But they need to

---

[3]*Stepford wives:* A reference to the 1975 film *The Stepford Wives* that portrays an affluent Connecticut town where the housewives seem to be strangely and permanently contented and blissful.

appropriate alcohol on their own terms and with their own biochemistry in mind — weighing the harms and the benefits, and then learning, very carefully, how to use it.

Read It Now: "Girls and Alcohol: Closing the Gender Gap?" by Allyson Shafter, **bedfordstmartins.com/americanow,** Chapter 6. This piece, included at the Web site for the National Clearinghouse for Alcohol and Drug Information, discusses the findings of the report by the *Journal of American College Health* (referred to by Barbara Ehrenreich). Other resources include a fact sheet, "Alcohol Use among Girls."

Read It Now: "Women on a Binge," by Jodie Morse, at Time.com, **bedford stmartins.com/americanow,** Chapter 6. Morse asks whether the rise in teen and college women's drinking is "girl power gone awry."

Vocabulary/Using a Dictionary

1. Look up the noun *scandal* in the dictionary to explain how the adjective *scandalized* (para. 3) evolved.
2. What is the origin of the adjective *puritanical* (para. 5)?
3. What is the origin of *redoubt* (para. 6)?

Responding to Words in Context

1. Define *binge drinking* (para. 1). Look up the word *binge* in the dictionary if you need to.
2. Ehrenreich writes, "Today, of course, we have both chocolate martinis and women's suffrage, '*grrrl* power' and a variety of tasty wine coolers for the kids" (para. 4). She repeats the term *grrrl* again, explaining, "So if you're seventeen and want to express your *grrrl*-ish toughness, while simultaneously kicking sand in Mom's face, what better way than to go out and get 'roofed' on a pint of cranberry vodka?" (para. 5). What two words might the term *grrrl* combine? What do you think *grrrl power* (para. 4) and *grrrl-ish toughness* (para. 5) mean?
3. In describing the results of the women's movement in the business world, Ehrenreich notes "today's *alpha* gals aspire to resemble the men, warts and hangovers included" (para. 4). What do you think the word *alpha* refers to in this context? What implications does such a term carry?

4. In describing drinking practices in sororities, Ehrenreich concludes, "Within them, bingeing seems to be more of a *nihilistic* escape than a rebellion of any kind" (para. 6). What do you think *nihilistic* means in this context? To answer this question, think about how a *nihilistic escape* contrasts with *feminist rebellion.*

5. Ehrenreich decides, "Whatever is behind female bingeing — conformity, *crypto-feminism,* ennui — it's hardly a feminist act" (para. 7). Looking at the invented term *crypto-feminism* in the context of Ehrenreich's argument, explain what the phrase means.

Discussing Main Point and Meaning

1. How does the question in the title capture Ehrenreich's argument? In particular, consider the double meaning of the word *libation.*

2. In both the introduction and near the end of the essay, Ehrenreich alludes to Mullah Omar. She imagines that he "must be smirking in his safe house as he reads the Harvard School of Public Health study showing that college women are now drinking as fast and barfing as hard as the guys" (para. 1). And she asserts that binge drinking occurs "not in the women's center, as Mullah Omar might imagine, but in the sorority houses" (para. 6). Who is Mullah Omar? What can you assume about his thoughts on the connection between women's drinking and their liberation? How do his views serve as a contrast to Ehrenreich's own?

3. How is an ancient play by Euripides (para. 2) relevant to Ehrenreich's argument? What point does she want to make in using this example?

4. What is the connection between the suffrage movement and the temperance crusade? What point does Ehrenreich want to make with this history lesson?

5. Ehrenreich reasons, "But the theory linking feminism to female drunkenness gets into trouble when you discover where the hard-drinking women can be found on most college campuses" (para. 6). How does the essay present a "theory linking feminism to female drunkenness?" How does Ehrenreich challenge this theory?

Examining Sentences, Paragraphs, and Organization

1. Briefly describe the essay's organizational structure. How effective is the structure in shaping Ehrenreich's argument?

2. In distinguishing second-wave feminists from third wavers, Ehrenreich vividly describes how "second-wave feminists, meaning those who forged the movement in the 1970s, were, as third wavers never tire of pointing out, just a wee bit on the puritanical side — washing down their tofu with Celestial Seasonings and constantly harping on the danger of date rape" (para. 5). Explain how the details Ehrenreich uses define "the puritanical side" of second-wave feminists.

3. In clarifying her view of sororities, Ehrenreich explains, "Now sororities are no longer training grounds for Stepford wives, but neither are they redoubts for militant feminism" (para. 6). What does Ehrenreich mean by "redoubts for militant feminism"? What image of sororities does Ehrenreich create in this sentence?

4. The ultimate point of Ehrenreich's argument doesn't unfold until the conclusion. Summarize the main ideas in this paragraph.

Thinking Critically

1. Ehrenreich gives a particularly apt description of the changes of the feminist movement when she declares, "Just as the daughters of the suffragists became the cigarette-smoking flappers of the 1920s, the rebellious daughters of second-wave feminists may help account for the recent rise of binge drinking at some of the historically feminist-leaning colleges" (para. 5). What does this sentence suggest about the changes in the feminist movement, why they occurred, and the explanation for binge drinking among women? What other examples of reactionary movements in generations, politics, or culture can you think of?

2. Ehrenreich speculates, "And while the feminist foremothers aimed to make men more like women — nicer, that is, and sober — today's alpha girls aspire to resemble men, warts and hangovers included" (para. 4). What irony about the women's movement is Ehrenreich noting? In general, think about the changes the women's movement has brought about. Have men become more like women or women more like men?

3. How does Ehrenreich characterize sororities? How valid do you find her characterization?

In-Class Writing Activities

1. Brainstorm a list of changes in gender roles for both men and women in the twentieth century. Identify which changes are largely positive and which negative for each sex.

2. Write a brief essay that analyzes binge drinking on your campus. How large of a problem does it seem to be? If you do not think it is a problem, speculate on why. What do drinking habits say about the student body? Have campus administrators set up policies to reduce the problem of binge drinking? If you do think binge drinking is a problem on your campus, analyze the sources of the problem and try to come up with appropriate solutions.

Discussing the Unit

Suggested Topic for Discussion

So how different are men from women, boys from girls? How many of these differences are related to sex (biology) or gender (cultural expectations based on sex)? How do gender expectations create problems for both sexes? Should women be eliminated from the draft because they are women?

Preparing for Class Discussion

1. Analyze the differences between males and females discussed in Dave Barry's "Punch and Judy" and the advertisements from the Supporting Our Sons organization. Which differences seem to be based on sex? Which ones stem from gender roles?

2. In this chapter, both of the essays by women consider equality within the context of traditionally male-dominated spheres.

Barbara Ehrenreich writes that "women are finally nearing equality" in the field of binge drinking (para. 1) and that many women, especially within corporate culture, see getting drunk as "a good way to get along with the guys" (para. 4). In Jana Larsen's essay, a feminist states that "drafting women would simply be a logical consequence of equality" (para. 13). How is women's equality characterized in these essays? How is the idea of equality shaped and worked toward within the framework of traditionally male-dominated institutions such as the corporation or the military? How would women's equality best be achieved within these institutions?

3.   What assumptions about gender roles underlie the arguments expressed in each essay in this chapter? How do the assumptions compare? Which ones do you agree with and why?

From Discussion to Writing

1.   Write two essays for or against drafting women into the military. Keep in mind the difference between sex (biology) and gender (cultural expectations). In one essay, base your argument on sex. In another essay, base your argument on gender. Your stance on the issue may change depending on which factor you are considering.

2.   In an essay, take up one difference between males and females discussed in one or more of the selections in this unit. Discuss how this difference is a result of culturally prescribed gender roles. If you perceive this difference as a problem, recommend a potential solution. Use your own observations, analysis, and examples as well as at least one of the selections in this unit to develop your ideas.

3.   Does the 1890 Jacob Riis photograph of "Homeless Boys" support the arguments made by the advertisements produced for "Supporting Our Sons?" In a short essay, consider the Jacob Riis photo and the accompanying remarks from his book in light of the two advertisements. In your opinion, do the Riis selections make a comment on gender differences or do they reflect the general social conditions of the time? Be sure to explain why you think one way or the other.

Topics for Cross-Cultural Discussion

1. Describe gender expectations for males and females in a non-U.S. culture. How do they compare to those in the United States? What problems, opportunities, or privileges for each sex do these gender expectations create?

2. Discuss the role of women in the military in another country. How large of a role do they play, if any? What kind of military service, if any, does the country require of its citizens? Are women included in these requirements? How does women's role in the military reflect gender expectations?

7

Sexism and Language: Do Pronouns Make a Difference?

How often do you find yourself as a writer trying to avoid the use of a masculine pronoun? Do you make a conscious effort to write *he* or *she* or use some other construction? Do you prefer to write *they* or *them* to remain neutral even when your subject is singular? Or do you think it's trivial to worry about such matters? In this unit we examine the social and political importance of gender terms in writing.

Could a "gender-neutral Bible" bring us "one step closer to a gender-neutral society"? In "The His-and-Hers Bible," Emily Nussbaum reports on a new translation of the Bible that eliminates old-fashioned but inessential male pronouns and expressions; for example, "he who believes" becomes in the new translation "whoever believes." So far so good, Nussbaum maintains, but "copy-editing the contradictions out of the Bible is not the same thing as resolving them — it merely papers over the problem, literally." Yet the effort to produce a gender-neutral Bible strongly appeals to University of Nebraska senior, Elizabeth Hansen. "What is wrong with writing a religious text that is inclusive?" she asks in "Defining 'Woman' without the 'Man.'" For Jason Gillikin, however, at Western Michigan University, "people who get upset at the use of masculine pronouns have

entirely too much time on their hands." Besides, he suggests, don't
they know the fundamental rules of English grammar?

***

EMILY NUSSBAUM

The His-and-Hers Bible

[THE NEW YORK TIMES MAGAZINE / February 10, 2002]

Before You Read

Do you read the Bible? Would a gender-neutral version of the Bible
make you more or less inclined to read it? Why?

Words to Learn

semiotics (para. 2): study of relationships between signs and symbols, particularly in language (n.)

quotidian (para. 3): commonplace;
   everyday (adj.)

laudable (para. 4): commendable;
   praiseworthy (adj.)

hep (para. 4): hip; aware of current
   trends (adj.)

pragmatic (para. 5): dealing with
   facts or actual occurrences (adj.)

subterfuge (para. 6): deception or
   artifice used to avoid criticism or
   confrontation (n.)

parchment (para. 7): paper made
   from sheep skin (n.)

***

Emily Nussbaum (b. 1966) is the former editor of Nerve Magazine. *Her
features have appeared in the* New York Times Magazine, Lingua Franca,
Slate, *and* Discover. *She lives in New York City.*

After several years of internal debate, the International Bible Society is releasing a gender-neutral alternative to the best-selling New International Version (N.I.V.) — the rather nervously titled Today's New International Version (T.N.I.V.). This "inclusive" New Testament, full of "children of God" where once there were only "sons," goes on sale in April [2002], alongside the more traditional edition. 1

Unsurprisingly, many fundamentalist Christians — a prime market for the N.I.V. — are less than thrilled. And they are right to be concerned. Like any Brown [University] semiotics major, conservative Christians know that symbols matter; they affect the way we view the world. A gender-neutral Bible is one step closer to a gender-neutral society. And while liberals and feminists might support such a goal, they should still join in the fight against degendering the Good Book. For copy-editing the contradictions out of the Bible is not the same thing as resolving them — it merely papers over the problem, literally. 2

T.N.I.V. translators argue that these changes are necessary to keep the Bible up to date. God's message, says Dr. Ronald Youngblood, a member of the group that developed T.N.I.V., must be communicated "in the language of the day." And indeed, the substitutions are fairly quotidian — "whoever believes" for "he who believes" and so on — and affect only followers. The creator and his son stay resolutely male. Some of the alterations are even justified by the original language. But others are triumphs of ideology over semantics: an "oops" to the exclusion of women in practically every verse. 3

Of course, saying "sisters and brothers" has one obvious, laudable effect: it makes half the congregation feel included. Even as an adolescent at Temple Israel in White Plains, I remember reading Bible verses and feeling a part-cynical, part-bemused sense that this wasn't really meant for me. Who could object to making women feel more a part of God's message? (Well, some people could, but let's just leave it rhetorical.) Certainly, there's nothing new about crunchier, more user-friendly versions of the Testaments: 1985's New Jerusalem Bible was the first official gender-neutral Roman Catholic version, and Reconstructionist and Reform Jews have long used inclusive texts. A 1966 version of the Gospel called "God Is for Real, Man" even featured hep "street" translations ("the Lord is like my probation officer"). For those who view the Bible as philosophical poetry or a historical 4

Conservative Christians know that symbols matter; they affect the way we view the world.

record — or perhaps simply as the final whispered message in a cultural game of telephone, what Northrop Frye[1] called "literature
plus" — there is justification for such approaches. Anything that increases the text's communicative power is good. Say "people" instead
of "men" long enough and the religion itself alters: a whistle-a-
happy-tune experiment in social change.

But as appealing — and pragmatic — as such arguments are, they   5
are also, in the end, rationalizations, and the T.N.I.V. controversy
makes that clear. Because when you make literal changes for a readership that takes the Bible literally, you bump up against the fact that
men and women in the Bible are not even remotely equal. Men owned
things: slaves, land, women. They had the moral authority, and with
it, the moral responsibility. To cite an obvious example: "Wives, be
subject to your husbands, as to the Lord. For the husband is the head
of the wife as Christ is the head of the church, his body, and is himself
its Savior. As the church is subject to Christ, so let wives also be subject in everything to their husbands." Gender-neutralize that!

Perhaps the real issue is that the translation doesn't go far   6
enough, dealing, as it does, with only the flock, not the shepherd(ess).
Without masculinity, how would God's authority, or God's mercy,
change in our eyes? How would we change — made, as we are, in the
creator's image? Linguistic changes of this sort are conceivable in
English in a way they are not in the romance languages, where each
noun — hat, chair, arm, leg — is assigned a gender from the start. But
in English, we can escape this constraint, free to be inclusive (men
and women) or neutral (people) or to avoid the subject altogether
with grammatical subterfuge.

To translate the Bible this way is understandably tempting, but   7
it's also a lie. I'm reminded of a modern Orthodox co-worker I once
had, who said, "Look, being Jewish is a game with a set of rules: go
ahead and move the pieces anyplace you want, but don't call it
chess." A truly gender-neutral interpretation of the Bible would
quickly begin to fall apart at the seams — laws about rape or slavery
rising up like invisible ink from ancient parchment. One solution, of
course, is to reject the Bible entirely. Another is to regard it merely as
a parable whose historical foundation can be ignored. But for anyone
who wants to take religion seriously, neither solution truly suits. Instead, it seems necessary to confront the contradictions in the text —

[1]*Northrop Frye* (1912–1991): A noted Canadian scholar, literary critic, and commentator on society and culture.

to keep the pronouns as they are and wrestle instead with the messy truth, like, well, manly Jacob[2] with his angel. It's a more difficult task, but it's the only honest way out.

Vocabulary/Using a Dictionary

1. How does *laudable* (para. 4) resemble another word, which means "to clap in approval"?

2. The prefix *sub-* in *subterfuge* (para. 6) means "under." What goes or is put "under" when one practices *subterfuge*?

Responding to Words in Context

1. Nussbaum calls the International Bible Society's "gender-neutral" version "rather nervously titled" (para. 1). What makes the title seem *nervous*? How is this use of *nervous* different from more common uses?

2. Of some of the changes in the T.N.I.V., Nussbaum writes, "But [other alterations] are triumphs of ideology over semantics; an 'oops' to the exclusion of women in practically every verse" (para. 3). Why does she use the word *oops* in this context? How does this word reveal her opinion of the new Bible version?

Discussing Main Point and Meaning

1. Is Nussbaum arguing that the Bible is fine the way it is? Or does she have some other reason for criticizing the T.N.I.V.'s pronoun changes?

2. How does Dr. Youngblood explain the controversial changes to the Bible (para. 3)? Do you find his reasoning compelling? Why or why not?

3. In paragraph 5, Nussbaum argues that "when you make literal changes for a readership that takes the Bible literally, you bump up against the fact that men and women in the Bible are not even remotely equal." How does this point contribute to her overall argument? Do you think this is how most opponents of the gender-neutral Bible might describe their argument?

---

[2]*Jacob:* From the Bible; second son of Isaac and Rebekah, brother of Esau.

4. Nussbaum speculates that the new translation of the Bible might not "go far enough" (para. 6), since it does not seek to question the masculinity of God in Christianity. How would this change be different from the linguistic changes in the gender-neutral Bible?

5. What does the author mean when she says that "a truly gender-neutral interpretation of the Bible would quickly begin to fall apart at the seams — laws about rape or slavery rising up like invisible ink from ancient parchment" (para. 7)?

Examining Sentences, Paragraphs, and Organization

1. Where can you find the thesis of Nussbaum's essay?

2. Paragraphs 5 and 6 make two points — one about the literal question of sexism and inequality in the content of the Bible, and one about how equality or inequality are conveyed in the English language. Paraphrase each of these points and explain their relationship to each other.

3. At the end of this article, Nussbaum makes reference to the biblical struggle of "manly Jacob" and the angel he fought with until he proved his strength (the angel subsequently renamed Jacob "Israel") (para. 7). Why would she choose such an image to close out her argument?

4. Examine the tone Nussbaum uses in this article: "let's just leave it rhetorical" (para. 4), "crunchier" (para. 4), "whistle-a-happy-tune" (para. 4), "Gender-neutralize that!" (para. 5), "manly Jacob with his angel" (para. 7). How would you characterize her tone, and how does it contribute to her argument?

Thinking Critically

1. The International Bible Society released the new version of its Bible as an *alternative* to the "more traditional edition" (para. 1). Do you think there should be multiple versions of the Bible so that people can choose a version according to their own beliefs and values, or does this negate the whole point of having a religious doctrine or belonging to a religious community?

2. "One solution," Nussbaum writes, "is to reject the Bible entirely" (para. 7). What problem is this a solution to? Does this seem to be a shocking or extreme suggestion? Does it seem logical, given the extent of the problem of interpreting the Bible's meaning?

In-Class Writing Activities

1. It is commonly understood and accepted that the stories and books of the Bible were written by a number of different men. Choose a story from the Bible (for example, Eve and the apple, Noah's ark, Moses's receipt of the Ten Commandments, Lot's wife turning into a pillar of salt, the prodigal son) and retell it as if from the point of view of a woman. In what ways would it be different?

2. Most major religions allocate different roles for men and women. What are your thoughts on this practice? Is this true of any religion you have practiced or currently follow in your life? Describe your experience or understanding of this treatment. Should men and women be treated or valued differently in a spiritual practice? Why or why not?

ELIZABETH HANSEN

Defining "Woman" without the "Man"

[DAILY NEBRASKAN, UNIVERSITY OF NEBRASKA–LINCOLN / March 1, 2002]

Before You Read

Does it matter to you that masculine nouns and pronouns are meant to account for both women and men, according to conventional English grammar? Does this practice reinforce gender inequality?

Elizabeth Hansen (b. 1980) is an opinion writer for the Daily Nebraskan. *Her work has been recognized by the University of Nebraska's Women Studies program for promoting a positive image of feminism. Hansen, a survivor of lymphoma, expects to graduate in December 2002.*

Words to Learn

discourse (para. 18): formal and lengthy discussion on a subject (n.)
patriarchal (para. 19): of or pertaining to a male-dominated society (adj.)
archaic (para. 20): no longer current; belonging to an earlier time (adj.)
misogynistic (para. 20): expressing hatred of women (adj.)

"Long afterward, Oedipus,[1] old and blinded, walked the roads. He smelled a familiar smell. It was the Sphinx.[2]   1

"Oedipus said, 'I want to ask one question. Why didn't I recognize my mother?'   2

"'You gave the wrong answer,' said the Sphinx.   3

"'But that was what made everything possible,' said Oedipus.   4

"'No,' she said. 'When I asked, What walks on four legs in the morning, two at noon and three in the evening, you answered, Man. You didn't say anything about woman.'   5

"'When you say Man,' said Oedipus, 'you include women too. Everyone knows that.'   6

"She said, 'That's what you think.'"   7

Muriel Rukeyser[3] wrote this story. It is short, simple, and to the point. Language is exclusionary. When one says man, does it mean women too? I argue no. Women are supposed to identify with the term "man," but men are not supposed to identify with the term "woman." Who decided this load of crap?   8

The very term "woman" suggests women are a part of man. But the term man is singular — it stands alone and does not identify with the other half of what are known as "people." We are mankind, female, she, and woman.   9

What if we do not want to describe ourselves or identify with men? What can we say that we are?   10

Women have no way of describing their person without including men, but men can continually describe themselves without including women. We are expected to identify ourselves with men, while men have the license to have their own identity.   11

The new translation of the Bible known as the "gender-neutral" version has been a source of great controversy, but why? What is wrong with writing a religious text that is inclusive?   12

[1]*Oedipus:* A tragic figure in two plays by Sophocles, doomed to kill his father and marry his mother. He became ruler of Thebes by answering the riddle of the Sphinx.
[2]*Sphinx:* Mythological figure with the body of a lion and the head of a man.
[3]*Muriel Rukeyser* (1913–1980): Twentieth-century American poet.

Some, like a local chaplain, told this paper the Bible is accept- 13
able in the present masculine form. He said when the Bible refers to
"a man, people interpret it as a person." Do they?

I do not consider myself included in the term "man."

Our friend Oedipus in Rukeyser's story was 14
told differently. I am telling the chaplain and others like him that many have not interpreted it that
way. Certainly the founders of our country did not
believe that "man" included woman. If the Constitution included woman, we would not have
needed an amendment to give women the right to vote.

Of course, we could go further back in time and find numerous 15
instances when the term "man" in versions of the Bible meant
"man." This version of the Bible helped defend slavery and the subjugation of people on a world scale. This version of the Bible created
one world citizen — the white man.

This "man" interpreted the Bible in any way that suited his 16
newest conquest and the very women who were included in the term
"man" were raped, beaten, and treated like property. These women
who were defined in the term "man" had no legal rights and nothing
to call their own, not even their children.

I do not consider myself included in the term "man." I refuse to 17
fall into that linguistic pit. I will not identify myself as a counterpart
to the male of the species, forced to link my gender identity with his
and him not showing me the same respect. The same people who say
that "man" includes "woman" are the same ones who do not want
women to work, think, or speak.

Getting back to the main reason for this discourse, I think the 18
new Bible is a good thing. I never have believed one translation is
good enough. We should have the option of looking at many translations. While I would love to learn ancient Greek and Hebrew and
translate the Bible my own way, I really do not have that luxury right
now. So I will look at different versions, hopefully there will be more,
and decide which one I like the best.

It will not, however, be the masculine, exclusive one that has 19
been used to breed prejudice and sexist thought. It will be an inclusive one that concentrates on the meanings of faith and Christianity,
not on reproducing a patriarchal society.

After all, isn't that what counts — the meaning? Translation is a 20
sticky business because of meaning. Words are not mathematical
equations that balance out. Words are carriers of thought, culture,
and systems. The very term "man" is a carrier of the cultural idea

that men are superior to women. This term is no longer acceptable in a society where we are attempting to promote the idea that people are equal. The term "man" is an archaic remnant from a time in the past. We must acknowledge its misogynistic meaning and discard it. Killing a word is not killing a language. Language is alive, and we continually stop using words without even thinking about it. This particular meaning of "man" needs to go, especially in texts and discourses that holds so much weight in the minds of many people.

Web **Read It Now:** Gender: Sexist Language and Assumption, **bedfordstmartins** **.com/americanow**, Chapter 7. This brief article is from *The American Heritage Book of English Usage*.

Web **Read It Now:** Non-Sexist Language Guidelines (NCTE), **bedfordstmartins** **.com/americanow**, Chapter 7. These guidelines are from the National Council of Teachers of English, posted at the Purdue University Online Writing Lab.

Vocabulary/Using a Dictionary

1. Some words that come from the same root as *patriarchal* (para. 19) are *paternal, patron,* and *patriot*. Look up the definitions for these words and compare them to *patriarchal*. What would you guess is the meaning of the root word *pater*?

2. Can you guess the meanings of these words related to *archaic* (para. 20): *archives, archaeology,* or *archetype*?

3. Split the word *misogynistic* (para. 20) into its parts *miso-, gyn-, -istic,* and try to discern the meaning of each part based on what you know the whole definition to be.

Responding to Words in Context

1. At the bottom of paragraph 8, Hansen asks, "Who decided this load of crap?" Why do you think she uses such strong and casual language to question the "inclusive" use of masculine nouns and pronouns?

2. When Hansen says that men "have the license to have their own identity" (para. 11), what does she mean by this? How does this use of *license* compare to more literal uses (for example, driver's license)?

3. What image is the phrase "linguistic pit" (para. 17) meant to conjure up in the reader's mind?

Discussing Main Point and Meaning

1. Hansen makes an implicit connection between the Bible and the U.S. Constitution in paragraphs 13 and 14, when she is arguing about the noninclusive effects of the "neutral" use of masculine nouns and pronouns. What is your response to this comparison? Does it make sense to look at a religious and a legal document in the context of the same argument?

2. "Words are carriers of thought, culture, and systems" (para. 20), Hansen writes. Does it make sense to you to describe words as *carriers*? Explain why or why not.

3. If, as Hansen argues, "Language is alive" (para. 20), what does it feed on? And if it lives, then can it "die"?

Examining Sentences, Paragraphs, and Organization

1. Why does Hansen's essay open with the presentation of a story about Oedipus?

2. "We are mankind, female, she, and woman" (para. 9). What point is this sentence trying to make? How does it relate to the overall point of the paragraph?

3. Hansen cites "the main reason for [her] discourse" in paragraph 18. Is this an announcement of her thesis? If so, does it come too late in the essay? Or did she need time to build up to this announcement?

4. When Hansen asks "isn't that what counts — the meaning?" (para. 20), does she mean for the reader to answer this question? How would you answer it?

Thinking Critically

1. Does Hansen's argument presume that women and men want to be treated the same or differently? If there were words to describe women that were not derived from the words that describe men, do you think those words would make women seem more equal to men? Or is it possible that the words would still connote

something inferior? What is gender equality? Does it mean that both genders are treated according to exactly the same standards, or does it mean that the differences between men and women are valued equally? Could it be some combination of the two positions?

2. If the Bible is founded on such sexist assumptions, why not ignore it entirely? Why bother trying to update a text that may seem out of step with our times?

In-Class Writing Activities

1. The Muriel Rukeyser story Hansen discusses in her article takes a well-known fictional character (Oedipus) and presents another side of that character, or another chapter in the story of that character. Choose another well-known literary figure (for example, Hester Prynne from *The Scarlet Letter* or Bigger Thomas from *Native Son*), and write an essay from the perspective of that character. How important is the role of language in relation to that character's quest for freedoms and equality? Support your argument with specific passages from the text.

2. Write a letter to Hansen's newspaper, the *Daily Nebraskan,* supporting or challenging her argument. Cite quotes from her text to make specific points about.

JASON GILLIKIN

Inclusive Language:
A Problem That Isn't

[THE WESTERN HERALD, WESTERN MICHIGAN UNIVERSITY / June 14, 2001]

Before You Read

Should grammar rules be preserved for their own sake? Why would anyone be offended by the use of masculine terms to refer to both men and women? Does grammatical correctness outweigh political correctness?

Words to Learn

truism (para. 1): statement of an obvious truth (n.)

neuter (para. 2): neither masculine nor feminine; asexual (n.)

uncontested (para. 3): unchallenged; accepted (adj.)

eradicated (para. 3): erased; removed (adj.)

progressive (para. 5): favoring reform (adj.)

advocate (para. 5): to recommend or support (v.); one who recommends or supports (n.)

maliciously (para. 5): with a desire to harm (adv.)

adage (para. 6): short maxim or proverb (n.)

JASON GILLIKIN (b. 1976) graduated from Western Michigan University in 2002, where he served as the opinion editor of the Western Herald. *Gillikin, who wrote this piece as a senior, commented that it prompted many letters to the newspaper and classroom debates. He feels that the responses to his column highlight the ongoing debate of the use of politically correct language.*

It seems to be a truism of academic liberalism that any grammatical construction that would exclude somebody is inferior to those constructions deemed inclusive. The classic example, of course, is the use of the word *he* to refer to individuals of unknown sex. On the surface, this seems to be an entirely rational and correct-thinking position. But is anyone actually being excluded?

I went through elementary and high school having been taught that English has three natural genders (masculine, feminine, and neuter), but four grammatical genders. The fourth grammatical gender, called common, uses masculine constructions but refers to indeterminate or mixed natural gender. The technical term for this practice is "masculine preferred"; that is, the masculine grammatical gender is preferred when making reference to males, females, or mixed company.

Some contemporary grammarians have claimed that the masculine preferred system is based on the everyday practices of our linguistic forefathers, for whom male domination was an uncontested reality; the use of male-only pronouns to refer to indeterminate gender ought to be eradicated, as a sign of modern society's seriousness of cleansing the wounds of sexism. This argument, however, is open to criticism. Most significantly, the masculine preferred system had been understood to be a grammatical issue long before women began their fight for social, political, and economic equality. *Fundamentals of English Composition,* written in 1925, makes it clear that masculine preferred constructions have nothing to do with the sex of the person referred to, but rather with the unique demands of English grammar.

> *Those pronouns have got to go!*

One less technical criticism is that people who get upset at the use of masculine pronouns have entirely too much time on their hands. Of all the things to get worked up about, I find it hard to figure out how grammar rises to the top of anybody's list. Forget world peace, feeding the hungry, stopping child labor, or saving the environment: those pronouns have got to go!

The inclusive language movement has fallen prey to a unique danger of contemporary progressive thought — advocating symbolism over substance. Inclusive language is a problem that isn't. The advocates of grammatical reform are either mistaken about or maliciously disregard the reality of the masculine preferred construction: *he* or *his* do not refer exclusively to males when the pronouns are, or could be, referring to people of mixed or unknown gender. There is no defect in English grammar to correct. When allegedly gender-neutral constructions became prevalent in academia, it was considered a sign of being right-minded about diversity to use them. Those obstinate folks who persist in using "exclusive" language are apparently unenlightened — even though they're the people using the English language correctly!

For those inclined to prefer style over logic, consider this: "He or   6
she who establishes his or her argument by noise and command shows that his or her reason is weak." Michel de Montaigne's[1] famous adage — easily applied to the inclusive language crowd — loses something after being vandalized by inclusive language. So when I see sentences containing *he-or-she*'s or *him-or-her*'s or — God forbid! — the construction *s/he*, I chuckle. For people who make such a point of appearing to be intelligent and sophisticated and tolerant, I find it deliciously ironic that the device they use to proclaim their right-thinking is, itself, little more than a basic grammatical error.

Vocabulary/Using a Dictionary

1. *Uncontested* (para. 3) contains the word *contest*. How does the meaning of *uncontested* involve or relate to having a *contest*?

2. The word *maliciously* (para. 5) is related to the term *malice,* which is used frequently in a legal context. What do you think *malice* means according to the law?

Responding to Words in Context

1. Gillikin describes inclusive language as *vandalizing* (para. 6) meaning. What does he mean by this? What does *vandalism* usually involve?

2. Why does Gillikin find the use of neutered language to be "deliciously ironic" (para. 6)?

Discussing Main Point and Meaning

1. In paragraph 2, Gillikin refers to a technical grammatical term "masculine preferred." Were you taught this term? Why do you think Gillikin takes the time to define and present such a specific

---

[1]*Michel de Montaigne* (1533–1592): French essayist.

technical term? How does it help him to support his general argument?

2. Gillikin offers "one less technical criticism" (para. 4) of those in favor of neutered language. What is that criticism? Does it help Gillikin's argument? If so, how?

3. Do you think Gillikin would be opposed to the use of a "feminine preferred" system to refer to men and women alike? Why or why not?

Examining Sentences, Paragraphs, and Organization

1. Trace the tone of Gillikin's essay from beginning to end. How would you characterize it? Does it shift at all, or is it consistent throughout?

2. Examine paragraph 3. What is Gillikin's main point here? Why does he cite a text published in 1925?

3. The quoted passage from Montaigne in paragraph 6 could be paraphrased as saying people get loud and pushy when trying to hide that they have no point. Gillikin chooses the passage to demonstrate that use of both gendered pronouns (he or she; his or her) would cause a "loss" of meaning. What meaning would be lost? Are there any other gender-neutral ways of presenting this passage without affecting the meaning?

Thinking Critically

1. Many grammatical conventions and word meanings in English have changed over the years to suit the needs of an evolving society. Why shouldn't the grammatical conventions related to gender change, given the extent of their effects?

2. Would it make any difference to you if this essay had been written by a woman? Why or why not?

In-Class Writing Activities

1. Rewrite the following passage to make it gender-neutral. Use a combination of pronouns, the neutral pronoun *one*, second-person pronouns, or plural pronouns, according to your preference. Whatever you choose, be consistent. Discuss whether the changes affect the meaning of the passage in any way.

These days a professional athlete must be on guard about many things. As always, he must realize first and foremost that his body is his main asset, and that his number one priority should be the maintenance and preservation of that asset. An athlete will be distracted by the sudden money and fame that now accompany his profession, however, and this will threaten his priority. Furthermore, the press will make every effort to expose his faults and secrets, not caring a whit about his privacy or reputation. Finally, fans will expect a lot from an athlete who earns more than just about anyone else in society: He'd better perform consistently or he'll lose their support in an instant.

Discussing the Unit

Suggested Topic for Discussion

As the saying goes, "the Devil is in the details." Why do we argue about the use of male pronouns in the Bible? What do we accomplish? Are we merely distracting ourselves from larger, more important examples of sexism and other forms of discrimination (spousal abuse, child prostitution, poverty, and so on), or is it important to fight this battle on all fronts?

Preparing for Class Discussion

1. Do you think altering major cultural documents like the Bible, the U.S. Constitution, or the rules of an institution such as English grammar have significant effects on our society? Why or why not?

2. While the general person or "indeterminate case" may be referred to as male, other sexless objects are often referred to as female (for example, nature, ships, cars, countries, continents). Would this pose a problem for any of the authors in this unit? Does it pose a problem for you?

From Discussion to Writing

1. How important is it to you that language be neutral about or inclusive of your sex? Does language add anything to or detract anything from your participation in society? Write a short essay

answering these questions and also imagining the consequences of your position on "the other sex."

2. Jason Gillikin calls for gender-neutral language, "advocating symbolism over substance" (para. 5). What is a symbol's relationship to substance? Many people think that the desecration of the U.S. flag should be illegal because what the flag stands for is so important to us. In most religions, symbols take on a sacred quality and carry significant meaning from generation to generation. In fashion, a brand name signifies the difference between authentic quality and a cheap imposter. How important are symbols to you? Write a brief essay on this issue, citing some examples of symbols that you believe are substantive.

Topics for Cross-Cultural Discussion

1. Do you speak another language that uses masculine pronouns to denote men and women collectively? How do the pronouns and "neutral" nouns of that language compare to those in English? Do these differences play any role in or reflect other cultural differences?

2. Is "inclusiveness" in language an issue in other countries? Has language usage ever changed in other countries as a result of changing cultural values?

8

Can Words Be Dangerous?

Do the words we use matter personally, socially, and politically? Does it make any difference whether we say *girl* instead of *woman* or *colored people* instead of *people of color*? How and why do words take on such power? Do our words sometimes speak louder than our actions?

Do African Americans operate with a "double standard" when it comes to the N-word, using it themselves but finding it offensive when used by anyone not black? This issue is closely examined by Yvonne Bynoe in "The N-Word: We're Talking Out of Both Sides of Our Mouths," where she looks at how the term has been internationally popularized by black comedians and rap stars. What about other kinds of "bad words" — profanity, curses, and vulgar expressions? In "The Power of Profanity," DePauw University student Scott Weaver finds himself at home in the world of vulgar language and argues that cursing is a valid form of expression. Since the attacks of September 11, 2001, Americans have encountered an important political term: *terrorism.* The word is used regularly by the military, the government, and the media, but do we have any clear idea of what it means? In "'Terrorism': The Word Itself Is Dangerous," John V. Whitbeck suggests that words can speak louder than actions. "The greatest threat to world peace today," he claims, "is clearly 'terrorism' — not the behavior to which the word is applied, but the word itself."

YVONNE BYNOE

The N-Word: We're Talking Out of Both Sides of Our Mouths

[AFRICANA.COM / April 14, 2001]

Before You Read

How do you react when you hear the term *nigger?* Is this word always racially derogatory? Does it depend on who uses the word and in what context?

Words to Learn

familial (para. 4): characteristic of or pertaining to a family (adj.)

nuances (para. 4): shades of difference; delicate variations in tone or meaning (n.)

duality (para. 6): the condition of having a double character or nature (n.)

pejorative (para. 6): having negative connotations; disparaging (adj.)

egregious (para. 7): notably bad; flagrant (adj.)

cavalierly (para. 7): disdainfully; haughtily (adv.)

excise (para. 8): to remove by or as if by cutting out (v.)

ministerial (para. 8): relating to a high officer of state who heads a division of government (adj.)

mandate (para. 8): an authoritative command (n.)

arbiters (para. 8): those having the power to decide; judges (n.)

Yvonne Bynoe *is the president and cofounder of Urban Think Tank, Inc. She is currently a fellow at the Du Bois Bunche Center for Public Policy at Medgar Evers College, City University of New York. Bynoe has contributed to* Popmatters.com, PoliticallyBlack.com, Africana.com, TheSource .com, *and* The Black World Today *online.*

On the heels of Senator Robert Byrd's recent use of the term   1
"white nigger" and California Lieutenant Governor Cruz Bustamente's
Freudian slip[1] at the Black Trade Unionists annual dinner, the N-word
has resurfaced as a focal point for public debate. What is ironic is that
while the majority of black Americans have expressed dismay, if not
outrage, over the use of the word by these nonblack public officials, as
a group we have been relatively silent about the rampant use of the
N-word by black entertainers, particularly rap artists and comedians.

The sad fact is that while the vast majority of Americans —   2
black, white, and other — are not particularly interested in the utter-
ances of either Byrd or Bustamente, they are familiar with everything
said by black celebrities like Chris Rock or DMX. And now the cultural products of the United States are exported abroad, so a global
audience is increasingly under the impression that the N-word is a
content-neutral, equal-opportunity term.

If the majority of black Americans are still offended by the use of   3
the N-word by anyone not black, then they must show the same
vocal indignation when a black person uses the word — our current
double standard does not send a clear message of where black Americans stand on this issue.

Through the many, many years of the word's history, black   4
Americans have internalized the word and many of us even use it in
our private conversations. Younger black Americans involved with
the Hip Hop community have made some weak
attempts to distinguish "nigga" as a familial term
from "nigger," a slur. Unfortunately, these nuances, which are largely dependent on vocal inflec-
tions and the intent of the speaker, are lost on
many white Americans and foreigners.

*At its core the
N-word is
connected with
the subjugation
of black people.*

This became unnervingly apparent on a recent   5
trip to South Africa, where young black American
males could expect to be greeted with "What's up, my nigger?" by
misled natives. The casual and frequent use of the N-word by black
American rap artists, whose music is heavily imported into the country, didn't help young black South Africans see that the term is a slur.
Similarly, white Europeans also steeped in American culture see no
problem with using the N-word in our presence, whether they are
reciting an American rap lyric or having a conversation.

---

[1]*Freudian slip:* An unintentional mistake that seems to reveal a subconscious intention.

In the public sphere the N-word cannot have duality: Either it is   6
a flatly forbidden racial insult, or else it is just another word because
its pejorative meaning has dissipated.

By and large, black Americans still see the N-word as an egre-   7
gious slur because, despite its various manipulations, at its core the
N-word is connected with linguistic violence and the subjugation of
black people. For older black Americans, the word still conjures up
memories of the degradation of segregation and racial discrimination.
Younger black Americans can look to the atrocities committed
against James Byrd, Amadou Diallo, and Abner Louima[2] for sufficient evidence that the original concept of a "nigger" as a sub-human
still exists in America. Black Americans who stand for justice should
not disrespect our history or our present-day realities by cavalierly
using the N-word or allowing anyone else to do so.

Artistic freedom as supported by the First Amendment is often   8
used as the justification for the use of the N-word in creative works.
Many rap artists flatly state that the N-word is such an integral part
of their language and that of their audiences, they couldn't possibly
excise it from their lyrics: the old "keepin' it real" excuse. The key
question to be asked is whether or not the use of the N-word helps to
illuminate the breadth and scope of a creative expression; does it educate the audience, or does its use simply perpetuate ignorance and old
stereotypes? Art is subjective and personal, and obviously there
should never be a ministerial mandate that the N-word should never
be used, but black Americans themselves need to be better arbiters of
when it is appropriate and in what contexts.

What is most disturbing is that black Americans are allowing   9
corporate media entities, be they record companies, radio stations,
television stations, or film companies, to define our group identity. At
the end of the day, the majority of black entertainers or cultural
workers cannot produce or broadcast any material that is not sanctioned by a white executive, while these white executives, under the
guise of entertainment, are quite comfortable allowing blacks to use
the N-word as well as a host of other derogatory terms.

As descendants of African people, inheritors of an oral tradition   10
that has provided this country with much of its artistic and concep-
tual framework, we should understand the weight of words. Words
like "nigger," "buck," "coon," "mammy," and "bitch" were used to
dehumanize us and therefore helped to rationalize the brutality

---

[2]*James Byrd, Amadou Diallo, and Abner Louima:* All three were recent victims of horrible crimes.

leveled against us for centuries. Therefore black Americans have to decide publicly whether they have indeed become "niggers" and have no reason to restrict the usage of the word, or whether they are human beings who demand that their history and their pain be respected around the world by rejecting this slur. For the record, I am down with Hip Hop, but don't call me "nigger."

Web **Read It Now:** That Word, **bedfordstmartins.com/americanow**, Chapter 8. Randall Kennedy, author of *Nigger: The Strange Career of a Troublesome Word*, comments in this *Atlantic Unbound* interview on his book and on language and its boundaries.

Web **Read It Now:** The N Word, **bedfordstmartins.com/americanow**, Chapter 8. In this *Salon.com* review of Randall Kennedy's book *Nigger: The Strange Career of a Troublesome Word*, Charles Taylor asks whether it's ever okay to use the word.

Web **Read It Now:** Black Perspectives on the "N-Word," **bedfordstmartins.com/americanow**, Chapter 8. Should the word *nigger* be banned? This article by Cynthia Greenlee for Africana.com considers this question in regard to the word's significance on the Internet, within the legal system, and within popular culture.

Vocabulary/Using a Dictionary

1. How are *egregious* (para. 7) and *segregation* (para. 7) related?
2. What is the origin of *cavalierly* (para. 7)?
3. List four suitable synonyms for *mandate* (para. 8).

Responding to Words in Context

1. Bynoe mentions Senator Byrd's use of the term *white nigger* and Lieutenant Governor Bustamente's "*Freudian slip* at the Black Trade Unionists annual dinner" (para. 1). What do you think the term *white nigger* means? What is Bynoe referring to when she mentions Bustamente's *Freudian slip*?
2. What would it mean to "have *internalized* the [N-]word" (para. 4)?
3. How might using "'nigga' as a *familial* term" (para. 4) distinguish it from *nigger*?

4. The writer contends "the N-word is connected with *linguistic violence*" (para. 7). What do you think she means by *linguistic violence*?

Discussing Main Point and Meaning

1. Look at the title. What does the expression "talking out of both sides of our mouths" mean? How does this idiomatic expression in the title reflect the essay's argument? To whom does the pronoun *our* refer? Who is the audience for this essay?

2. According to Bynoe, why should black Americans avoid the N-word?

3. In this essay, Bynoe considers the reasons why some members of the African American community defend their use of the N-word. What are their reasons? How does Bynoe refute them?

4. In paragraph 7, Bynoe looks at the historical context of the N-word. What purpose did the N-word serve in the past? What purpose does it serve today? How is this paragraph a central point in Bynoe's argument?

Examining Sentences, Paragraphs, and Organization

1. Bynoe contends, "And now the cultural products of the United States are exported abroad, so a global audience is increasingly under the impression that the N-word is a content-neutral, equal-opportunity term" (para. 2). What are the cultural products Bynoe refers to? What does it mean for the N-word to be a "content-neutral, equal-opportunity term?"

2. In paragraph 9, Bynoe finds it disturbing "that black Americans are allowing corporate media entities...to define our group identity." She ends the paragraph by concluding, "these white executives, under the guise of entertainment, are quite comfortable allowing blacks to use the N-word as well as a host of other derogatory terms." Look closely at her word choice. What is Bynoe implying in this paragraph?

3. Bynoe concludes, "Therefore black Americans have to decide publicly whether they have indeed become 'niggers' and have no reason to restrict the usage of the word, or whether they are human beings who demand that their history and their pain be respected around the world by rejecting this slur" (para. 10).

What does it mean to make a public decision? What does Bynoe mean by "they have indeed become 'niggers'?"

4. In the last sentence, Bynoe adds, "For the record, I am down with Hip Hop, but don't call me 'nigger'" (para. 10). What tone does this sentence create? Why do you think Bynoe felt it necessary to add this line?

Thinking Critically

1. Why do you think Bynoe consistently uses the term *N-word* instead of *nigger* unless she is quoting someone else's words? How does this word choice reflect her argument about the term?

2. Several times in this essay Bynoe makes an either-or argument. Either the N-word is a racial insult or just another word. It cannot be both (para. 6). To paraphrase Bynoe, black Americans become "niggers" in adopting the term or human beings in rejecting it (para. 10). Representing only two possibilities when more exist is known as the either-or fallacy. Has Bynoe committed the either-or fallacy? Explain your answer.

3. Bynoe condemns black Americans who reject the use of the N-word by nonblacks but accept it when the speaker is black. Why might some blacks reject the word in one instance and use it in another? Do you agree with Bynoe that "they must show the same vocal indignation when a black person uses the word" (para. 3)?

In-Class Writing Activities

1. Bynoe agrees that "art is subjective and personal, and obviously there should never be a ministerial mandate that the N-word should never be used." However, she goes on to argue that "black Americans themselves need to be better arbiters of when it is appropriate and in what contexts" (para. 8). In a brief essay, take up this issue of artistic and consumer responsibility. How responsible should artists be in producing works that do not promote harm? How responsible should consumers be in rejecting harmful works? Consider these questions by focusing on a very specific example. For instance, you might want to look at the N-word in the context of a comedic monologue or a rap song, a film that many critics have deemed too violent, or a New

York art exhibit that received great public criticism because it featured a concentration camp made out of Legos.

2. Bynoe argues, "Words like 'nigger,' 'buck,' 'coon,' 'mammy,' and 'bitch' were used to dehumanize us and therefore helped to rationalize the brutality leveled against us for centuries" (para. 10). Respond to this sentence in a freewrite in which you explain how words can dehumanize and rationalize atrocities.

3. Words like *nigga, bitch,* and *queer* are examples of words that originally carried a pejorative meaning but have been adopted by the very groups insulted by the term. Bynoe's essay offers the example of black Americans using the N-word. In addition, some women proudly declare themselves *bitches* to proclaim their pride in their assertiveness, and many members of the gay community embrace the term *queer* with pride. In defense of such a use of these racist, sexist, homophobic terms, those adopting them might argue they rob both the word and their oppressors of their power if they can control the term themselves. Do you agree with such an argument, or do you side with Bynoe's rejection of the pejorative term? Respond in a brief essay that focuses on one of these terms.

SCOTT WEAVER

The Power of Profanity

[THE DEPAUW.COM, DEPAUW UNIVERSITY / March 7, 2001]

Before You Read

How comfortable are you with profanity? How would you react if you encountered vulgar language in a college newspaper or classroom? How is your own attitude about profanity shaped by the environments in which you grew up? Why do you think people are offended by foul language?

Words to Learn

vulgarity (para. 2): something that is crude, course, lacking in taste; offensive; lewdly indecent (n.)

profanity (para. 3): the use of language that serves to debase what is holy; irreverent language (n.)

dialect (para. 6): a regional variety of language (n.)

canon (para. 7): an official or authoritative list (such as the literary canon) (n.)

marginalize (para. 8): to exclude from or exist outside the mainstream of society or a group (v.)

I remember the first time I cursed in front of my grandmother. She's an old farm wife, straight Midwest and God-fearing. She looked at me, still dishing out homemade fried chicken and said, "Only stupid people cuss. It's because they can't think of any way else to say what they want to say."   1

Scott Weaver *(b. 1978) recently graduated from DePauw University with a B.A. in creative writing. He has received various awards for his sports, fiction, and column writing. Weaver, who wrote this essay as a senior, commented that he "likes the power of the profane" and says that "the exclusion of these words gives them their punch." He is currently an M.F.A. candidate at George Mason University.*

This was my introduction to the large group of people who don't like the way I talk. But it really wasn't my fault. I was raised in a baseball dugout crowd. My dad coached a team of semi-pro players who were to vulgarity what Jimi Hendricks was to the guitar.

Most of them were young, early twenties, and would string together a profanity-laced sentence better than Michelangelo could paint ceilings. Then they would look down at my skinny, six-year-old face, take a short breath, and say, "Don't ever say that."

Telling me not to repeat the new words I was picking up weekly was like giving a sixteen-year-old a new car and saying, "Hey, don't drive that."

So I grew up into who I am. I speak English adequately, Spanish horribly, and Profanity fluently. I thrive on it. I live through it. I'm only comfortable in class if the professor lets some curse words slip. Vulgar language is my home.

Not everybody agrees. My mom has slapped me a couple times after I explained myself in my expanded vocabulary. I turned heads in church, when I used to go. This very student newspaper has argued, deleted, and belittled my dialect. The higher-ups and I — present and past — have gone the equivalent of a twelve-round, heavyweight fight over what most people consider vulgarity and I consider words.

But when it comes down to it, the canon of "bad words" are just that — words. Each elicits a certain response from the listener or the reader. It's the difference of these responses that give these words their power. And what a power it is.

There are words in the English language we are not allowed to say on either television or radio. We are not allowed to print them. These words hold so much power that, as far as certain people are concerned, they do not exist. It's funny. These same people who marginalize these words give them their power, a power that people like me use when we force these "nonexistent" words into existence. Thank you.

Vulgar language is my home.

As much as I love my grandmother, she's wrong about some things. One of them is profanity. People don't use vulgar words because they can't think of "real" words to express what they want to say. They use them because the vulgarity expresses exactly what they want to say. It provides a depth and scope to our language that makes it come alive, makes it fly, and at the same time firmly roots it back to the ground.

So who's stupid? The person who can't say exactly what they mean because they have a limited vocabulary? Or is it the person who says exactly what they want to, taking the English language by the . . . uh, throat and using every possible form of expression? I think by now you know how I'd answer that question. 10

But maybe not. In the above five hundred words, I didn't curse once. If I had, I could have told you exactly how I feel about the issue of profanity, something I think is essential to our language. I could have backed it all up with colorful stories that you'd probably laugh about with your friends while you eat lunch on Tuesday. I could have made you explode with laughter, or anger, or whatever reaction a well-placed curse word sets off in you. But I didn't. 11

Vocabulary/Using a Dictionary

1. What is the origin of the word *vulgarity* (para. 2)? What does the origin tell you about who is associated with vulgar language?

2. What is the origin of the word *profanity* (para. 3)? What does the origin tell you about why some people regard *profanity* as offensive?

Responding to Words in Context

1. The essay opens with the author considering the first time he "*cursed* in front of [his] grandmother" (para. 1). How does a *curse* differ from a *vulgarity*? Why would "an old farm wife, straight Midwest and God-fearing" (para. 1) object to a curse?

2. What does Weaver suggest about his use of profanity by calling it a *dialect* (para. 6)?

3. What does Weaver suggest about profanity by calling it a "canon of 'bad words'" (para. 7)?

Discussing Main Point and Meaning

1. How does the essay attempt to prove that there is power in profanity?

2. What point does Weaver make about the power of bad words? How does he use this claim to defend his cursing?

3. The first paragraph ends with Weaver's grandmother's claim that, "Only stupid people cuss." How does the writer turn around this claim to defend his use of vulgarity?

Examining Sentences, Paragraphs, and Organization

1. In describing the environment in which he grew up, Weaver writes, "My dad coached a team of semi-pro players who were to vulgarity what Jimi Hendricks was to the guitar" (para. 2). What is the effect of this analogy?

2. In describing semi-pro players, Weaver admires their ability to "string together a profanity-laced sentence better than Michelangelo could paint ceilings" (para. 3). What is the effect of this analogy?

3. What point does Weaver make with the analogy in paragraph 4?

4. Weaver writes, "I speak English adequately, Spanish horribly, and Profanity fluently" (para. 5). Aside from the humor, assume this sentence makes a serious point. What is it?

Thinking Critically

1. The writer reasons, "[bad] words hold so much power that, as far as certain people are concerned, they do not exist" (para. 8). Explain what Weaver means and evaluate the soundness of his claim.

2. Weaver points out the irony that "these same people who marginalize these words give them their power, a power that people like me use when we force these 'nonexistent' words into existence" (para. 8). Who do you think gives profanity its real power, those who forbid the words or those who use them frequently? Explain your reasoning.

3. In contrast to his grandmother, Weaver asserts people who cuss are not stupid (para. 9) because they do use word choice consciously. "They use [bad words] because the vulgarity expresses exactly what they want to say. It provides a depth and scope to our language that makes it come alive, makes it fly, and at the same time firmly roots it back to the ground" (para. 9). Do you agree with Weaver's characterization of profanity and its speakers? Explain.

4. In the conclusion, Weaver bemoans what his essay has lost because of the lack of profanity. Why do you think the essay lacks profanity? Do you think the essay loses its impact without vulgar language?

In-Class Writing Activities

1. Weaver uses different terms to describe "bad words," including *cursing, vulgarity,* and *profanity.* Each of these carries a slightly different meaning. Break up offensive language into different categories according to the nature of the offense. Use these categories to explain why people are offended. Finally, rank your categories from the most offensive to the least. How would you define *obscenity?* What is "swearing?"

2. Weaver refers to his use of profanity in terms of self-identity, proclaiming "So I grew up into who I am" (para. 5). Weaver attributes his speech to the "baseball dugout crowd" he grew up with (para. 2) in contrast to his "old farm wife, straight Midwest and God-fearing" grandmother (para. 1). Thus, the essay suggests subcultures create language preferences. In a freewrite, discuss the different cultural forces that have shaped your own attitude toward profanity, vulgarity, or cursing. If you do use foul language, you might explain why you use it in some situations and social contexts and not in others.

3. Assume you are the parent of a four-year-old who has recently learned what you or others would consider a bad word. How would you react? As you draft your response, you'll want to specify the offensive word and decide how harmful you think the word is. If you want your child to stop using the word, explain what you think the best plan of action would be.

JOHN V. WHITBECK

"Terrorism": The Word Itself Is Dangerous

[WASHINGTON REPORT ON MIDDLE EAST AFFAIRS, WRMEA.COM / March 2002]

Before You Read

How would you define *terrorism*? What examples of terrorism come to mind? Is this a word that has a clear definition? Can you think of instances when the word *terrorism* has been abused or misused? Who tends to the use the word, and which groups of people or political movements is it used to describe?

Words to Learn

truisms (para. 2): undoubted or self-evident truths (n.)

notorious (para. 2): generally known and talked of, especially widely and unfavorably known (adj.)

inherent (para. 3): established as an essential part of something; intrinsic (adj.)

statute (para. 4): a law enacted by a legislative body (n.)

epithet (para. 6): a characterizing and often abusive word or phrase (n.)

abomination (para. 6): something odious, loathsome, detestable (n.)

insurgency (para. 7): a movement that revolts against civil authority or government (n.)

bandwagon (para. 7): a movement that attracts growing support; a current or fashionable trend (n.)

reprehensible (para. 7): deserving blame or censure; culpable (adj.)

carte blanche (para. 7): full discretionary power (from French) (n.)

self-determination (para. 8): the free choice of one's own acts, without external compulsion; the right of a people to decide its own form of government (n.)

JOHN V. WHITBECK *(b. 1946) is an international lawyer who has published over 350 articles on the Middle East in the international press. Whitbeck was born and raised in New York City and currently practices law in Saudi Arabia.*

The greatest threat to world peace today is clearly "terrorism" —   1
not the behavior to which the word is applied, but the word itself.

For years, people have recited the truisms that "one man's terror-   2
ist is another man's freedom fighter" and that "terrorism, like
beauty, is in the eye of the beholder." With the world's sole super-
power declaring an open-ended, worldwide "war on terrorism,"
however, the notorious subjectivity of this word is no longer a joke.

It is no accident that there is no agreed definition of "terrorism,"   3
since the word is so subjective as to be devoid of any inherent meaning. At the same time, the word is extremely dangerous, because people
tend to believe that it does have meaning and to use and abuse the
word by applying it to whatever they hate as a way of avoiding rational thought and discussion and, frequently, excusing their own illegal
and immoral behavior.

There is no shortage of precise verbal formulations for the di-   4
verse acts to which the word "terrorism" often is applied. "Mass
murder," "assassination," "arson," and "sabotage" are available (to
all of which the phrase "politically motivated" can be added if appropriate). Such crimes, moreover, are already on the statute books, rendering specific criminal legislation for "terrorism" unnecessary. Such
precise formulations, however, do not carry the overwhelming, de-
monizing, and thought-deadening impact of the word "terrorism,"
which is, of course, precisely the charm of the word for its more cyni-
cal and unprincipled users and abusers. If someone commits "politically motivated mass murder," people might be curious as to the
cause or grievances which inspired such a crime, but no cause or
grievance can justify (or even explain) "terrorism," which, all right-
thinking people agree, is the ultimate evil.

Most acts to which the word "terrorism" is applied (at least in   5
the West) are tactics of the weak, usually (although not always)
against the strong. Such acts are not a tactic of choice but of last resort. To cite one example, the Palestinians certainly would prefer to
be able to fight for their freedom by "respectable" means, using
F-16s, Apache attack helicopters and laser-guided missiles such as
those the United States provides to Israel. If the United States provided such weapons to Palestine as well, the problem of suicide
bombers would be solved. Until it does, and for so long as the Palestinians can see no hope for a decent future, no one should be surprised or shocked that Palestinians use the "delivery systems" available to them — their own bodies. Genuine hope for something better

than a life worse than death is the only cure for the despair which inspires such gruesome violence.

The Poor, the Weak, and the Oppressed Rarely Complain about "Terrorism"

In this regard, it is worth noting that the poor, the weak, and the oppressed rarely complain about "terrorism." The rich, the strong, and the oppressors constantly do. While most of mankind has more reason to fear the high-technology violence of the strong than the low-technology violence of the weak, the fundamental mind-trick employed by the abusers of the epithet "terrorism" (no doubt, in some cases, unconsciously) is essentially this: The low-technology violence of the weak is such an abomination that there are no limits on the high-technology violence of the strong which can be deployed against it.

Perhaps the only honest and globally workable definition of "terrorism" is "violence which I don't support."

Not surprisingly, since September 11, virtually every recognized state confronting an insurgency or separatist movement has eagerly jumped on the "war on terrorism" bandwagon, branding its domestic opponents (if it had not already done so) "terrorists" and, at least implicitly, taking the position that, since no one dares to criticize the United States for doing whatever it deems necessary in its "war on terrorism," no one should criticize whatever they now do to suppress their own "terrorists." Even while accepting that many people labeled "terrorists" are genuinely reprehensible, it should be recognized that neither respect for human rights nor the human condition are likely to be enhanced by this apparent carte blanche seized by the strong to crush the weak as they see fit.

Writing in the *Washington Post* on October 15, deputy editor Jackson Diehl cited two prominent examples of the abuse of the epithet "terrorism": "With their handshake in the Kremlin, Sharon and Putin exchanged a common falsehood about the wars their armies are fighting against rebels in Chechnya and the West Bank and Gaza. In both cases, the underlying conflict is about national self-determination: statehood for the Palestinians, self-rule for Chechnya. The world is inclined to believe that both causes are just.... Sharon and Putin both have tried to convince the world that all their opponents are terrorists, which implies that the solution need not involve political concessions but merely a vigorous counterterrorism campaign."

Perhaps the only honest and globally workable definition of "ter-   9
rorism" is an explicitly subjective one — "violence which I don't support." Anyone who reads both the Western and Arab press cannot
help noticing that the Western press routinely characterizes as "terrorism" virtually all Palestinian violence against Israelis (even against
Israeli occupation forces within Palestine), while the Arab press routinely characterizes as "terrorism" virtually all Israeli violence against
Palestinians. Only this formulation would accommodate both charac-
terizations, as well as most others.

A Devalued Word

However, the word has been so devalued that even violence is no   10
longer an essential prerequisite for its use. In recently announcing a
multibillion-dollar lawsuit against ten international tobacco companies, a Saudi Arabian lawyer told the press: "We will demand that tobacco firms be included on the lists of terrorists and those financing
and sponsoring terrorism because of the large number of victims that
smoking has claimed the world over."

If everyone recognized that the word "terrorism" is fundamen-   11
tally an epithet and a term of abuse, with no intrinsic meaning, there
would be no more reason to worry about the word now than prior to
September 11. However, with the United States relying on the word
to assert, apparently, an absolute right to attack any country it dislikes (for the most part, countries Israel dislikes) and with President
George W. Bush repeatedly menacing that "either you're with us or
you're with the terrorists" (which effectively means, "either you
make our enemies your enemies or you'll be our enemy — and you
know what we do to our enemies"), many people around the world
must feel a genuine sense of terror (dictionary definition: "a state of
intense fear") as to where the United States is taking the rest of the
world.

Meanwhile, in America itself, the Bush administration appears to   12
be feeding the U.S. Constitution and America's traditions of civil liberties, due process, and the rule of law (the finest aspects of American
life, and the principal reasons why the country used to be admired
abroad) into a shredder — mostly to domestic applause or acquies-
cence. Who would have imagined that nineteen angry men armed
only with knives could accomplish so much, provoking a response,
beyond their wildest dreams, which threatens to be vastly more damaging to their enemies even than their own appalling acts?

If the world is to avoid a descent into anarchy, in which the only   13
rule is "might makes right," every "retaliation" provokes a "counter-
retaliation" and a genuine "war of civilizations" is ignited, the world —
and particularly the United States — must recognize that "terrorism"
is simply a word, a subjective epithet, not an objective reality, and
certainly not an excuse to suspend all the rules of international law
and domestic civil liberties which have, until now, made at least some
parts of our planet decent places to live.

Web **Read It Now:** What is Terrorism? **bedfordstmartins.com/americanow**, Chapter 8. This site, "Terrorism: Questions and Answers," hosted by the Council
of Foreign Relations and the Markle Foundation, offers an analysis of terrorism and in-depth coverage of Afghanistan, terrorist groups, 9/11 and its aftermath, and U.S. responses and policies.

Web **Read It Now:** Presidential Speech on 9/11, **bedfordstmartins.com/americanow**,
Chapter 8. Read the text of George Bush's speech on the evening of September 11, 2001 in which he addresses terrorism.

Web **Read It Now:** "The Wrong War," by Grenville Byford, **bedfordstmartins.com/
americanow**, Chapter 8. Originally published in _Foreign Affairs Magazine_
(September, 2002), this article explores the definition and use of the word
terrorism and critiques the "rhetoric of the 'war on terror.'"

Vocabulary/Using a Dictionary

1. What are four synonyms for _truism_ (para. 2)?

2. Look up _terrorism_ in the dictionary. Based on this definition, do
    you agree with Whitbeck's claim that "the word is so subjective
    as to be devoid of any inherent meaning" (para. 3)?

3. Whitbeck lists four terms that he believes are "precise verbal for-
    mulations for the diverse acts to which the word 'terrorism' often
    is applied[:] '_mass murder_,' '_assassination_,' '_arson_,' and '_sabo-
    tage_'" (para. 4). Look up one of these terms in the dictionary.
    How does the denotative meaning compare to _terrorism_? Is it
    more precise and less subjective than _terrorism_? How does the
    word's connotative meaning compare to _terrorism_?

4. Look up the literal meaning of _bandwagon_ (para. 7) to see where
    its figurative meaning derives.

5. What is the literal translation of the French term *carte blanche* (para. 7)?

Responding to Words in Context

1. In paragraph 5, why does Whitbeck put quotation marks around *respectable*? What point is he making in doing so? How would the meaning of the sentence change if *respectable* were not in quotation marks?

2. What kind of term is *delivery systems* (para. 5)? Why do you think Whitbeck uses it to describe the bodies of Palestinian suicide bombers?

3. Look at the writer's use of the word *anarchy* in paragraph 13's conclusion. Do you think the general meaning for *anarchy* of "utter chaos" applies best, or does the more specific meaning of "a social structure without government or law and order" seem more appropriate here? Explain you answer by looking at the word in the context of paragraph 13.

Discussing Main Point and Meaning

1. According to Whitbeck, how does the subjectivity of *terrorism* make it a dangerous word?

2. According to the essay, who complains about terrorism? What point is Whitbeck making in setting up this distinction?

3. What examples does Whitbeck give of insurgencies or separatist movements that have been labeled as *terrorist*?

4. What example does Whitbeck offer to argue *terrorism* is a devalued word? Does Whitbeck think *terrorism* is merely a devalued word? Explain.

5. How is the issue of civil liberties relevant to Whitbeck's discussion of *terrorism* as a dangerous word?

Examining Sentences, Paragraphs, and Organization

1. Paragraph 4 compares *terrorism* to "precise verbal formulations for the diverse acts to which the word 'terrorism' often is applied." What points does Whitbeck raise in comparing *terrorism*

to these other words? How are these points central to his argument?

2. Paragraph 6 ends with Whitbeck's conclusion that "while most of mankind has more reason to fear the high-technology violence of the strong than the low-technology violence of the weak, the fundamental mind-trick employed by the abusers of the epithet 'terrorism' (no doubt, in some cases, unconsciously) is essentially this: The low-technology violence of the weak is such an abomination that there are no limits on the high-technology violence of the strong which can be deployed against it." Explain how the abuse of the word *terrorism* is a "mind-trick." What example does Whitbeck offer earlier in the essay that this sentence would relate to? Do you agree with Whitbeck's point here?

3. Paragraph 7 ends with the following sentence: "Even while accepting that many people labeled 'terrorists' are genuinely reprehensible, it should be recognized that neither respect for human rights nor the human condition are likely to be enhanced by this apparent carte blanche seized by the strong to crush the weak as they see fit." What potential concerns of his readers is Whitbeck addressing here? Do you find his response to those concerns in this sentence adequate?

4. Paragraph 11 concludes with the idea that "many people around the world must feel a genuine sense of terror (dictionary definition: 'a state of intense fear') as to where the United States is taking the rest of the world." What does this sentence imply about the United States?

Thinking Critically

1. Whitbeck compares Palestinian suicide bombers to Israel's use of high-technology weapons. The only difference, he speculates, is that the Palestinians are deemed *terrorists* because they use low-technology violence (para. 5). How justifiable is this comparison?

2. What do you think of Whitbeck's characterization of the men responsible for September 11th (para. 12)? Do you think Whitbeck would call them terrorists? Why or why not? What do you think the most fitting term for them would be? What is Whitbeck referring to when he claims they "provok[ed] a response, beyond their wildest dreams?" Do you agree with Whitbeck's claim that this

response is "vastly more damaging to their enemies even than their own appalling acts"? What is Whitbeck implying here?

In-Class Writing Activities

1. The author cites President Bush's repeated assertion to other countries that "'either you're with us or you're with the terrorists'" (para. 11). Evaluate Bush's statement. What groups does Bush consider to be terrorist? If another country does not join the United States in its fight against terrorism, does it mean that country supports terrorists? Is Whitbeck's interpretation of Bush's statement valid?

2. Whitbeck's argument hinges on the premise that the subjectivity of *terrorism* makes it a dangerous word because of its potential for abuse. If you disagree with Whitbeck, write a response in which you defend the use of the word *terrorism*. If you agree with Whitbeck, write a brief essay in which you analyze another word whose very subjectivity makes it dangerous. Define the word both in the dictionary and in practice, being sure to offer specific examples of its abuse. Some examples of words to consider are *communist* or *communism, democracy, fascism, totalitarianism,* and *anarchy.*

Discussing the Unit

Suggested Topic for Discussion

What gives particular words their power? Is it the speakers who use them, those who forbid the word, the definition of the word, the connotation of the word, or its history? Can some words actually cause harm? The selections in this unit ask readers to ponder these questions.

Preparing for Class Discussion

1. Are some words acceptable in one social context or one group of people but not another? How would Yvonne Bynoe answer this question about the N-word, Scott Weaver about the "canon of 'bad words,'" and John Whitbeck about the word *terrorism*?

Also answer this question yourself by making a list of potentially offensive or harmful words or categories for such words and explain which words or categories are unacceptable in all contexts and which are acceptable in some contexts but not others. (See "Read It Now" below)

2. Our use of certain words or the potential of words to cause harm depend heavily on the culture surrounding the words. Discuss how culture plays a role in Bynoe's analysis of the N-word, Weaver's defense of cursing, and Whitbeck's condemnation of the word *terrorism*. More specifically, think about each author's explanation of who uses and who does not use the word and why. How does the term reflect a particular culture or subculture or the vested interests of a particular culture's or group's ideologies?

Web   **Read It Now:** More Dangerous Words, **bedfordstmartins.com/americanow,** Chapter 8. Read additional essays that consider such words as *jihad.*

From Discussion to Writing

1. Write an essay about a word that you think becomes dangerous in its use. Look at its dictionary definition, its origin, and its history, considering whether the meaning has changed over time. (Here the *Oxford English Dictionary* will be helpful.) Pay particular attention to the connotation of the term. Use specific examples and reasoning to support your argument that the word is dangerous. Your analysis will be more insightful if you can choose a word that your readers do not already accept as harmful. For example, Bynoe is writing to an audience of African Americans who accept the use of the N-word by black entertainers. And most readers probably would not perceive *terrorism* to be a dangerous word prior to reading Whitbeck's essay. Thus, you'll want to write an essay that proves to readers that the word is more harmful than they think. If you cannot think of a word that fulfills the demands of this question, then choose a word your audience would perceive as dangerous and explain why it is *not,* defending the usefulness of the word.

2. Write an essay in which you compare the N-word to the word *terrorism,* using your analysis of Bynoe's and Whitbeck's essays as the basis of your argument. Are both words equally harmful epithets? Who uses each word and to what end? Do both words

serve the interests of the strong oppressors to govern the oppressed? In comparing these words, consider to what extent you accept and reject each writer's argument, what their arguments have in common, where they might differ, and what your own ideas about each word are. Use the texts and your own reasoning and examples to develop your ideas.

Topics for Cross-Cultural Discussion

1. A major point in Bynoe's argument is her claim that "a global audience is increasingly under the impression that the N-word is a content-neutral, equal-opportunity term" (para. 2). Can you think of a country that has access to "the cultural products of the United States" (para. 2) containing the N-word? If so, is Bynoe's argument supported or challenged by how people in your native country perceive the N-word?

2. What is the equivalent of the word *terrorism* in other languages that you speak? Based on the use of the equivalent of the word *terrorism* in that language, do you agree or reject Whitbeck's assertion that "the poor, the weak, and the oppressed rarely complain about 'terrorism'" (para. 6)?

3. Make a list of words or categories of potentially offensive terms in other languages. Do they mirror offensive terms in English? Are some types of words more offensive or harmful in your native culture than others?

9

God and the Constitution: How Separate Must They Be?

When a U.S. Court of Appeals ruled in June 2002 that the phrase "under God" in the Pledge of Allegiance violated the First Amendment of the U.S. Constitution, its decision immediately provoked a heated controversy, one that received top-story coverage throughout the nation's media. But this was only one more skirmish in what will continue to be a battle between Americans who believe that God is an inseparable part of the nation's fundamental principles and traditions and those who believe that by bringing God into the political sphere we violate the separation between church and state. Current movements recommend removing the U.S. motto "In God We Trust" from our currency and classrooms, restricting the use of the word *God* in national songs, and making sure that references to God do not appear in any state mottoes or public displays in government offices or state property.

The intense controversy stems from just sixteen words contained in the First Amendment to the U.S. Constitution: "Congress shall make no law respecting an establishment of religion, or prohibiting the free exercise thereof." This is generally referred to as the Establishment Clause. Do these sixteen words simply mean that the U.S. government can institute no established church, no single state-authorized religion, as did some nations and even several states at the time the Constitution was ratified? Or does it mean, as modern courts have increasingly interpreted it, that no religious expression —

including the word *God* itself — can appear in political documents or be used in such a way that religion appears to be endorsed by the state?

Recently, as courts and legislators have moved towards a strict secularism that strives to maintain the wall of separation between church and state, the nation has been faced with what looks like glaring inconsistencies between our laws and our traditions. Doesn't all of our currency contain the phrase "In God We Trust"? Must we one day issue an entirely new currency with that phrase removed? Since the phrase also happens to be our national motto, must that be changed? And what about patriotic songs? Do we need to eliminate parts of "The Star Spangled Banner" and prohibit ballpark performances of "God Bless America"? What should we do with the opening sentences of our most treasured document, the Declaration of Independence, with its reference to "Nature's God" and a "Creator" from which all our rights are derived? Though not a legal document like the Constitution, will the Declaration of Independence eventually be prohibited from classrooms, public buildings, or state property because it appears to endorse a belief in God and may offend various groups of nonbelievers? Since the Declaration not only directly refers to God but also states that the Creator is the ultimate source of all human rights, will courts eventually rule that schoolroom displays or recitals of the Declaration of Independence violate the Constitution?

We examine in this unit how the Establishment Clause relates to two recent issues: (1) whether the phrase "under God" must be removed from the Pledge of Allegiance and (2) whether the nation's motto "In God We Trust" can be displayed in public school classrooms. The first two selections examine the recent controversy over a federal court's decision to remove the phrase "under God" from the Pledge of Allegiance. The phrase had been added in 1954 (see "Three Versions of the Pledge of Allegiance"). As Judge Alfred T. Goodwin argues in his judicial ruling, "The text of the official pledge, codified in federal law, impermissibly takes a position with respect to the purely religious question of the existence and identity of God." Although it endorses the separation of church and state, a *San Francisco Chronicle* editorial believes the "under God" ruling "exceeds the bounds of rationality" and "makes a mockery of the very serious issue of encroachment of religion on public policy in this nation."

The second issue is raised by the editorial board of the *Arizona Daily Wildcat,* the school paper of the University of Arizona in Tucson. After providing a brief history of the nation's motto, it asks students: "What do you think? Is it appropriate to place the motto 'In God We Trust' in public schools?" The responses of six University of Arizona students demonstrate the variety of opinion surrounding the place of religion in public schools. Although many Americans regard a policy of strictly separating church and state as a restraint on religious practice, the Anti-Defamation League believes otherwise. In one of its public service advertisements, the League suggests that, on the contrary, "the wall separating church and state" has allowed religion in America "to flourish free from government interference."

Three Versions of the Pledge of Allegiance

The pledge that millions of schoolchildren have recited for over a century has an interesting history. Originally written by a leading Boston socialist and clergyman, Francis Bellamy (1855–1931), it was first published in a family-oriented magazine in 1892. Over the years, the pledge got longer as two significant additions were made.

1892

"I pledge allegiance to my Flag, and to the Republic for which it stands, one nation, indivisible, with liberty and justice for all."

1923

"I pledge allegiance to the Flag of the United States of America, and to the Republic for which it stands, one nation, indivisible, with liberty and justice for all."

1954

"I pledge allegiance to the Flag of the United States of America, and to the Republic for which it stands, one nation, under God, indivisible, with liberty and justice for all."

Web **Hear It Now:** A Short History of the Pledge, **bedfordstmartins.com/ americanow**, Chapter 9. In this NPR interview, John Baer, author of *The Pledge of Allegiance: A Short History* (1992), provides context for today's debate.

Should the Words "Under God" Be Struck from the Pledge of Allegiance?

Before You Read

Do the words "under God" in the Pledge of Allegiance refer to a specific god? Are they enough of a religious reference to violate our constitutional separation of church and state? Can laws keep church and state separate?

Words to Learn [Goodwin]

monotheism (para. 1): doctrine of belief that there is only one god (n.)

normative (para. 1): establishing or prescribing a norm or standard (n.)

codified (para. 1): arranged in a system (v.)

inculcate (para. 1): instill or indoctrinate by repeating over and over (v.)

Words to Learn [Editorial Board]

absolutism (title): belief in a particular idea as unquestionable or unconditional (n.)

trump (para. 1): outrank at an opportune moment (v.)

doctrinaire (para. 1): dogmatic or dictatorial (adj.)

appellate (para. 3): having power to hear appeals and overturn decisions (adj.)

pluralism (para. 5): a condition of society in which numerous groups coexist in one nation (n.)

proscription (para. 6): prohibition; ban (n.)

amorphous (para. 6): vague; unstructured (adj.)

encroachment (para. 6): intrusion; infringement (n.)

preclude (para. 11): rule out; disqualify (v.)

JUDGE ALFRED T. GOODWIN

From The Opinion, Newdow vs. U.S. Congress

[THE NEW YORK TIMES / June 27, 2002]

In the context of the pledge, the statement that the United States is a nation, "under God," is an endorsement of religion. It is a profession of a religious belief — namely, a belief in monotheism. The recitation that ours is a nation "under God" is not a mere acknowledgment that many Americans believe in a deity. Nor is it merely descriptive of the undeniable historical significance of religion in the founding of the republic. Rather, the phrase "one nation, under God" in the context of the pledge is normative. To recite the pledge is not to describe the United States; instead, it is to swear allegiance to the values for which the flag stands: unity, indivisibility, liberty, justice, and — since 1954 — monotheism. The text of the official pledge, codified in federal law, impermissibly takes a position with respect to the purely religious question of the existence and identity of God. A profession that we are a nation "under God" is identical, for Establishment Clause purposes, to a profession that we are a nation "under Jesus," a nation "under Vishnu," a nation "under Zeus," or a nation "under no god," because none of these professions can be neutral with respect to religion. "The government must pursue a course of complete neutrality toward religion." Furthermore, the school dis-

The government must pursue a course of complete neutrality toward religion.

JUDGE ALFRED T. GOODWIN (b. 1923) was appointed to the U.S. Court of Appeals for the Ninth Circuit by President Nixon in 1971. In June 2002, he wrote the majority opinion that declared the reciting of the Pledge of Allegiance in public schools is unconstitutional due to the inclusion of the phrase "one nation, under God."

trict's practice of teacher-led recitation of the pledge aims to inculcate in students a respect for the ideals set forth in the pledge, and thus amounts to state endorsements of these ideals. Although students cannot be forced to participate in recitation of the pledge, the school district is nonetheless conveying a message of state endorsement of a religious belief when it requires public school teachers to recite, and lead the recitation, of the current form of the pledge. . . .

The pledge, as currently codified, is an impermissible government 2 endorsement of religion because it sends a message to unbelievers "that they are outsiders, not full members of the political community, and an accompanying message to adherents that they are insiders, favored members of the political community."

Web **Read It Now:** "Separation of Church and State," **bedfordstmartins.com/ americanow**, Chapter 9. Where does this phrase originate? Read historical document #510 at the University of Virginia online archive to find out.

Web **Read It Now:** The Opinion: Newdow vs. U.S. Congress, **bedfordstmartins.com/ americanow**, Chapter 9. Read the full text of the Court of Appeals decision written by Judge Goodwin and argued on March 14, 2002.

EDITORIAL BOARD

Allegiance to Absolutism

[SAN FRANCISCO CHRONICLE / June 27, 2002]

Common sense was trumped by doctrinaire thinking in a court 1 ruling barring the Pledge of Allegiance from including the phrase "under God."

A three-judge panel of the Ninth Circuit U.S. Court of Appeals in 2 San Francisco wants the thirty-one-word pledge trimmed of the two-word mention of God, which was added to the pledge by Congress in 1954.

Because the deity is mentioned, even generically, the pledge crosses 3 the line separating church and state, the appellate court declared.

"None of these professions can be neutral with respect to reli- 4 gion," wrote Judge Alfred Goodwin, who saw no distinction, for example, between the phrase "one nation under God" and "one nation under Jesus" or "one nation under Vishnu."

We disagree. This country's founders were wise to build a wall between church and state. No set of religious beliefs should have sway over others in a democracy built on the values of pluralism.

But the appellate court exceeds the bounds of rationality. Its proscription of the pledge because of two words — cast in an amorphous way — makes a mockery of the very serious issue of encroachment of religion on public policy in this nation. Adherents of any faith can project their own beliefs onto the phrase "one nation, under God." And the Supreme Court has made it clear that atheists cannot be compelled to recite those words.

In the past, courts have sensibly barred prayers at school graduations and sports events. The Ten Commandments likewise were forbidden from classroom walls. These were examples of distinct religious beliefs being sanctioned by government — and the courts justifiably tossed them out.

> *Constitutional rights, while sacred, are not absolute.*

With its ruling, the appellate court has declared open season on a wide range of more vague and benign mentions of God in public life. Does this country really want to reach the point where every mention of religion needs to be eliminated in the name of constitutional purity?

"In God We Trust" is printed on currency and coins. Does this amount to a religious intrusion?

The list goes on. Elected leaders from the president on down to a town council member swear on a Bible or with a raised hand to uphold their office "so help me God." Witnesses in court promise to tell the truth under a similar oath.

Constitutional rights, while sacred, are not absolute. They provide room for reason. The First Amendment does not offer a right to shout "fire!" in a crowded theater. And the separation of church and state should not preclude Americans from reciting the Pledge of Allegiance.

Web   Read It Now: "Leave 'the Pledge' Alone," **bedfordstmartins.com/americanow**, Chapter 9. Alan Wolfe, a professor of political science at Boston College, argues for the phrase "under God" in this Salon.com editorial.

Web   Hear It Now: "Fight for the Pledge: Two Views on the 'Under God' Debate" **bedfordstmartins.com/americanow**, Chapter 9. Listen to or read this PBS Online NewsHour debate in which the president of Americans United for the

Separation of Church and State takes on the American Center for Law and Justice, a group affiliated with the Christian coalition.

Vocabulary/Using a Dictionary

1. Break the word *monotheism* (Goodwin, para. 1) into its parts. What does each part mean? Do you know any other words that contain either of the parts?

2. How is *codified* (Goodwin, para. 1) related to the more familiar word *code*?

3. What is *pluralism* (Editorial Board, para. 5)? Is it the same thing as *multiculturalism*?

4. Use *preclude* (Editorial Board, para. 11) in a sentence of your own.

Responding to Words in Context

1. The adverb *impermissibly* appears in paragraph 1 and the related adjective *impermissible* appears in paragraph 2. Why do you think the concept of *impermissibility* is so central to Judge Goodwin's opinion?

2. Examine the phrase "under God." What does it mean? Could it mean different things to different people?

3. "With its ruling, the appellate court has declared open season on a wide range of more vague and benign mentions of God in public life" (Editorial Board, para. 8). Does the capitalization of *God* in this sentence pose any problem for the argument these authors are trying to make? Explain.

Discussing Main Point and Meaning

1. Why does Goodwin believe that the phrase "under God" is analogous to the phrases "under Jesus," "under Vishnu," "under Zeus," and "under no god" (para. 1)?

2. Why does Goodwin have a problem with the practice of "teacher-led recitation of the pledge" (para. 1)?

3. How does the pledge in its present state affect our country's notion of equality, according to Goodwin? Reread paragraph 2 for help with this question.

4. Why doesn't the Editorial Board agree with Judge Alfred Goodwin's opinion on the use of the phrase "under God" in the Pledge of Allegiance?

5. "Adherents of any faith can project their own beliefs onto the phrase 'one nation, under God'" (Editorial Board, para. 6). What does this sentence mean? Do you agree with it?

Examining Sentences, Paragraphs, and Organization

1. How does the excerpt from Goodwin's legal opinion compare to other types of material you've read? Describe the tone, writing style, and argument of this legal document.

2. The first sentence in paragraph 5 is "We disagree." Why is it so short? Is it an effective sentence, in your opinion?

Thinking Critically

1. What if the phrase "under God" was changed so that *God* was in lowercase, making it a common noun rather than a proper noun? Would using the more generic term have any effect on the meaning of the phrase? Would it have any effect on Goodwin's opinion?

2. Does the fact that students "cannot be forced to participate in recitation of the pledge" (Goodwin, para. 1) have any bearing on your opinion of this issue? Would your opinion change if students were routinely disciplined or expelled for refusing to recite the "Pledge of Allegiance"?

3. The Editorial Board authors concede points to their opposition in paragraphs 5 and 7. Why do they do this? Does it hurt or help their argument?

4. In paragraphs 9 and 10, the Editorial Board authors list a few of the ways religious references are inserted into public life: on money, in council meetings, and in court proceedings. What point are they trying to make?

In-Class Writing Activities

1. Write a one-paragraph brief for your school's newspaper that summarizes Goodwin's opinion. Use your own words as much as possible, but quote small phrases from Goodwin's text if necessary.

2. How does the "commonsense" argument put forth by the Editorial Board apply to other constitutional issues? For example, does common sense need to be used with respect to the First Amendment, which grants all citizens the right to free speech? Consider the problems of pornography, slander, or racist language used in the workplace. Another example is the Second Amendment, the right to bear arms. Should people be allowed to carry loaded weapons on the subway? Should guns be available at WalMart? Or what about the example of the Fifth Amendment, the right not to incriminate oneself in court? Are there some cases in which a witness should be compelled to testify no matter what? Write a short essay about the role of common sense in the application of one of these constitutional rights.

3. In what subtle ways besides the Pledge of Allegiance does religion seep into public life? Do you notice religious references made by professional athletes during competition? Do you hear religious references in movies, on TV, or in the music you listen to? Write a short list of all the ways that religion presents itself to you even when you are not engaged in any form of worship.

Is It Appropriate to Place the Motto "In God We Trust" in Public Schools?

Before You Read

Have you ever noticed the motto "In God We Trust" on U.S. currency? Do you think the motto violates the constitutional separation of church and state? Many states are seeking to place this motto in public school classrooms. Do you think this is a good idea? This question is posed by the Editorial Board at the *Arizona Daily Wildcat* and responded to in the essays that follow by students at the University of Arizona in Tucson. How do you imagine the students will respond? What arguments might they make to support their responses?

Words to Learn [Editorial Board]

motto (para. 1): a sentence, phrase, or word inscribed that identifies a philosophy (n.)

precedent (para. 3): something said or done that may serve to authorize or justify further words or acts of the same or similar kind (n.)

momentum (para. 4): impetus; the force with which a body moves against resistence (n.)

constitutionality (para. 6): the quality or state of being constitutional (n.)

secular (para. 6): not sacred or ecclesiastical (adj.)

Words to Learn [Winsky]

impressionable (para. 2): easily molded or influenced (adj.)

myriad (para. 3): an indefinitely large number (n.)

travesties (para. 3): imitations that make crude fun of something (n.)

Words to Learn [Cucher]

mandate (para. 2): an authoritative command (n.)

transcendence (para. 3): state of existing apart from the material (n.)

Words to Learn [Hall]

endorsement (para. 1): approval,
  sanction (n.)
testimony (para. 1): evidence based
  on observation or knowledge (n.)
immutable (para. 3): unchangeable,
  unchanging (n.)

proclamation (para. 4): an official
  public announcement (n.)
unison (para. 5): harmonious agreement or union; accord (n.)

Words to Learn [Durrani]

rationalism (para. 3): the practice of
  guiding one's own actions and

opinions solely by what seems
reasonable (n.)

EDITORIAL BOARD

In God We Trust — In Public Schools?

[ARIZONA DAILY WILDCAT, UNIVERSITY OF ARIZONA (TUCSON) / March 6, 2002]

From U.S. coins, to the national motto, to classrooms, the phrase   1
"In God We Trust" found its way into American history when it was
minted onto the 1864 two-cent coins as part of the increased religious sentiment during the Civil War.

In a letter dated November 20, 1861, Secretary of the Treasury   2
Salmon P. Chase instructed James Pollack, director of the mint at
Philadelphia, to arrange a motto: "Dear Sir: No nation can be strong
except in the strength of God, or safe except in His defense. The trust
of our people in God should be declared on our national coins. You
will cause a device to be prepared without unnecessary delay with a motto expressing this national
recognition."

*But what about
the separation
between church
and state?*

Placing the motto on that coin set a precedent   3
for the design of all coins since.

Nearly a century later, the motto again gained   4
momentum. On July 30, 1956, Congress passed a
law declaring "In God We Trust" as the official
national motto of the United States. Paper money adapted the motto
in 1957.

But now, in a the rise of patriotism spawned by September 11, many states are looking to place the motto in all public school classrooms. "If putting these mottos in the schools can help build patriotism, it has served its purpose," said Florida's Clay County School Superintendent David Owens.

But what about the separation between church and state? "It's been tested for its constitutionality in federal court," said Michigan State Representative Stephen Ehardt, a Republican. "It is secular. It's not a religious statement, and it's something we should be proud of — it's our national motto."

What do you think? Is it appropriate to place the motto "In God We Trust" in public schools?

SHANE DALE

What about the Money and the Pledge?

Every school day, kids recite the Pledge of Allegiance, along with the words "one nation, under God." Every school day, kids pay for their lunches with currency that has "In God We Trust" inscribed on it.

God has always played a part in our public school system. The question in this case is, will posting our national motto in public school classrooms inhibit any student's freedom of religion?

If we say "yes," we might have to do away with the Pledge and money at school, too. Maybe we should have parents prepay for their kids' school lunches, and give the kids pretend "school bucks" instead, so they can still learn the value of money.

Quit nodding. I'm not serious.

It's no big surprise that the group who started this whole push was a fundamentalist Christian organization from the Deep South.

SHANE DALE (b. 1980) wrote this piece as a junior at the University of Arizona, where he won the Award for Excellence in Column Writing at the Arizona Daily Wildcat in 2001–2002. He is currently working on a book regarding liberalism at universities.

These people obviously want to further bridge the gap between church and state by doing this.

Regardless, I say go for it. Slap the motto on classroom walls, if   6
for no other reason than to watch the ACLU [American Civil Liberties Union] throw another fit.

Read It Now: Religion in the Public Schools, American Civil Liberties Union (ACLU), **bedfordstmartins.com/americanow**, Chapter 9. This statement outlines the position held by the ACLU and other organizations on specific issues such as school prayer and religious literature.

LAURA WINSKY

Not the Right Trend

In God we trust. Whose God? My God? Your God? And just   1
who is represented by "we"? All of us? Or does that exclude the roughly six percent who don't believe in God at all?

The "national motto" doesn't belong on our coins, on our paper   2
money, or on our government buildings. And it certainly doesn't belong plastered on our school walls and forced into young, impressionable minds. Let's look at the source. This movement of requiring schools to post the phrase began in Tupelo, Mississippi. I've never been, but this is the same state that voted last year to continue to proudly wave the Confederate flag. Is this the state that should be counseling the rest of the country on a new moral trend?

> *The "national motto" doesn't belong on our school walls.*

I'd like to paraphrase Marc Stern, the legal director of the American Jewish Conference, when   3
he said that these types of post-9/11 movements are an exploitation of the tragedies. I couldn't agree more. This topic falls right in with the myriad of other travesties that have become acceptable since 9/11 but weren't before: dictator-like com-

---

LAURA WINSKY *wrote this piece as a senior majoring in Spanish and political science at the University of Arizona.*

ments such as "axis of evil," anti-Arab American hatred, and now this.

Leave the "trusting of God" to our hearts and our places of worship. That's where it belongs.

DANIEL CUCHER

In Mottos I Trust

This issue must be divided into two questions: (1) Should any national motto be displayed in every classroom? (2) Is there anything wrong with the national motto "In God We Trust"? For a lack of space, I shall deal only with the latter question.

Every time the issue of God in our national motto has been challenged, it has been promptly shot down because, according to the terms and intent of the Constitution, such language does not violate the separation of church and state. It does not oppress any religion, nor does it mandate the practice of any one religion.

Most people believe in a God, whether in nature, humanity, plurality, unity, science, transcendence, and so on, ad infinitum. There are more ideas about God than there are humans in existence. But at the very least, the term "God" can simply be taken to mean, "that which is greater than me," or for those who feel singularly divine, "me."

The concept of something far greater than a country, in which a country places its confidence, is an overwhelmingly positive influence. Although it can be manipulated as political propaganda, it also has the effect of creating a sense of humility among people.

And if there's one thing humanity needs, it is to be humbled.

DANIEL CUCHER *wrote this piece as a senior majoring in creative writing at the University of Arizona.*

CAITLIN HALL

What Do They Mean, "We"?

Should the phrase "In God We Trust" become part of our edu-   1
cation system? Absolutely not. Should it even be our national motto?
No. Federal endorsement of such a statement is a testimony to the degree that religious intolerance still pervades our government.

How many people are really included in that "we," after all? The   2
phrase doesn't refer to any god, it refers to THE God. Capital "g."
No Yahweh. No Allah. No Supreme Being.

I realize that a majority of the people in this country believe in a   3
deity of some kind, and a majority of those believe in the Christian
God. However, this type of "we" is not the same as that of the statement "we voted George Bush into office." It is immutable, eternal,
and wrong. In matters of belief, popular opinion does not justify
blanket statements.

Furthermore, having such a proclamation imposed upon our edu-   4
cation system introduces new problems. Even if the Supreme Court
has been unwilling to completely abolish religious influence in secular
policy, it has been clear on the presence of religion in schools.

In considering this issue, let us weigh the influence of our heads,   5
hearts, and Constitution. Hopefully they speak in unison.

CAITLIN HALL (b. 1983) *writes a weekly column in the* Arizona Daily
Wildcat. *Hall, who wrote this piece as a freshman, is currently a sophomore
majoring in biochemistry and philosophy at the University of Arizona.*

MARIAM DURRANI

No on Religion, Yes on Pride

I am a strong opponent of religion in public schools. The school I   1
went to was so poor that art and music weren't offered the last two
years I was there.

So teaching religion in school would be another cost for public   2
schools when most of them already are scrounging for money.

However, you also have to maintain a degree of rationalism in   3
the debate to use the "In God We Trust" motto in public schools.
This motto is called "tra-di-shun."

Tradition is the glue that connects us to the past.

Tradition is something that has lost a lot of its   4
place in society, but it is also the glue that connects us to the past. It has been our national motto
since 1864. Of course, the norm that everyone is
Christian has changed since then, but simply placing the motto in public schools is not necessarily
teaching religion. It is teaching our national motto
in schools in order to honor America and its history.

This is not a sneaky way to preach to kids but a way to inspire   5
them. If we really are in America, then the simple wording of a
hundred-year-old phrase will not inhibit the mission of these words:
to inspire and unite us in the American spirit.

---

*MARIAM DURRANI (b. 1981) was born in Pakistan and grew up in Ari-
zona and Germany. She has worked for the* Arizona Daily Wildcat *since
2001 and expects to graduate from the University of Arizona in 2003 with a
B.S. in systems engineering.*

KENDRICK WILSON

By All Means, Let's Avoid the Real Issues

Another bad idea from the Christian right — just one from a seemingly infinite supply. Our education system is falling apart, especially in Arizona. Qualified teachers are being forced out of the profession because they cannot afford to teach with rock bottom salaries, classes are so overcrowded that some students don't have chairs to sit at (remember the young girl mentioned in the Gore/Bush debates in 2000?), and textbooks are outdated. Our schools are crumbling, and, along with walls, fall test scores. 1

What a depressing topic! Denial is always a good way of dealing with it. Rather than discussing how to improve our crumbling schools, the Christian right is intent on driving the debate toward whether "In God We Trust" should be displayed in public schools. Never mind the fact that schools won't be able to afford the paper these words will be printed on. 2

While the Christian right seems to prefer "In God We Trust," what's wrong with our nation's original official motto, "E Pluribus Unum" (Latin for "from many, one")? These words could not be more patriotic — unless the Christian right could enlighten me as to how our national motto is not the highest display of patriotism — and should not be offensive to anyone. 3

Vocabulary/Using a Dictionary

1. What is the Latin origin of the word *motto* (Editorial Board, para. 1)?

2. What other words is *precedent* (Editorial Board, para. 3) related to?

KENDRICK WILSON (b. 1982) is a sophomore majoring in political science. He writes for the Arizona Daily Wildcat's "Perspectives" column. Wilson enjoys writing about the environment but finds the issue of the Pledge especially interesting, because "it focuses on a social issue involving the Christian right."

3. What is the root of *travesty* (Winsky, para. 3)? How does *travesty* relate to *vestment*? How does the connotation of *travesty* differ from its denotative definition?

4. What does *plurality* (Cucher, para. 3) mean in a religious sense?

5. *Transcendence* (Cucher, para. 3) as a theological idea is the opposite of *immanence*. Look up *immanence* in the dictionary and explain the difference.

6. What are the roots of *unison* (Hall, para. 5)?

Responding to Words in Context

1. The motto "In God We Trust" grew out of "increased religious *sentiment* during the Civil War" (Editorial Board, para. 1). What does the word *sentiment* tell you about why the motto came about?

2. In using the word *secular* to describe the motto "In God We Trust," what argument does Representative Ehardt make (Editorial Board, para. 6)?

3. Cucher contends the concept of "In God We Trust" "can be *manipulated* as political propaganda" (para. 4). Do you agree?

4. In analyzing the word *we* in the motto "In God We Trust," Hall reasons that "this type of 'we' is not the same as that of the statement 'we voted George Bush into office'" (para. 3). How might the use of the word *we* differ in each circumstance? What point is Hall trying to make?

5. When Durrani claims "you also have to maintain a degree of *rationalism* in the debate to use the 'In God We Trust' motto in public schools" (para. 3), what is she implying about the nature of the debate thus far?

6. Durrani writes, "This motto is called 'tra-di-shun'" (para. 3). Why does Durrani sound out *tradition*? What does she assume about her readers?

Discussing Main Point and Meaning

1. Why was the motto "In God We Trust" placed on U.S. coins in the first place, and why is there a renewed interest in the motto now (Editorial Board, paras. 1–5)?

2. What would be an objection to the motto "In God We Trust?" What response to this objection does the article by the Editorial Board cite?

3. In one sentence for each, summarize the main point of students' responses.

4. After reading all the student responses to the question "Is it appropriate to place the motto 'In God We Trust' in public schools?" categorize the responses. What kinds of questions or concerns appear more than once?

Examining Sentences, Paragraphs, and Organization

1. How would you describe the tone of the letter from Salmon P. Chase to James Pollack (para. 2)? Why might the *Wildcat* editorial writers have chosen to include the excerpt?

2. Briefly describe the article's organizational structure. Why do the *Wildcat* editorial writers wait until the last two paragraphs to question the issue?

3. What is Dale referring to when he supports putting the motto "In God We Trust" in public schools "if for no other reason than to watch the ACLU throw another fit" (para. 6)? Who is the ACLU? What would it mean for them to "throw a fit"? Why does Dale think the ACLU would object to the motto in public schools? How would you describe Dale's tone here?

4. In paragraph 3, Winsky associates the attempt to place the motto "In God We Trust" in classrooms with movements that "are an exploitation of the [9/11] tragedies." What is Winsky's point in this paragraph? Do you agree with her analysis?

5. In paragraph 2, Wilson claims, "Denial is always a good way of dealing with it." What is Wilson referring to? Do you agree with his interpretation?

Thinking Critically

1. Do you believe Representative Ehardt's claim that the motto "In God We Trust" is secular? Why or why not?

2. Dale asserts that if we decide to prohibit displaying "In God We Trust" from public schools, "we might have to do away with the Pledge and money at school, too" (para. 3). Why does he make this claim? How strong is his reasoning?

3. Compare Winsky's interpretation of the word *God* in the motto (para. 1) to Cucher's (para. 3) and Hall's (para. 2). Whose points are similar? Which points differ? Whose point do you find the most convincing and why?

4. In looking at the origin of the movement to place the national motto in public schools, Winsky notes that Mississippi is the same state "that voted lasted year to continue to proudly wave the Confederate flag." She concludes, "Is this the state that should be counseling the rest of the country on a new moral trend?" (para. 2). What is Winsky implying here? How logical do you find her reasoning?

5. Both Cucher (para. 2) and Hall (para. 4) use federal court interpretations of the First Amendment to support their respective arguments on whether the motto "In God We Trust" should be placed in public schools. What point does each writer make? Whose point do you find the most persuasive and why?

6. Wilson's response centers on the lack of funding for public schools (paras. 1–2). How is this issue related to placing the motto in public schools? How sound is Wilson's reasoning?

In-Class Writing Activities

1. The First Amendment to the Constitution begins, "Congress shall make no law respecting an establishment of religion." What do you think this sentence means? Does the national motto "In God We Trust" establish a religion?

2. Examine the difference between placing the motto "In God We Trust" on U.S. currency and in public schools. Is there a significant difference? What are the implications of the motto on U.S. money? What might be the result of putting the motto in our nation's schools? Would the fact that the motto is already on U.S. money affect your decision to place the motto in schools? Would it be unconstitutional to frame a dollar bill and hang it on a public school wall? Why or why not?

3. Instead of placing "In God We Trust" in classrooms, Wilson suggests the alternative official motto of our nation "E Pluribus Unum" (para. 3). Write a brief essay defending which motto you would favor placing in classrooms. To focus your writing, consider the meaning of each term. How would the different idea each motto conveys support your argument in favor of one term over the other?

4. Interpret the meaning of the terms *God, we,* and *trust* in the national motto. Do you think the financial connotations of *trust* make the motto more appropriate for U.S. currency? Compare your interpretations to the students' responses in this selection.

5. The idea to place the motto "In God We Trust" in public schools came about as a response to the tragedies of 9/11. Is this movement, as Winsky argues, "an exploitation of the tragedies" or an appropriate response? Which of these student responses reflect on the needs of the nation after September 11? How well do you think the motto "In God We Trust" responds to those needs? If you do not think it is a suitable response, brainstorm some alternative responses.

ANTI-DEFAMATION LEAGUE

[2000]

Before You Read

What is the purpose of the separation of church and state? Does it allow for greater religious freedom? How seperate are church and state in the U.S.?

Words to Learn

flourish (sent. 1): to blossom; to grow vigorously (v.)
vitality (sent. 2): the power and strength to live or go on living (n.)
defamation (sent. 3): detraction, slander, libel, attacking or injuring the reputation or honor of by false or malicious statements (n.)

Read It Now: Separation of Church and State: First Amendment Primer, Anti-Defamation League, **bedfordstmartins.com/americanow**, Chapter 9. This four-part essay argues for separation of church and state and addresses the question of religion in public schools.

Vocabulary/Using a Dictionary

1. The first sentence of the advertisement reads: "For over 200 years, the separation of Church and State in America has allowed religions to *flourish* free from government interference." In this context, what does the word *flourish* mean? What else does the word mean? What are the origins of *flourish*?

2. What is *vitality* (sent. 2)? What word do you think it comes from?

Responding to Words in Context

The Anti-Defamation League, which works "hard on local, state, and Federal levels to keep both policy makers and the public aware of First Amendment violations" (sent. 3), posted the advertisement you've just read. In the context of this advertisement, what do you think *anti-defamation* means?

Discussing Main Point and Meaning

1. What does the separation of church and state in the United States allow? For how long have the church and state been separate in the United States?

2. Why does the Anti-Defamation League wish to continue to keep religion and government apart?

3. According to the advertisement, what does the Anti-Defamation League do?

Examining Sentences, Paragraphs, and Organization

1. Looking at the first line of the advertisement in large-size font that reads "Religious freedom is only as strong as the wall separating church and state," which words in this line of the advertisement are most prominent? Why do you think they were enlarged?

2. What do you think the reader will find by following the advice given by the Anti-Defamation League in the final sentence of the advertisement?

Thinking Critically

1. Do you agree with the Anti-Defamation League's claims in the first sentence? Do you ever think about why we have separation between church and state in the United States?

2. Would you support the Anti-Defamation League in its work "on local, state, and Federal levels to keep both policy makers and the public aware of First Amendment violations and to repair cracks in the wall" (sent. 3)? Would you call them for a free newsletter or visit their Web site?

In-Class Writing Activities

Hugo L. Black (1886–1971), the late U.S. Supreme Court Justice, once said:

> The "establishment of religion" clause of the First Amendment means at least this: Neither a state nor the Federal Government can set up a church. Neither can pass laws which aid one religion, aid all religions, or prefer one religion over another.
>
> The First Amendment has erected a wall between church and state. That wall must be kept high and impregnable. We could not approve the slightest breach.

Freewrite a response to the second part of Black's quote. Why do you think Black feels that the wall between church and state must be "high and impregnable?" Why should the U.S. Supreme Court not approve "the slightest breach?"

Discussing the Unit

Suggested Topic for Discussion

After September 11, both patriotism and attendance at religious services increased substantially. How does the movement to place the motto "In God We Trust" in public schools relate to those increases? What about the outcry over the appellate court's decision to strike the phrase "under God" from the Pledge of Allegiance? Are these responses primarily patriotic or religious in intent? Are we seeing a new crack in the wall separating church and state?

Preparing for Class Discussion

1. How do you imagine the Anti-Defamation League would respond to the movement to place the motto "In God We Trust" in public schools?

2. The Anti-Defamation League ad states, "For over 200 years, the separation of Church and State in America has allowed religions to flourish free from government interference." Look back at the history of the national motto "In God We Trust" that the Editorial Board of the *Arizona Daily Wildcat* discusses. To what degree does the history of the motto challenge this statement?

3. What would Judge Alfred Goodwin say to the *San Francisco Chronicle*'s argument that "common sense" should be applied to the debate over the phrase "under God" in the Pledge of Allegiance?

From Discussion to Writing

1. Write your own essay in response to the question, "Is it appropriate to place the motto 'In God We Trust' in public schools?" Your essay should consider opposing views to your thesis and respond in defense of your own argument. Use your own reasoning and examples as well as appropriate selections in this unit to represent opposing views and help you develop your argument.

2. Compare and contrast the debates over "In God We Trust" and "under God." Which debate is more significant, in your opinion? How do you think each issue will be resolved?

Topics for Cross-Cultural Discussion

1. Identify a country that seems less diverse in its religious groups than the United States. How large a role does the government play in religious life and vice versa? How do you think the lack of religious diversity affects the relationship between church and state?

2. This unit begins with the history of the motto "In God We Trust," which first appeared on U.S. coins and thereafter on paper currency. Compare a U.S. dollar bill to the equivalent cur-

rency of another country. What do the images and the text on the currency reveal about what each country values or honors?

3. Do other countries have a "document" similar to the United States's 'Pledge of Allegiance'? If you know of one, does it contain religious references? If not, consider national anthems for non-U.S. countries that you have heard. Do those anthems contain references to religion, unlike the U.S. national anthem?

10

What Does Patriotism Mean?

The eighteenth-century British writer Samuel Johnson memorably defined patriotism as "the last refuge of a scoundrel." He meant that it's easy for certain people to hide evil intentions under the guise of appearing patriotic, and therefore we ought to be suspicious of overly patriotic gestures: The flag in the window may merely be window-dressing. So how do we determine when patriotic sentiments are noble or ignoble, sincere or sinister? Does a true patriot always say, "My country, right or wrong"? Or do true patriots have an obligation to take an opposing stance when they believe their country is in the wrong?

If you do decide to wave the American flag, however, what sort of flag will it be — a traditional stars and strips or a psychedelic banner? In "The Meaning of That Star-Spangled Hard Hat," the opinion-page editor for the *New York Times,* Brent Staples, describes the new patriotism he witnessed in his neighborhood after the terrorist attacks on the World Trade Center. He traces this new patriotism back to the antiwar movement of the 1960s, which he claims "rejected the notion that there was only one way to be patriotic" as it "broadened the definition of patriotism and created a new, less formal identity for the American flag." But could the new "postmodern patriotism" Staples describes be merely symbolic and superficial, demanding too little of American citizens? In "All-Consuming Patriotism," Ian Frazier wonders how shopping became a patriotic duty and contrasts our current brand of consumer-oriented patriotism with the more rigorous demands put on citizens during past wars who were asked to make more meaningful sacrifices, as the World War II advertisements on page 243 reminds us. "I want to participate, to do something," Frazier writes, as he contemplates the more heroic efforts of past generations, "and shopping isn't it." Yet not all Americans after the attacks of September 11, 2001, took such a reflective attitude toward patriotism. As Laura Sahramaa, a University of Virginia student, points out, many citizens went "gung-ho about America." In "When Patriotism Runs Amuck," she looks at the fear, anxiety, and intolerance patriotism can breed. "Americans should love their country," she acknowledges, "but not to the extent that they forget what it stands for."

BRENT STAPLES

The Meaning of That Star-Spangled Hard Hat

[THE NEW YORK TIMES / November 9, 2001]

Before You Read

What does the American flag mean to you? How do you react when you see traditional flags? How do you react when you see wreaths made out of flags, houses brightly painted with the American flag, flag clothing, and even psychedelic flags? Are these varied flags symbols of the different forms patriotism can take, or do you see them as a violation of a sacred tradition?

BRENT STAPLES *(b. 1951) has been an editorial writer for the* New York Times *since 1983. His work has appeared in* The Nation, Time, *the* New York Review of Books, *and other magazines. He is also the author of* Parallel Time: Growing Up in Black and White *(2000).*

Words to Learn

postmodern (para. 3): a term used to describe recent art, architecture, or literature characterized by multiple styles and self-conscious expression; coming after, and usually in reaction to, modernism in the 20th century (adj.)

reviled (para. 5): abused verbally; railed at (v.)

incensed (para. 6): made extremely angry (v.)

camp (para. 7): something so outrageous, inappropriate, or theatrical as to be amusing (n.)

kitsch (para. 7): shoddy or cheap artistic or literary material (n.)

retro (para. 7): short for retrograde: moving or leaning backward (adj.)

personified (para. 7): embodied, incarnated (v.)

The trade center disaster came to my neighborhood as a dark 1 thunderhead of smoke that boiled over the river into Brooklyn, showering the streets with burning papers from the desks of the dead. Charred documents were still falling when the first American flag went up along our street. Within 48 hours this tree-lined block of nineteenth-century brownstones was flying more flags than it ever has. The flags have already created a new subset of petty crime. Like bicycles, they get stolen, leaving their owners to rustle up new ones in the midst of a flag shortage.

My wife is a flag purist. Tattered, ill-kept banners offend her. She 2 tolerates the plastic, paper, and synthetic flags that have blossomed since September, but does not view them as "real." A "real" flag for my wife is made of heavy-gauge cotton, sewn together piece by piece so that the seams are visible between the stripes and the flag furls gracefully. No seams, no authenticity.

I was a teenager during the Vietnam War, when the meaning of 3 the flag was hotly disputed, and never became a flag purist. The flags that speak to me most come in nontraditional, Pop Art designs. They were regarded as desecration when they first appeared in the 1960s but are now viewed simply as flags of another color. In my neighborhood I've seen a flag used as a garland, snaked through the railings of window grates and fire escapes, and a flag improvised from red, white, and blue bandannas. There is a spectacular flag painted across the full width of a house with glossy paint like the moist icing on a cake, with chrome yellow stripes instead of white ones. The composition speaks of patriotism with a postmodern twist.

Since September 11 conservative critics have been saying that the 4 60s generation has finally come round to a patriotism that it despised in the Vietnam era. But this generation did not reject patriotism. It rejected the notion that there was only one way to be patriotic. The protest era broadened the definition of patriotism and created a new, less formal identity for the American flag.

The psychedelic-flag hard hat that was worn by Dick Cheney when   5
he visited the trade center site shows how design liberties with the flag have been embraced by groups that would have reviled them in the past. Hats like the vice president wore would have been unwelcome — and might even have gotten you roughed up — on construction sites during the late 60s. Then, the term "hard hat" referred to the working-class white ethnics who were soon to bolt the Democratic Party for Ronald Reagan. The clashes between hard hats and antiwar demonstrators were particularly nasty in New York, especially during the building of the World Trade Center. The hard hats worn when I was a shipyard worker in high school were buckets, in basic colors. The flag decals that appeared on them later in the decade were in response to criticism of the country's policy in Vietnam. A longhair who was smart went the other way when he saw group of flagheads bunched together.

The protest era created a less formal identity for the American flag.

I never burned a flag, never saw one burned.   6
But as a teenager growing up around the shipyards on the Delaware River, I was threatened with tire irons by angry dockworkers who were incensed by flag clothing, most notably the flag that an eccentric friend made into a sash and wore to a Jimi Hendrix concert.

The art critic Jed Perl of the *New Republic* has described this as   7
partly a fashion issue, arguing that young people wished to see the flag "as camp, as Kitsch, or retro chic." But the thing went deeper than that. When the rock diva Grace Slick was photographed nude, wrapped in a flag, during the Vietnam War she personified a generation's desire to seize ownership of a symbol from which we were profoundly estranged.

As a black teenager with a huge cloud of hair, I would have   8
avoided a flag-draped street like the one I live on now, wanting no trouble with the kind of people who flew the colors from their homes. But cruising the same streets today, I note the funky, psychedelic banners among the "real" ones and understand that what we have now is a spacious, postmodern patriotism.

Web **See It Now:** 1960s Protest Images, **bedfordstmartins.com/americanow**, Chapter 10. Take a look at some images from the protest era of the 1960s. This substantial archive at U.C. Davis includes images of student demonstrations against the Vietnam War, the shootings at Ohio State University, and the riot at the 1968 Democratic convention in Chicago.

Vocabulary/Using a Dictionary

1. What is the best antonym for *desecration* (para. 3)?
2. How is *patriotism* (para. 3) related to *patriarchy*?
3. List at least four synonyms for *eccentric* (para. 6).

Responding to Words in Context

1. What does it mean to be a *flag purist* (para. 2)? Define the term both by using a dictionary and looking at Staples's description of the way his wife views the flag.
2. In referring to nontraditional flags, Staples explains they "were regarded as *desecration* when they first appeared" (para. 3). What does the word *desecration* imply about the way traditionalists view the flag?
3. In analyzing the significance of Dick Cheney's psychedelic-flag hard hat, Staples claims it "shows how design *liberties* with the flag have been embraced by groups that would have reviled them in the past" (para. 5). Given Staples's argument, what double meaning does the word *liberties* carry in this sentence?
4. In describing the tension surrounding the flag in the 1960s, Staples explains, "A *longhair* who was smart went the other way when he saw a group of *flagheads* bunched together" (para. 5). Looking at this sentence in the context of paragraph 5, define *longhair* and *flagheads* and explain their differing political philosophies.

Discussing Main Point and Meaning

1. The title of the essay emphasizes the image of the hard hat. Why is the hard hat such an important symbol for Staples? How does it represent changing attitudes about the American flag and the meaning of patriotism?

2. What were the conflicting attitudes about the flag during the 1960s? How did the debate about the representation of the flag mirror conflicting political views?

3. According to Staples, what is the relationship between the flag and patriotism? How does the acceptance of different versions of the flag reflect a change in the definition of patriotism?

Examining Sentences, Paragraphs, and Organization

1. Describe the organizational structure of the essay, considering the function of each paragraph. How effectively does the organization convey Staples's argument?

2. Look closely at the first sentence of the essay. How does it work in capturing the reader's attention?

3. Paragraph 7 rests on a comparison of art critic Jed Perl's interpretation of flag clothing with Staples's. How do their interpretations differ? What does it mean to personify "a generation's desire to seize ownership of a symbol from which we were profoundly estranged" (para. 7)?

Thinking Critically

1. Staples twice uses the word *postmodern* to explain the changing definition of patriotism. In describing the variety of flags on his block, he explains, "The composition speaks of patriotism with a *postmodern* twist" (para. 3). And he concludes the essay with the appreciation "that what we have now is a spacious, *postmodern* patriotism" (para. 8). Explain what you think Staples means by *postmodern patriotism* both in terms of flag design and a new way of thinking about patriotism.

2. As Staples suggests in his essay, wearing a flag often makes a political statement. What did wearing the American flag on their hard hats mean for construction workers building the World Trade Center in the 1960s (para. 5)? How does this compare to Grace Slick's wearing of the American flag during the Vietnam War (para. 7)? When you see someone wearing the American flag after September 11, what kind of political statement do you think it makes? Or do you agree with Perl that wearing the flag has more to do with fashion (para. 7)?

In-Class Writing Activities

1. The treatment of the American flag is a matter of much controversy. For flag purists, such as Staples's wife, there is an entire ritual surrounding the ceremony of the flag. For instance, the flag must never touch the floor and should be folded in a very specific way. For someone like Staples, variations of the American flag and wearing the flag as clothing reflect a variety of perspectives on patriotism. And then there are those who burn the American flag, something Staples briefly alludes to (para. 6). Of course, this last practice is a matter of great controversy. Some argue the act is so offensive as to constitute a crime while others see burning the flag as a legitimate sign of protest in a democratic society. Where do you stand on this issue? How should we treat the flag? Write a brief essay in which you defend your position on this question. You may want to defend or write against the view of flag purists, Staples's position, or flag burning.

2. Staples credits the 1960s with rejecting the "notion that there was only one way to be patriotic. The protest era broadened the definition of patriotism and created a new, less formal identity for the American flag" (para. 4). In a freewrite, define patriotism yourself, offering very specific examples of acts you see as patriotic.

IAN FRAZIER

All-Consuming Patriotism

[MOTHER JONES / March–April 2002]

Before You Read

After September 11, signs appeared on shop windows in which the American flag took on the shape of a shopping bag labeled with the words "America: Open for Business." Surely, the September 11 attacks had a negative impact on an economy already weakened by the failure of so many "dotcom" companies. The toll on the travel industry alone was huge. So in the wake of September 11, is it our patriotic duty to shop to stimulate the economy? Or does consumerism stand in the way of real acts of patriotism — acts that require us to sacrifice and give something back to our communities?

Words to Learn

exhorted (para. 2): urged, advised, or warned earnestly (v.)

girth (para. 2): a measure around something (n.)

atmospherics (para. 4): radio noise from atmospheric, electrical phenomenon (n.)

intangibles (para. 4): that which is impalpable; that which is not easily defined (n.)

aura (para. 4): a distinctive atmosphere surrounding a given source (n.)

obliquely (para. 4): not straightforwardly; indirectly (adv.)

antiscorbutics (para. 6): treatments for scurvy (n.)

suffrage (para. 6): the right to vote (n.)

forbears (para. 7): ancestors, forefathers, progenitors (n.)

precedents (para. 9): things said or done that may serve to justify or authorize further words or acts of the same or similar kind (n.)

IAN FRAZIER *(b. 1951) is an essayist and journalist. He was a staff writer for* The New Yorker *for twenty-one years. His publications include* Great Plains *(1989),* On the Rez *(2000), and most recently,* Fish Stories: Essays about Angling and the Outdoors *(2002).*

I think of myself as a good American. I follow current events, come to a complete stop at stop signs, show up for jury duty, vote. When the government tells me to shop, as it's been doing recently, I shop. Over the last few months, patriotically, I've bought all kinds of stuff I have no use for. Lack of money has been no obstacle; years ago I could never get a credit card, due to low income and lack of a regular job, and then one day for no reason credit cards began tumbling on me out of the mail. I now owe more to credit card companies than the average family of four earns in a year. So when buying something I don't want or need, I simply take out my credit card. That part's been easy; for me, it's the shopping itself that's hard. I happen to be a bad shopper — nervous, uninformed, prone to grab the first product I see on the shelf and pay any amount for it and run out the door. Frequently, trips I make to the supermarket end with my wife shouting in disbelief as she goes through the grocery bags and immediately transfers one wrongly purchased item after another directly into the garbage can.

It's been hard, as I say, but I've done my duty — I've shopped and then shopped some more. Certain sacrifices are called for. Out of concern for the economy after the terror attacks, the president said that he wanted us to go about our business, and not stop shopping. On a TV commercial sponsored by the travel industry, he exhorted us to take the family for a vacation. The treasury secretary, financial commentators, leaders of industry — all told us not to be afraid to spend. So I've gone out of my comfort zone, even expanded my purchasing patterns. Not long ago I detected a look of respect in the eye of a young salesman with many piercings at the music store as he took in my heavy middle-aged girth and then the rap music CD featuring songs of murder and gangsterism that I had selflessly decided to buy. My life is usually devoid of great excitement or difficulty, knock wood and thank God, and I have nothing to cry about, but I've also noticed in the media recently a strong approval for uninhibited public crying. So now, along with the shopping, I've been crying a lot, too. Sometimes I cry and shop at the same time.

As I'm pushing my overfull shopping cart down the aisle, sobbing quietly, moving a bit more slowly because of the extra weight I've lately put on, a couple of troubling questions cross my mind. First, I start to worry about the real depth of my shopping capabilities. So far I have more or less been able to keep up with what the government expects of me. I'm at a level of shopping that I can stand. But what if, God forbid, events take a bad turn and the national crisis worsens, and more shopping is required? Can I shop with greater intensity than I am shopping now? I suppose I could eat even more than I've been eating, and order additional products in the mail, and go on costlier trips, and so on. But I'm not eager, frankly, to enter that "code red" shopping mode. I try to tell myself that I'd be equal to it, that in a real crisis I might be surprised by how much I could buy. But I don't know.

My other worry is a vague one, more in the area of atmospherics,   4
intangibles. I feel kind of wrong even mentioning it in this time of trial. How can I admit that I am worried about my aura? I worry that my aura is not . . . well, that it's not what I had once hoped it would be. I can explain this only by comparison, obliquely. On the top shelf of my bookcase, among the works vital to me, is a book called *Trials and Triumphs: The Record of the Fifty-Fifth Ohio Volunteer Infantry*, by Captain Hartwell Osborn. I've read this book many times and studied it to the smallest detail, because I think the people in it are brave and cool and admirable in every way.

I want to participate, to do something — and shopping isn't it.

The Fifty-Fifth was a Union Army regiment,   5
formed in the Ohio town of Norwalk, that fought throughout the Civil War. My great-great-grandfather served in the regiment, as did other relatives. The book lists every mile the regiment marched and every casualty it suffered. I like reading about the soldiering, but I can't really identify with it, having never been in the service myself. I identify more with the soldiers' wives and mothers and daughters, whose home-front struggles I can better imagine. *Trials and Triumphs* devotes a chapter to them, and to an organization they set up called the Soldiers' Aid Society.

The ladies of the Soldiers' Aid Society worked for the regiment   6
almost constantly from the day it began. They sewed uniforms, made pillows, held ice-cream sociables to raise money, scraped lint for bandages, emptied their wedding chests of their best linen and donated it all. To provide the men with antiscorbutics while on campaign, they pickled everything that would pickle, from onions to potatoes to artichokes. Every other day they were shipping out a new order of home-made supplies. Some of the women spent so much time stooped over while packing goods in barrels that they believed they had permanently affected their postures. When the war ended the ladies of the Soldiers' Aid said that for the first time in their lives they understood what united womanhood could accomplish. The movements for pro-

hibition and women's suffrage that grew powerful in the early 1900s got their start among those who'd worked in similar home-front organizations during the war.

I don't envy my forebears, or wish I'd lived back then. I prefer   7
the greater speed and uncertainty and complicatedness of now. But I can't help thinking that in terms of aura, the Norwalk ladies have it all over me. I study the pages with their photographs, and admire the plainness of their dresses, the set of their jaws, the expression in their eyes. Next to them my credit card and I seem a sorry spectacle indeed. Their sense of purpose shames me. What the country needed from those ladies it asked for, and they provided, straightforwardly; what it wants from me it somehow can't come out and ask. I'm asked to shop more, which really means to spend more, which eventually must mean to work more than I was working before. In previous wars, harder work was a civilian sacrifice that the government didn't hesitate to ask. Nowadays it's apparently unwilling to ask for any sacrifice that might appear to be too painful, too real.

But I *want* it to be real. I think a lot of us do. I feel like an idiot   8
with my tears and shopping cart. I want to participate, to do something — and shopping isn't it. Many of the donors who contributed more than half a billion dollars to a Red Cross fund for the families of terror attack victims became angry when they learned that much of the money would end up not where they had intended but in the Red Cross bureaucracy. People want to express themselves with action. In New York City so many have been showing up recently for jury duty that the courts have had to turn hundreds away; officials said a new surplus of civic consciousness was responsible for the upsurge. I'd be glad if I were asked to — I don't know — drive less or turn the thermostat down or send in seldom-used items of clothing or collect rubber bands or plant a victory garden or join a civilian patrol or use fewer disposable paper products at children's birthday parties. I'd be willing, if asked, just to sit still for a day and meditate on the situation, much in the way that Lincoln used to call for national days of prayer.

A great, shared desire to *do* something is lying around mostly un-   9
tapped. The best we can manage, it seems, is to show our U.S.A. brand loyalty by putting American flags on our houses and cars. Some businesses across the country even display in their windows a poster on which the American flag appears as a shopping bag, with two handles at the top. Above the flag-bag are the words "America: Open for Business." Money and the economy have gotten so tangled

up in our politics that we forget we're citizens of our government, not its consumers. And the leaders we elect, who got where they are by selling themselves to us with television ads, and who often are only on short loan from the corporate world anyway, think of us as customers who must be kept happy. There's a scarcity of ideas about how to direct all this patriotic feeling because usually the market, not the country, occupies our minds. I'm sure it's possible to transform oneself from salesman to leader, just as it is to go from consumer to citizen. But the shift of identity is awkward, without many precedents, not easily done. In between the two — between selling and leading, between consuming and being citizens — is where our leaders and the rest of us are now.

We see the world beyond our immediate surroundings mostly   10
through television, whose view is not much wider than that of a security peephole in a door. We hear over and over that our lives have forever changed, but the details right in front of us don't look very different, for all that. The forces fighting in Afghanistan are in more danger than we are back home, but perhaps not so much more; everybody knows that when catastrophe comes it could hit anywhere, most likely someplace it isn't expected. Strong patriotic feelings stir us, fill us, but have few means of expressing themselves. We want to be a country, but where do you go to do that? Surely not the mall. When Mayor Giuliani left office at the end of 2001, he said he was giving up the honorable title of mayor for the more honorable title of citizen. He got that right. Citizen is honorable; shopper is not.

Web **Hear It Now:** Commentary on Patriotism, **bedfordstmartins.com/americanow**, Chapter 10. In this brief radio essay aired on National Public Radio, commentator Kathy Young expresses her dismay about flag waving, patriotism, and profiling. (Scroll to "Flags.")

Web **See and Read It Now:** "Patriotic Advertising?" **bedfordstmartins.com/americanow**, Chapter 10. Is using patriotism to sell products in bad taste or is it a civic duty? This article at ABCNews.com raises this question and provides examples of ads that try to tap consumer patriotism.

Vocabulary/Using a Dictionary

1. Give three synonyms for *exhort* (para. 2).
2. What is the best anonym for *intangible* (para. 4)?

Responding to Words in Context

1. In describing his shopping habits, Frazier confesses, "So I've gone out of my *comfort zone*, even expanded my *purchasing patterns*" (para. 2). What do the jargon phrases *comfort zone* and *purchasing patterns* mean? Why do you think Frazier uses jargon in this paragraph?

2. Frazier offers a specific example of a shopping moment in which he "detected a look of respect in the eye of a young salesman with many piercings . . . as he took in my heavy middle-aged girth and then the rap music CD featuring songs of murder and gangsterism that I had *selflessly* decided to buy" (para. 2). What does *selflessly* mean? How is Frazier's act a *selfless* one? How would you characterize his tone here?

3. The writer declares he is "not eager, frankly, to enter that '*code red*' shopping mode" (para. 3). To what does *code red* refer? Why do you think Frazier uses this term?

4. What do the words *atmospherics, intangibles,* and *aura* in paragraph 4 all have in common? How do they serve to mark an important shift in the essay?

5. Frazier uses the word *surplus* to describe the "civic consciousness . . . responsible for the upsurge" in New York City citizens showing up for jury duty after 9/11 (para. 8), but he bemoans the "*scarcity* of ideas about how to direct all this patriotic feeling" (para. 9). What do these antonyms have in common? Why are they particularly appropriate terms given the subject matter of the essay?

Discussing Main Point and Meaning

1. What argument does the essay make about shopping and consumerism?

2. How would Frazier define "true patriotism?" What examples does he offer?

3. What are the two meanings of *all-consuming* in the title "All-Consuming Patriotism?" How does each definition of the term reflect the essay's argument?

4. What point does the writer want to make with the example of the ladies of the Norwalk Soldiers' Aid Society?

Examining Sentences, Paragraphs, and Organization

1. The essay's structure can be divided into three parts. Paragraphs 1–3 discuss the author's shopping experiences. Paragraphs 4–7 describe the Norwalk ladies of the Soldiers' Aid Society. Paragraphs 8–10 contrast citizenship with consumerism. How would you characterize the tone and argument of each part of the essay? How effective are the organizational structure and tone shifts in conveying Frazier's argument?

2. Look at the three opening sentences of Frazier's essay. How do they foreshadow the argument the author will make?

3. Frazier claims, "We see the world beyond our immediate surroundings mostly through television, whose view is not much wider than that of a security peephole in a door" (para. 10). Consider this sentence in the context of paragraph 10. What point does Frazier want to make by comparing the television to a security peephole?

Thinking Critically

1. Frazier notes in paragraph 1 that he uses his credit card to buy things he doesn't need.

   > Lack of money has been no obstacle; years ago I could never get a credit card, due to low income and lack of a regular job, and then one day for no reason credit cards began tumbling on me out of the mail. I now owe more to credit card companies than the average family of four earns in a year. So when buying something I don't want or need, I simply take out my credit card.

   Of course, Frazier exaggerates for humorous effect, but how valid a point do you think he makes about his purchasing habits? How does this point relate to his larger argument?

2. Frazier discusses President Bush's request that Americans, after September 11, "go about our business, and not stop shopping. On a TV commercial sponsored by the travel industry, he exhorted us to take the family for a vacation. The treasury secretary, financial commentators, leaders of industry — all told us not to be afraid to spend" (para. 2). What point does Frazier want to make with these examples? Do you agree with him? Why or why not?

3. At the end of paragraph 2, Frazier associates shopping with crying. And in paragraph 8, he concedes "I feel like an idiot with my

tears and shopping cart." Why do you think Frazier connects shopping with crying? What point is he trying to make? Do you agree with his reasoning?

4. The author speculates on why the government is asking us to shop, reasoning in paragraph 7 that

> What the country needed from those [Norwalk] ladies it asked for, and they provided, straightforwardly; what it wants from me it somehow can't come out and ask. I'm asked to shop more, which really means to spend more, which eventually must mean to work more than I was working before. In previous wars, harder work was a civilian sacrifice that the government didn't hesitate to ask. Nowadays, it's apparently unwilling to ask for any sacrifice that might appear too painful, too real.

How persuasive do you find Frazier's analysis of why the government is asking us to shop?

5. Frazier concludes, "Money and the economy have gotten so tangled up in our politics that we forget we're citizens of our government, not its consumers" (para. 9). What would it mean to be a citizen of a government rather than a consumer? To what extent do you agree with Frazier's analysis?

In-Class Writing Activities

1. "All-Consuming Patriotism" traces the harmful effects of consumerism on our ability to feel a sense of civic consciousness. What do you think are the consequences of consumerism? Does it have any positive effects? Do you see any negative consequences in terms of personal or public life? Is the United States a consumer culture? Why or why not?

2. In tracing the influence of money on politics, Frazier notes that we often elect politicians on the basis of television commercials and that these politicians are only "on short loan from the corporate world anyway" (para. 9). In a freewite, explain how big a problem you think money is in the realm of politics. Are politicians with the biggest campaign funds the most likely to get elected? If you perceive the influence of money in politics to be problematic, brainstorm ideas on what can be done to fix the problem.

3. Frazier notes that there is plenty of willingness on the part of citizens to sacrifice for their country, but also that "there's a scarcity

of ideas about how to direct all this patriotic feeling" (para. 9). In paragraph 8, Frazier offers his suggestions. Working in small groups, evaluate Frazier's suggestions and come up with your own ideas for invigorating the country with meaningful acts of patriotism. Submit what you agree to be the best three ideas in the form of a proposal.

LAURA SAHRAMAA

When Patriotism Runs Amuck

[THE CAVALIER DAILY, UNIVERSITY OF VIRGINIA / October 23, 2001]

Before You Read

After September 11, we witnessed many noble acts of patriotism. But can you think of any incidents in which love of country turned into hatred of others? Why do you think these incidents happen?

Words to Learn

amuck (para. 1): in a violent, frenzied, or uncontrolled manner (adj.)
overt (para. 2): not secret (adj.)
subtle (para. 2): hardly noticeable (adj.)
treasonous (para. 3): characterized by the offense of attempting to overthrow the government of

one's own country or of assisting its enemies in a time of war (adj.)
rabid (para. 4): being fanatical or extreme (adj.)
recitation (para. 6): reciting, recital (n.)

LAURA SAHRAMAA *(b. 1981) is studying American government at the University of Virginia. Born in Finland and raised in Virginia, Sahramaa is passionate about American politics, commenting, "I can't even vote in the American elections I get so riled up about." She received a first-place award in general column writing from the Society of Professional Journalists' Mark of Excellence contest in 2002.*

What happens when patriotism runs amuck? While the last month has shown that patriotism can bring out the best in Americans, it has also been seen to bring out the worst. It can make Americans betray their own principles; it can become something that incites anxiety, even fear — something it should never be. When patriotism runs amuck, it becomes something that divides rather than unites. 1

Of all places, the most overt example of out-of-control patriotism can be found in Wisconsin. In order to comply with a state law that requires a daily show of patriotism in public schools, the Madison School Board decided to eliminate saying the Pledge of Allegiance as an option. They wanted to avoid making students of different backgrounds uncomfortable; also, some parents were concerned about the religious aspect of the line containing "one nation, under God."[1] Instead of having students recite the pledge, the board instead decided that schools would play an instrumental version of the Star-Spangled Banner every day. They felt it would be a more subtle form of patriotism and would ensure that students of all religions and backgrounds would feel comfortable in school. 2

Their decision was met with outrage. The school board received over 20,000 angry phone calls and e-mails, many from out of state. Some people suggested that the school board "move to Afghanistan"; others called the board's decision a "treasonous act." One woman wrote, "I am sick of weak individuals [like you] who are afraid to stand up to the minority voices in this country, and are afraid to tell them to 'get a life.'" "If you can't pledge allegiance to this flag, then go somewhere else," one Madison resident said. Sadly, the Madison School Board caved into the tremendous pressure and reversed its position. 3

When patriotism runs amuck, bad things happen.

Patriotism is out of control when normally reasonable people become a shouting mob that throws around words like "treason," when an instrumental version of the Star-Spangled Banner just isn't patriotic enough. Wherever Americans are acting like this, they need to take a step back: They need to remember who they are and look at what they're doing. If they do not, things that previously have been valued greatly in this country — principles like tolerance and acceptance — will go out the window in the face of this new, almost rabid brand of patriotism. 4

---

[1]For more on this issue, see Unit 9, "God and the Constitution: How Separate Must They Be?" (p. 196).

Americans always have been proud of seeing their country as a   5
"melting pot," but now people seem to be forgetting — or just not
caring — that people who live here come from many different backgrounds. Multiculturalism, and the tolerance of differences that goes
along with it, used to be hailed as a part of what makes America
great. For generations, the United States has been looked to as a place
where you can be whoever you are without fear of being punished for
it. Now, it looks as if anyone who feels loyalty to their home countries or simply isn't gung-ho about America should go along with the
crowd if they don't want trouble.

Now, kids in Madison — as well as in other regions where the   6
Pledge of Allegiance is said in schools — will feel peer pressure to say
the pledge even if it conflicts with their beliefs. Those who oppose the
recitation of the pledge are worried that students who don't want to
participate will be harassed. In conditions such as these, the pledge
becomes forced; it becomes something ugly and artificial. Students
may begin saying it not because they believe in the words, but because they are afraid of what will happen if they don't say them. It is
doubtful that the author of the pledge meant for it to be that way.

The initial wave of patriotism was self-medicating, a way for the   7
country to deal with the terrorist attacks. But when patriotism runs
amuck, bad things happen. People who hold different beliefs are divided when they should be feeling close to each other. Americans
begin robbing themselves of things they used to pride themselves on,
like multiculturalism and tolerance. Americans should love their
country, but not to the extent that they forget what it stands for.

Vocabulary/Using a Dictionary

1. What is the origin of the term *amuck* (para. 1), also spelled
    amok? The *Oxford English Dictionary* can provide you with the
    most complete answer.

2. What is the origin of *overt* (para. 2)? What is its most suitable
    antonym?

3. In describing the community reaction to the Madison School
    Board decision to play the national anthem instead of the Pledge
    of Allegiance, Sahramaa calls it "this new, almost rabid brand of
    patriotism" (para. 4). *Rabid* comes from the Latin *rabere* mean-
    ing "to rave, rage, or be made mad." What are two other defini-
    tions of the term *rabid*, besides "being fanatical or extreme," that

share this original meaning? Considering these other definitions, what does Sahramaa imply about school board critics by describing their patriotism as rabid?

Responding to Words in Context

1. The writer notes that *"multiculturalism . . .* used to be . . . what makes America great" (para. 5). Break the word *multiculturalism* up into its prefix *multi-*, root *cultural*, and suffix *-ism* to define the term.

2. Sahramaa contends, "Multiculturalism, and the tolerance of differences that goes along with it, used to be *hailed* as a part of what makes America great" (para. 5). What connotation does *hailed* carry to make it a particularly appropriate term to use in this context?

3. In analyzing the consequences of the insistence on the Pledge of Allegiance, the writer concludes, "Now, it looks as if anyone who feels loyalty to their home countries or simply isn't *gung-ho* about America should go along with the crowd if they don't want trouble" (para. 5). What does *gung-ho* mean, and what is its origin? How well does the term work in this context given your understanding of its meaning and its origin?

Discussing Main Point and Meaning

1. According to the author, what bad things happen when "patriotism runs amuck" (para. 1)?

2. What is the Madison School Board's reasoning for preferring to play an instrumental version of the Star-Spangled Banner rather than asking the students to recite the Pledge of Allegiance?

3. How did people across the country respond to the school board's decision?

Examining Sentences, Paragraphs, and Organization

1. In the opening sentence to paragraph 2, Sahramaa observes, "Of all places, the most overt example of out-of-control patriotism can be found in Wisconsin." She ends the paragraph by explaining the Madison School Board's decision to play the national anthem instead of asking students to recite the Pledge of Allegiance:

"They felt it would be a more subtle form of patriotism." How do these sentences work to set up contrasting images of patriotism? What do they indicate about Sahramaa's own attitude toward patriotism?

2. Sahramaa describes the "initial wave of patriotism [as] *self-medicating,* a way for the country to deal with the terrorist attacks" (para. 7). What does *self-medicating* mean? In what sense is the term usually used? What does it mean to use the term *self-medicating* to describe patriotism? What is the writer suggesting about her own attitude toward patriotism? How would you describe acts of patriotism after 9/11? Would you also use the term *self-medicating* to describe them? Why or why not?

Thinking Critically

1. What do you think of the Madison School Board's decision to play an instrumental version of the Star-Spangled Banner instead of asking the students to recite the Pledge of Allegiance? To what extent do you agree with members' reasoning?

2. Evaluate the logic of the responses to the school board decision. In particular, look at the suggestions that the members of the school board "'move to Afghanistan'" and the claim, "'If you can't pledge allegiance to this flag, then go somewhere else,'" as well as the charge that the decision not to include the Pledge of Allegiance is treasonous (para. 3).

3. Do you think Sahramaa's predictions in paragraph 6 on what will happen as a result of the school board's decision to reinstate the Pledge of Allegiance are well founded?

4. Sahramaa waxes nostalgic for an America that once prided itself on being a melting pot. She thinks that in the past, America "has been looked to as a place where you can be whoever you are without fear of being punished for it" (para. 5). Do you agree with Sahramaa's interpretation of American history? Why or why not?

In-Class Writing Activities

1. In a freewrite, consider a current or historical example that you know about in which "patriotism runs amuck, [so that] it becomes something that divides rather than unites" (para. 1). What

do you think are the reasons behind "this rabid brand of patriotism" (para. 4)?

2. Assume you are a member of the Madison School Board, and you must "comply with a state law that requires a daily show of patriotism in public schools" (para. 2). Working in small groups, brainstorm a list of options. Agree on at least two plans and write a proposal identifying and defending your choices.

AMERICA THEN . . . 1942
WORLD WAR II POSTERS

Ian Frazier's "All-Consuming Patriotism" criticizes the limited ways citizens today are encouraged to express their patriotism as opposed to the more rigorous sacrifices demanded of Americans during past wars. During World War II, for example, many advertisements and posters asked civilians to help the war effort through a wide variety of means, from consuming less to working harder. In an address to the nation on December 9, 1941, a few days after the attack on

Pearl Harbor, President Roosevelt reminded Americans that "We are now in this war. We are all in it all the way. Every single man, woman, and child is a partner in the most tremendous undertaking of our American history. We must share together the bad news and the good news, the defeats and the victories — the changing fortunes of war." The posters "Put your muscle on a war basis!" and "We Can't Win Without Them" represent just two of countless appeals conducted by the United States government in its attempt to persuade noncombatants to do their part.

Web **See It Now:** World War II Poster Collection, **bedfordstmartins.com/ americanow**, Chapter 10. View more than 300 posters by U.S. federal agencies from the onset of World War II through 1945, collected by the Northwestern University Library.

Discussing the Unit

Suggested Topic for Discussion

When you hear the term *patriotism,* how do you react? What symbols, songs, sayings, and actions come to mind? Do you view it as something generally positive, or do you think its repercussions are sometimes negative? How have the influences surrounding you — family, friends, school, media, community, and country — shaped your view of patriotism? Have any of the selections in this unit changed the way you think about patriotism?

Preparing for Class Discussion

1. As the selections in this unit demonstrate, patriotism can take on many different forms, from Brent Staples's sense that we now have a "spacious, postmodern patriotism" (para. 8) to Ian Frazier's dual admonition against and argument for an "All-Consuming Patriotism" to Laura Sahramaa's example of a patriotism "that divides rather than unites" (para. 1). Make a list of the different examples of patriotism that appear in the selections in this unit, looking at both positive and negative examples from each essay. In determining whether each example is a generally positive or negative display of patriotism, first consider the au-

thor's attitude toward the display or act and then articulate your own response, either concurring with the author's position or challenging it. Offer reasons for your own view in either case.

2. Staples's essay focuses on the American flag as a significant symbol of patriotism and embraces the many nontraditional flags that line his Brooklyn street, seeing them as the embodiment of a more varied definition of patriotism. Considering Frazier's and Sahramaa's arguments, how do you think each author would respond to nontraditional flags as a form of patriotic display? Support your answers with evidence from the texts.

From Discussion to Writing

1. Sahramaa's essay centers around the furor that arose over the Madison School Board's decision to eliminate the Pledge of Allegiance as an option to comply with a state mandate requiring public schools to institute "a daily show of patriotism" (para. 2). Is such a law a good idea? If it is, what display of patriotism would be appropriate?

2. Specifically, *nationalism* is "an ideology based on the premise that the individual's loyalty and devotion to the nation-state surpass other individual or group interests" (*Encyclopedia Britannica Online*), but more generally one can define *nationalism* as "devotion to one's nation" (*Oxford English Dictionary*). In this more general sense of the word, *nationalism* is almost synonymous with *patriotism,* or a love of one's country. In an 1844 edition of the British periodical *Fraser's Magazine,* an anonymous author writes, "Nationalism is another word for egotism." Replace the word *nationalism* with *patriotism* and write an essay in which you explore patriotism as a form of egotism. Rather than merely writing for or against such an idea, analyze what it means. What does *egotism* mean? Why would someone associate patriotism with egotism? What kind of patriotism, both in thought and action, could constitute egotism? When is patriotism not a form of egotism? What kind of thought or action would be the opposite of an egotistic display of patriotism? As you develop your response, take into account the examples of patriotism in the selections in this unit. Do you think the World War II ads could be interpreted as "egotistic"?

Topics for Cross-Cultural Discussion

1. How large of a role does patriotism play in other countries? What different forms does it take? How has patriotism had a positive influence in other countries? Can you think of any negative consequences of patriotism?

2. In other countries, how important is the national flag? What rituals or ceremonies surround the display of the flag? Outside of the U.S., are there any versions of nontraditional flags such as the ones Staples discusses in his essay? In other countries, how do attitudes toward the national flag illustrate definitions of patriotism?

11

Guns and Violence: Is There a Connection?

Does the availability of guns in America make us a more violent nation? Would serious gun control legislation cut down on violent crime? When we allow children to play with toy guns or violent videos are we sending a message that killing can be exciting and fun? In this chapter we examine these and related questions as we look into the connection between guns and violence. We begin with a parental debate: "Do Toy Guns Teach Violence?" "Yes," argues Wendy Dutton, a mother of four, who believes that when "you put a toy gun in a kid's hands, you are encouraging that child to practice using a real gun." But even though Elizabeth Crane admits she hates guns, her answer is "No": "I would wager," she writes, "that kids who work out their feelings about guns and power as children are healthier adolescents." This decades-old debate is then depicted in comic strip form by *Progressive* cartoonist Lloyd Dangle, who in "Freeze or I'll Shoot" imagines the fate of a child who never took "to guns like a normal child." The debate between those who want to restrict and regulate guns and the gun lobby that supports every American's right to bear arms is also vigorously conducted in the advertising pages of major periodicals, as recent ads for the National Crime Prevention Council and the National Rifle Association illustrate. These ads try to persuade us with imagery and personal testimony, but in "What Can We Do to Curb Gun Violence?" Georgetown University student Peter Denton uses different persuasive tactics: statistics and research. Most Americans, he writes, "do not realize that approximately eighty-two people, including ten children, are killed each day by firearms." Opposing views on guns and violent crime have long maintained that guns are not a source of danger but a major means of protection. An advertisement from 1915 clearly demonstrates the longevity of that argument.

OPPOSING VIEWS

Do Toy Guns Teach Violence?

Before You Read

Did you ever play with toy guns as a child? If so, do you think they made you more prone to violence? Do you think parents should allow their children to play with toy guns?

Words to Learn [Dutton]

atrocity (para. 1): an act or object that is savagely brutal, cruel, or wicked (n.)

unequivocal (para. 3): leaving no doubt; clear (adj.)

renegade (para. 8): a deserter from one faith, principle, or party for another (n.)

illicit (para. 8): not permitted; unlawful (adj.)

innate (para. 10): existing in, belonging to, or determined by factors present in an individual from birth; native (adj.)

spoiler (para. 11): an entity (e.g., a person, idea, or object) that corrupts, mars, or renders something useless (n.)

Words to Learn [Crane]

demystifying (para. 4): taking away the mystery; making clear (v.)

mystique (para. 4): an air or attitude of mystery and reverence

developing around something or someone (n.)

WENDY DUTTON

Yes

[BRAIN, CHILD / Spring 2001]

Listen: In Michigan a six-year-old went to school, took a gun out of his pants, and shot and killed his classmate. Following just a few weeks after the atrocity in Columbine, this kind of thing can no longer be treated as a freak incident. The courts agree: The mother of the boy in Michigan received fifteen years in prison. This is a wake-up call for parents across the country to get real about guns with their kids. No toy guns. No real guns. No stun guns. No gun-guns.

There are not many reasons why kids should *not* play with guns. In fact, there is only one reason. Guns kill. Yes, real guns kill; toy guns only give the illusion of killing. Whoopie. When you put a toy gun in a kid's hands, you are encouraging that child to practice using a real gun. They are practicing aiming. They are practicing pulling the trigger. They are practicing gun noises. They are practicing ways to stand with a gun, ways to conceal a gun, and ways to whip it out. They are acting out the many scenarios when a gun might come in handy — war, showdowns, ambush, revenge, and maybe a little espionage and thievery. And while a toy gun is just a toy, it represents a real gun every time.

This is no longer a gray-line issue. Kids do know the difference between real guns and toy guns. If you can understand the allure that toy guns have for kids, then you can understand the allure that real guns also hold for kids. Rather than fostering confusion about that, we must be unequivocal in our condemnation of guns.

Not a real gun, not a toy gun, not a red gun, not a blue gun, not in a video game, not in a movie, not with an action hero, not with the kid next door.

WENDY DUTTON (b. 1963) has published articles in Hip Mama, Mother's Underground, the Single Mother's Companion, Commentary, World Literature Today, the Threepenny Review, and Farmer's Market and won the Pushcart Prize for fiction in 1997. She is the mother of four children and lives in Oakland, California, where she helps to run a landscaping business.

If you send a zero-tolerance message to your children about guns   5
from age one, at least they will know that even when they really
really want to play with guns, they can't. And even when they really
really want to blow away all the popular kids in school, they can't.
Kids deserve a consistent and clear message about guns. Guns kill.
Killing is bad.

Forgive me if I sound extreme. I'm just saying that it's no longer   6
a worry that kids steeped in violent toys may grow up to be violent
adults. They are not even growing up before the crossover from toy
guns to real guns takes place. When children take up arms, we need
an extreme response.

(Of course, who am I to talk? At the very time of writing this my   7
two-and-a-half-year-old son is downstairs, using pieces of his train
track like guns. He's shooting from both hips. POW POW POW.
There is a cookie monster lying dead on the floor.)

This is a family issue now. Schools are clear about this. Toy guns   8
and action figures were long ago banned from
schools; now they are installing metal detectors.
In most preschools toy guns and action figures
are seen as un-PC. Teachers will also tell you
that they don't have toy weapons because they
cause too much trouble. The kids fight too
much over who gets to play with the gun. My
friend who runs a preschool where weapon toys are not allowed always has a renegade band of children who are smuggling in imaginary guns anyway. At least they know it's illicit. At least when she
says, "Is that an imaginary gun you've got?" they say, "No, no, it's a
bow and arrow."

We must be unequivocal in our condemnation of guns.

(Okay, I've been downstairs and I have confiscated the double-   9
barreled train tracks. Forrest screamed at me and told me to go outside. Then he accepted my offer of crayons. Now he is drawing hurri-
canes — his specialty.)

I understand that gun love is innate. Forrest is living proof. Just   10
because he is going to turn every one of his toys into a gun doesn't
mean I have to promote it or go along with it. And I don't have to
keep my mouth shut about it either. In fact, it's my moral obligation
as a parent to speak up against guns.

The spoiler of the argument is squirt guns. When I told my family   11
no guns were allowed, their first response was a collective wail, "Even
squirt guns?" Let's face it: squirt guns are fun. On a very hot day squirt
guns are really fun. But consider this: water balloons are fun too.

I know, I know, they're going to go to a friend's house, and   12
they're going to play with squirt guns, and they're going to have a
great time, and I'll be Miss Killjoy when they come home and I say,
"Now what would have happened if that was bullets coming out of
the gun instead of water?" I'm going to say it anyway. Even if my
kids are going to think I am the biggest squarest mom on all the
planet, I'm going to be boringly black and white on this issue. No
guns.

Not even squirt guns.   13

ELIZABETH CRANE

No

[BRAIN, CHILD / Spring 2001]

I hate guns. I do. But I've fired a gun, and I know that if I had to   1
I could fire one again. I am not afraid of guns, but I am afraid of
what guns in the hands of ignorant thrill-seekers can do. That is why
I am firmly in favor of toy gun play for preschool-age children. I believe that you can bring guns down from their status as something illicit and desirable and turn them into just another thing from which
children can learn.

Children should be free to experiment. Obviously, I am not say-   2
ing that kids should be issued Colt revolvers and told to find out
what happens when they pull the trigger. What I am saying is that by
banning guns and gun play from preschool, we are squashing a natural impulse toward exploration. Kids are curious. They want to
know why they are not allowed to have guns: This is the perfect opportunity to let them in on the idea that guns kill people.

ELIZABETH CRANE (b. 1965) has published articles in Woman's Day,
Working Woman, MSN Underwire, and HipMama. Commenting on this
piece, Crane said, "As the mother of boys, I feel strongly about issues that involve violence and control. I always champion information over suppression,
which often means more work for me, but I think my sons will be better men
because of it."

If you forbid something, it becomes that much more attractive. You can't expect children to understand that gun play is "bad" — they merely learn that it is something interesting that they are not allowed to do, so they do it when you're not around and get that sweet illicit thrill of having fun and being disobedient without really hurting anything. You create guilt. I do not believe that gun play in children creates violent adults; I have never read a study that claims anything close. If anything, I would wager that kids who work out their feelings about guns and power as children are healthier adolescents.   3

Power is a heady concept. Some kids really need to feed on their own power, which to my mind is where gun play comes from. Kids figure out what the leaders and followers do, and work out what fair play means to them. It's quite a lengthy process — in my experience it lasts years — and pointing things at each other (sticks, Duplo blocks, anything) is part of the learning. They need to know that if they say, "Bang, you're dead" to their friend, their friend is not actually dead. They need to know that if they hit their friend, their friend will be hurt (in more ways than one). They need to know (from you) that real guns kill people on purpose as well as by accident. Demystifying guns is part of our job as parents. Without their mystique, guns are just tools that mankind has used for good as well as ill. Allowing gun play is not a license to kill, it is a teaching tool that, when handled sensitively and intelligently, can give your child the reasoning and the strength behind the ability to stay gun-safe and gun-smart.   4

> *If you forbid something, it becomes that much more attractive.*

At a recent parent meeting, it was proposed that our co-op nursery school ban all gun play. We sat there at our meeting and shifted uncomfortably. We talked a little about how our school operates well without a lot of burdensome rules. Then one mother got up and spoke.   5

She has a boy who, when he was preschool age, loved to dress in little girls' dresses. When she started him in a different preschool, he was told that little boys do not wear dresses. She promptly removed him from that school and enrolled him in our school, where he quite happily dressed in frilly dresses and no one batted an eye. He's now ten and doing fine, thank you very much. His younger brother, however, is now in our preschool, and he seems to have been born with his hand in the shape of a gun. This kid shoots at anything, and he always has. His mother is no more in favor of her son actually shooting people than anybody would be, but she doesn't see the point in trying to squash who he is in order to satisfy a societal fear about gun play,   6 any more than she felt it necessary to make her dress-loving son wear pants in order to satisfy some grown-up idea of gender. Her gun-loving boy needs a safe environment to experiment with appropriate behaviors, and he will eventually learn that most adults don't like guns pointed at them, and that some children don't like gun play at all, and hey, let's go try on some frilly dresses instead. The point is, children need to be free to be who they are and to learn to express that in ways that are societally acceptable. It is unreasonable to expect a four-year-old to mask his true self, and if that true self involves issues of power and dominance then that should be worked with, not covered up. The blanket rule against gun play was voted down.

I still won't buy toy guns, but my boys know about guns, and they at least seem properly respectful of the idea that guns are dangerous. I will continue to give them the information they need to make intelligent choices about guns when they are confronted with the real thing, and I will continue to work with and learn from the power play in my preschool and in my home.

7

Web Read It Now: Kids and Guns in America, bedfordstmartins.com/americanow, Chapter 11. Published by the Brady Campaign to Prevent Gun Violence, this brief report includes statistics.

Web Read It Now: Where School Shooters Get Their Guns, bedfordstmartins.com/americanow, Chapter 11. This article from *The Christian Science Monitor* provides details on how students obtain weapons.

Vocabulary/Using a Dictionary

1. What is the best antonym for *unequivocal* (Dutton, para. 3)?

2. Use a dictionary to find the origin of *renegade* (Dutton, para. 8).

3. Look up the definition of *confiscate* in the dictionary. Why do you think Dutton chooses to use *confiscated* rather than simply *taken away* when she writes, "I have *confiscated* the double-barreled train tracks" (para. 9)?

Responding to Words in Context

1. In paragraph 8, Dutton explains, "In most preschools toy guns and action figures are *un-PC*." Considering the context of the sentence, try to define *un-PC*.

2. In using the word *innate* to describe her son's love of guns (para. 10), how does Dutton acknowledge points Crane explicitly makes?

3. In paragraph 8, Dutton uses the word *illicit,* a term that also appears in paragraphs 1 and 3 of Crane's essay. How does each author use the word to serve a very different point?

Discussing Main Point and Meaning

1. Dutton asserts in paragraph 2 that she will offer only one reason to support her argument. What is her reason? Why does she argue she needs to offer only one reason? Does she really offer only one reason?

2. Notice the parenthetical observations of her own child Dutton makes in paragraphs 7 and 9. Are these paragraphs placed in parentheses as merely humorous asides to her main argument, or do these paragraphs play a central role in shaping Dutton's argument? Explain your answer.

3. What kind of evidence do Dutton and Crane use to support their arguments on the relationship between toy guns and real violence? How convincing is each writer's use of evidence?

4. What are Crane's main reasons for supporting toy gun play?

Examining Sentences, Paragraphs, and Organization

1. Examine the opening sentences of each essay. How effective are they in getting your attention?

2. How does Dutton use repetition in paragraph 2? What is the effect of this repetition?

3. Dutton ends paragraphs 1 and 5 with fragments and short sentences. What is the effect of this sentence structure?

Thinking Critically

1. Compare Dutton's point in paragraph 3 to Crane's point in paragraph 4. What point does each writer make about the difference between real guns and toy ones? How does the specific point support each writer's larger argument? Whose point do you find more convincing and why?

2. How does Dutton's point on the relationship between toy guns and real violence in paragraph 6 compare to Crane's examination of the issue in paragraph 3? Whose point do you find more convincing and why?

3. In paragraph 6, Crane compares a preschool's decision not to allow a boy to dress in female clothes to the discussion of whether to allow toy guns in preschool. Crane explains that a mother "doesn't see the point in trying to squash who he [her son who loves guns] is in order to satisfy a societal fear about gun play, any more than she felt it necessary to make her dress-loving son wear pants in order to satisfy some grown-up idea of gender." Would you justify such a comparison between dressing up in clothes to gun play? Explain your answer.

4. Dutton admits her own son simulates gun play with other toys (para. 7, 9, and 10) and Crane ends by asserting "I still won't buy toy guns" (para. 7). Look separately at each author's confession. What effect does the confession have on the persuasiveness of the argument?

In-Class Writing Activities

1. Write an essay in which you defend either Dutton's or Crane's thesis. You should consider an opposing view using the arguments of the author with whom you disagree. Use your own observations as well as the author's argument you agree with to refute the opposing view and support your own argument. Qualify your argument whenever necessary.

2. Assume you are either a parent who has denied a child's request to play with a toy gun or a preschool owner who has banned toy guns in school. Now you must come up with creative alternatives to toy guns. Brainstorm a list of ideas. Discuss your list with the class.

LLOYD DANGLE

Freeze or I'll Shoot

[THE PROGRESSIVE / April 2001]

Before You Read

What factors do you think contribute to the rash of school shootings? What are potential solutions to the problem? What do you think about gun control as a potential solution?

Words to Learn

haiku (frame 3): an unrhymed Japanese verse form of three lines containing five, seven, and five syllables respectively (n.)

Vocabulary/Using a Dictionary

1. Use the dictionary to find the different meanings of the word *alien*. How does *alien* relate to its Latin root word, *alius*? How does *alien* relate to the word *alienate* (frame 4)?

2. The word *rage* (frame 4) is a variation on the Latin word *rabere*, which means "to be mad." In what sense is the word *mad* used in this definition? What other words stem from the root word *rabere*?

Responding to Words in Context

1. The police officer in the strip uses the phrase "thoroughly discredited notion" (frame 5). Is this a phrase that is commonly used in spoken English? Who do you think may have done the *discrediting* of the *notion*? What is the cartoonist's intent in including this phrase, and why might he have the police officer say it?

Lloyd Dangle *(b. 1961) has been a self-employed cartoonist and illustrator since 1986. His work has appeared in over one hundred newspapers, magazines, and comic anthologies and has been exhibited internationally.*

2. Consider the phrase "straighten him out" (frame 6). The word *straight* comes from the root word *strecchen*, which means "to stretch"; and one of the many meanings of *straight* is "exhibiting no deviation from what is accepted as usual, normal or proper." Why would the parents in this comic want to "straighten out" their son? What do the parents in this comic strip consider as "normal" or proper?

Web **Read It Now:** Homicide Trends in the United States, U.S. Department of Justice, Bureau of Justice Statistics, **bedfordstmartins.com/americanow**, Chapter 11. This overview includes visuals, statistical information, and a link to the full Bureau of Justice report.

Discussing Main Point and Meaning

1. What argument does this cartoon make about the causes of school shootings?

2. The second frame of the cartoon refers to "committing suicide by police." What do you think this means? How is this reference a point in the cartoonist's larger argument?

3. What solution does the arrested boy propose to stop school shootings?

4. In the sixth frame, the mother bewails her son's repulsion to guns and suggests he should spend more time in the video arcade. What social debate is Dangle referring to here? Why does he include this reference in the cartoon?

Examining Details, Imagery, and Design

1. When you read about the boy's haiku in frame 3, what do you expect it to be about? What is it really about? How does this organizational design serve Dangle's point?

2. Look at the pictures of all the guns in the cartoon. What do you notice about the police officer's guns compared to the parents'? What point do these images make about gun ownership?

3. Analyze the emotions of the police officer and parents in frames 2, 4, and 6. What point does Dangle want to make with their moods and the content of their discussion?

Thinking Critically

1. Schoolchildren in this cartoon are arrested for their artwork. How does this parody play off of a serious social debate about the role of teachers in detecting signs of potential violence? What do you think about this issue?

2. What does the cartoon imply about gun control as a means to solve the problem of school shootings? What do you think about this solution?

3. What point does the cartoon seem to make about video arcades? What effect, if any, do you think violent video games have on actual acts of violence?

In-Class Writing Activities

1. Brainstorm a list of factors you think contribute to school shootings. Next, put the list in order from the most significant factor to the least. Discuss your list with the class.

2. In small groups, come up with a list of potential solutions to solve the problem of school shootings. Come up with as many ideas as you can.

3. What do you think the boy's haiku said? Try writing an antigun haiku.

Kalie Was My Baby Sister

[THE AD COUNCIL AND THE NATIONAL CRIME PREVENTION COUNCIL / 2001]

Before You Read

Do you know of anyone who has been a victim of a gun firearms accident or have you heard news stories about such victims? What circumstances usually cause those accidents? How could they have been prevented?

Kalie was my baby sister.

She loved pink.

We were playing with her dolls.

I found a gun in the drawer.

It went off.

I made Kalie go away.

I hate me.

An unlocked gun could be the death of your family.
Please lock up your gun.

Responding to Words in Context

How does the advertisement's language — phrases such as "I made Kalie go away" — reveal what its sponsors are trying to achieve? Try substituting other words and phrases for each line of the ad. Would other word choices have been more effective? Why or why not?

Discussing Main Point and Meaning

1. What is the cause of the accident portrayed in the ad? Who is responsible?

2. To whom is the ad directed? What is the message and purpose of the ad?

Examining Details, Imagery, and Design

1. How do lines four, five, and six of the ad reflect the child's understanding of the shooting? What is the effect of these lines?

2. What do the style of the drawing and the images reveal about the ages of the victim and shooter? What does the placement of the gun suggest? What effect does the child's drawing have on you as a viewer?

Thinking Critically

1. The caption at the bottom of the ad states, "An unlocked gun could be the death of your family." How does the phrase "death of your family" work on both a literal and figurative level?

2. The National Crime Prevention Council sponsored the ad. Does this ad portray a crime or an accident? Explain your response. If this is a crime, who is responsible? What would be a fit punishment?

In-Class Writing Activities

1. Working in a group, design your own ad promoting gun safety. Make decisions on what audience you would target, what message you want to send, and what purpose you want the ad to achieve. Describe text, design, and images that will have a powerful effect on the viewer.

2. Suppose you live in a house with small children. Would you decide to keep a gun in the house? Why or why not? Freewrite your response.

THE NATIONAL RIFLE ASSOCIATION

I'm the NRA

[NATIONAL REVIEW / September 25, 2000]

Before You Read

Do you agree with the current gun control laws, or do you think they should be less stringent? More stringent? How do you interpret the Second Amendment covering the right to bear arms? What is the position of the National Rifle Association (NRA) in regard to gun control and the Second Amendment?

Vocabulary/Using a Dictionary

1. Use a dictionary to look up the meanings of the word *defame* (para. 3). How do they compare to the word *defend*?

2. What are some synonyms of the word *restore* (para. 4)?

Responding to Words in Context

1. What does Heston mean by the phrase "rightful, respected place" (para. 4)?

I've never been afraid of doing the right thing, even if it's the unpopular thing. That's why I marched for civil rights in the early '60s, *long before it was fashionable.*

That's also why I answered the call to lead the NRA. I believe the Second Amendment is worthy of my time...and of yours.

Just like its companions in the Bill of Rights — freedoms of speech and religion and the press — the right to bear arms welcomes all who believe in its core principles of freedom. *It also welcomes differing views about how it's exercised.* Our mutual commitment must be to defend the freedom, not to defame its critics.

I hope you'll help the NRA restore gun ownership and the shooting sports to their rightful, respected place in mainstream American life. *And if you won't, please let me know why.* **I'm The NRA.**

Charlton Heston
Actor

EDDIE

© 2000 National Rifle Association of America • 11250 Waples Mill Road • Fairfax, VA 22030

Eddie Eagle®

Did You Know ... "Nobody does more to prevent childhood firearm accidents than the NRA. We've invested $20 million to teach youngsters not to touch guns through our Eddie Eagle GunSafe® Program. Since 1988, 13 million schoolkids have learned its simple lifesaving message about guns: 'Stop, Don't Touch, Leave The Area, Tell An Adult.'"

Wayne LaPierre, NRA Executive Vice President

2. How would marching for civil rights be considered *fashionable* (para. 1)?

3. Note the multiple appearance of the word *freedom*. What effect does this have on the argument presented in the advertisement?

Discussing Main Point and Meaning

1. To whom do you think this advertisement is directed? More specifically, what can you assume about the audience's political beliefs? Support your answer with evidence from the ad.

2. What does the NRA want to do? How do they use the Second Amendment to support the goals of their organization?

3. What does the Eddie Eagle GunSafe Program do?

Examining Details, Imagery, and Design

1. Notice the text in italics. Why are these phrases in italics? What do the italicized sentences have in common? To what kind of person are they directed? What kind of image of the NRA and its leader Charlton Heston do they create?

2. Much of the ad centers on the picture of Charlton Heston. Who is he? How would you describe his image in the photo? What kind of image does he give to the NRA?

3. Look at the NRA mascot, Eddie Eagle. Why do you think the NRA chose this mascot?

Thinking Critically

1. Heston begins the text to the ad by declaring he fought for civil rights before it was fashionable. Why does he mention this? Who is he appealing to? What connection does he make between his support for civil rights and the NRA?

2. In paragraph 3 the ad refers to "core principles of freedom" and claims, "Our mutual commitment must be to defend the freedom, not to defame its critics." What different freedoms is Heston referring to? Who do you think he means by the word *our*? Who do you think Heston means by "its critics"? Would you link all the freedoms listed in the Bill of Rights together the way Heston does? Why or why not?

3. The NRA's goal is to "restore gun ownership and the shooting sports to their rightful, respected place in mainstream American life" (para. 4). What does Heston mean here? Do you agree with him? Why or why not?

4. Critics of the NRA charge its massive lobbying power has blocked crucial laws to regulate the firearms industry, resulting in numer-

ous firearm accidents involving children. How does the NRA respond to this criticism in the ad? Is the response sufficient?

In-Class Writing Activities

1. Heston ends his comments by inviting readers to respond back if they disagree with him. Write a short letter to Heston explaining why you do or do not agree with him.

2. Choose a spokesperson or mascot to represent your stance on gun control. If you agree with the NRA, you'll still want to choose your own spokesperson or mascot. In a freewrite, explain how your spokesperson or mascot reflects your decision.

PETER DENTON

What Can We Do to Curb Gun Violence?

[THE HOYA, GEORGETOWN UNIVERSITY / February 27, 2001]

Before You Read

What do you think are the leading causes of gun violence? Would you own a gun or keep one in your home? How regulated do you think the firearm industry is?

PETER DENTON (b. 1981) was a sophomore at Georgetown University when he wrote this piece for The Hoya, Georgetown's student newspaper. In 2001, Denton served as the president of the Georgetown chapter of the Campus Alliance to End Gun Violence. Denton, who is interested in politics and social responsibility, has also written for the Sarasota Herald-Tribune and the Bradenton Herald.

Words to Learn

bane (para. 3): woe; harm (n.)
chamber (para. 10): the part of the firearm that holds the cartridge or powder charge during firing (n.)
magazine (para. 10): a container in a gun for holding cartridges (n.)
unobtrusive (para. 10): not bold; inconspicuous (adj.)

bipartisan (para. 11): representing or composed of members of two parties (adj.)
categorically (para. 12): absolutely and without qualifications (adv.)
grassroots (para. 13): society at the local level as distinguished from the centers of political leadership (n.)

While discussing the issue of gun violence recently with a few conservative-minded friends, I realized that there are many misconceptions concerning the gun control movement. 1

While recent tragedies such as those in Columbine, Paducah, and Atlanta highlight the massive scourge of gun violence in our nation, most Americans do not realize that approximately eighty-two people, including ten children, are killed each day by firearms. According to Kris Christoffel, author of *Children's Environments,* the plague of gun violence is ten times larger than the polio epidemic of the first half of this century. 2

However, many still view gun violence as a uniquely urban dilemma caused primarily by drugs and gang violence. Others see the bane of gun violence as all the more reason to own a firearm for self-protection. In reality, the majority of gun violence is caused by the availability of firearms, not premeditated actions or gang warfare. Crimes of passion, attempted suicides, and accidents all become deadly when a gun is readily accessible. 3

The statistics are stunning. *The National Crime Victimization Survey Report* showed that Americans are three times more likely to be attacked at home by a person they know than by a stranger. According to the *FBI Uniform on Crime Reports,* in 1997, approximately half of murder victims were killed by someone they knew. And according to a 1998 report by the *New England Journal of Medicine,* guns kept in the home for self-protection are twenty-two times more likely to be used to kill their owner or someone the owner knows than they are to kill in self-defense. 4

So it is obvious that firearm violence presents a clear and present danger to the American public. The question remains — what can we do to curb gun violence? 5

Many of the common misconceptions about the gun control movement concern this crucial question. The National Rifle Association 6 paints a picture of liberal Democrats in favor of banning the personal ownership of guns. The majority of the gun control movement, led by groups such as James Brady's Handgun Control, Inc., is not trying to ban guns but rather to make them safer.

Firearms are one of the least regulated consumer products in America, and an average of one person dies every day because guns lack basic safety features. Guns are specifically exempt from the kind of federal product safety standards that apply to nearly every consumer product. When the Consumer Product Safety Commission was created in 1976, Congressman John Dingell (D-Mich.), an NRA board member at the time, inserted a provision expressly prohibiting the commission from regulating firearms or ammunition.   7

In contrast, between 1994 and 1997, eight models of teddy bears were recalled because they could pose choking hazards. In fact, at least four federal safety regulations apply to teddy bears: sharp edges and points, small parts, hazardous materials, and flammability.   8

> *Firearms are one of the least regulated consumer products in America.*

Because guns are unregulated, however, they do not have to comply with any product safety standards governing their design and manufacture, and many have design flaws that result in unintentional shootings. The fact remains that there are simple, proven, low-tech safety devices that can prevent unintentional shootings.   9

Chamber load indicators make sure the gun is unloaded. Magazine disconnect safeties prevent the gun from firing when the magazine has been removed. Grip safeties require a mature person's hand to fire. These relatively unobtrusive solutions, which the firearm industry refuses to voluntarily enforce, could save hundreds of lives each year.   10

Basic safety regulation of the gun industry is a commonsense measure that should attract bipartisan support. In fact, according to the Johns Hopkins University Center for Gun Policy and Research, 88 percent of Americans favor childproofing guns, 82 percent support magazine disconnect safeties, and 73 percent favor loaded-chamber indicators.   11

The NRA, however, adamantly claims that there are already too many regulations on the gun industry and categorically attacks any new legislation offered in Congress. One of the most powerful industry lobbies in Washington, D.C., the NRA's money and influence, similar to that of the tobacco industry, has succeeded for decades in misleading Americans about the gun control movement.   12

While the lobby may donate millions upon millions of dollars to   13
political campaigns, right here at Georgetown a grassroots effort is
underway to take on the NRA. As one of the first chapters of the national Campus Alliance to End Gun Violence, Georgetown students
are organizing letter-writing campaigns to Congress and lobbying
trips to Capitol Hill.

Firearm violence is preventable, but the silent majority of Ameri-   14
cans who support commonsense gun safety legislation must speak up
and be heard over the roar of the NRA's bank account.

Web **Read It Now:** Crime and Victims Statistics, **bedfordstmartins.com/
americanow,** Chapter 11. Read a summary of the National Crime Victimization Survey mentioned in Denton's essay and access data gathered during the
survey.

Vocabulary/Using a Dictionary

1. Look up the two different meanings of the noun *scourge.* Which
   one best applies to its use in paragraph 2?

2. Look up the different meanings of *dilemma* in the dictionary.
   Which one best applies to its use in paragraph 3?

3. Investigate the origin of the term *grassroots* (para. 13). You may
   need to use the *Oxford English Dictionary* or another dictionary
   that provides the etymology of words.

Responding to Words in Context

1. Denton argues most gunfire deaths are not the result of *premeditated* actions (para. 3). How does the word *premeditated* serve
   the writer's larger point in paragraph 3?

2. In paragraph 12, Denton uses *adamantly* to describe NRA claims
   and *categorically* to define their attacks on gun control legislation. What portrait does the writer create of the NRA by using
   these words?

Discussing Main Point and Meaning

1. What misconceptions about guns and the gun control movement
   does the writer identify?

2. According to Denton, why is the firearms industry unregulated? What are the consequences of this lack of regulation?

3. What evidence does the writer use to support his claims?

Examining Sentences, Paragraphs, and Organization

1. Explain the organizational structure of the essay. How effective is it?

2. Look at the last sentence of the essay. How well does it capture the writer's argument? Has he earned his conclusion?

3. What is the function of paragraph 8?

4. What is the effect of comparing the NRA to the tobacco industry in paragraph 12?

Thinking Critically

1. In paragraph 3, the writer rejects the notion that gun violence is just a problem affecting urban areas. What is the effect of thinking gun violence is limited to inner cities?

2. What kind of compromise does the essay offer between the NRA and those who indeed do want to ban guns? Do you think the author's proposal is reasonable, too strict, or not strict enough? Explain why.

3. How does the writer characterize the NRA? Is this a fair characterization?

4. How convincing do you find the writer's argument? Explain your answer.

In-Class Writing Activities

1. Did this essay change your view of the gun control movement or provide you with any surprising or new facts or information? Explain your response in a freewrite.

2. Based on this essay, would you decide to own a gun? Why or why not? Freewrite your response.

3. Write a brief essay in which you argue for or against the regulation of the gun industry by comparing it to other regulated industries.

AMERICA THEN . . . 1915 IVER JOHNSON REVOLVER, GUN ADVERTISEMENT

Protection of one's family and property has long been a key sales point of handgun marketing, as the 1915 advertisement for Iver Johnson revolvers on page 271 clearly shows, with its emphatic connection between increased drug use and burglaries. Purchasing any kind of gun then was much easier than it is now, although a few years before this ad (in 1911) New York passed the Sullivan Law, which required a police permit for handgun ownership. Over time, other states began enacting similar laws and placing greater restrictions on handgun sales. The Sullivan Law was passed around the same time that New York City experienced its heaviest influx of immigrants in a single day: nearly 18,000 people passed through Ellis Island on April 17, 1911. Part of the motivation for the law was to keep guns out of the hands of a swelling foreign-born population that many Americans considered a potential danger. The imagery of the advertisement also alludes to this fear.

Discussing the Unit

Suggested Topic for Discussion

Deciding what place guns should have in American life requires us to make many personal and public decisions. Would you let your child play with toy guns? Would you own a gun to protect yourself in your home? Would you support candidates who favor gun control?

Preparing for Class Discussion

1. Consider the issue of guns in American life in a historical perspective. To do so, analyze the meaning of the Second Amendment: "A well regulated Militia, being necessary to the security of a free State, the right of the people to keep and bear Arms, shall not be infringed." What do you think the framers of the Constitution had in mind when they wrote these words? How did the colonists use guns in Revolutionary War America? Does the Second Amend-

The Use of Drugs is Making More Criminals Every Year!

Every drug fiend is at heart a criminal of the most dangerous type, for while under the influence of drugs he is reckless, unscrupulous and irresponsible. The use of drugs has grown enormously during the last few years.

Increase of burglar insurance rates is an alarming indication of the growth of those crimes which expose the criminal to danger.

Is your home protected? The

IVER JOHNSON
Safety Automatic REVOLVER

is guarding over two million homes. No weapon can be compared to it for accuracy, speed and absolute safety. It cannot be accidentally discharged. You can with safety drop it, throw it against a wall or "Hammer the Hammer."

$6 at Hardware or Sporting Goods Stores

Send for 84-page book which tells all about Iver Johnson Revolvers, Shotguns, Bicycles and Motorcycles.

IVER JOHNSON'S ARMS & CYCLE WORKS
146 River Street, Fitchburg, Mass.
99 Chambers St., New York   717 Market St., San Francisco

ment apply today? How has the range and design of guns changed since colonial America? How has the use of guns changed since that time? Does the Second Amendment protect an inherent, timeless right of the American people, or should we make changes to the amendment to reflect the changes in America?

2. How much control should the government have over the firearms industry? Should the government regulate the design and manufacture of firearms to insure their safety or require manufacturers to install safety devices? Should the government require gun buyers to undergo a waiting period to conduct thorough background checks? Should the government ban private ownership of handguns and automatic weapons? In answering these questions, consider the arguments put forth in the selections of this unit.

From Discussion to Writing

1. Assume you are a kindergarten teacher and your principal has asked you to educate your class about gun safety. You have the following options to choose from:

    • Having children engage in toy gun play (see Dutton's and Crane's essays)

    • Showing the children the "Kalie Was My Baby Sister" ad

    • Bringing the NRA's Eddie Eagle GunSafe Program to class

    • Designing your own exercise

    You may choose all or any number of these options. Write up a proposal for your principal in which you explain why you've adopted some measures and rejected others. If you design your own exercise, be sure to explain and justify it.

2. The NRA wants to "restore gun ownership and the shooting sports to their rightful, respected place in mainstream American life." Write an essay in which you articulate what the role of guns should be in American life. Are they an inherent part of American culture and a necessary means of protection as the 1915 ad for Iver Johnson revolvers suggests? Are guns safe so long as we lock them up, install safety devices, and keep them away from children? Should we support gun ownership and educate children about their dangers? Or do guns play a central role in a violent society? Do toy guns teach children violence? Does the widespread availability of guns increase the likelihood of

deadly accidents? Your essay should not attempt to answer all these questions; they are here to help prod your thinking and guide you toward a potential thesis. As you develop your argument, support it with your own observations, examples, and reasoning. Use relevant texts from this unit for further support.

3. Write an essay in which you ponder the source of violence in American society. This is a broad topic, so you'll want to focus your argument carefully. To do so, reread the selections by Dutton, Crane, Dangle, and Denton. Consider some of the questions these texts ask. To what degree are some people aggressive by nature? To what extent do toy guns teach violence? What other aspects of our culture promote violence? Does the availability of firearms increase the chances of violence? While considering various factors that promote violence, your essay should focus on the factor you find most significant.

Topics for Cross-Cultural Discussion

1. What are the rules regulating the firearms industry and gun ownership in a country other than America? Does the country's constitution provide any specific right to bear arms? Do you think the U.S. would benefit from following the approach to guns of this other country? Why or why not?

2. What are the rates of violence in a country other than America? How does the violence compare to that of American culture? What are factors that promote or curb violence in this country?

12

Can We Prevent Racial Profiling?

Is racial profiling an efficient and effective means of ensuring public safety and combating serious crime? Or is it instead a type of racial discrimination impermissible in our society? After the terrorist attacks of September 11, 2001, which resulted in stepped-up airport security measures, would it have made sense to single out Middle Eastern men for extra scrutiny since all the nineteen hijackers were in fact of Arab descent? Or would it be wrong to do so? In "Profiles in Courage," James Q. Wilson and Heather R. Higgins argue that "it would be impossible for law enforcement to do its job without taking into account the observable features of people." Yet these "observable features" may not be so easily or accurately identified, as Annie Kiefhaber, a Northern Arizona University student maintains. Although identifying potential criminals through stereotypical features may make us feel more in control, she writes, we actually have little control because "literally any type of person is capable of just about any type of crime imaginable." Her point is dramatically conveyed by a popular advertisement for the American Civil Liberties Union (ACLU), which shows why a convicted mass murderer would have a better chance of eluding police surveillance than one of the nation's most respected public figures. The ad, though it doesn't use the words, ought to remind us that the term *racial profiling* first emerged out of studies in the early 1990s that conclusively showed black drivers were far more likely than white drivers to be stopped by police officers.

In the unit's final selection, we look at racial profiling from a different perspective. Why do so many opposed to racial profiling support affirmative action and so many against affirmative action favor racial profiling, asks the prominent African American law professor, Randall Kennedy. In "Blind Spot" he takes an incisive look at the issue of racial discrimination as it is reflected in two hotly contested and closely related areas — racial profiling and affirmative action.

JAMES Q. WILSON AND
HEATHER R. HIGGINS

Profiles in Courage

[THE WALL STREET JOURNAL / January 10, 2002]

Before You Read

Profiling is part of the process by which law enforcement authorities form a portrait of a suspect. How are people profiled by the police? Consider the profiling done by airport security. Are random searches at airports a fair and effective means of security? Or is any type of profiling an intrusion upon a person's civil liberties?

Words to Learn

profile (title): a concise biographical sketch (n.)

consternation (para. 1): amazed dismay and confusion (n.)

manifestly (para. 3): easily understood; obviously (adv.)

maligned (para. 5): spoken evil of; defamed (v.)

JAMES Q. WILSON (b. 1931) is a well-known political scientist who has written extensively on human nature and ethics. His publications include The Ethics of Human Cloning *(1998),* Bureaucracy *(2000), and* The Marriage Problem *(2002). HEATHER R. HIGGINS (b. 1959) is a frequent political commentator and a senior fellow at the Progress & Freedom Foundation, a thinktank for the study of digital technology and its cultural impact.*

dodgy (para. 8): appearing to avoid or evade (adj.)

beatific (para. 11): giving or indicative of great joy or bliss (adj.)

polarized (para. 16): broken up into opposing groups (v.)

These days, it seems every evening's news leads with another story of consternation by somebody over the use of "racial profiling." But before the country is carried away with slogans, we ought to spend a little time being honest about the question. That means recognizing that most profiling is not racial, that some profiling (even when it involves race) is essential under some circumstances, and that it would be impossible for law enforcement to do its job without taking into account the observable features of people. 1

Young men are vastly more likely to commit crimes than are young women or older men. When the police scan the streets looking for people to question, should they stop men and women, old and young at equal rates? Black men are six to eight times more likely to commit violent crimes than are white men. When the police patrol the streets trying to prevent crime, should they stop white and black men at the same rate? 2

Notice, please, that we say "stop," not "arrest." The police have a right to question citizens, but they only have a right to arrest them if they have evidence they have committed a crime. It would be manifestly wrong to arrest or issue so much as a traffic ticket to a person simply because of his age, sex, or race. "Driving While Black" (or while young or male) is not an offense with which anyone should be charged. 3

We do not doubt that pedestrians or motorists have been stopped because of their race, but we suspect that if someone did a decent study of police behavior (instead of relying on the complaints of politicians and activists) they would discover that in most cases (if unhappily, not in all of them), there were more cues leading to the stop than just sex or race. 4

Consider the case of the Street Crimes Unit in the New York Police Department. This group, while much maligned, took thousands of guns off the street, helping drive down that city's murder rate. It did so by stopping and patting down people on the street. Heather MacDonald reported that the unit frisked 45,000 people during a two-year period, leading to 9,500 arrests and the seizure of 2,500 illegal guns. 5

Getting one gun off the street for every eighteen stops is a pretty   6
good outcome, considering that those not carrying guns, or doing
something otherwise illegal, were merely inconvenienced for a few
minutes. No doubt some people regarded the stop as worse than an
inconvenience and no doubt some stops may have been hard to justify. But the hassle factor has to be evaluated in the light of the great
gains: 2,500 fewer dangerous weapons in dangerous hands.

Now, in the aftermath of September 11 the task of law enforce-   7
ment has been taken to a different level. It must figure out how to
prevent a tiny fraction of the millions of people who use our airports
from carrying knives, guns, and bombs onto airliners. For people
working airport security stations, the risks to society of their failure
are vastly greater than for the Street Crimes Unit.

In just a few seconds, a screener must decide whether to pat   8
down a person who is hurrying to a plane. Trained properly, these
screeners must be able to notice some bits of behavior or body language that may be a tip-off — a nervous, hurried
manner, perhaps, or dodgy eyes or a guilty look.
But not all terrorists are basket cases. And for
many of those serving as the country's final line of
defense against terrorism in the skies, physical features may be all they have to go on. As Professor
Peter H. Schuck of Yale Law School recently
pointed out, the screeners have no choice but to
rely on stereotypes to make a reasonable judgment.

> *A stereotype is halfway between an error and a fact.*

So, stereotypes. The word has come to connote any irrational   9
prejudice. But stereotypes are not in fact any different from the fleet-
ing impressions and judgments we all use to govern our daily lives.
We are cautious about people who have a rough appearance or speak
in an erratic manner just as we are drawn to people who are attractive and well-spoken. And while those instincts of avoidance or attraction are not always reliable, indulging ourselves with the luxury
of waiting for conclusive evidence would mean either meeting no one,
or everyone.

As Mr. Schuck says, a stereotype is halfway between an error and   10
a fact. We should try to use it cautiously.

When James Wilson's wife, Roberta, recently went flying, she   11
was picked out at the boarding gate by American Airlines for a complete search. She is the least threatening person one could image —
five feet tall, blonde hair, older than she would like to be, and with a

beatific expression on her face. She was picked, the airline agent said, "at random."

When Heather Higgins went to Reagan National Airport, Delta   12
Airlines selected fifteen passengers for complete searches. Though all terrorists involved in September 11 were young Middle Eastern males, Delta picked three elderly men (one an Asian), six Caucasian women, including one with two children, and two Hispanic women. Yet in the line of seventy or so passengers, there were six individuals who were not only Middle Eastern but young, male, and traveling alone. Not one of them was checked. When asked, Delta said the only searches they would do were at random.

By contrast, when a male Secret Service agent armed with a gun   13
left on his airplane seat his bag and some books, apparently written in Arabic, the flight attendants became alarmed. The pilot reviewed the man's paperwork and found it incomplete. When asked to fill out a new form, the agent became anxious and then hostile. As Christopher Caldwell has pointed out in *The Weekly Standard,* had the agent been named John Smith instead of Walied Shater, there would have been no incident. But Mr. Shater and the Council on American Islamic Relations claimed he was the victim of ethnic profiling.

Mrs. Wilson and Mrs. Higgins get searched, and they pass it off.   14
But a Near Eastern male carrying a gun and claiming he was going to see the president on the basis of incomplete forms starts complaining about profiling?

This is nonsense. Doing only random searches and not ques-   15
tioning an armed Middle Eastern male can only be justified if your only goal is to avoid the charge of "profiling." If your goal instead is to prevent somebody from carrying a shoe bomb or box cutters onto an airplane, then the search should not be random but deliberate, using all available facts to form a useful, if not entirely reliable, stereotype.

Of course, to do that exposes the airline to charges of "profil-   16
ing." And indeed it is profiling. But it is not a profile based exclusively or even chiefly on race, but on hints — that is, useful stereotypes — supplied by judgments made by rational people. Unfortunately, political leaders and civil rights activists have so polarized the discussion of profiling that an entirely defensible screening policy is now regarded as a threat to our fundamental liberties and is replaced by an irrational screening policy that threatens our safety.

The more we study terrorists, the more we will learn about them   17
and the better our screening profiles — our stereotypes — will be-

come. If we apply that knowledge, fewer innocent people will face any burden and more real terrorists will be caught. We will overcome slogans about "racial profiling" and instead become a bit safer.

Web **Read It Now:** American Civil Liberties Union: Racial Profiling, **bedford stmartins.com/americanow**, Chapter 12. This page at the ACLU Web site provides updated information and articles about racial profiling and an archive of reports including the ACLU report "Driving While Black."

Vocabulary/Using a Dictionary

1. What does *manifestly* (para. 3) have in common with *manicure*? Use a dictionary to find the answer.

2. Look in the dictionary to make a list of words related to the meaning of *maligned* (para. 5).

3. *Beatific* (para. 11) stems from *beatify*. Look up the different definitions of *beatify*. Based on these definitions, describe the connotation of *beatific*. Why do you think Wilson uses this word to describe his wife? What point is he trying to make?

Responding to Words in Context

1. How do the authors describe *profiling* in paragraph 1? How does this definition set the stage for their argument?

2. In paragraphs 9 and 10, how do the writers attempt to redefine *stereotype*? What point are they trying to make? How sound is their explanation of the term?

Discussing Main Point and Meaning

1. How does the title convey the argument Wilson and Higgins make? The title deliberately refers to a famous book by President John F. Kennedy, *Profiles in Courage*. Why do you think this title was borrowed for the essay?

2. What two different types of profiling do the writers consider? What arguments do they offer to support both types of profiling?

Examining Sentences, Paragraphs, and Organization

1. The writers begin with a discussion of profiling in policing and then move on to airport security. Where and how do the writers make the transition between the two parts of their argument? How does the organization serve the argument?

2. What do you see as the purpose of paragraph 2? Does this paragraph make the argument more or less persuasive? Explain.

3. Look at paragraph 3. What point do the authors want to make about evidence? How valid is their point?

4. What is the effect of the paraphrase of Peter Schuck in paragraph 8?

Thinking Critically

1. In paragraph 2, Wilson and Higgins discuss crime rates and statistics followed by questions asking whether police should stop men and women, young and old, black and white at the same rates. How do you think the writers would answer these questions? How would you answer them? Defend your response.

2. The writers defend the practice of profiling in policing and argue for it in security searches at airports. Would you support or argue against both practices? Would you argue for profiling in one area but not the other? Explain your answers.

3. Look at the specific example of a random search the writers discuss in paragraph 12. What are they suggesting with this example? What assumptions do they make? Are these assumptions valid?

In-Class Writing Activities

1. Working in small groups, consider the various options for airport security. Think about other procedures in addition to the random searches and searches based on stereotyped screening profiles the writers discuss. What are the potential benefits and drawbacks of each measure?

2. Wilson and Higgins conclude, "Unfortunately, political leaders and civil rights activists have so polarized the discussion of profil-

ing that an entirely defensible screening policy is now regarded as a threat to our fundamental liberties and is replaced by an irrational screening policy that threatens our safety" (para. 16). Write a brief essay in which you weigh the need for liberty against the need for security. Is it possible to balance the two? If so, how? If not, which need should take precedence and why?

ANNIE KIEFHABER

Criminal Profiling: Not as Simple as Black and White

[THE LUMBERJACK ONLINE, NORTHERN ARIZONA UNIVERSITY / January 16, 2002]

Before You Read

What do you think criminal profiling involves? Do you think this process is effective? Recall your reaction to the federal government's warnings to remain on high alert regarding terrorist threats. How did you react? Did you become a criminal profiler of sorts?

Words to Learn

perpetrator (para. 3): a guilty person; someone who has committed a crime (n.)
segregation (para. 9): the act of cutting off from others, especially the practice of separating by races (n.)

RHIANNON "ANNIE" KIEFHABER (b. 1982) attends Northern Arizona University where she is studying journalism and criminal justice. She has worked as a general assignment reporter and events columnist for the Lumberjack.

Though as a society we don't like to admit it, we generally think in a very black and white sort of way. This is especially true when it comes to the criminal justice system, which is why the process of criminal profiling is such an important issue.

How is it fair to create a profile strictly based on a criminal justice system that unfairly represents society? Blacks, for example, make up a smaller portion of society than whites, but encompass a considerably larger portion of those involved with the criminal justice system. Does this simple fact mean blacks commit more crimes or get caught more often? People argue the merits of both theories, but either way, it does not mean it is acceptable to assume a black person is more likely than a white to fit a certain profile.

In many cases, criminal profiling just doesn't work. It's hard to see how it could have been helpful in the recent rape case that occurred on campus. Fortunately, the victim was able to identify the perpetrator as a former Northern Arizona University football player through some evidence that was left behind. But what if she had been unable to do so?

Criminal profiling provokes fear and fuels discrimination.

The criminal profiling process begins after the victim's statement is recorded. According to professional profilers, analysis begins with the rapist's words and behavior as witnessed during the crime. Next, law-enforcement officials try to determine if the rapist's mentality is what they term "unselfish" or "selfish." Officials say this classification gives them a better idea of the suspect's motives and danger level. Generally, FBI profiles also describe what type of person the rapist is believed to be, and whether they are likely to strike again. If at all possible, a basic description of the rapist is determined, including race, height, and age.

Whenever race is involved, there is the possibility of discrimination. In this specific rape case, since the suspect comes from Pago Pago in American Samoa, it seems possible that he could have been misidentified as Native American or Hispanic. Is profiling worth it when a simple mistake such as this creates a profile that can generate unnecessary fear across the campus and in the community, especially when someone fits the description?

A similar fear is prevalent nationally and even globally on a daily basis right now.

The federal government has specifically asked everyone to remain on high alert in case of any terrorist activity or further attacks. But what exactly are we to be "looking out" for? Well, people have obviously become much more cautious toward those with dark features, beards, and other stereotypically Middle Eastern traits. I'm sure many people today are much more aware of whom they sit next to on planes, trains, and buses. But really, none of this awareness has made a drastic improvement in public safety; however, it makes us feel like we are taking control.

In actuality, we have little control though because as we have   8
seen in the past, literally any type of person is capable of just about any type of crime imaginable. Who would have thought that such a caring and seemingly normal woman as Susan Smith could watch as her children sat inside a car headed straight into a lake? Then she said an African American male was the suspect, and instantaneously a search began, raising a certain level of fear, for this fictitious man.

It seems criminal profiling is really just a way for law enforce-   9
ment officials to say they have started a "hunt." While some may defend the practice as the obvious, or only place, to start an investigation, there are definitely more cons than pros involved in that way of thinking. In reality, criminal profiling simply provokes unnecessary fear and fuels further discrimination and segregation.

Vocabulary/Using a Dictionary

1. What is the most suitable synonym for *perpetrator* (para. 3)?

2. Look up the Latin origin of *segregation* (para. 9). How does the origin parallel the definition?

Responding to Words in Context

1. What double meaning does the term "black and white" carry in the title and paragraph 1?

2. The writer uses the term *criminal profiling* rather than *racial profiling* (para. 1). What do you perceive as the difference between the two terms? Explain which term you think is the most effective within the context of the essay.

3. What does *seemingly* (para. 8) mean? What point does the writer make by using this word to describe Susan Smith?

Discussing Main Point and Meaning

1. What problems does Kiefhaber identify with criminal profiling?
2. What examples does Kiefhaber offer to support her argument? What point does she want to make with each example? How effective are these examples?

Examining Sentences, Paragraphs, and Organization

1. Describe the logic behind the order of the essay's specific examples. How effective is the organization?
2. Look at Kiefhaber's use of questions in paragraphs 2, 3, 5, and 7. How effectively does she answer her own questions? Why does she leave some questions unanswered?
3. In paragraph 2, the author claims "People argue the merits of both theories." What two theories is Kiefhaber referring to? What might be the merits of each theory? Kiefhaber goes on to argue that "either way, it does not mean it is acceptable to assume a black person is more likely than a white to fit a certain profile" (para. 2). Has Kiefhaber reached a fair conclusion about one of the theories? Explain.

Thinking Critically

1. In paragraph 4, Kiefhaber discusses the process of criminal profiling. What factors other than race do profilers consider? Are these other factors as problematic as considering race? Why or why not?
2. In discussing the effect of American caution around people of Middle Eastern appearance after September 11, 2001, Kiefhaber concludes, "But really, none of this awareness has made a drastic improvement in public safety; however, it makes us feel like we are taking control. In actuality, we have little control though, because as we have seen in the past, literally any type of person is capable of just about any type of crime imaginable" (paras. 7 and 8). Based on your own observations, explore the validity of this conclusion.
3. Kiefhaber asserts in her conclusion, "While some may defend the practice [of criminal profiling] as the obvious, or only place, to start an investigation, there are definitely more cons

than pros involved in that way of thinking" (para. 9). Has Kiefhaber sufficiently proven this point in the essay? Explain your answer.

In-Class Writing Activities

1. Create a role-playing game in class to test the success of criminal profiling. In groups, have one group construct a crime scenario with a specific criminal in mind. Students in this group should invent a detailed description of the crime as well as the criminal. For the sake of the exercise, choose as the fictitious criminal a well-known celebrity or public figure. Have in mind both a physical and mental description of the person. Another group will work as criminal profilers, trying to develop a profile of the suspect to identify the criminal. This group should consider the nature of the crime and then develop a profile of the suspect based on the description of the crime. Next, the group should ask ten questions to the creators of the criminal to try to correctly identify the suspect. Finally, each group should draft a response summarizing their conclusions on the effectiveness of criminal profiling based on the game. However, keep in mind the limitations of the game and avoid forming overly broad assumptions about actual incidents of criminal profiling.

2. Assume you are a government official who has just received word of a probable terrorist attack from a credible source. Would you decide to put the nation on a state of high alert? If you do decide to put the country on a state of high alert, is there any way you could avoid incidents of racial profiling of citizens of Middle Eastern appearance? Write a brief essay in which you defend your decisions and explain your stance.

AMERICAN CIVIL LIBERTIES UNION

It Happens Every Day
on America's Highways

Before You Read

Are drivers who are African American or Hispanic more likely to be pulled over by police than white drivers? Do police engage in racial and ethnic profiling? Is the "stop and search" process legal?

Web **Read It Now:** Racial Profiling and the Law, **bedfordstmartins.com/ americanow,** Chapter 12. Read the most current legislation, selected articles, and government documents on racial profiling at a page hosted by the U.S. Department of State.

Vocabulary/Using a Dictionary

1. *Civil liberty* is defined as "freedom from arbitrary government interference." What does the word *arbitrary* mean?

2. What is the Latin root of the words *violate* and *violation*?

Responding to Words in Context

1. How is the word *constituted* used in this ad? How is it related to the word *constitution*?

2. What is the difference between *humbling* and *humiliating*? Why does the ACLU choose the word *humiliating*?

Discussing Main Point and Meaning

1. What point does the ACLU want to make with the caption above the photographs and the photographs themselves?

2. What argument does the advertisement make? What evidence does it use to support the argument?

3. What legal argument does the advertisement make?

4. What does the advertisement want viewers to do?

Examining Details, Imagery, and Design

1. Who is the man in the photograph on the left? Who is the man in the photograph on the right? What is the effect of using these two people? What message does the ACLU send with these images? Do you think the positions of left and right were arbitrarily selected?

2. What phrases are in the largest font? Why do you think the advertisers designed the ad this way?

3. The advertisement looks like a "wanted" poster from the Old West. What message does the ACLU send with this choice of design?

Thinking Critically

1. Which do you find more powerful, the images in the advertisement or the statistics in the ad? Explain your answer.

2. Does the ACLU advertisement support its conclusion that "police stop drivers based on their skin color rather than for the way they are driving"? Explain why or why not.

3. What questions would you ask the ACLU about its statistics to determine their credibility?

4. Who do you think is the target audience for this advertisement? Explain your reasoning.

5.   Why do you think the term *racial profiling* does not appear in the advertisement?

In-Class Writing Activities

The Department of Justice defines racial profiling as "any police-initiated action that relies on race, ethnicity, or national origin rather than the behavior of an individual." Assume you are the chief of police in Florida. What can your department do to identify whether racial profiling is a problem in your state? If it does prove to be a problem, what action would you use to prevent racial profiling? Answer in the form of a freewrite.

RANDALL KENNEDY

Blind Spot

[THE ATLANTIC MONTHLY / April 2002]

Before You Read

How would you define racial profiling and affirmative action? Do you see any significant similarities and differences between the two practices?

RANDALL KENNEDY *(b. 1954) is a professor at Harvard Law School, where he teaches courses on freedom of expression and the regulation of race relations. He was awarded the 1998 Robert F. Kennedy Book Award for* Race, Crime, and the Law *(1998). His most recent publication is* Nigger: The Strange Career of a Troublesome Word *(2002), and his forth-coming* Interracial Intimacies: Sex, Marriage, Identity, and Adoption *will be published in 2003.*

Words to Learn

obfuscates (para. 2): confuses (v.)

foiling (para. 2): preventing from obtaining an end; defeating (v.)

unassailable (para. 4): not liable to doubt, attack, or questioning (adj.)

presumptively (para. 4): by reasonable assumption (adv.)

illicit (para. 4): not permitted; unlawful (adj.)

communal (para. 5): of or relating to a commune or community (adj.)

purported (para. 5): conveyed or implied meaning (adj.)

contending (para. 6): striving; struggling; antagonistic (adj.)

What is one to think about "racial profiling"? Confusion abounds about what the term even means. It should be defined as the policy or practice of using race as a factor in selecting whom to place under special surveillance: If police officers at an airport decide to search Passenger A because he is twenty-five to forty years old, bought a first-class ticket with cash, is flying cross-country, and is apparently of Arab ancestry, Passenger A has been subjected to racial profiling. But officials often prefer to define racial profiling as being based *solely* on race; and in doing so they are often seeking to preserve their authority to act against a person *partly* on the basis of race. Civil rights activists, too, often define racial profiling as solely race-based; but their aim is to arouse their followers and to portray law-enforcement officials in as menacing a light as possible. 1

The problem with defining racial profiling in the narrow manner of these strange bedfellows is that doing so obfuscates the real issue confronting Americans. Exceedingly few police officers, airport screeners, or other authorities charged with the task of foiling or apprehending criminals act solely on the basis of race. Many, however, act on the basis of intuition, using race along with other indicators (sex, age, patterns of past conduct) as a guide. The difficult question, then, is not whether the authorities ought to be allowed to act against individuals on the basis of race alone; almost everyone would disapprove of that. The difficult question is whether they ought to be allowed to use race *at all* in schemes of surveillance. If, indeed, it is used, the action amounts to racial discrimination. The extent of the discrimination may be relatively small when race is only one factor among many, but even a little racial discrimination should require lots of justification. 2

The key argument in favor of racial profiling, essentially, is that taking race into account enables the authorities to screen carefully and at less expense those sectors of the population that are more likely than others to contain the criminals for whom officials are searching. Proponents of this theory stress that resources for surveillance are scarce, that the dangers to be avoided are grave, and that reducing these dangers helps everyone — including, sometimes especially, those in the groups subjected to special scrutiny. Proponents also assert that it makes good sense to consider whiteness if the search is for Ku Klux Klan assassins, blackness if the search is for drug couriers in certain locales, and Arab nationality or ethnicity if the search is for agents of al Qaeda.

Some commentators embrace this position as if it were unassailable, but under U.S. law racial discrimination backed by state power is presumptively illicit. This means that supporters of racial profiling carry a heavy burden of persuasion. Opponents rightly argue, however, that not much rigorous empirical proof supports the idea of racial profiling as an effective tool of law enforcement. Opponents rightly contend, also, that alternatives to racial profiling have not been much studied or pursued. Stressing that racial profiling generates clear harm (for example, the fear, resentment, and alienation felt by innocent people in the profiled group), opponents of racial profiling sensibly question whether compromising our hard-earned principle of anti-discrimination is worth merely speculative gains in overall security.

> *Even a little racial discrimination should require lots of justification.*

A notable feature of this conflict is that champions of each position frequently embrace rhetoric, attitudes, and value systems that are completely at odds with those they adopt when confronting another controversial instance of racial discrimination — namely, affirmative action. Vocal supporters of racial profiling who trumpet the urgency of communal needs when discussing law enforcement all of a sudden become fanatical individualists when condemning affirmative action in college admissions and the labor market. Supporters of profiling, who are willing to impose what amounts to a racial tax on profiled groups, denounce as betrayals of "color blindness" programs that require racial diversity. A similar turnabout can be seen on the part of many of those who support affirmative action. Impatient with talk of communal needs in assessing racial profiling, they very often have no difficulty with subordinating the interests of individual white candidates to the purported good of the whole. Opposed to race consciousness in policing, they demand race consciousness in deciding whom to admit to college or select for a job.

The racial-profiling controversy — like the conflict over affirmative action — will not end soon. For one thing, in both cases many of the contestants are animated by decent but contending sentiments. Although exasperating, this is actually good for our society; and it would be even better if participants in the debates acknowledged the simple truth that their adversaries have something useful to say.   6

Web **Read It Now:** Racial Profiling Debate, **bedfordstmartins.com/americanow,** Chapter 12. Read a range of opinions on racial profiling from the archives of *The Atlantic Monthly,* the magazine that published Randall Kennedy's essay.

___

Vocabulary/Using a Dictionary

1. Look up the word *courier* (para. 3) in the dictionary. Does the definition fit with the author's use of the term? Why or why not?

2. Look up the definition of *empirical* (para. 4) in the dictionary. What does the definition tell you about what kind of evidence Kennedy expects proponents of racial profiling to provide?

3. What is another definition for the verb *compromising* (para. 4) other than "exposing to suspicion or loss of reputation"? How do the connotations of the two different definitions compare? Now look up *compromise* as a noun. How does the noun allow for the two different definitions of the verb?

4. Use the dictionary to define *speculative* (para. 4). Based on this definition, explain what Kennedy means by "speculative gains in overall security."

5. Look up the dictionary definition of *rhetoric* (para. 5). Do you think Kennedy uses the word the same way as the dictionary? Explain your answer.

Responding to Words in Context

1. How does Kennedy define *racial profiling* (para. 1)? How reasonable do you find this definition?

2. The author writes, "The problem with defining racial profiling in the narrow manner of these strange bedfellows is that doing so

obfuscates the real issue confronting Americans" (para. 2). Define *strange bedfellows,* using a dictionary if you need to. Who is Kennedy referring to here? What point is he making?

3. How does Kennedy define *affirmative action* (para. 5)? Do you agree with his definition? Why or why not? How do you think a supporter of affirmative action might define the term?

4. What do you think Kennedy means by *racial tax* when he writes, "Supporters of profiling . . . are willing to impose what amounts to a racial tax on profiled groups" (para. 5)? What point is he trying to make?

Discussing Main Point and Meaning

1. Look at the title of the article. How does it reflect the author's purpose and argument?

2. According to the essay, what reasons do proponents of racial profiling offer in defense of their stance? Why would they argue against affirmative action?

3. According to the essay, what reasons do opponents of racial profiling offer in defense of their stance? Why would they argue in support of affirmative action?

4. What do you think Kennedy's stances on racial profiling and affirmative action are? Explain your answer using textual support.

Examining Sentences, Paragraphs, and Organization

1. Explain the organizational structure of the essay. How effective is it in fulfilling Kennedy's purpose?

2. In paragraph 1, Kennedy offers two different definitions of racial profiling — one from officials and the other from civil rights activists. How are the definitions similar? How do they serve different agendas?

3. In paragraph 2, Kennedy rejects the idea that racial profiling is based solely on race. Why? He ends the paragraph by defining the real question at issue. What is really of concern when analyzing racial profiling, according to the writer? How accurately do you think he has identified the difficult question?

4. What does Kennedy mean when he argues "under U.S. law racial discrimination backed by state power is presumptively illicit" (para. 4)?

5. Look at the conclusion of the essay. How does this last paragraph explain Kennedy's purpose in comparing racial profiling to affirmative action in paragraph 5?

Thinking Critically

1. How fairly do you think Kennedy represents the argument for racial profiling in paragraph 3? Do you find these reasons persuasive? Why or why not?

2. In paragraph 4, is Kennedy's tone neutral or does he favor the argument against racial profiling? Explain your answering using evidence from this paragraph. How persuasive do you find the argument against racial profiling?

3. How legitimate do you find Kennedy's comparison between racial profiling and affirmative action in paragraph 5?

In-Class Writing Activities

1. Which of the following best describes your position on racial profiling and affirmative action:

   a. *For* racial profiling but *against* affirmative action

   b. *Against* racial profiling but *for* affirmative action

   c. *Against* both racial profiling and affirmative action

   d. *For* both racial profiling and affirmative action

   Freewrite the reasons for your position. Compare your position to that of Kennedy.

2. Kennedy ends his essay by pointing out that "in both cases many of the contestants are animated by decent but contending sentiments" (para. 6). He encourages both sides on the issues of racial profiling and affirmative action to acknowledge "the simple truth that their adversaries have something useful to say." What do you think are some of the "decent but contending sentiments"?

Discussing the Unit

Suggested Topic for Discussion

What different forms can law enforcement and security profiles take? Is profiling inherently racist? If it does involve race, is it ever justified? How effective is profiling in preventing or solving crime? What different forms has profiling taken after September 11, 2001?

Preparing for Class Discussion

1. All the writers in this unit, whether explicitly or implicitly, define profiling. Articulate the definition of profiling according to each piece in this unit. Explain which definition you find to be most effective. If you find none of the definitions satisfactory, come up with one of your own.

2. Both James Wilson and Heather Higgins in "Profiles in Courage" and Annie Kiefhaber in "Criminal Profiling: Not as Simple as Black and White" begin with examples of police profiling and then move on to profiling in response to the September 11 terrorist attacks. Are the writers' initial views on profiling at all changed by the events of September 11? Have your own? What kind of conversation do you imagine Wilson and Higgins would have with Kiefhaber over security issues and profiling after September 11?

3. All the writers in discussing profiling address the issues of effectiveness in preventing or solving crime or civil liberties. Based on the merits of their respective arguments, to what degree do you think profiling is an effective law enforcement tool? To what degree do you think it is a violation of civil liberties?

From Discussion to Writing

1. Write a dialogue about two key issues: racial profiling and affirmative action. Have Kennedy serve as the moderator of the discussion trying to get opposing sides to see the merit in the other's argument. The debate should occur between Wilson and Higgins and a lawyer from the ACLU. We know from their respective

pieces that Wilson and Higgins defend profiling whereas the ACLU does not. The ACLU also supports affirmative action. For the sake of this exercise, assume that Wilson and Higgins oppose affirmative action. Use textual support from the essays and the ad to help you create the dialogue.

2. Write an essay in which you focus on one form of profiling (FBI profiling, racial profiling, screening profiles at airports, or terrorist warnings that may result in citizens profiling). Defend or argue against this form of profiling. Also, respond to opposing views. Would you make a distinction between racial and ethnic profiling? Use the texts in this unit to help you develop your argument.

3. Assume you are the Director of Homeland Security and it is your job to protect the nation from terrorist attacks. At the same time, you must also protect the civil liberties of individuals. Design a proposal in which you attempt to do both at once. Your proposal should cover only one specific issue. Here are examples of issues you could write on:

    • Alerting the public of terrorist threats

    • Improving searches of passengers at airports

    • Interrogating suspects

    • Scrutinizing suspects under surveillance

    • Requiring national identity cards for everyone in the United States

Topics for Cross-Cultural Discussion

1. Describe law enforcement techniques in a country other than the U.S. What problems, if any, do citizens have with the police? Is racial profiling an issue in this country? Do problems seem to occur in specific regions of the country, or are they widespread? How does the justice system in this country shape law enforcement?

2. Describe the security measures in an airport outside of the U.S. either prior to or after September 11, 2001. How stringent is the security compared to pre- and post-September 11 America? How effective do you think the security is in protecting the safety of air travel? Do you see any infringement of civil liberties in these methods?

13

Do Animals Possess Rights?

Many groups and prominent individuals believe that we must stop using animals in scientific and medical research. Some groups take more extreme positions than others, but by and large nearly all agree that human beings bear a moral responsibility to animals. But does that responsibility mean that rats and chimpanzees should never under any circumstances be used in medical experimentation? Or that no animal should live in captivity either on farms, in zoos, or even as domestic pets? Does it mean that people should refrain from wearing leather and fur, and from eating beef, fish, pork, or fowl? Where do we draw the line? Do animals, for example, possess constitutional rights? In this unit we examine a spectrum of opinions concerning animal experimentation and the rights of animals in general.

In "A Question of Ethics," the author and animal activist Jane Goodall succinctly describes the "fuzzy" distinction between humans and chimpanzees, and maintains that we need to question the "assumption that animals are essential to medical research." This commonly held assumption is regularly attacked by two leading groups that hope to end animal experimentation, the Student Organization for Animal Rights (SOAR) and In Defense of Animals (IDA). As their advertisement indicates, these groups often join forces on college campuses, such as the University of Minnesota, where they take an active role in working to abolish primate experimentation. Their views do not go unopposed, however, as groups such as Americans for Medical Progress (AMP) are also busy producing advertisements arguing that primate research is "absolutely essential to progress on diseases that still plague and threaten our society." At the University of Utah, Kristien Hixson encounters the SOAR people but isn't persuaded. "Comparing the worth of a human being to a Drosophila fly is demeaning and a disgrace to the intelligence of mankind," she writes in "A SOARing Insult to Science."

If animals are granted legal rights, will that put an end to animal research and our control over animals in general? If cattle are granted legal rights will the hamburger become a dim memory? The final selection raises the stakes of the issue as it examines the possibility of moving from ethical to legal considerations. In "Why Animals Deserve Legal Rights," Steven M. Wise wonders, "What accounts for the legal personhood of all of us and the legal thinghood of all of them?" As we learn more about the intelligence and emotions of animals — especially primates — we now "know that they have what it takes for basic legal rights. The next step," he concludes, "is obvious."

JANE GOODALL

A Question of Ethics

[NEWSWEEK INTERNATIONAL / May 7, 2001]

Before You Read

Should we use animals to advance medical technologies for humans? Are animals — especially primates — more like us than we want to admit?

JANE GOODALL (b. 1934) has spent more than three decades studying the behavior of wild chimpanzees. Her work has resulted in a wealth of writings, books, and awards. Her most recent publications include Reason For Hope: A Spiritual Journey (1999) and a children's book, The Chimpanzees I Love (2001). In recent years, Goodall has become a spokesperson for the humane treatment of captive primates.

Words to Learn
sentient (para. 3): conscious; responsive (adj.)
systemic (para. 4): general; universal (adj.)

David Greybeard first showed me how fuzzy the distinction between animals and humans can be. Forty years ago I befriended David, a chimpanzee, during my first field trip to Gombe in Tanzania. One day I offered him a nut in my open palm. He looked directly into my eyes, took the nut out of my hand, and dropped it. At the same moment he very gently squeezed my hand as if to say, I don't want it, but I understand your motives.

1

Since chimpanzees are thought to be physiologically close to humans, researchers use them as test subjects for new drugs and vaccines. In the labs, these very sociable creatures often live isolated from one another in 5-by-5-foot cages, where they grow surly and sometimes violent. Dogs, cats, and rats are also kept in poor conditions and subjected to painful procedures. Many people would find it hard to sympathize with rats, but dogs and cats are part of our lives. Ten or fifteen years ago, when the use of animals in medical testing was first brought to my attention, I decided to visit the labs myself. Many people working there had forced themselves to believe that animal testing is the only way forward for medical research.

2

> *Once we accept that animals are sentient beings, is it ethical to use them in research?*

Once we accept that animals are sentient beings, is it ethical to use them in research? From the point of view of the animals, it is quite simply wrong. From our standpoint, it seems ridiculous to equate a rat with a human being. If we clearly and honestly believe that using animals in research will, in the end, reduce massive human suffering, it would be difficult to argue that doing so is unethical. How do we find a way out of this dilemma?

3

One thing we can do is change our mind-set. We can begin by questioning the assumption that animals are essential to medical research. Scientists have concluded that chimpanzees are not useful for AIDS research because, even though their genetic makeup differs from ours by about 1 percent, their immune systems deal much differently with the AIDS virus. Many scientists test drugs and vaccines on animals simply because they are required to by law rather than out of scientific merit. This is a shame, because our medical technology is beginning to provide alternatives. We can perform many tests on cell and

4

tissue cultures without recourse to systemic testing on animals. Computer simulations can also cut down on the number of animal tests we need to run. We aren't exploring these alternatives vigorously enough.

Ten or fifteen years ago animal rights activists resorted to violence against humans in their efforts to break through the public's terrible apathy and lack of imagination on this issue. This extremism is counterproductive. I believe that more and more people are becoming aware that to use animals thoughtlessly, without any anguish or making an effort to find another way, diminishes us as human beings.   5

Web **Read It Now:** U.S. Policy on Animal Research, **bedfordstmartins.com/ americanow**, Chapter 13. Read the report that lays out the government's policy on animal testing, published by the Office of Laboratory Animal Welfare at the National Institutes of Health. You will also find the latest government reports and legislation and alternatives to animal testing.

Vocabulary/Using a Dictionary

1. How do you think the words *systemic* (para. 4) and *system* are related?

2. Use *apathy* (para. 5) or its adjective form, *apathetic,* in a sentence of your own.

Responding to Words in Context

1. Comment on Goodall's use of the word *fuzzy* in paragraph 1.

2. "Many people working there had forced themselves to believe that animal testing is the only way forward for medical research" (para. 2), Goodall writes. Examine the phrase, "forced themselves to believe." Does Goodall really know how these people come to believe what they believe? Or is her point more subjective?

Discussing Main Point and Meaning

1. What is surprising to Goodall about David Greybeard's refusal of the nut she offered him (para. 1)?

2. Describe what happens to the social skills of animals confined and isolated in small cages. Do you think humans would behave the same way?

3. "We can begin by questioning the assumption that animals are essential to medical research" (para. 4), Goodall says. How does she begin to do this questioning in the sentences that follow?

4. Why did some animal rights activists turn to violence to protest animal testing?

Examining Sentences, Paragraphs, and Organization

1. Reread Goodall's introductory paragraph. Why does she introduce David Greybeard by name before revealing his species? What is the purpose of including the anecdote about the nut?

2. Goodall concludes, "I believe that more and more people are becoming aware that to use animals thoughtlessly, without any anguish or making an effort to find another way, diminishes us as human beings." Describe the tone in this sentence. Do you find this conclusion upbeat or critical? Why does Goodall end her essay this way?

3. This essay combines an abstract philosophical argument with concrete descriptions and illustrations. Is there enough of each? Does one outweigh the other?

Thinking Critically

1. Goodall argues that we should question "our assumption that animals are essential to medical research" (para. 4) by citing the failure of using chimpanzees for AIDS research. Is this enough evidence for you to be persuaded of her point?

2. Some argue that animals have also benefited medically from animal testing, as human medicine often informs veterinary medicine. Does this make animal testing any more ethical?

In-Class Writing Activities

1. What is your position regarding animal testing in medical research? Do you think it's all bad? All good? Is it acceptable to use animals for research on the most serious illnesses but not for the less serious? Or would you draw the line somewhere in between systemic testing (even if the animals must be killed in the process) and no testing at all? Write a short essay in answer to these questions.

2. In what ways are animals like humans? How are humans like animals? Brainstorm a list of the similarities and differences you observe in animal and human behavior. Are the similarities more significant than the differences, or vice versa? Discuss your results.

OPPOSING VIEWS

Should Animals Be Used for Research?

STUDENT ORGANIZATION FOR ANIMAL RIGHTS (SOAR)
There is No Excuse . . . for Animal Abuse

AMERICANS FOR MEDICAL PROGRESS (AMP)
Primates in Research: A Record of Medical Progress

KRISTIEN McDONALD
A SOARing Insult to Science

Before You Read
Do research universities play a role in animal cruelty or are they improving the lives of humans with cutting edge experiments? Do you know of any animal research going on at your school?

Words to Learn [SOAR advertisement]
primate: a member of the order of Primates, which includes humans, apes, monkeys, and related mammals (such as lemurs and tarsiers) (n.)

Words to Learn [AMP advertisement]
hepatitis: an inflammation of the liver, caused by infectious or noxious agents (n.)
immunosuppressive: tending to suppress a natural immune system response of an organism (adj.)
arteriosclerosis: chronic disease in which thickening or hardening of the arterial walls interferes with blood circulation (n.)
congenital: existing at birth but not hereditary (adj.)

rhesus macaque: brown, short-tailed monkey species from India, used frequently in biological experimentation (n.)

SIV: Simian Immunodeficiency Virus; the monkey form of AIDS

sickle cell anemia: a chronic disease found primarily in African Americans, characterized by oxygen-deficient red blood cells (n.)

endometriosis: painful thickening of the uterine lining that can cause infertility (n.)

Lyme disease: a disease carried and transferred by deer ticks that is characterized by joint pain, fatigue, and mental confusion; It is especially harmful to children and the elderly

retina: delicate, light-sensitive lining of the inner eyeball (n.)

Words to Learn [McDonald]

demographic (para. 5): of or related to the statistical study of human populations (adj.)

ephemeral (para. 6): lasting briefly; short-lived (adj.)

STUDENT ORGANIZATION
FOR ANIMAL RIGHTS (SOAR)

[THE MINNESOTA DAILY, UNIVERSITY OF MINNESOTA / 2002]

If you have information or documentation regarding experimentation or other animal abuse
occuring on campus call 415-388-9641 or 612-624-0422.

Web **See It Now:** Ads against Animal Testing, **bedfordstmartins.com/americanow,**
Chapter 13. See additional opinion ads posted by the Student Organization
for Animal Rights (SOAR).

AMERICANS FOR MEDICAL PROGRESS [2002]

Primates in Research:
A Record of Medical Progress

Of laboratory animals used in medical research, only about one third of one percent are nonhuman primates. Nevertheless, primate research has, and will continue to be, absolutely essential to progress on diseases that still plague and threaten our society, such as Alzheimer's disease, drug addiction, cancer, cardiovascular disease and AIDS.

One illustration of the importance of primates to medical research is that polio has been eliminated in the Western Hemisphere. We are on the verge of eradicating the disease worldwide. Should we discontinue using monkeys in the development and testing of the vaccine, polio will return, killing and paralyzing thousands of children.

Among other numerous medical advances, nonhuman primate research has enabled scientists to:

☆ develop vaccines against **rubella** and **hepatitis B.**

☆ identify an immunosuppressive virus in monkey that is a model for understanding the mechanisms of **HIV** infection and disease in humans.

☆ demonstrate the influence of psychological and social phenomena and stress on the development of **arteriosclerosis**.

☆ clone and sequence a monkey version of a newly identified human herpesvirus that seems to be a co-factor in causing **Kaposi's sarcoma**, which causes skin lesions and organ tumors in many **AIDS** patients.

☆ contribute to an understanding of the development of the visual system in the brain that has permitted therapies to prevent **vision loss** due to congenital eye defects.

☆ demonstrate in the female rhesus macaque SIV model that it is possible to develop a vaccine to prevent heterosexual transmission of **HIV** by induction of an immune response in the genital tract.

☆ discover that **herpes** viruses can cause **leukemia** and identify viral genes necessary to initiate disease.

☆ provide the first data leading to the use of hydroxyurea for the treatment of **sickle cell anemia**.

☆ develop and characterize a nonhuman primate model for **inflammatory bowel disease** and **colon cancer.**

☆   help explain how the brain's release of growth hormone signals the pituitary gland to secrete hormones that regulate the ovary—knowledge that is being used to treat **infertility, endometriosis** and **prostate cancer.**

☆   devise new drugs and novel imaging techniques for the diagnosis and assessment of therapy for **Parkinson's disease.**

☆   establish a rhesus monkey model for *in vitro* **fertilization-embryo transfer** (IVF-ET) research that facilitates efforts to improve the human IVF-ET **pregnancy** rates, explore new approaches to **contraception**, and study early development of the embryo.

☆   perfect methods and therapies for **organ transplants.**

☆   discover new drugs that reduce **cholesterol** levels.

☆   develop procedures to study factors that control the beginning of labor—a study that may help prevent **premature birth.**

☆   develop a vaccine against one of the primary causes of **periodontal disease**, a condition that causes tooth loss and gum erosion in more than 500,000 Americans each year.

☆   discover the potential of gene therapy for long-term delivery of therapeutic agents to combat the effects of **Alzheimer's** and the neurodegenerative diseases.

☆   develop a rhesus monkey model of **Lyme disease.**

☆   establish the efficacy and safety of synthetic peptide surfactants in the premature rhesus monkey model for the treatment of newborns with **respiratory distress syndrome.**

☆   develop and test the efficacy of oral **birth control** medication.

☆   explore the color circuitry of the macaque retina, which is virtually identical to that in humans, and obtain a number of clues to the cause of **retinal diseases.**

For more information on animal research, contact:

AMP
AMERICANS FOR MEDICAL PROGRESS

908 King Street ● Suite 201 ● Alexandria, VA 22314-3067 ● Phone (703) 836-9595 ● Fax (703) 836-9594
● E-mail AMP@AMProgress.org ● http://www.AMProgress.org

Web Read It Now: Are Animals Necessary to Medical Research? **bedford stmartins.com/americanow**, Chapter 13. Read reports, articles, fact sheets, and surveys by the Americans for Medical Progress.

KRISTIEN McDONALD

A SOARing Insult to Science

[THE DAILY UTAH CHRONICLE, THE UNIVERSITY OF UTAH / April 19, 2001]

How much do you like those nice leather Doc Marten sandals? How important is your violin bow to you, or perhaps your mink coat? I suppose we could all get by without the furs and fancy accessories, but I wonder how important your mother is to you, or a sibling, or even a child.

1

I find it annoying that members of the Student Organization for Animal Rights (SOAR) take advantage of the benefits of animal experimentation while protesting that scientists bash bunnies upside their heads with clubs. I find it annoying that there truly are people out there who have a problem with developing a vaccine for otherwise devastating sicknesses. I find it annoying that there are people out there who have a problem with granting a small child life because it may be at the expense of an earthworm.

2

However, I thought it worth fifty minutes of my life to enlighten my mind a bit with the stimulating views of these social activists. I found that the experience stimulated my appetite far more than it did my intellect. In the end, I don't view such an idea as the ethical comparison of a human baby to swine very appealing or worthy of my signature on their petition.

3

A compelling theme of the activists' defense was that every animal used for experimentation on campus can feel pain and that no scientist has the supreme right to inflict such pain on a creature that can experience it. I work in a radiobiology lab in Research Park, and the procedures we perform on our lab rats are far from painful. We study the effects of pregnancy and lactation on their bones and not once from the day they're born to the day they die do we inflict any form of pain upon them. Yet, every time we have to endure an inspection, we are reprimanded by an inspector who has never performed a lab experiment for not "de-gassing" a rat's lungs after

4

Kristien McDonald *is an opinion columnist at the* Daily Utah Chronicle *at the University of Utah.*

putting it under anesthesia or giving it aspirin through a stomach tube when it "appears" to be in pain. You tell me how to de-gas a rat's lung and perhaps we can work something out.

I found it fairly amusing to hear a group of humanities students explain to me their ideologies concerning the advancement of research and how if scientists would simply abandon tests on animals, far better, kinder, and effective alternatives would just show up spontaneously. They tried to convince me that alternatives such as cell and organ cultures and population studies were sufficient for scientific study. Who wants to be the first to try a drug that has been approved by a chart of demographic statistics? Don't be afraid — it's just a drug.

Or we could just do the research on dead human bodies. We'll disregard the fact there could not possibly be enough available cadavers to supplement the constant demands of science. Perhaps it's not such a terrible idea to dig Grandma's bones back up — just try not to disturb the ephemeral glory of the pill bugs underneath.

Animal experimentation is not prejudice; it is progress.

Unfortunately, as members of SOAR imply, it is not merely social or economic distress that causes medical problems. It is not simply due to increased stress or poor health habits that the human population is stricken with lung cancer. Why not try telling that to a five-year-old with leukemia. "Well, if you had just listened to your father and not swallowed your dinner so fast, this might not have happened." Many medical conditions are strictly just that — medical conditions. Some are purely genetic, and the only way to study preventive means is through animal experimentation.

I don't buy the idea that all animals are the "cousins" of humanity as SOAR tries to persuade us to believe. Comparing the worth of a human being to a Drosophila fly is demeaning and a disgrace to the intelligence of mankind. A leader of SOAR claims that it is arrogant of scientists and researchers like me to exercise prejudice against a creature because it is weaker and more helpless.

Animal experimentation is not prejudice; it's progress.

Perhaps the most radical idea proposed by SOAR is that if research were performed on rats for the benefit of rats, then it would be ethically acceptable. I suppose that after we discover a cure for AIDS, lung cancer, heart disease, multiple sclerosis, and arthritis (and all through studying only cell cultures, mind you), it might not be such a bad idea to research how to increase the life span of a rat from two years to three.

But maybe they have a point here. Lab rats shouldn't be forced to   11
be "martyrs" for the human race. So perhaps on your way to lunch
you could volunteer yourself for cancer research.

Vocabulary/Using a Dictionary

1. Why do you think the SOAR ad ("There Is No Excuse") uses the word *primates* in the headline rather than *monkeys?*

2. What more familiar word can you see in *arteriosclerosis* ("Primates in Research")? Do you have any idea what *multiple sclerosis* might be? Look it up in the dictionary if you need to, and find out what *arteriosclerosis* and *multiple sclerosis* have in common.

3. Use *ephemeral* in a sentence (McDonald, para. 6).

Responding to Words in Context

1. Why do you think SOAR chose to use only two sentences in this ad? What is the effect of the rhyme (in sentence two)?

2. Note the use of the starred list in the Americans for Medical Progress advertisement (page 305, para. 3). Each word that begins a starred item is an active verb. How does the quality of these verbs — such as *contribute* and *discover* — work to persuade the reader? Do these word choices affect your reading of the ad? Your opinion of AMP's perspective?

3. Identify in the McDonald essay (page 307) each word or phrase that might be termed hyperbolic, humorous, or sarcastic. How do these words and phrases contribute to the essay's overall tone? How do they affect the essay's persuasiveness?

Discussing Main Point and Meaning

1. Does the SOAR ad ask the reader to take specific action?

2. The Americans for Medical Progress ad says that "one-third of one percent" of animals used in laboratory research are primates (para. 1). Why do they use such a specific number here? What point is this statistic meant to convey?

3. What kind of research is the lab McDonald works at involved in?

4. What is McDonald's problem with "humanities students" (para. 5)?

5. Describe the general tone of McDonald's editorial. How would you characterize her voice? Is the tone appropriate to the subject matter?

Examining Details, Imagery, and Design

1. What is the purpose and the intended audience of the SOAR ad? Examine the picture featured; describe the effect it has on you. Is the image an effective tool given SOAR's purpose and audience?

2. What audience is the AMP trying to persuade through the ad "Primates in Research"? Identify all words that you think were chosen specifically to persuade the reader.

3. The SOAR ad refers to "primate experimentation" while the AMP ad refers to "primates in research". What do these word choices tell you about the views of these organizations?

4. The phrase "I find it annoying" appears three times in paragraph 2 of Kristien McDonald's article. Why does she use repetition here?

Thinking Critically

1. Aside from an image of an animal in a lab, SOAR chooses to provide no evidence or argument to support their stance against animal experimentation. Compare this approach to that of the AMP. As a persuasive strategy, is an appeal to emotion as effective as a supported argument? Why or why not?

2. McDonald suggests that there are "people out there who have a problem with granting a small child life because it may be at the expense of an earthworm" (para. 2). Do you think this is an exaggeration? If it is, why is it used?

In-Class Writing Activities

1. In small groups, design two ads of your own — one that represents that pro-animal research position and one that represents the opposition to animal testing. Describe the graphics, layout, and slogans you would use and draw up sketches to present to the class.

2. Rewrite McDonald's essay with a different tone of voice, as if her goal were to educate people with no knowledge of this issue rather than to criticize those who disagree. Be sure to touch on all of the same substance, but make changes to word choice, voice, and overall perspective.

STEVEN M. WISE

Why Animals Deserve Legal Rights

[THE CHRONICLE OF HIGHER EDUCATION / February 2, 2001]

Before You Read

How rational is our legal definition of *personhood*? Why aren't animals more recognized by our legal system? Do you think animals should have rights?

Words to Learn

theologian (para. 3): one who studies religion and spirituality (n.)
canon law (para. 3): religious principles or rules (n.)
proffer (para. 4): hold out; extend (v.)
inference (para. 7): assumption; conclusion (n.)

drub (para. 10): thrash; defeat (v.)
Machiavellian (para. 11): like or pertaining to the crafty and duplicitous political principles and methods of Niccolò Machiavelli; deceitful; cunning (adj.)
alpha male (para. 11): dominant male in a group or pack (n.)

For centuries, the right to have everything that makes existence worthwhile — like freedom, safety from torture, and even life itself— has turned on whether the law classifies one as a person or a thing. Although some Jews once belonged to Pharaoh, Syrians to Nero, and African Americans to George Washington, now every human is a person in the eyes of the law. 1

All nonhuman animals, on the other hand, are things with no rights. The law ignores them unless a person decides to do something to them, and then, in most cases, nothing can be done to help them. According to statistics collected annually by the Department of Agriculture, in the United States this year, tens of millions of animals are 2

Steven M. Wise (b. 1950) has been an animal rights lawyer for over twenty years. He is the author of Rattling the Cage: Toward Legal Rights for Animals *(2000) and* Drawing the Line: Science and the Case for Animal Rights *(2002).*

likely to be killed, sometimes painfully, during biomedical research; 10 billion more will be raised in factories so crowded that they're unable to turn around, and then killed for food. The U.S. Fish and Wildlife Service and allied state agencies report that hundreds of millions will be shot by hunters or exploited in rodeos, circuses, and roadside zoos. And all of that is perfectly legal.

What accounts for the legal personhood of all of us and the legal thinghood of all of them? Judeo-Christian theologians sometimes argue that humans are made in the image of God. But that argument has been leaking since Gratian, the twelfth-century Benedictine monk who is considered the father of canon law, made the same claim just for men in his *Decretum*. Few, if any, philosophers or judges today would argue that being human, all by itself, is sufficient for legal rights. There must be something about us that entitles us to rights.

Philosophers have proffered many criteria as sufficient, including sentience, a sense of justice, the possession of language or morality, and having a rational plan for one's life. Among legal thinkers, the most important is autonomy, also known as self-determination or volition. Things don't act autonomously. Persons do.

Evidence has been accumulating that at least some nonhuman animals have extraordinary minds.

Notice that I said that autonomy is "sufficient" for basic legal rights; it obviously isn't necessary. We don't eat or vivisect human babies born without brains, who are so lacking in sentience that they are operated on without anesthesia.

But autonomy is tough to define. Kant thought that autonomous beings always act rationally. Anyone who can't do that can justly be treated as a thing. Kant must have had extraordinary friends and relatives. Not being a fulltime academic, I don't know anyone who always acts rationally.

Most philosophers, and just about every judge, reject Kant's rigorous conception of autonomy, for they can easily imagine a human who lacks it, but can still walk about making decisions. Instead, some of them think that a being can be autonomous — at least to some degree — if she has preferences and the ability to act to satisfy them. Others would say she is autonomous if she can cope with changed circumstances. Still others, if she can make choices, even if she can't evaluate their merits very well. Or if she has desires and beliefs and can make at least some sound and appropriate inferences from them.

As things, nonhuman animals have been invisible to civil law   8
since its inception. "All law," said the Roman jurist Hermogenianus,
"was established for men's sake." And why not? Everything else was.

Unfortunately for animals, many people have believed that they   9
were put on earth for human use and lack autonomy. Aristotle
granted them a few mental abilities: They could perceive and act on
impulse. Many Stoics, however, denied them the capacities to perceive, conceive, reason, remember, believe, even experience. Animals
knew nothing of the past and could not imagine a future. Nor could
they desire, know good, or learn from experience.

For decades, though, evidence has been accumulating that at   10
least some nonhuman animals have extraordinary minds. Twelve
years ago, seven-year-old Kanzi—a bonobo who works with Sue
Savage-Rumbaugh, a biologist at Georgia State University—drub-
bed a human two-year-old, named Alia, in a series of language-
comprehension tests. In the tests, both human and bonobo had to
struggle, as we all do, with trying to make sense of the mind of a
speaker. When Kanzi was asked to "put some water on the vacuum
cleaner," he gulped water from a glass, marched to the vacuum
cleaner, and dribbled the water over it. Told to "feed your ball some
tomato," he could see no ball before him. So he picked up a spongy
toy Halloween pumpkin and pretended to shove a tomato into its
mouth. When asked to go to the refrigerator and get an orange,
Kanzi immediately complied; Alia didn't have a clue what to do.

In the forty years since Jane Goodall arrived at Gombe, she and   11
others have shown that apes have most, if not all, of the emotions
that we do. They are probably self-conscious; many of them can recognize themselves in a mirror. They use insight, not just trial and
error, to solve problems. They form complex mental representations,
including mental maps of the area where they live. They understand
cause and effect. They act intentionally. They compare objects, and
relationships between objects. They count. They use tools—they
even make tools. Given the appropriate opportunity and motivation,
they have been known to teach, deceive, and empathize with others.
They can figure out what others see and know, abilities that human
children don't develop until the ages of three to five. They create cultural traditions that they pass on to their descendants. They flourish
in rough-and-tumble societies so intensely political that they have
been dubbed Machiavellian, and in which they form coalitions to
limit the power of alpha males.

Twenty-first-century law should be based on twenty-first- 12
century knowledge. Once the law assumed that witches existed and
that mute people lacked intelligence. Now it is illegal to burn
someone for witchcraft, and the mute have the same rights as anyone else.

Today we know that apes, and perhaps other nonhuman ani- 13
mals, are not what we thought they were in the pre-scientific age
when the law declared them things. Now we know that they have
what it takes for basic legal rights. The next step is obvious.

Vocabulary/Using a Dictionary

1. What are the parts of the word *theologian* (para. 3), and what do
    they mean? What are the definitions for the related words *apoth-
    eosis* and *monotheistic*?

2. *Alpha* (para. 11) is the first word in the Greek alphabet. Why do
    you think a dominant male is referred to as the *alpha male*?

Responding to Words in Context

1. Wise writes that the idea that the law should recognize as persons
    those made in the image of God is an "argument [that] has been
    leaking" since the twelfth century (para. 3). Why does he use the
    word *leaking*? What imagery does this word choice conjure up?

2. This article uses both the term *human* and the term *person*, but
    not interchangeably. Can you infer the difference between these
    words from Wise's point of view?

Discussing Main Point and Meaning

1. Does Wise argue that nonhuman animals should be treated
    equally under the law to all humans or with a different degree of
    "personhood"?

2. Summarize Kant's definition of autonomy and subsequent
    philosophers' objections to it.

3. List some of the examples of categories of human beings who
    Wise compares to nonhuman animals to support his argument
    that the legal standard for personhood is inconsistent.

Examining Sentences, Paragraphs, and Organization

1. Wise reasons, "We don't eat or vivisect human babies born without brains, who are so lacking in sentience that they are operated on without anesthesia" (para. 5). What effect do you think this sentence is meant to have on the reader?

2. The last line of this article is "The next step is obvious." Is it? If so, what is it? Why do you think Wise doesn't directly articulate what that step is here?

3. Paragraph 11 enumerates the mental abilities of apes. Describe the manner in which the examples Wise lists build on one another. What is their cumulative effect on the reader?

Thinking Critically

1. If, as Wise suggests, nonhuman animals are so close to humans in intellect, behavior, and character, why are they so easily subjugated by man? If they are so much like humans, shouldn't nonhuman animals be capable of fighting on their own behalf?

2. What other kinds of legal issues would be complicated or called into question if nonhuman animals had rights? Would the laws around human reproduction, mental competency, or children's rights change? Would farmers, pet owners, or veterinarians have to be regulated in new ways?

3. Is it fair for Wise to compare the abilities of a two-year-old toddler with the abilities of an adult chimpanzee?

In-Class Writing Activities

1. Write a rebuttal to Wise that presents examples of how nonhuman animals are not like humans and thus do not deserve the same legal status. Refer directly to his examples in your rebuttal as necessary.

2. Many pet owners personify (assign human characteristics to) their cats, dogs, or other pets. Describe a pet you are familiar with, citing examples of its humanlike behaviors or its humanlike role in its owners' lives.

Discussing the Unit

Suggested Topic for Discussion

Do animals have any rights that you know of? Should they? In general, would you say that human health and comfort takes precedence over the rights of animals?

Preparing for Class Discussion

1. Do you think most Americans are for or against animal research?

2. How do the ads against animal cruelty relate to the arguments in Jane Goodall's and Steven Wise's articles? Do the ads seem more or less extreme than the writers? How does the message in an ad need to be presented as compared to an article?

From Discussion to Writing

1. Where do you personally draw the line in the debate over animal testing? Is the quality of life for human beings always more important than the lives of animals? Are there just a few exceptions where you would support experimentation on animals (for example, for research on specific diseases or using only certain types of animals)? Or do you believe all animals should be treated with the same respect for life with which society treats human beings? Would you include insects as part of animal life?

2. What is the role of science in society? Are scientists more important than teachers or firefighters? How much scrutiny should be used in deciding the legal boundaries of scientific research? Who should monitor scientific experiments: nonscientists, who may not have full intellectual understanding of their work? Or other scientists, who may have a bias towards progress over ethics?

3. Using the articles of Goodall and Wise, write a rebuttal to Kristien McDonald. Quote from all three articles as necessary and describe any points of commonality you find. Alternately, use McDonald to rebut either Goodall's or Wise's argument. In either case, be very clear about whom you are quoting and paraphrasing, and use proper citation format.

Topics for Cross-Cultural Discussion

1. Do you know of another culture in which there is a debate over the use of animals in laboratory research? Would the ads presented in this unit, for example, receive a supportive or dismissive response in the newspapers of other countries with large research industries?

2. Many Americans keep pets, whom they view as members of their families, and yet the United States arguably conducts the most comprehensive animal research programs in the world. How would you describe Americans' view of animals?

14

Should Human Cloning
Be Allowed?

Just four years after the news of the first successfully cloned sheep in 1997, Americans learned that a Massachusetts lab had cloned a human embryo. Though the prospects of using cloning techniques to produce a child are still in the distance, the rapid pace of biomedical research has worried many ethicists and legislators who view cloning as a blind leap into a science fiction nightmare. Supporters of cloning, however, point to the countless lives the new biomedical research could save if the science of cloning is publicly encouraged and sufficiently funded. With the latest cloning news, the debate has turned from what happens "if" to what happens "when."

This unit presents a debate — two opposing views and a response to both — that demonstrates how both advocates and opponents are framing what will undoubtedly remain a controversial issue for years. Published in the *Wall Street Journal,* this debate features libertarians versus conservatives, as cloning supporter Virginia Postrel argues that the future medical benefits of cloning outweigh its political liabilities. Should human cloning be allowed? Her answer is "Yes, Don't Impede Medical Progress." On the opposing side, however, are conservative thinkers Eric Cohen and William Kristol who say "No, It's a Moral Monstrosity." The opposing views stimulated many letters in response; one of these, by biology professor Michael A. Goldman, argues that the debate, for all the good points it raised, needed to be framed differently and a careful distinction drawn between reproductive and therapeutic cloning. Though the debate touches on a number of related issues — such as abortion and eugenics — it is essentially grounded in a dilemma familiar to all who've watched science fiction films: the moral problems that arise when scientific experiments go awry and threaten our common notion of human identity. It was inevitable that once cloning became a popular scientific topic in the 1970s that a film such as *The Clones* would appear to confront the general public — as the poster in this unit depicts — with the horrors of science and technology gone immeasurably beyond control.

It's no surprise, then, that University of Oregon student Pat Payne alludes to the fears about cloning raised by such science fiction films as *The Boys from Brazil* and *Star Trek II:* "For too many years," writes Payne, "when people heard the word 'clone,' they thought of depictions in the popular media that almost universally portrayed cloning as a tool of evil or, at best, a force of nature better left untapped." Also from the University of Oregon, cartoonist Steve Baggs offers readers a way of picturing the new organ transplant industry.

OPPOSING VIEWS

Should Human Cloning Be Allowed?

Before You Read

What should happen when science and government are in conflict? Should the moral imperative of government outweigh the medical benefits of biochemistry? Does the prospect of human cloning excite or appall you?

Words to Learn [Postrel]

embryo (para. 1): the fertilized egg of a vertebrate animal (n.)
islet (para. 2): "little island"; in the pancreas, cluster of cells related to production of insulin (n.)

stem cells (para. 3): cells that can differentiate into other kinds of cells (n.)

immunosuppressant (para. 3): having the ability to suppress the immune system (adj.)

moratorium (para. 10): suspension; halt; cessation (n.)

cytoplasm (para. 12): the life-giving substance outside a cell nucleus (n.)

dystopia (para. 14): imaginary place where only bad things happen; opposite of *utopia* (n.)

eugenics (para. 14): the controversial movement devoted to improving the human species through the control of hereditary factors in mating (n.)

Words to Learn [Cohen and Kristol]

ethicist (para. 6): an expert in moral philosophy (n.)

untenable (para. 8): not defensible; unsuitable for use (adj.)

czar (para. 9): authority; leader (n.)

despotism (para. 10): tyranny; absolute rule (n.)

utopia (para. 12): idealistic condition or place of perfection (n.)

chimera (para. 13): mythological organism created from at least two genetically distinct parents (n.)

Words to Learn [Goldman]

monolithic (para. 1): huge, massive; characterized by a rigidly fixed uniformity (adj.)

chromosome (para. 4): a strand of DNA that contains genes, the

necessary information for cell life (n.)

genome (para. 4): the total genetic content of an organism (n.)

VIRGINIA POSTREL

Yes, Don't Impede Medical Progress

[THE WALL STREET JOURNAL / December 5, 2001]

To many biologists, the recently announced creation of a cloned human embryo was no big deal. True, researchers at Advanced Cell

1

VIRGINIA POSTREL *served as the editor of* Reason *magazine from 1989 to 2000. She is the founder of the Franklin Society, an organization that advocates free scientific inquiry and innovation, and the author of* The Future and Its Enemies *(1998).*

Technology (ACT) replaced the nucleus of a human egg with the genetic material of another person. And they got that cloned cell to start replicating. But their results were modest. It took seventy-one eggs to produce a single success, and in the best case, the embryo grew to only six cells before dying. That's not a revolution. It's an incremental step in understanding how early-stage cells develop.

And it's far from the one hundred or so cells in a blastocyst, the   2
hollow ball from which stem cells can be isolated. Scientists hope to coax embryonic stem cells into becoming specialized tissues such as nerve, muscle, or pancreatic islet cells. Therapeutic cloning, or nucleus transplantation, could make such treatments more effective.

In theory, it would work like this: Suppose I need new heart tissue   3
or some insulin-secreting islet cells to counteract diabetes. You could take the nucleus from one of my cells, stick it in an egg cell from which the nucleus had been removed, let that develop into stem cells, and then trigger the stem cells to form the specific tissue needed. The new "cloned" tissue would be genetically mine and would not face rejection problems. It would function in my body as if it had grown there naturally, so I wouldn't face a lifetime of immunosuppressant drugs.

But all of that is a long way off. ACT and others in the field are   4
still doing very basic research, not developing clinical therapies. Indeed, because of the difficulty of obtaining eggs, therapeutic cloning may ultimately prove impractical for clinical treatments. It could be more important as a technique for understanding cell development or studying the mutations that lead to cancer. We simply don't know right now. Science is about exploring the unknown and cannot offer guarantees.

Politics, however, feeds on fear, uncertainty, and doubt, and the   5
word "cloning" arouses those emotions. While its scientific importance remains to be seen, ACT's announcement has rekindled the campaign to criminalize nucleus transplantation and any therapies derived from that process. Under a bill passed by the House and endorsed by the president, scientists who transfer a human nucleus into an egg cell would be subject to ten-year federal prison sentences and $1 million fines. So would anyone who imports therapies developed through such research in countries where it is legal, such as Britain. The bill represents an unprecedented attempt to criminalize basic biomedical research.

The legislation's backers consider the fear of cloning their best   6
hope for stopping medical research that might lead to gene-level therapies. Opponents make three basic arguments for banning therapeutic cloning.

The first is that a fertilized egg is a person, entitled to full human rights. Taking stem cells out of a blastocyst is, in this view, no different from cutting the heart out of a baby. Hence, we hear fears of "embryo farming" for "spare parts."

This view treats microscopic cells with no past or present consciousness, no organs or tissues, as people. A vocal minority of Americans, of course, do find compelling the argument that a fertilized egg is someone who deserves protection from harm. That view animates the anti-abortion movement and exercises considerable influence in Republican politics.

> *Politics feeds on fear, uncertainty, and doubt, and the word "cloning" arouses those emotions.*

But most Americans don't believe we should sacrifice the lives and well-being of actual people to save cells. Human identity must rest on something more compelling than the right string of proteins in a petri dish, detectable only with high-tech equipment. We will never get a moral consensus that a single cell, or a clump of one hundred cells, is a human being. That definition defies moral sense, rational argument, and several major religious traditions.

So cloning opponents add a second argument. If we allow therapeutic cloning, they say, some unscrupulous person will pretend to be doing cellular research but instead implant a cloned embryo in a woman's womb and produce a baby. At the current stage of knowledge, using cloning to conceive a child would indeed be dangerous and unethical, with a high risk of serious birth defects. Anyone who cloned a baby today would rightly face, at the very least, the potential of an enormous malpractice judgment. There are good arguments for establishing a temporary moratorium on reproductive cloning.

But the small possibility of reproductive cloning does not justify making nucleus transfer a crime. Almost any science might conceivably be turned to evil purposes. This particular misuse is neither especially likely — cell biology labs are not set up to deliver fertility treatments — nor, in the long run, especially threatening.

Contrary to a lot of scary rhetoric, a healthy cloned infant would not be a moral nightmare, merely the not-quite-identical twin of an older person. (The fetal environment and egg cytoplasm create some genetic variations.) Certainly, some parents might have such a baby for bad reasons, to gratify their egos or to "replace" a child who died. But parents have been having children for bad reasons since time immemorial.

Just as likely, cloned babies would be the cherished children of couples who could not have biological offspring any other way.

These children might bear an uncanny resemblance to their biological parents, but that, too, is not unprecedented. Like the "test tube babies" born of in vitro fertilization, cloned children need not be identifiable, much less freaks or outcasts.

Why worry so much about a few babies? Because, say opponents, even a single cloned infant puts us on the road to genetic dystopia, a combination of Brave New World and Nazi Germany. A cloned child's genetic makeup is too well known, goes the argument, and therefore transforms random reproduction into "manufacturing" that robs the child of his autonomy. This is where the attack broadens from nucleus transfer to human genetic engineering more generally. An anti-therapeutic cloning petition, circulated by the unlikely duo of conservative publisher William Kristol and arch-technophobe Jeremy Rifkin, concludes, "We are mindful of the tragic history of social eugenics movements in the first half of the twentieth century, and are united in our opposition to any use of biotechnology for a commercial eugenics movement in the twenty-first century." 14

But the "eugenics" they attack has nothing to do with state-sponsored mass murder or forced sterilization. To the contrary, they are the ones who want the state to dictate the most private aspects of family life. They are the ones who want central authorities, rather than the choices of families and individuals, to determine our genetic future. They are the ones who demand that the government control the means of reproduction. They are the ones who measure the worth of human beings by the circumstances of their conception and the purity of their genetic makeup. They are the ones who say "natural" genes are the mark of true humanity. 15

Winners in the genetic lottery themselves, blessed with good health and unusual intelligence, they seek to deny future parents the chance to give their children an equally promising genetic start. In a despicable moral equivalency, they equate loving parents with Nazis. 16

Biomedicine does have the potential to alter the human experience. Indeed, it already has. Life expectancy has doubled worldwide in the past century. Childbirth is no longer a peril to mother and infant. Childhood is no longer a time for early death. The pervasive sense of mortality that down through the ages shaped art, religion, and culture has waned. 17

Our lives are different from our ancestors' in fundamental ways. We rarely remark on the change, however, because it occurred incrementally. That's how culture evolves and how science works. We should let the process continue. 18

ERIC COHEN AND
WILLIAM KRISTOL

No, It's a Moral Monstrosity

[THE WALL STREET JOURNAL / December 5, 2001]

Dr. Michael West, the lead scientist on the team that recently   1
cloned the first human embryos, believes his mission in life is "to end
suffering and death." "For the sake of medicine," he informs us, "we
need to set our fears aside." For the sake of health, in other words,
we need to overcome our moral inhibitions against cloning and eugenics.

The human cloning announcement was not a shock. We have   2
been "progressing" down this road for years, while averting our gaze
from the destination. Now we have cloned human embryos. That
means that women's eggs were procured, their genetic material removed, the DNA[1] from someone else inserted, and the resulting
cloned embryos manufactured as genetic replicas of an existing person. In Dr. West's experiments, the embryos died very quickly. But
the hope is that someday these embryos will serve as a source of
rejection-free stem cells that can help cure diseases.

For now, this is science fiction, or a rosy form of speculation. No   3
one has ever been treated with "therapeutic cloning" or embryonic

---

[1]DNA: Deoxyribonucleic acid; a sequence of chromosomes that determines individual
hereditary characteristics.

ERIC COHEN has published numerous articles in the Wall Street Journal,
the Weekly Standard, First Things, and the Washington Times. From 2000 to
2002 he was a fellow at the new American Foundation, a public policy institute currently chaired by James Fallows. WILLIAM KRISTOL has been the editor
and publisher of the Weekly Standard since 1995 and the chairman of the
Project for the New American Century since 2001. Kristol makes regular appearances on ABC's This Week. Cohen and Kristol are coeditors of The Future Is Now: America Confronts the New Genetics (2002).

stem cells. There have been no human trials. But it is true that this research may work in the future (though the benefits would likely be decades away). In addition, beyond cloning, scientists have larger ambitions, including "tinkering" with DNA before it is placed in an egg, and adding designer genes that would make clones into "super clones," stem cells into "super stem cells."

Yet while Dr. West and his colleagues say that they have no interest in creating cloned humans — on the grounds that doing so is not yet safe — they do not seem too frightened by the prospect of laying the groundwork for those who would do just that. "We didn't feel that the abuse of this technology, its potential abuses, should stop us from doing what we believe is the right thing in medicine," Dr. West said.   4

The Senate, it seems, is also not very concerned. Majority Leader Tom Daschle wants to put off until spring [2002] a vote on the Human Cloning Prohibition Act, which the House passed by 265–162 in July [2001]. And on Monday [December 3, 2001] the Senate chose not to consider a six-month moratorium on all human cloning. As Sen. Harry Reid has said, a moratorium for "six months or two months or two days would impede science." And that, he believes, we cannot do.   5

> *Once we begin stockpiling cloned embryos for research, it will be virtually impossible to control how they are used.*

It is understandable that many senators want to avoid a decision on this controversial issue, and no surprise that those driven by a desire to advance science and to heal the sick at any cost resist a ban. But as the ethicist Paul Ramsey wrote, "The good things that men do can be complete only by the things they refuse to do." And cloning is one of those things we should refuse to do.   6

The debate is usually divided into two issues — reproductive cloning (creating cloned human beings) and therapeutic cloning (creating cloned human embryos for research and destruction). For now, there is near-universal consensus that we should shun the first. The idea of mother-daughter twins or genetically identical "daddy juniors" stirs horror in us. Our moral sense revolts at the prospect because so many of our cherished principles would be violated: the principle that children should not be designed in advance; that newborns should be truly new, without the burden of a genetic identity already lived; that a society where cloning is easy (requiring a few cells from anywhere in the body) means anyone could be cloned without knowledge or consent; and   7 that replacing lost loved ones with "copies" is an insult to the ones lost, since it denies the uniqueness and sacredness of their existence. For these reasons, Americans agree that human cloning should never happen — not merely because the procedure is not yet "safe," but because it is wrong.

Many research advocates say that they, too, are against "reproductive cloning." But to protect their research, they seek to restrict only the implantation of cloned embryos, not the creation of cloned embryos for research. This is untenable: Once we begin stockpiling cloned embryos for research, it will be virtually impossible to control how they are used. We would be creating a class of embryos that, by law, must be destroyed. And the only remedy for wrongfully implanting cloned embryos would be forced abortions, something neither pro-lifers nor reproductive rights advocates would tolerate, nor should.   8

But the cloning debate is not simply the latest act in the moral divide over abortion. It is the "opening skirmish" — as Leon Kass, the president's bioethics czar, describes it — in deciding whether we wish to "put human nature itself on the operating table, ready for alteration, enhancement, and wholesale redesign." Lured by the seductive promise of medical science to "end" suffering and disease, we risk not seeing the dark side of the eugenic project.   9

Three horrors come to mind: First, the designing of our descendants, whether through cloning or germ-line engineering, is a form of generational despotism. Second, in trying to make human beings live indefinitely, our scientists have begun mixing our genes with those of cows, pigs, and jellyfish. And in trying to stamp out disease by any means necessary, we risk beginning the "compassionate" project of killing off the diseased themselves, something that has already begun with the selective abortion by parents of "undesirable" embryos.   10

Proponents of the biogenetic revolution will surely say that such warnings are nothing more than superstitions. Naive to the destructive power of man's inventions, they will say that freedom means leaving scientists to experiment as they see fit. They will say that those who wish to stop the unchecked advance of biotechnology are themselves "genetic fundamentalists," who see human beings as nothing more than their genetic make-ups. Banning human cloning, one advocate says, "would set a very dangerous precedent of bringing the police powers of the federal government into the laboratories."   11

But the fact is that society accepts the need to regulate behavior for moral reasons — from drug use to nuclear weapons research to   12 dumping waste. And those who say that human identity is "more than a person's genetic make-up" are typically the ones who seek to crack man's genetic code, so that they might "improve" humans in the image they see fit. In promising biological utopia, they justify breaching fundamental moral boundaries.

C. S. Lewis[2] saw this possibility long ago in *The Abolition of Man*. As he put it, "Each new power won by man is a power over man as well." In order to stop the dehumanization of man, and the creation of a post-human world of designer babies, man-animal chimeras, and "compassionate killing" of the disabled, we may have to forgo some research. We may have to say no to certain experiments before they begin. The ban on human cloning is an ideal opportunity to reassert democratic control over science, and to reconnect technological advance with human dignity and responsibility. 13

Web **Read It Now:** Stem Cells: A Primer, bedfordstmartins.com/americanow, Chapter 14. Published by the National Institutes of Health, this four-page document answers questions such as "What is a stem cell?"

Web **Read It Now:** Stem Cells: Scientific Progress and Future Research Directions, bedfordstmartins.com/americanow, Chapter 14. This comprehensive report from the National Institutes of Health explores the potential of stem cell applications.

---

[2]*C. S. Lewis:* British writer and scholar (1898–1963) who, besides many books on morality and religion, is also the author of the famous children's series, the *Chronicles of Narnia.*

MICHAEL A. GOLDMAN

Is Our Fear of Cloning Unnecessary?

[THE WALL STREET JOURNAL / December 14, 2001]

In the December 5th editorial-page debate, "Should Human   1
Cloning Be Allowed?" authors pro and con made excellent points.
But both articles view the cloning question as monolithic, failing, like
the House of Representatives, to recognize that reproductive and
therapeutic cloning must be addressed seperately. The authors also
ignore a very important limitation of reproductive cloning — it is all
but impossible.

The Europeans seem to have drawn a sensible distinction between   2
reproductive and therapeutic cloning, even if we Americans continually intertwine these issues and even that of genetic modification. Any
rational discussion must consider two questions, not one. The first
question is, "Should experiments aimed at the development of therapeutic cloning be permitted?" The second is, "Should we undertake
reproductive cloning to produce a child?"

An understanding of the science behind reproductive cloning sug-   3
gests that the joyful world Virginia Postrel envisions, in which
"cloned babies would be the cherished children of couples who could
not have biological offspring" and Eric Cohen and William Kristol's
contention that the "idea of mother-daughter twins stirs horror in
us" are both off the mark. Not a shred of evidence today says that we
will ever achieve more than a 5 percent success rate in reproductive
cloning. Despite the report of "healthy cloned cows" with an 80 percent
survival rate from Advanced Cell Technologies, the true measure of

MICHAEL A. GOLDMAN *is a professor of biology at San Francisco State
University, where he teaches genetics, developmental biology, and ethical issues in science. His editorials and letters have appeared in the* New York
Times, Los Angeles Times, *and* San Francisco Chronicle; *and he has also
published technical articles in* Science *and* Nature *and* Genetics. *Professor
Goldman considers "the public understanding of science as a key need if science and society are to thrive."*

survival from single-cell embryo to adult remains low. (The 80 percent survival in cloned cows actually refers to survival from birth to an age of one to four years.)

The reasons for this are complex, and apparently related to the 4 differential "marking" of the maternal and paternal genomes or chromosome sets that normally occurs in sperm and egg prior to fertilization. So marked or "imprinted," dozens of the genes inherited from the mother function differently from those inherited from the father, especially during some of the critical early steps in development. Cloning by nuclear transfer skips the critical stages of sperm and egg development in which these important changes occur, and in which many errors in the genetic material are screened out by specialized cell divisions. The process of cloning is not limited by the dexterity of the technician manipulating the eggs and nuclei, but by the very fundamental processes of genetic reprogramming essential to reproduction.

> *Whether we consider cloning to reproduce a child a gift from God or a reprehensible act, we aren't going to see it soon, and we aren't going to see it often.*

Whether we consider cloning to reproduce a child a gift from God 5 or a reprehensible act, we aren't going to see it soon, and we aren't going to see it often.

Messrs. Cohen and Kristol charge that scientists who claim to be 6 against reproductive cloning yet in favor of therapeutic cloning are in an "untenable" position. Like many others, these authors envision little to stop a collection of embryos cloned for cell therapy from turning into a collection of cloned children. But while the process of inserting a nucleus into an enucleated egg cell is common to both reproductive and therapeutic cloning, the procedures are nearly as different as chiseling rock to build a highway and sculpting a masterpiece. Producing a clump of cells that can be coddled in the laboratory to grow as a flat sheet, and maybe later to grow into a few specialized cell types, as opposed to fashioning an embryo capable of self-directing its own progress through the most challenging stages any of us faced in our lives — the development of an organized body plan from a formless mass of cells — are vastly different problems.

Should human reproductive cloning be allowed? No, because it is 7 probably unnecessary and it is just about impossible anyway. Should cloning to produce ideal cells for experiments leading to new and better therapies be allowed? Yes, and preferably with generous federal support.

Vocabulary/Using a Dictionary

1. Postrel fears a "genetic dystopia" (para. 14), while Cohen and Kristol warn of promises for a "biological utopia" (para. 12). What is a *dystopia*? What is a *utopia*? How are the words related? Can you guess what the root of the words is?

2. Both essays here distinguish between *reproductive cloning* and *therapeutic cloning*, though the terms refer essentially to the same process. What is the difference between *reproductive* and *therapeutic* cloning? Why does Goldman criticize the debate as *monolithic*?

3. Look up *czar* (Cohen and Kristol, para. 9) in your dictionary to find out what language and political system originated the term. How is the origin of *czar* different from its present American usage?

4. *Moratorium* (Postrel, para. 10) comes from the same Old French root, *demorer,* of the word *demur,* which mean "to delay" and "to raise objections," respectively. How are these older words related to *moratorium*? How do you think *moratorium* evolved from *demorer*?

Responding to Words in Context

1. What does Postrel mean when she calls the results of the experiments by Advanced Cell Technology "modest" (para. 1)?

2. Postrel calls Jeremy Rifkin an "arch-technophobe" (para. 14). What do you think this term means?

3. Do you think that the words *cloning* or *clone* generally have a positive or negative connotation? Or do you think they are neutral?

4. While Postrel refers to cloning human embryos as "basic research" (para. 4), "biomedical research" (para. 5), "cellular research" (para. 10), or even "human genetic engineering" (para. 14), Cohen and Kristol continually use the term *eugenics.* How do these examples of word choice reveal the authors' arguments?

5. Cohen and Kristol define *therapeutic cloning* as "creating cloned human embryos for research and destruction" (para. 7). What word do you think Postrel would substitute for *destruction*? What term would Goldman substitute?

6. "The ban on human cloning is an ideal opportunity to reassert democratic control over science" (para. 13), Cohen and Kristol write.

Examine the phrase "democratic control." What do you think the authors mean by this? How does Goldman respond to this idea?

Discussing Main Point and Meaning

1. Postrel argues that, "Science is about exploring the unknown and cannot offer guarantees" (para. 4). How does this general statement about science connect to the more specific example of human cloning? How is it meant to answer critics of human cloning?

2. What are the "three basic arguments for banning therapeutic [human] cloning" (para. 6) Postrel presents in her essay? Summarize the arguments and Postrel's objections to them. Does Goldman agree with Postrel's suggestion?

3. Each essay shows how this issue is related to the abortion debate (Postrel, para. 8, and Cohen and Kristol, para. 8). What is the relationship between these issues, in your opinion?

4. Explain the C. S. Lewis quote used by Cohen and Kristol in paragraph 13. How does this quote relate to the research discussed in these articles? How do you think Goldman would respond to this quote?

5. Cohen and Kristol draw an analogy between human cloning regulation and the regulation of drug use, nuclear power, and dumping environmentally hazardous waste (para. 12). How do each of the examples compare to cloning? Do you think any of the three is a stronger analogy than the others?

Examining Sentences, Paragraphs, and Organization

1. Examine Postrel's tone and word choice in the following passage: "But most Americans don't believe we should sacrifice the lives and well-being of actual people to save cells" (para. 9). How is Postrel's position revealed here?

2. When Postrel asks, "Why worry so much about a few babies?" (para. 14) are you surprised? Do you think Postrel wanted the reader to respond to this question in a particular way? Is she making any assumptions about her audience when she asks this question?

3. The phrase "they are the ones" is used five times in paragraph 15 of Postrel's article. Why does Postrel use repetition here?

4. Cohen and Kristol frequently set words off with quotation marks: "progressing" (para. 2); "tinkering," "super clones," and "super stem cells" (para. 3); "daddy juniors" (para. 7); "compassionate" and "undesirable" (para. 10); "genetic fundamentalists" (para. 11); and "more than a person's genetic makeup" and "improve" (para. 12). Why are these words set off in this manner? How are these quotation marks different in kind and effect from the ones used to signal direct quotes in paragraphs 1, 4, 5, 6, 9, and 13? How do all of the quotes combined affect the content of this essay?

Thinking Critically

1. An *ad hominem* attack is an error in reasoning that occurs when a speaker slanders or discredits an opponent in place of presenting compelling evidence or logic to challenge that opponent's argument. In your opinion, are paragraphs 15–16 of Postrel's article an example of *ad hominem* attack? Why or why not?

2. Postrel argues that "parents have been having children for bad reasons since time immemorial" (para. 12) in answer to the criticism that human cloning would encourage people to create new versions of themselves or to recreate a dead child. Do you find this logic compelling or flimsy?

3. "Once we begin stockpiling cloned embryos for research, it will be virtually impossible to control how they are used" (para. 8), Cohen and Kristol write. Is this necessarily true? Or is this an example of "slippery slope" logic, where the speaker insists that allowing one action or event will necessarily cause a chain reaction of increasingly more extreme results until the worst possible case is achieved?

4. Goldman argues that reproductive cloning "is just about impossible" and that there's no evidence we could "ever achieve more than a 5 percent success rate." In your opinion, does that small possibility suggest that reproductive cloning remains an insignificant issue? What do you think Goldman's position would be if the success rate of reproductive cloning was 50 percent?

In-Class Writing Activities

1. Identify what you think to be the most compelling passage in each of these articles (even if you agree more with one article than

the other). In a paragraph or two use those passages to construct a "middle ground" argument.

2. Do you think Postrel, Cohen, and Kristol would be persuaded by Goldman's analysis of their debate? In two paragraphs, summarize how you think either side would respond to Goldman's solution to the cloning issue.

AMERICA THEN . . . 1973

The Clones

The idea of cloning human beings existed in science fiction long before the process became experimentally feasible. There has always been something inherently scary about creating people who are duplicates of other people. The concept of cloning threatens one of the fundamental certainties of human life: that every person is a unique individual.

Since science fiction writers enjoy challenging our everyday, commonsense notions of reality, they have found in cloning an irresistible subject. The 1973 poster for one of the first sci-fi films to capitalize on cloning appears here.

PAT PAYNE

Factory "Seconds" Could Save Lives

[OREGON DAILY EMERALD, UNIVERSITY OF OREGON,
EUGENE / Februrary 5, 2002]

Before You Read

Many moral arguments consist of one side maintaining that "the end justifies the means" while the opposing side takes the position that we cannot do something improper even if the results are beneficial. How do you see these perspectives as affecting the cloning debate?

Words to Learn

sacrosanct (para. 3): very sacred, holy, or inviolable (adj.)
eugenics (para. 4): the controversial movement devoted to improving the human species through the control of hereditary factors in mating (n.)

PAT PAYNE *is a senior at the University of Oregon in Eugene where he studies journalism and serves as a commentary editor for the* Oregon Daily Emerald. *Payne's investigative reporting for the student paper at El Camino College (California) has won him awards from the Journalism Association of Community Colleges and he has interned at the* Palos Verdes Peninsula News. *He hopes one day to work for the Associated Press.*

STEVE BAGGS *is a senior majoring in multimedia design at the University of Oregon in Eugene. Baggs, a staff illustrator and cartoonist for the* Oregon Daily Emerald, *is also an animator whose work appears in the 2003 Spike and Mike's Classic Festival of Animation. He plans to work on special effects for the film and video game industries and also aims to become a syndicated political cartoonist.*

The new technological revolution has begun yet again. In Massachusetts, scientists at Advanced Cell Technology have cloned a cow's kidney from an embryo. While this could be an amazing feat, what is even more astounding is that the cloned organ actually functioned in most of the ways that an (for lack of a better term) "organic" kidney would and was not rejected by the cow's body. By extracting the stem cells just as they began to specialize into a kidney function and colonizing them in what is known as a "biocompatible scaffolding" — basically a mold of the organ to be created — they were able to "create" a kidney. This new science will have a major impact on medicine by allowing a patient in a life-threatening situation to receive vital organs more quickly. More than that, it clears the path for a near-limitless organ supply.

However, there is one thing standing in the way of this advance   2
in medical science. We have a deep-seated mistrust of cloning and cloning technology. The sources of this mistrust are two-fold: one is religious in nature — people have been taught that to clone a human being or any part of a human is little more than "playing God." Others feel that an embryo, no matter how early in its development stage, is a human being and therefore sacrosanct. This course in the debate over cloning has been picked up by anti-abortion advocates who feel, through a leap in logic, that cloning is therefore tantamount to abortion.

The second source of mistrust is the average American's science-   3
fictional view of the dangers of genetic engineering. For too many years, when people heard the word "clone,"
they thought of depictions in the popular media
that almost universally protrayed cloning as a
tool of evil or, at best, a force of nature better
left untapped. Two memorable instances are:
the book and motion picture *The Boys from
Brazil,* which features Nazi doctor Josef Men-
gele turning out numerous clones of Adolf
Hitler, and *Star Trek II: The Wrath of Khan,*
starring Ricardo Montalban as the genetically
engineered supercriminal Khan Noonien Singh,
a genocidal tyrant who abuses his strength to
take over the world.

*This new science
will have a major
impact on medicine
by allowing a
patient in a life-
threatening
situation to receive
vital organs more
quickly*

The upcoming *Star Wars* prequel is also rumored to be set dur-   4
ing a "clone war" where clone soldiers are churned out by the bushel to fight for the bad guys. Then there is the real world's actual experi-ence in eugenics, where — in Nazi Germany, Europe more generally, and even for a brief period in this country — there were attempts to "purify" the genetic pool by using brutal methods. With these no-tions in our collective memory, is it any wonder that we fear any ap-plication of cloning?

But we live in an age where the terrors of some unchecked,   5
cloned "superman" on the silver screen is far less horrific than what thousands of families are going through at this very moment. Organ donations are still nowhere near enough to cover the 76,000 on organ waiting lists in this country. More than 6,000 people die each

year in the United States because a donor couldn't be found fast enough to save the life of someone who desperately needed a kidney, heart, liver, or a lung. And those family members who donate their own organs (kidneys and parts of the liver) while they're still alive run serious risks, including death. If cloning could save those 6,000 lives, then I say fears be damned. We now hold in our hands the promise of a future in which no person would have to die needlessly because a donor organ could not be found in time.

Web **Hear It Now:** President Bush on Stem Cell Research, **bedfordstmartins.com/ americanow**, Chapter 14. Listen to the president's remarks delivered on August 9, 2001 (transcript also available).

Web **Read It Now:** "The Scientists Speak: No Human Cloning," by Jessica Reaves, Time.com, **bedfordstmartins.com/americanow**, Chapter 14. Read the recommendations of the National Academy of Sciences on cloning of embryos for research purposes.

Vocabulary/Using a Dictionary

1. What common terms are related to "sacrosanct" (para. 2)? What would lead you to think the word has religious significance?

2. How do you think the term "genocidal" (para. 3) was formed? In what way does it resemble "suicidal?" Can you think of other words it closely resembles?

3. What is the origin of the word "eugenics?" What common words does it resemble? In what way is it related to "Eugene," the town in Oregon that is the home of Payne's university?

Responding to Words in Context

1. What sort of word is "prequel" (para. 4)? In what contexts do you see it used? How and why do you think the term came to be coined?

2. Why does Payne put the word "purify" (para. 4) in quotation marks? What connotations does the word possess? How can the concept of "purity" have negative connotations?

3. Consider the essay's title. What does Payne mean by "factory 'seconds'"? Where have you heard this expression and what image

does it convey? How did Steve Baggs pick up on Payne's title for his cartoon?

Discussing Main Point and Meaning

1. What position does Payne advocate in this essay? What does he believe is the primary benefit of cloning?
2. What are the two primary reasons, according to Payne, that Americans distrust and fear cloning?
3. Note that after the sci-fi film references, Payne introduces the "eugenics" issue (para. 4). Is this related to the science fiction films or is it a seperate source of public mistrust?

Examining Sentences, Paragraphs, and Organization

1. Note Payne's opening sentence. Why do you think he says that a "new technological revolution has begun yet again?" Why is this different from simply saying a "new technological revolution has begun?"
2. How does Payne's final paragraph support the issue he raises in the first paragraph? How successfully in your opinion does he lock-in his conclusion to his introduction?
3. Payne's paper is a near-perfect example of what many writing teachers refer to as the "five paragraph theme." How does each paragraph work in this organization? How does Payne introduce his point, develop it, and form his conclusion? Are there any parts of the essay you think don't fit the format?

Thinking Critically

1. In his second paragraph, Payne connects the religious mistrust of cloning to abortion, claiming that "through a leap in logic," pro-life advocates see cloning as similar to abortion. But Payne doesn't explain what's wrong with their logic. What do you think the explanation would be?
2. After offering several science fiction films as reasons behind the public's mistrust of cloning technology, Payne then introduces the "real world's own experiences in eugenics" as another

source of mistrust, arguing that "With these notions in our collective memory, is it any wonder that we fear any application of cloning." Do you think there's a distinction to be made between the sci-fi movies and the Nazi practice of eugenics? What has eugenics to do with cloning? And how does Payne get past the seriousness of the question he raises? Does his final paragraph, in your opinion, confront the question that ends paragraph four?

3. Many scientists intended eugenics to be used as a means of improving the human species by ensuring reproduction of only genetically desirable characteristics — in that sense, they were justifying their methods by looking at end results. Payne — who appears to believe eugenics should make us skeptical about cloning — would nevertheless like to employ cloning technology as an effective way to save human life through organ transplants. Explain whether you think the basis of his argument is similar or dissimilar to those who promoted eugenics?

4. If the supply of donor organs could be increased and delivery sped up, thus making cloned organs less necessary, do you think Payne would still argue in favor of cloning? To what extent does his argument depend on the inefficiency of our current donor organ procedure?

In-Class Writing Activities

1. Imagine you just read Payne's essay in your college paper. Write a quick letter in which you respond by either agreeing or disagreeing with his main point.

2. Payne mentions a main reason for supporting the technology of cloning — it could save lives through organ transplants. After breaking into small groups, discuss other reasons for either supporting or opposing cloning. Make a list of these additional reasons to support cloning along with the objections a mistrusting public may bring towards them.

Discussing the Unit

Suggested Topic for Discussion

The potential development and uses of human cloning inspire heated debate in major newspapers, student newspapers, and cartoons. Where do you stand based on your current understanding of the procedures involved and the intended applications? Are all human eggs and embryos sacred, even partially manufactured in a lab? Or must we keep first in our minds the millions of people who are right now suffering from tragic illnesses on a daily basis?

Preparing for Class Discussion

1. To what extent do concepts of "ends and means" shape the cloning debate? Would you agree or disagree that therapeutic cloning should proceed because of the medical benefits it promises? Would reproductive cloning also offer medical benefits?

2. To what extent does "slippery slope" logic (see p. 332) shape the cloning debate? Do you think that if some types of cloning are permitted that it would open the way for all types of cloning to be allowed?

From Discussion to Writing

1. Write a letter to your local representative expressing your view on human cloning and your opinion on whether scientists should be able to continue their research. Quote from at least two selections in this unit to support your argument.

2. Write an essay that discusses the relationship between religion and politics in U.S. society, using the debate around this issue as a primary illustration. Is this relationship the way it should be? Should religion and politics be more separate or more entwined? What lessons should we learn from the cloning controversy?

Topics for Cross-Cultural Discussion

1. Who controls medical and other scientific research in other countries with which you are familiar? Does the government have to approve all research? Are any religious groups influential? Or are scientists almost completely autonomous?

2. What role do science fiction films play in another country or culture that you know? Are they an entertaining source of information on scientific issues? Would a film such as *The Clones* be popular in that country?

15

Should Reparations Be Paid for Slavery?

In the months before the terrorist attacks of September 11, 2001, the most heated issue on American campuses was whether African Americans should receive reparations for slavery. The case for reparations had been passionately argued by a black Harvard law professor, Randall Robinson, in his bestseller, *The Debt: What America Owes to Blacks* (2000), but the reparations controversy began in earnest in March 2001 after a former radical turned conservative, David Horowitz, took out an ad in several college newspapers provocatively proposing "Ten Reasons Why Reparations for Blacks Is a Bad Idea — and Racist Too." A number of college papers refused to run the ad, and some of those that did found themselves subjected to protests and harassment, allowing Horowitz to complain that his free speech rights were being denied him because of a repressive climate of political correctness on American campuses that is enforced by a liberal orthodoxy and docile administrations. In the spring of 2002, Horowitz rekindled the conflict by publishing an entire book about his ad and its reception, *Uncivil Wars: The Controversy over Reparations for Slavery*. Some prominent African American writers and commentators subsequently tried to wrestle the issue back from Horowitz, who, they argued, had deliberately distorted and reframed the debate to promote his own conservative agenda.

The reparations issue is complex. This unit examines a variety of opinions from different perspectives. First, we look briefly at the background of today's reparations movement. Although the media coverage has centered mainly around the Randall Robinson book and the Horowitz advertisement, it's important to note that the issue has a deeper history. Shortly after the Civil War, freed slaves were offered "forty acres and a mule" so they could begin their lives anew, but this offer was rescinded by Lincoln's successor, President Andrew Johnson, who believed it was the slaveholders themselves who should be receiving reparations for the loss of their property. Over the years, the case for reparations would occasionally be raised but would have little impact. A major incident in the quest for reparations occurred in May 1969 when a black civil rights activist, James Forman, interrupted a church service in New York City with a "manifesto" that called for white Christian churches and Jewish synagogues to pay $500 million to African Americans as reparations for centuries of exploitation. Forman's demands went nowhere. As the *New York Times* reported (May 6, 1969) in an editorial titled "Is Nothing Sacred?": "James Forman, a black militant, accompanied by his aides, pushed past two elderly ushers to mount the chancel steps and read staggering demands for the payment of 'reparations' to Negroes.... The unreasonableness of the demands was exceeded only by the outrageousness of the episode." Forman's manifesto, nevertheless, served to stimulate one of the first systematically laid-out legal briefs for reparations, *The Case for Black Reparations,* published in 1973 by a Yale Law School professor, Boris I. Bittker.

In January 1989, Michigan congressman John Conyers Jr., one of the leaders of the Black Caucus, first introduced a bill into the House of Representatives that would establish a commission to study the impact of slavery on today's African American community and to recommend appropriate remedies. Conyers, who was instrumental in establishing the Martin Luther King Jr. Holiday, has been introducing the reparations bill unsuccessfully every year since. But the extensive media coverage the issue has been receiving, along with the popularity of Randall Robinson's *The Debt* and a growing grassroots movement in many cities in support of Conyers's bill, suggests that a congressional study may find the support it needs. In the spring of 2002, a number of prominent African American writers, lawyers, and political figures began a movement to sue corporations who profited in the past from slavery or the slave trade. These cases will be watched closely by a media that is now beginning to take the issue more seriously, though the economic climate after 9/11 is not nearly as encouraging as it was for reparations activists during the boom years of 1999 and 2000 when Randall Robinson's arguments were first being aired, both in his book and in articles that he wrote for various magazines, such as "America's Debt to Blacks," which appeared in *The Nation* (March 13, 2000).

The unit's second part focuses on the controversy provoked by the Horowitz advertisement. Horowitz's ad was not a direct rebuttal of Robinson's book, as many commentators on the issue have erroneously suggested. Robinson devotes only several pages of *The Debt* to specifics. Although at one point Horowitz alludes to Robinson's book, he apparently summarized various claims for reparations that had been surfacing in proposals, resolutions, and manifestos at the time. Most of the early responses to the ad were emotionally charged and highly personalized attacks against Horowitz, but a few systematic responses to Horowitz's advertisement did appear, one of the best being "Ten Reasons: A Response to David Horowitz" by two African American professors, Robert Chrisman and Ernest Allen Jr. Other prominent black intellectuals soon joined the fray, though within the African American community sentiments over reparations could be divided, as the selections by John Hope Franklin and Shelby Steele demonstrate.

Since the controversy was initially ignited by college newspapers, it's not surprising that reparations quickly emerged as a dominant issue on campuses throughout the nation. In the unit's third part we look at a spectrum of responses that appeared in both print and online publications at the University of Michigan, the University of Minnesota, the University of Wisconsin–Madison, Purdue University, and the University of Louisville. Although these essays necessarily represent only a tiny fraction of responses to the controversy, they reflect the diversity of student opinion. As you examine the issue in your own classroom debates, forums, or papers, keep in mind Monique Luse's point about the necessity of "open discussion" on the topic. As she puts it, "To address reparations is to engage in real economic, social, philosophical, and political discourse."

I. BACKGROUND

Before You Read

Do you think it's possible to repair the damage that slavery has done to the African American community? Can the movement to gain reparations for slavery's descendants right the wrongs of the past?

Words to Learn [Robinson]

heinous (para. 1): monstrous; evil (adj.)

hegemony (para. 1): domination; control (n.)

contemporaneousness (para. 1): quality of existing at the same time or belonging to the same age (n.)

covenant (para. 3): agreement; convention (n.)

redline (para. 3): exclude from the budget (v.)

myriad (para. 3): countless; innumerable (adj.)

ephemera (para. 5): something short-lived or temporary; matter of passing interest (n.)

behoove (para. 5): to be appropriate for; to be fitting (v.)

de jure (para. 6): Latin, in law (adj.)

de facto (para. 6): Latin, in fact (adj.)

Words to Learn [Conyers]

polarize (para. 2): to cause opposition; to separate into contrasting positions (v.)

uncontroverted (para. 4): without opposition; inarguable (adj.)

broach (para. 8): introduce; mention; raise (v.)

grassroots (para. 9): originating outside of a major political center (adj.)

pilfer (para. 13): steal; appropriate (v.)

garner (para. 14): acquire; get (v.)

internment (para. 15): imprisonment; confinement (n.)

RANDALL ROBINSON

America's Debt to Blacks

[THE NATION / March 13, 2000]

Well before the birth of our country, Europe and the eventual   1
United States perpetrated a heinous wrong against the peoples of
Africa and sustained and benefited from the wrong through the continuing exploitation of Africa's human and material resources. America followed slavery with more than a hundred years of legal racial
segregation and discrimination of one variety or another. It was only
in 1965, after nearly 350 years of legal racial suppression, that the
United States enacted the Voting Rights Act. Virtually simultaneously, however, it began to walk away from the social wreckage that
centuries of white hegemony had wrought. Our country then began
to rub itself with the memory-emptying salve of contemporaneousness. (If the wrong did not *just* occur, then it did not occur in a way
that would render the living responsible.)

But when the black living suffer real and current consequences as   2
a result of wrongs committed by a younger America, then contemporary America must shoulder responsibility for those wrongs until
such wrongs have been adequately righted. The life and responsibilities of a nation are not limited to the life spans of its mortal con-
stituents. Federal and state governments were active participants not
only in slavery but also in the exclusion and dehumanization of
blacks that continued legally up until the passage of key civil rights
legislation in the sixties. Black calls for reparations began almost
from the moment that slavery officially ended in 1865. However, although our calls far predate those of either the Japanese or the Jews,
only the latter two communities have been responded to in a spirit of
sober compassion and thoughtful humanity.

RANDALL ROBINSON *(b. 1941) is a civil and human rights activist and author. He founded the organization TransAfrica to attempt to alter American
foreign policy concerning predominantly black nations. Robinson is the author of* The Debt: What America Owes to Blacks *(2000) and, more recently,*
The Reckoning: What Blacks Owe to Each Other *(2002).*

In response to our call, individual Americans need not feel defensive or under attack. No one holds any living person responsible for slavery or the later century-plus of legal relegation of blacks to substandard education, exclusion from home ownership via restrictive covenants and redlining, or any of the myriad mechanisms for pushing blacks to the back of the line. Nonetheless, we must all, as a nation, ponder the repercussions of those acts.

There are many ways to begin righting America's massive wrong. But resolving economic and social disparities so long in the making will require great resources (in the form of public initiatives, not personal checks) and decades of national fortitude. Habit is the enemy. Whites and blacks see each other the only way they can remember seeing each other — in a relationship of economic and social inequality. The system, which starts each child where its parents left off, is not fair. This is particularly the case for African Americans, whose general economic starting points have been rearmost because of slavery and its aftermath.

> *Slaves for two and a half centuries saw not just their freedom taken from them but their labor as well.*

Slaves for two and a half centuries saw not just their freedom taken from them but their labor as well. Were it a line item in today's gross national product report, that value would undoubtedly run into billions of dollars.

America has made an art form by now of grinding its past deeds, no matter how despicable, into mere ephemera. And African Americans, unfortunately, have accommodated this amnesia all too well. It would behoove African Americans to remember that history forgets first those who forget themselves. To do what is necessary to accomplish anything approaching psychic and economic parity in the next half-century will require a fundamental shift in America's thinking. Before the country in general can be made to understand, African Americans themselves must come to understand that this demand is not for charity. It is simply for what they are owed on a debt that is old but compellingly obvious and valid still. (Do not be fooled by individual examples of conspicuous black success. They have closed neither the economic nor the psychic gaps between blacks and whites, and are statistically insignificant.)

The blacks of Rosewood, Florida, and Greenwood, Oklahoma, have successfully brought their case for reparations to national attention. Indeed, in Oklahoma a biracial commission has just concluded that justice demands that reparations be paid to the victims of Oklahoma's Greenwood massacre. Congressman John Conyers has introduced H.R. 40, a bill "to examine the institution of slavery," subsequent "de jure and de facto discrimination against freed slaves and their descendants," the impact of these forces "on living African Americans" and to make recommendations to Congress on "appropriate remedies." Passage of this bill is crucial; even the making of a well-reasoned case for broader national restitution will do wonders for the spirits of blacks.

This is a struggle that African Americans cannot lose, for in the   7
very making of it we will discover, if nothing else, ourselves. And it is a struggle that all Americans must support, as the important first step toward America's having any chance for a new beginning in which all its inhabitants are true co-owners of America's democratic ideals.

Web **Read It Now:** Excerpt from *The Debt,* **bedfordstmartins.com/americanow,** Chapter 15. Read a five-page excerpt in *Essence* magazine from *The Debt: What America Owes to Blacks,* by Randall Robinson. In his argument for reparations for slavery, Robinson writes: "Black people worked long, hard, killing days, years, centuries — and they were never paid. The value of their labor went into other pockets."

JOHN CONYERS JR.

The Commission to Study Reparations Proposals for African Americans Act

[REPARATIONS PAGE, U.S. HOUSE OF REPRESENTATIVES / 2002]

In January of 1989, I first introduced the bill H.R. 40. Commis-   1
sion to Study Reparation Proposals for African Americans Act. I have reintroduced H.R. 40 every Congress since 1989, and will continue to do so until it's passed into law.

JOHN CONYERS JR. *(b. 1929) has served nineteen terms in office as a representative of the fourteenth district of Michigan. Representative Conyers is the Democratic leader on the House Judiciary Committee, where he continues to oversee constitutional, consumer protection, and civil rights issues. He is also the founder of the congressional Black Caucus.*

One of the biggest challenges in discussing the issue of reparations in a political context is deciding how to have a national discussion without allowing the issue to polarize our party or our nation. The approach that I have advocated for over a decade has been for the federal government to undertake an official study of the impact of slavery on the social, political and economic life of our nation.

Over 4 million Africans and their descendants were enslaved in the United States and its colonies from 1619 to 1865, and as a result, the United States was able to begin its grand place as the most prosperous country in the free world.

It is uncontroverted that African slaves were not compensated for their labor. More unclear however, is what the effects and remnants of this relationship have had on African Americans and our nation from the time of emancipation through today.

I chose the number of the bill, 40, as a symbol of the forty acres and a mule that the United States initially promised freed slaves. This unfulfilled promise and the serious devastation that slavery had on African American lives has never been acknowledged officially by the United States Government.

My bill does four things:

1. It acknowledges the fundamental injustice and inhumanity of slavery.
2. It establishes a commission to study slavery, its subsequent racial and economic discrimination against freed slaves.
3. It studies the impact of those forces on today's living African Americans.
4. The commission would then make recommendations to Congress on appropriate remedies to redress the harm inflicted on living African Americans.

The commission established would also shed light on the capture and procurement of slaves, the transport and sale of slaves, the treatment of slaves in the colonies and in the United States. It would examine the extent to which federal and state governments in the United States supported the institution of slavery and examine federal and state laws that discriminated against freed African slaves from the end of the Civil War to the present.

Many of the most pressing issues, which have heretofore not been broached on any broad scale, would be addressed. Issues such as the lingering negative effects of the institution of slavery, whether an apology is owed, whether compensation is warranted and, if so, in what form and who should eligible would also be delved into.

H.R. 40 has strong grassroots support within the African American community, including major civil rights organizations, religious organizations, academic and civic groups from across the country. This support is very similar to the strong grassroots support that proceeded another legislative initiative: the Martin Luther King Jr. Holiday bill. It took a full fifteen years from the time I first introduced it on April 5, 1968, to its passage in the fall of 1983. Through most of those fifteen years, the idea of a federal holiday honoring an African American civil rights leader was considered a radical idea. [9]

Like the King Holiday bill, we have seen the support for this bill increase each year. Today we have over forty cosponsors, more than at any time in the past. What is also encouraging is the dramatic increase in the number of supporters for the bill among members of Congress who are not members of the congressional Black Caucus. Just this past month my colleague Tony Hall from Ohio introduced a bill calling for an apology as well as the creation of a reparations commission. So now, for the first time, we have two bills in Congress that call for the creation of a commission. [10]

We are also encouraged by the support of city councils and other local jurisdiction that have supported our bill. Already the city councils in Detroit, Cleveland, Chicago, and Atlanta have passed bills supporting H.R. 40. And just this past month a councilman in Los Angeles, the site of our 2000 convention, has introduced a bill with the strong support of the Los Angeles community. Also, there are presently two bills in the Michigan State House of Representatives addressing the issue of reparations. [11]

It is a fact that slavery flourished in the United States and constituted an immoral and inhumane deprivation of African slaves' lives, liberty, and cultural heritage. As a result, millions of African Americans today continue to suffer great injustices. [12]

But reparation is a national and a global issue, which should be addressed in America and in the world. It is not limited to Black Americans in the United States but is an issue for the many countries and villages in Africa, which were pilfered, and the many countries, which participated in the institution of slavery. [13]

Another reason that this bill has garnered so much resistance is because many people want to leave slavery in the past — they contend that slavery happened so long ago that it is hurtful and divisive to bring it up now. It's too painful. But the concept of reparations is [14] not a foreign idea to either the U.S. government or governments throughout the world.

Though there is historical cognition for reparations and it is a   15
term that is fairly well known in the international body politic, the question of reparations for African Americans remains unresolved. And so, just as we've discussed the Holocaust, and Japanese internment camps, and to some extent the devastation that the colonists inflicted upon the Indians, we must talk about slavery and its continued effects.

Web **Read It Now:** Text of the Reparations Bill, **bedfordstmartins.com/ americanow**, Chapter 15. Read the full text of the reparations for slavery bill (H.R. 40) that Representative John Conyers Jr. has presented to each Congress since 1989. Among the goals of the bill is to acknowledge the cruelty and injustice of slavery and to establish a commission to examine slavery and its impact on African Americans today.

Vocabulary/Using a Dictionary

1. What antonym for *uncontrovertible* (Conyers, para. 4) shares its root?

2. What words do you see *interment* (Conyers, para. 15) being related to? How are the meanings of those words the same? How are they different? What related adjective do you see in the word *contemporaneousness* (Robinson, para. 1)

3. The original meaning of *covenant* (Robinson, para. 3) is "coming together." How does this meaning relate to the words *convent, convention, venue, coven,* and *convenient*? Use your dictionary as necessary.

4. If "de jure" discrimination (Robinson, para. 6) means discrimination that is instituted by law (for example, slave owning before the Civil War), what does "de facto" discrimination (Robinson, para. 6) mean? Can you think of any examples of de facto discrimination?

Responding to Words in Context

1. Why do you think Conyers uses the word *pilfered* in paragraph 13 rather than *overtaken* or *used*?

2. Examine and analyze Robinson's metaphorical use of the word *salve* in paragraph 1. Do you find the metaphor effective? Why or why not?

3. Robinson writes in paragraph 5 that "African Americans, unfortunately, have accommodated this amnesia all too well." What is the meaning of *amnesia*? Is Robinson using the dictionary definition here, or a slightly different connotation?

Discussing Main Point and Meaning

1. What would bill H.R. 40 accomplish if, as Conyers hopes, it was passed by the House of Representatives and the Senate?

2. Why does Conyers compare his current bill (H.R. 40) to the Martin Luther King Jr. Holiday bill passed in 1983?

3. Do you know about any initiatives to make reparations to Holocaust survivors and Japanese interment camp victims, whom Conyers mentions in paragraph 15? How are the examples similar to the example of slavery reparations? How are they different?

4. "This is a struggle that African Americans cannot lose, for in the very making of it we will discover, if nothing else, ourselves" (Robinson, para. 7). What does Robinson mean by this? How will reparations lead to identity for African Americans?

Examining Sentences, Paragraphs, and Organization

1. Conyers introduces his essay by describing the number of times he has introduced his bill into Congress (and thus the number of times it has failed). Why does he begin this way rather than by enumerating the atrocities of slavery or the present state of the African American community?

2. Why do you think Conyers summarizes his bill in a list form (para. 6)?

3. Conyers spends several paragraphs (paras. 9–11) describing the growing support for his bill. How is this growth categorized in each of the paragraphs?

4. Examine Robinson's quotation of Conyers's bill in paragraph 6. Why doesn't he merely summarize or paraphrase Conyers? Why does he include specific words and phrases as quotes?

Thinking Critically

1. Would making reparations for slavery descendants open the door to other kinds of (albeit lesser) reparations, such as reparations for women, whose inheritances and dowries generally were passed directly to their husbands until late in the nineteenth century, or pay to descendants of Chinese laborers who were indentured (or paid very little) to build railroad tracks in the late nineteenth century?

2. Do you think the government has avoided making reparations for slavery because of all of the logistical problems that could arise (for example, determining who owes what and who gets what), because of the potential costs (the African American population has grown steadily since abolition), or because it finds reparations an unfair or illogical act?

In-Class Writing Activities

1. Write a short essay on how you think reparations to the descendants of slaves would change our society. Do you think relations between whites and blacks would improve? How would such reparations affect other racial minority groups?

2. In discussing early affirmative action initiatives, President Lyndon Johnson famously used a metaphor of several runners running a race, one runner wearing shackles around his ankles. Johnson asked whether merely removing the shackles halfway around the track would make the race "fair," suggesting that the government needed to do more for African Americans than merely stop discriminating — they needed to equalize the playing field. Does this same logic underlie the reparations movement? How is affirmative action similar to the idea of reparations? How is it different? Write a short essay comparing the two approaches to equalizing the playing field. (On this topic also see Randall Kennedy's "Blind Spot," p. 289.)

AMERICA THEN . . . 1847

$200 Reward

Few historical documents confront us with the bitter reality of slavery more dramatically than the advertisements and reward posters that regularly appeared in American towns and newspapers for three centuries. These ads and posters often notified customers of slave auctions or offered rewards for slaves who had run away from their owners. The reward poster here — one of thousands that have survived — is especially moving because it depicts an entire family attempting to escape to Chicago.

$200 Reward.

RANAWAY from the subscriber, on the night of Thursday, the 30th of Sepember,

FIVE NEGRO SLAVES,

To-wit : one Negro man, his wife, and three children.

The man is a black negro, full height, very erect, his face a little thin. He is about forty years of age, and calls himself *Washington Reed*, and is known by the name of Washington. He is probably well dressed, possibly takes with him an ivory headed cane, and is of good address. Several of his teeth are gone.

Mary, his wife, is about thirty years of age, a bright mulatto woman, and quite stout and strong.

The oldest of the children is a boy, of the name of FIELDING, twelve years of age, a dark mulatto, with heavy eyelids. He probably wore a new cloth cap.

MATILDA, the second child, is a girl, six years of age, rather a dark mulatto, but a bright and smart looking child.

MALGOLM, the youngest, is a boy, four years old, a lighter mulatto than the last, and about equally as bright. He probably also wore a cloth cap. If examined, he will be found to have a swelling at the navel.

Washington and Mary have lived at or near St. Louis, with the subscriber, for about 15 years.

It is supposed that they are making their way to Chicago, and that a white man accompanies them, that they will travel chiefly at night, and most probably in a covered wagon.

A reward of $150 will be paid for their apprehension, so that I can get them, if taken within one hundred miles of St. Louis, and $200 if taken beyond that, and secured so that I can get them, and other reasonable additional charges, if delivered to the subscriber, or to THOMAS ALLEN, Esq., at St. Louis, Mo. The above negroes, for the last few years, have been in possession of Thomas Allen, Esq., of St. Louis.

WM. RUSSELL.

ST. LOUIS, Oct. 1, 1847.

Web **See It Now:** Slave Reward Posters, bedfordstmartins.com/americanow, Chapter 15. This archive at the Duke University Library includes images and transcripts of reward posters, bills of sale, and logs of slave ships.

Web **See and Read It Now:** Slave Narratives and Images, bedfordstmartins.com/americanow, Chapter 15. This collection at the Library of Congress, titled "Born in Slavery: Slave Narratives from the Federal Writers' Project, 1936–1938," offers more than 2,300 narratives and more than 500 photographs of former slaves, 200 of which have never before been publicly available.

II. "TEN REASONS": THE CONTROVERSY

Before You Read

Do reparations for slavery heal a wound or exacerbate it? Can such reparations be justified, or are they too late and too symbolic to do any good?

Words to Learn [Horowitz]

antebellum (para. 1): belonging to the pre–Civil War period (adj.)

GNP (para. 2): gross national product; total market value of goods and services produced by a nation for a given period (n.)

per capita (para. 2): per person (adj.)

redress (para. 8): rectify; remedy; put in balance (v.)

Words to Learn [Chrisman and Allen]

foment (para. 1): to fuel; to stimulate (v.)

polemic (para. 2): argumentative attack (n.)

sophistry (para. 2): plausible but misleading or fallacious argument (n.)

relativist (para. 3): pertaining to a state of dependence between two or more entities (adj.)

institutionalize (para. 5): formally establish or recognize as civic or public system (v.)

chandlery (para. 5): business of candle making and sales (n.)

indenture (para. 7): contract binding one party into the service of another for a specified term (n.)

conscript (para. 9): recruit; draftee (n.)

nominally (para. 11): by name; technically (adv.)

disfranchisement (para. 15): deprivation of a right of citizenship, especially voting (n.)

ideology (para. 20): philosophy or creed based on self-interest (n.)

paternalism (para. 24): system of providing for the needs of people without giving them responsibility or freedom (n.)

spurious (para. 25): false; illegitimate (adj.)

vestiges (para. 26): traces; relics; remnants (n.)

This advertisement, sponsored by political conservative David Horowitz, was published in March 2001 in college newspapers across the country. The full text of the ad is included on pages 358–362.

DAVID HOROWITZ

Ten Reasons Why Reparations for Slavery Is a Bad Idea — and Racist Too

[THE BROWN DAILY HERALD, BROWN UNIVERSITY / March 2001]

I
There Is No Single Group Responsible for the Crime of Slavery.

Black Africans and Arabs were responsible for enslaving the ancestors of African Americans. There were 3,000 black slave-owners in the antebellum United States. Are reparations to be paid by their descendants too? There were white slaves in colonial America. Are their descendants going to receive payments?

II
There Is No Single Group That Benefited Exclusively from Slavery.

The claim for reparations is premised on the false assumption that only whites have benefited from slavery. If slave labor has created wealth for Americans, then obviously it has created wealth for black Americans as well, including the descendants of slaves. The GNP of black America makes the African American community the tenth most prosperous "nation" in the world. American blacks on average enjoy per capita incomes in the range of twenty to fifty times that of blacks living in any of the African nations from which they were kidnapped.

DAVID HOROWITZ (b. 1939) is a Fox News analyst and a columnist for Salon.com. He has written over a dozen books including Hating Whitey and Other Progressive Causes (1999) and Uncivil Wars: The Controversy over Reparations for Slavery (2001).

III
Only a Minority of White Americans Owned Slaves, While Others Gave Their Lives to Free Them.

Only a tiny minority of Americans ever owned slaves. This is true even for those who lived in the antebellum South where only one white in five was a slaveholder. Why should their descendants owe a debt? What about the descendants of the 350,000 Union soldiers who died to free the slaves? They gave their lives. What morality would ask their descendants to pay again? If paying reparations on the basis of skin color is not racism, what is?

IV
Most Living Americans Have No Connection (Direct or Indirect) to Slavery.

The two great waves of American immigration occurred after 1880 and then after 1960. What logic would require Vietnamese boat people, Russian refuseniks, Iranian refugees, Armenian victims of the Turkish persecution, Jews, Mexicans, Greeks, or Polish, Hungarian, Cambodian and Korean victims of Communism, to pay reparations to American blacks?

V
The Historical Precedents Used to Justify the Reparations Claim Do Not Apply, and the Claim Itself Is Based on Race Not Injury.

The historical precedents generally invoked to justify the reparations claim are payments to Jewish survivors of the Holocaust, Japanese-Americans and African American victims of racial experiments in Tuskegee, or racial outrages in Rosewood and Oklahoma City. But in each case, the recipients of reparations were the direct victims of the injustice or their immediate families. This would be the only case of reparations to people who were not immediately affected and whose sole qualification to receive reparations would be racial. During the slavery era, many blacks were free men or slave-owners themselves, yet the reparations claimants make no attempt to take this fact into account. If this is not racism, what is?

VI

The Reparations Argument Is Based on the Unsubstantiated Claim That All African Americans Suffer from the Economic Consequences of Slavery and Discrimination.

No scientific attempt has been made to prove that living individuals have been adversely affected by a slave system that was ended nearly 150 years ago. But there is plenty of evidence that the hardships of slavery were hardships that individuals could and did overcome. The black middle class in America is a prosperous community that is now larger in absolute terms than the black underclass. Its existence suggests that present economic adversity is the result of failures of individual character rather than the lingering after-effects of racial discrimination or a slave system that ceased to exist well over a century ago. West Indian blacks in America are also descended from slaves but their average incomes are equivalent to the average incomes of whites (and nearly 25 percent higher than the average incomes of American-born blacks). How is it that slavery adversely affected one large group of descendants but not the other? How can government be expected to decide an issue that is so subjective?

VII

The Reparations Claim Is One More Attempt to Turn African Americans into Victims. It Sends a Damaging Message to the African-American Community and to Others.

The renewed sense of grievance — which is what the claim for reparations will inevitably create — is not a constructive or helpful message for black leaders to send to their communities and to others. To focus the social passions of African Americans on what some other Americans may have done to their ancestors 50 or 150 years ago is to burden them with a crippling sense of victimhood. How are the millions of nonblack refugees from tyranny and genocide who are now living in America going to receive these claims, moreover, except as demands for special treatment — an extravagant new handout that is only necessary because some blacks can't seem to locate the ladder of opportunity within reach of others, many of whom are less privileged than themselves?

VIII

Reparations to African Americans Have Already Been Paid.

Since the passage of the Civil Rights Acts and the advent of the Great Society in 1965, trillions of dollars in transfer payments have been made to African Americans in the form of welfare benefits and racial preferences (in contracts, job placements and educational admissions) — all under the rationale of redressing historic racial grievances. It is said that reparations are necessary to achieve a healing between African Americans and other Americans. If trillion-dollar restitutions and a wholesale rewriting of American law (in order to accommodate racial preferences) is not enough to achieve a "healing," what is?

IX
What about the Debt Blacks Owe to America?

Slavery existed for thousands of years before the Atlantic slave trade, and in all societies. But in the thousand years of slavery's existence, there never was an anti-slavery movement until white Anglo-Saxon Christians created one. If not for the anti-slavery beliefs and military power of white Englishmen and Americans, the slave trade would not have been brought to an end. If not for the sacrifices of white soldiers and a white American president who gave his life to sign the Emancipation Proclamation, blacks in America would still be slaves. If not for the dedication of Americans of all ethnicities and colors to a society based on the principle that all men are created equal, blacks in America would not enjoy the highest standard of living of blacks anywhere in the world, and indeed one of the highest standards of living of any people in the world. They would not enjoy the greatest freedoms and the most thoroughly protected individual rights anywhere. Where is the acknowledgment of black America and its leaders for those gifts?

X
The Reparations Claim Is a Separatist Idea That Sets African Americans against the Nation That Gave Them Freedom.

Blacks were here before the Mayflower. Who is more American than the descendants of African slaves? For the African American community to isolate itself from America is to embark on a course whose implications are troubling. Yet the African American community has had a long-running flirtation with separatists, nationalists, and the political left, who want African Americans to be no part of America's social contract. African Americans should reject this temptation.

For all America's faults, African Americans have an enormous stake in this country and its heritage. It is this heritage that is really under attack by the reparations movement. The reparations claim is one more assault on America, conducted by racial separatists and the political left. It is an attack not only on white Americans, but on all Americans — especially African Americans.

America's African American citizens are the richest and most privileged black people alive, a bounty that is a direct result of the heritage that is under assault. The American idea needs the support of its African American citizens. But African Americans also need the support of the American idea. For it is the American idea that led to the principles and created the institutions that have set African Americans — and all of us — free.

Web **Read It Now:** A Reparations Bibliography, **bedfordstmartins.com/ americanow**, Chapter 15. This extensive bibliography, compiled by David Horowitz and organized by national and student publications, is a hefty list of articles representing a range of opinion on reparations.

ROBERT CHRISMAN AND
ERNEST ALLEN JR.

Ten Reasons: A Response to David Horowitz

[THE BLACK SCHOLAR / Summer 2001]

David Horowitz's article, "Ten Reasons Why Reparations for Slavery Is a Bad Idea — and Racist Too," recently achieved circulation in a handful of college newspapers throughout the United States as a paid advertisement sponsored by the Center for the Study of Popular Culture. While Horowitz's article pretends to address the issues of reparations, it is not about reparations at all. It is, rather, a well-heeled, coordinated attack on Black Americans that is calculated to elicit division and strife. Horowitz reportedly attempted to place his article in some fifty student newspapers at universities and colleges across the country, and was successful in purchasing space in such newspapers at Brown, Duke, Arizona, UC Berkeley, UC Davis, University of Chicago, and University of Wisconsin, paying an average of $700 per paper. His campaign has succeeded in fomenting outrage, dissension, and grief wherever it has appeared. Unfortunately, both its supporters and its foes too often have categorized the issue as one centering on "free speech." The sale and purchase of advertising space is not a matter of free speech, however, but involves an exchange of commodities. Professor Lewis Gordon of Brown University put it very well, saying that "what concerned me was that the ad was both hate speech and a solicitation for financial support to develop antiblack ad space. I was concerned that it would embolden white su-

1

ROBERT CHRISMAN is editor-in-chief and publisher of The Black Scholar. He is also a professor of English and director of the African American Film Institute at Wayne State University in Detroit. ERNEST ALLEN JR. is a professor in the W. E. B. DuBois Department of Afro-American Studies at the University of Massachusetts.

premacists and antiblack racists." At a March 15 panel held at UC Berkeley, Horowitz also conceded that his paid advertisement did not constitute a free speech issue.

As one examines the text of Horowitz's article, it becomes apparent that it is not a reasoned essay addressed to the topic of reparations: It is, rather, a racist polemic against African Americans and Africans that is neither responsible nor informed, relying heavily upon sophistry and a Hitlerian "Big Lie" technique. To our knowledge, only one of Horowitz's ten "reasons" has been challenged by a black scholar as to source, accuracy, and validity. It is our intention here to briefly rebut his slanders in order to pave the way for an honest and forthright debate on reparations. In these efforts we focus not just on slavery, but also the legacy of slavery that continues to inform institutional as well as individual behavior in the United States to this day. Although we recognize that white America still owes a debt to the descendants of slaves, in addressing Horowitz's distortions of history we do not act as advocates for a specific form of reparations.

1. There is No Single Group Clearly Responsible for the Crime of Slavery

Horowitz's first argument, relativist in structure, can only lead to two conclusions: (1) societies are not responsible for their actions and (2) since "everyone" was responsible for slavery, no one was responsible. While diverse groups on different continents certainly participated in the trade the principal responsibility for internationalization of that trade and the institutionalization of slavery in the so-called New World rests with European and American individuals and institutions. The transatlantic slave trade began with the importation of African slaves into Hispaniola by Spain in the early 1500s. Nationals of France, England, Portugal, and the Netherlands, supported by their respective governments and powerful religious institutions, quickly entered the trade and extracted their pieces of silver as well. By conservative estimates, 14 million enslaved Africans survived the horror of the Middle Passage for the purpose of producing wealth for Europeans and Euro-Americans in the New World.

While there is some evidence of blacks owning slaves for profit purposes — most notably the creole caste in Louisiana — the numbers were small. As historian James Oakes noted, "By 1830 there were some 3,775 free black slaveholders across the South.... The evidence is overwhelming that the vast majority of black slaveholders were

free men who purchased members of their families or who acted out
of benevolence" (47–48).

2. There Is No Single Group That Benefited Exclusively
From Slavery

Horowitz's second point, which is also a relativist one, seeks to
dismiss the argument that white Americans benefited as a group from
slavery, contending that the material benefits of slavery could not accrue in an exclusive way to a single group. But such sophistry evades
the basic issue: Who benefited primarily from slavery? Those who
were responsible for the institutionalized enslavement of people of
African descent also received the primary benefits from such actions.
New England slave traders, merchants, bankers, and insurance companies all profited from the slave trade, which required a wide variety
of commodities ranging from sails, chandlery, foodstuffs, and guns,
to cloth goods and other items for trading purposes. Both prior to
and after the American Revolution, slaveholding was a principal path
for white upward mobility in the South. The white native-born as
well as immigrant groups such as Germans, Scots-Irish, and the like
participated. In 1860, cotton was the country's largest single export.
As Eric Williams and C. L. R. James have demonstrated, the free
labor provided by slavery was central to the growth of industry in
western Europe and the United States; simultaneously, as Walter
Rodney has argued, slavery depressed and destabilized the economies
of African states. Slaveholders benefited primarily from the institution, of course, and generally in proportion to the number of slaves
that they held. But the sharing of the proceeds of slave exploitation
spilled across class lines within white communities as well.

As historian John Hope Franklin recently affirmed in a rebuttal
to Horowitz's claims:

> All whites and no slaves benefited from American slavery. All blacks
> had no rights that they could claim as their own. All whites, including
> the vast majority who had no slaves, were not only encouraged but
> authorized to exercise dominion over all slaves, thereby adding
> strength to the system of control.
>
> If David Horowitz had read James D. DeBow's "The Interest in
> Slavery of the Southern Non-slaveholder," he would not have blun-
> dered into the fantasy of claiming that no single group benefited from
> slavery. Planters did, of course. New York merchants did, of course.
> Even poor whites benefited from the legal advantage they enjoyed

over all blacks as well as from the psychological advantage of having a group beneath them.

The context of the African American argument for reparations is confined to the practice and consequences of slavery within the United States, from the colonial period on through final abolition and the aftermath, circa 1619–1865. Contrary to Horowitz's assertion, there is no record of institutionalized white enslavement in colonial America. Horowitz is confusing the indenture of white labor, which usually lasted seven years or so during the early colonial period, with enslavement. African slavery was expanded, in fact, to replace the inefficient and unenforceable white indenture system (Smith).

Seeking to claim that African Americans, too, have benefited from slavery, Horowitz points to the relative prosperity of African Americans in comparison to their counterparts on the African continent. However, his argument that, "the GNP of black America makes the African American community the tenth most prosperous 'nation' in the world" is based upon a false analogy. GNP is defined as "the total market value of all the goods and services produced by a nation during a specified period." Black Americans are not a nation and have no GNP. Horowitz confuses disposable income and "consumer power" with the generation of wealth.

3. Only a Tiny Minority of White Americans Ever Owned Slaves, and Others Gave Their Lives to Free Them

Most white union troops were drafted into the union army in a war that the federal government initially defined as a "war to preserve the union." In large part because they feared that freed slaves would flee the South and "take their jobs" while they themselves were engaged in warfare with Confederate troops, recently drafted white conscripts in New York City and elsewhere rioted during the summer of 1863, taking a heavy toll on black civilian life and property. Too many instances can be cited where white northern troops plundered the personal property of slaves, appropriating their bedding, chickens, pigs, and foodstuffs as they swept through the South. On the other hand, it is certainly true that there also existed principled white commanders and troops who were committed abolitionists.

However, Horowitz's focus on what he mistakenly considers to be the overriding, benevolent aim of white union troops in the Civil War obscures the role that blacks themselves played in their own liberation. African Americans were initially forbidden by the Union to fight in the Civil War, and black leaders such as Frederick Douglass and Martin Delany demanded the right to fight for their freedom. When racist doctrine finally conceded to military necessity, blacks were recruited into the Union Army in 1862 at approximately half the pay of white soldiers — a situation that was partially rectified by an act of Congress in mid-1864. Some 170,000 blacks served in the Civil War, representing nearly one-third of the free black population.

By 1860, four million blacks in the United States were enslaved;   11
some 500,000 were nominally free. Because of slavery, racist laws, and racist policies, blacks were denied the chance to compete for the opportunities and resources of America that were available to native whites and immigrants: labor opportunities, free enterprise, and land. The promise of "forty acres and a mule" to former slaves was effectively nullified by the actions of President Andrew Johnson. And because the best land offered by the Homestead Act of 1862 and its subsequent revisions quickly fell under the sway of white homesteaders and speculators, most former slaves were unable to take advantage of its provisions.

4. Most Living Americans Have No Connection (Direct or Indirect) to Slavery

As Joseph Anderson, member of the National Council of African   12
American Men, observed, "the arguments for reparations aren't made on the basis of whether every white person directly gained from slavery. The arguments are made on the basis that slavery was institutionalized and protected by law in the United States. As the government is an entity that survives generations, its debts and obligations survive the lifespan of any particular individuals.... Governments make restitution to victims as a group or class" (*San Francisco Chronicle,* March 26, 2001, p. A21).

Horowitz's article is not a reasoned essay: It is a racist polemic against African Americans and Africans.

Most Americans today were not alive during   13
World War II. Yet reparations to Japanese Americans for their interment in concentration camps during the war was paid out of current government sources contributed to by contemporary Americans. Passage of time does not negate the responsibility of government in crimes against humanity. Similarly, German corporations are not the "same" corporations that supported the Holocaust; their personnel

and policies today belong to generations removed from their earlier criminal behavior. Yet, these corporations are being successfully sued by Jews for their past actions. In the same vein, the U.S. government is not the same government as it was in the pre-Civil War era, yet its debts and obligations from the past are no less relevant today.

5. The Historical Precedents Used to Justify the Reparations Claim Do Not Apply, and the Claim Itself Is Based on Race Not Injury

As noted in our response to "Reason 4," the historical precedents   14
for the reparations claims of African Americans are fully consistent with restitution accorded other historical groups for atrocities committed against them. Second, the injury in question — that of slavery — was inflicted upon a people designated as a race. The descendants of that people — still socially constructed as a race today — continue to suffer the institutional legacies of slavery some 135 years after its demise. To attempt to separate the issue of so-called race from that of injury in this instance is pure sophistry. For example, the criminal (in)justice system today largely continues to operate as it did under slavery — for the protection of white citizens against black "outsiders." Although no longer inscribed in law, this very attitude is implicit to processes of law enforcement, prosecution, and incarceration, guiding the behavior of police, prosecutors, judges, juries, wardens, and parole boards. Hence, African Americans continue to experience higher rates of incarceration than do whites charged with similar crimes, endure longer sentences for the same classes of crimes perpetrated by whites, and, compared to white inmates, receive far less consideration by parole boards when being considered for release.

Slavery was an institution sanctioned by the highest laws of the   15
land with a degree of support from the Constitution itself. The institution of slavery established the idea and the practice that American democracy was "for whites only." There are many white Americans whose actions (or lack thereof) reveal such sentiments today — witness the response of the media and the general populace to the blatant disfranchisement of African Americans in Florida during the last presidential election. Would such complacency exist if African Americans were considered "real citizens"? And despite the dramatic successes of the Civil Rights movement of the 1950s and 60s, the majority of black Americans do not enjoy the same rights as white Americans in the economic sphere. (We continue this argument in the following section.)

6. The Reparations Argument Is Based on the Unfounded Claim That All African American Descendants of Slaves Suffer from the Economic Consequences of Slavery and Discrimination

Most blacks suffered and continue to suffer the economic conse-   16
quences of slavery and its aftermath. As of 1998, median white family income in the United States was $49,023; median black family income was $29,404 just 60 percent of white income (*2001 New York Times Almanac,* p. 319). Further, the costs of living within the United States far exceed those of African nations. The present poverty level for an American family of four is $17,029. Twenty-three and three-fifths percent (23.6 percent) of all black families live below the poverty level.

When one examines net financial worth, which reflects, in part,   17
the wealth handed down within families from generation to genera-tion, the figures appear much starker. Recently, sociologists Melvin L. Oliver and Thomas M. Shapiro found that just a little over a decade ago, the net financial worth of white American families with *zero* or *negative* net financial worth stood at around 25 percent; that of Hispanic households at 54 percent; and that of black American households at almost 61 percent (Oliver & Shapiro, p. 87). The in-ability to accrue net financial worth is also directly related to hiring practices in which black Americans are "last hired" when the econ-omy experiences an upturn, and "first fired" when it falls on hard times.

And as historian John Hope Franklin remarked on the legacy of   18
slavery for black education: "laws enacted by states forbade the teaching of blacks any means of acquiring knowledge — including the alphabet — which is the legacy of disadvantage of educational priva-tization and discrimination experienced by African Americans in 2001."

Horowitz's comparison of African Americans with Jamaicans is   19
a false analogy, ignoring the different historical contexts of the two populations. The British government ended slavery in Jamaica and its other West Indian territories in 1836, paying West Indian slave-holders 20,000,000 pounds ($100,000,000 U.S. dollars) to free the slaves, and leaving the black Jamaicans, who comprised 90 percent of that island's population, relatively free. Though still facing racist obstacles, Jamaicans come to the United States as voluntary immi-grants, with greater opportunity to weigh, choose, and develop their options.

7. The Reparations Claim Is One More Attempt to Turn African Americans into Victims. It Sends a Damaging Message to the African American Community

What is a victim? Black people have certainly been victimized,   20
but acknowledgment of that fact is not a case of "playing the victim" but of seeking justice. There is no validity to Horowitz's comparison between black Americans and victims of oppressive regimes
who have voluntarily immigrated to these shores. Further, many
members of those populations, such as Chileans and Salvadorans,
direct their energies for redress toward the governments of their
own oppressive nations, which is precisely what black Americans
are doing. Horowitz's racism is expressed in his contemptuous
characterization of reparations as "an extravagant new handout
that is only necessary because some blacks can't seem to locate the
ladder of opportunity within reach of others, many of whom are
less privileged than themselves." What Horowitz fails to acknowledge is that racism continues as an ideology and a material force
within the United States, providing blacks with no ladder that
reaches the top. The damage lies in the systematic treatment of
black people in the United States, not their claims against those
who initiated this damage and their spiritual descendants who continue its perpetuation.

8. Reparations to African Americans Have Already Been Paid

The nearest the U.S. government came to full and permanent   21
restitution of African Americans was the spontaneous redistribution
of land brought about by General William Sherman's Field Order 15
in January, 1865, which empowered Union commanders to make
land grants and give other material assistance to newly liberated
blacks. But that order was rescinded by President Andrew Johnson
later in the year. Efforts by Representative Thaddeus Stevens and
other radical Republicans to provide the proverbial "forty acres and
a mule" that would have carved up huge plantations of the defeated
Confederacy into modest land grants for blacks and poor whites
never got out of the House of Representatives. The debt has not been
paid.

"Welfare benefits and racial preferences" are not reparations. The   22
welfare system was set in place in the 1930s to alleviate the poverty of
the Great Depression, and more whites than blacks received welfare.
So-called "racial preferences" come not from benevolence but from

lawsuits by blacks against white businesses, government agencies, and municipalities that practice racial discrimination.

9. What about the Debt Blacks Owe to America?

Horowitz's assertion that "in the thousand years of slavery's ex-   23
istence, there never was an antislavery movement until white Anglo-
Saxon Christians created one," only demonstrates his ignorance concerning the formidable efforts of blacks to free themselves. Led by
black Toussaint L'Ouverture, the Haitian revolution of 1793 over-
threw the French slave system, created the first black republic in the
world, and intensified the activities of black and white antislavery
movements in the United States. Slave insurrections and conspiracies
such as those of Gabriel (1800), Denmark Vesey (1822), and Nat
Turner (1831) were potent sources of black resistance; black abolitionists such as Harriet Tubman, Frederick Douglass, Richard Allen,
Sojourner Truth, Martin Delany, David Walker, and Henry Highland
Garnet waged an incessant struggle against slavery through agencies
such as the press, notably Douglass's *North Star* and its variants,
which ran from 1847 to 1863 (blacks, moreover, constituted some 75
percent of the subscribers to William Lloyd Garrison's *Liberator*
newspaper in its first four years); the Underground Railroad, the
Negro Convention Movement, local, state, and national antislavery
societies, and the slave narrative. Black Americans were in no ways
the passive recipients of freedom from anyone, whether viewed from
the perspective of black participation in the abolitionist movement,
the flight of slaves from plantations and farms during the Civil War,
or the enlistment of black troops in the Union army.

The idea of black debt to U.S. society is a rehash of the Christian   24
missionary argument of the seventeenth and eighteenth centuries: Because Africans were considered heathens, it was therefore legitimate
to enslave them and drag them in chains to a Christian nation. Following their partial conversion, their moral and material lot were improved, for which black folk should be eternally grateful. Slave ideo-
logues John Calhoun and George Fitzhugh updated this idea in the
nineteenth century, arguing that blacks were better off under slavery
than whites in the North who received wages, due to the paternalism
and benevolence of the plantation system that assured perpetual employment, shelter, and board. Please excuse the analogy, but if someone chops off your fingers and then hands them back to you, should
you be "grateful" for having received your mangled fingers, or en-
raged that they were chopped off in the first place?

10. *The Reparations Claim Is a Separatist Idea That Sets African Americans against the Nation That Gave Them Freedom*

Again, Horowitz reverses matters. Blacks are already separated   25
from white America in fundamental matters such as income, family
wealth, housing, legal treatment, education, and political representation. Andrew Hacker, for example, has argued the case persuasively
in his book *Two Nations*. To ignore such divisions, and then charge
those who raise valid claims against society with promoting divisive-
ness, offers a classic example of "blaming the victim." And we have
already refuted the spurious point that African Americans were the
passive recipients of benevolent white individuals or institutions that
"gave" them freedom.

Too many Americans tend to view history as "something that   26
happened in the past," something that is "over and done," and thus
has no bearing upon the present. Especially in the case of slavery,
nothing could be further from the truth. As historian John Hope
Franklin noted in his response to Horowitz:

> Most living Americans do have a connection with slavery. They have
> inherited the preferential advantage, if they are white, or the loath-
> some disadvantage, if they are black; and those positions are virtually
> as alive today as they were in the nineteenth century. The pattern of
> housing, the discrimination in employment, the resistance to equal
> opportunity in education, the racial profiling, the inequities in the ad-
> ministration of justice, the low expectation of blacks in the discharge
> of duties assigned to them, the widespread belief that blacks have
> physical prowess but little intellectual capacities, and the widespread
> opposition to affirmative action, as if that had not been enjoyed by
> whites for three centuries, all indicate that the vestiges of slavery are
> still with us.
>
> And as long as there are pro-slavery protagonists among us, hid-
> ing behind such absurdities as "we are all in this together" or "it
> hurts me as much as it hurts you" or "slavery benefited you as much
> as it benefited me," we will suffer from the inability to confront the
> tragic legacies of slavery and deal with them in a forthright and con-
> structive manner.
>
> Most important, we must never fall victim to some scheme de-
> signed to create a controversy among potential allies in order to divide
> them and, at the same time, exploit them for its own special purpose.

Bibliography

2001 New York Times Almanac (New York: Penguin Books, 2000).

Richard F. America, *Paying the Social Debt: What White America Owes Black America* (Westport, CT: Praeger, 1993).

J. D. B. DeBow, "The Interest in Slavery of the Southern Non-Slaveholder," in *Slavery Defended: The Views of the Old South,* ed. Eric L. McKitrick (Englewood Cliffs, NJ: Prentice-Hall, 1963), 169–77.

Ira Berlin and others, *Slaves No More: Three Essays on Emancipation and the Civil War* (Cambridge [England]; New York: Cambridge University Press, 1992).

Dalton Conley, *Being Black, Living in the Red: Race, Wealth, and Social Policy in America* (Berkeley: University of California Press, 1999).

LaWanda Cox, "The Promise of Land for the Freedmen," *Mississippi Valley Historical Review* 45 (December 1958): 413–40.

Dudley Taylor Cornish, *The Sable Arm: Black Troops in the Union Army, 1861–1865* (1956; rpt. Lawrence, KS: University Press of Kansas, 1987).

Eric Foner, *Free Soil, Free Labor, Free Men: The Ideology of the Republican Party before the Civil War* (New York: Oxford University Press, 1970).

John Hope Franklin and Alfred A. Moss, Jr., *From Slavery to Freedom: A History of African Americans,* 7th ed. (New York: McGraw-Hill, 1994).

Andrew Hacker, *Two Nations: Black and White, Separate, Hostile, Unequal,* rev. ed. (New York: Ballantine Books, 1995).

James Oliver Horton and Lois E. Horton, *In Hope of Liberty: Culture, Community, and Protest among Northern Free Blacks, 1700–1860* (New York: Oxford University Press, 1997).

James L. Huston, "Property Rights in Slavery and the Coming of the Civil War," *Journal of Southern History* 65 (1999): 249–86.

James Oakes, *The Ruling Race: A History of American Slaveholders* (New York: Vintage Books, 1983).

Melvin L. Oliver and Thomas M. Shapiro, *Black Wealth/White Wealth: A New Perspective on Racial Inequality* (New York: Routledge, 1995).

Benjamin Quarles, *Black Abolitionists* (New York: Oxford University Press, 1969).
———, *The Negro in the Civil War* (Boston: Little, Brown, 1953).

Walter Rodney, *How Europe Underdeveloped Africa,* rev. ed. (Washington, DC: Howard University Press, 1981).

Jack Salzman, David Lionel Smith, and Cornel West, eds., *Encyclopedia of African-American Culture and History,* 5 vols. (New York: Macmillan Library Reference, 1996).

Diana Jean Schemo, "An Ad Provokes Campus Protests and Pushes Limits of Expression," *New York Times,* 21 March 2001, pp. A1, A17.

Abbot Emerson Smith, *Colonists in Bondage; White Servitude and Convict Labor in America, 1607–1776* (Chapel Hill: Pub. for the Institute of Early American History and Culture at Williamsburg, Va., by the University of North Carolina Press, 1947).

Barbara L. Solow and Stanley L. Engerman, eds., *British Capitalism and Caribbean Slavery: The Legacy of Eric Williams* (New York: Cambridge University Press, 1987).

Eric Williams, *Capitalism & Slavery* (1944; rpt. New York: Russell & Russell, 1961).

Web **Read It Now:** "Horowitz's Provocation," bedfordstmartins.com/americanow,
Chapter 15. In this opinion piece published in *The Progressive* (May 2001)
Adolph L. Reed Jr. argues that response to Horowitz's ad should not center
on censorship and that the piece itself is not "worthy of reasoned debate."
Read this and a collection of articles on reparations and the Horowitz con-
troversy.

Vocabulary/Using a Dictionary

1. Horowitz uses the term *manifesto* (para. 5) to describe Randall
   Robinson's book *The Debt*. What does this word mean? Does it
   also describe Horowitz's "Ten Reasons?" Why or why not?

2. The words *sophistry* (Chrisman and Allen, para. 2) and *sophisticated* come from the same root, *sophós*. What do you think this
   root means?

3. *Ideology* (Chrisman and Allen, para. 20) is derived from the
   same source as the word *idea*. What relationship do you see between the meanings of the two words?

4. The word *vestiges* (Chrisman and Allen, para. 26) is related to
   the word *investigate*. How do the meanings of these words relate
   to each other? Which do you think came first?

Responding to Words in Context

1. Horowitz calls "one white in five" a "tiny minority" (para. 3)
   when referring to the number of slaveholders in the antebellum
   period. Is the use of the word *tiny* accurate here?

2. Why does Horowitz use the word *gifts* in paragraph 9 to describe
   the abolition of slavery, the high standard of living in the United
   States, and the freedoms associated with U.S. democracy?

3. What does Horowitz mean by the phrase "the American idea"
   (para. 12)?

4. How does your understanding of the label "black slaveholder"
   change after you read paragraph 4 in Chrisman and Allen's
   essay?

5. What does Chrisman and Allen's often-used phrase "blaming the
   victim" mean?

Discussing Main Point and Meaning

1. Horowitz opposes reparations for slavery largely because so many generations have come and gone since abolition, and therefore there are no direct participants to hold responsible. Based on what you've read in Horowitz's advertisement, do you think he would have made the same argument right after slavery was abolished?

2. Examine and summarize Horowitz's logic in paragraph 2, where he argues that "there is no single group that benefited exclusively from slavery." Is his argument here persuasive? Does he provide ample evidence to support his claim here?

3. What are the main differences between Horowitz's "Ten Reasons" and Chrisman and Allen's rebuttal in terms of breadth of scope and level of detail?

4. What recent examples of race-based injury do Chrisman and Allen use to support their position that the legacies of slavery continue to adversely affect African Americans? See paragraphs 14–18 and 26 for help.

Examining Sentences, Paragraphs, and Organization

1. Horowitz chooses a list structure (consisting of ten items) to present his argument against reparations for slavery. Why do you think he uses this format? Why do you think he divides the format into ten items? Finally, why do you think Chrisman and Allen echo Horowitz's format in their rebuttal?

2. Why do you think almost every one of Horowitz's list items ends with a question?

3. Chrisman and Allen quote heavily from historian John Hope Franklin. What effect do these quotes have? How do they contribute to Chrisman and Allen's rebuttal of Horowitz?

Thinking Critically

1. Does Horowitz indicate anywhere in his advertisement that slavery was an immoral institution that had an adverse effect on the African American community?

2. Horowitz writes that, "The black middle-class in America is a prosperous community that is now larger in absolute terms than the black underclass" (para. 6). Does he provide evidence for this claim? Does he need to?

3. Chrisman and Allen seem to persuasively rebut Horowitz's claims that no single group was responsible for slavery, that whites were the saviors of slaves, and that reparations were already paid to slaves and their descendants. But they also try to make the argument that there are specific and identifiable legacies of slavery in the present that can and should be addressed. Are you persuaded by their connection between past and present? Why or why not?

In-Class Writing Activities

1. Identify three of Chrisman and Allen's most persuasive rebuttal points. Write a response to those points from Horowitz's point of view.

2. Is there a middle-ground perspective between Horowitz's and Chrisman and Allen's points of view? Write a short essay in which you present a compromise position on reparations for slavery.

TWO AFRICAN AMERICAN PERSPECTIVES

Should Black Americans Support Reparations?

Before You Read

Would reparations dishonor the memory of the generations of slaves who established African American culture? Are reparations a trade of "honor for dollars?"

Words to Learn [Franklin]

diatribe (para. 1): tirade; attack (n.)
dominion (para. 2): power; command (n.)
privatization (para. 4): process of transforming a public entity or service into a privately owned one (n.)
prowess (para. 5): skill; aptitude (n.)

Words to Learn [Steele]

crucible (para. 2): a severe test or trial (n.)
scion (para 3): descendant or heir (n.)
inertia (para. 5): resistance to acceleration or motion (n.)
deference (para. 9): courteous yielding to the wishes of another (n.)
ward (para. 9): a person under the guard or protection of another (n.)

JOHN HOPE FRANKLIN

Horowitz's Hortatory Horror

[THE CHRONICLE, DUKE UNIVERSITY / March 29, 2001]

Here are a few things to bear in mind when reading the diatribe on slavery and reparations that appeared in *The Chronicle* a few days ago.   1

All whites and no slaves benefited from American slavery. All blacks had no rights that they could claim as their own. All whites, including the vast majority who had no slaves, were not only encouraged but authorized to exercise dominion over all slaves, thereby adding strength to the system of control.   2

If David Horowitz had read James D. DeBow's "The Interest in Slavery of the Southern Non-slaveholder," he would not have blun-   3

JOHN HOPE FRANKLIN (b. 1915) is the James B. Duke Professor Emeritus of History and for seven years was professor of legal history in the law school at Duke University. He is the author of countless publications, including From Slavery to Freedom: A History of African-Americans *(1947), and has won numerous honors and awards, among them the Presidential Medal of Freedom in 1995.*

dered into the fantasy of claiming that no single group benefited from slavery. Planters did, of course. New York merchants did, of course. Even poor whites benefited from the legal advantage they enjoyed over all blacks as well as from the psychological advantage of having a group beneath them.

Meanwhile, laws enacted by states forbade the teaching of blacks   4
any means of acquiring knowledge — including the alphabet — which is the legacy of disadvantage of educational privatization and discrimination experienced by African Americans in 2001.

Most living Americans do have a connection with slavery. They   5
have inherited the preferential advantage, if they are white, or the loathsome disadvantage, if they are black; and those positions are virtually as alive today as they were in the nineteenth century. The pattern of housing, the discrimination in employment, the resistance to equal opportunity in education,

All whites and no slaves benefited from American slavery.

the racial profiling, the inequities in the administration of justice, the low expectation of blacks in the discharge of duties assigned to them, the widespread belief that blacks have physical prowess but little intellectual capacities, and the widespread opposition to affirmative action, as if that had not been enjoyed by whites for three centuries, all indicate that the vestiges of slavery are still with us.

And as long as there are pro-slavery protagonists among us, hid-   6
ing behind such absurdities as "we are all in this together" or "it hurts me as much as it hurts you" or "slavery benefited you as much as it benefited me," we will suffer from the inability to confront the tragic legacies of slavery and deal with them in a forthright and constructive manner.

Most important, we must never fall victim to some scheme de-   7
signed to create a controversy among potential allies in order to divide them and, at the same time, exploit them for its own special purpose.

SHELBY STEELE

Reparations Enshrine Victimhood, Dishonoring Our Ancestors

[NEWSWEEK / August 27, 2001]

My father was born in the last year of the nineteenth century. His father was very likely born into slavery, though there are no official records to confirm this. Still, from family accounts, I can plausibly argue that my grandfather was born a slave. 1

When I tell people this, I worry that I may seem conceited, like someone claiming a connection to royalty. The extreme experience of slavery — its commitment to broken-willed servitude — was so intense a crucible that it must have taken a kind of genius to survive it. In the jaws of slavery and segregation, blacks created a life-sustaining form of worship, rituals for every human initiation from childbirth to death, a rich folk mythology, a world-famous written literature, a complete cuisine, a truth-telling comic sensibility, and, of course, some of the most glorious music the world has ever known. 2

Like the scion of an aristocratic family, I mention my grandfather to stand a little in the light of the black American genius. So my first objection to reparation for slavery is that it feels like selling our birthright for a pot of porridge. There is a profound esteem that comes to us from having overcome four centuries of oppression. 3

This esteem is an irreplaceable resource. In Richard Wright's *Black Boy,* a black elevator operator makes pocket money by letting white men kick him in the behind for a quarter. Maybe reparations are not quite this degrading, but when you trade on the past victimization of your own people, you trade honor for dollars. And this 4

SHELBY STEELE's *writing has appeared in* Harper's, *the* New York Times Magazine, Commentary, *the* Washington Post, *the* American Scholar, *and* The Best American Essays, *and he is the 1993 recipient of the* National Magazine Award. *His books include* The Content of Our Character *(1990) and* A Dream Deferred *(1998).*

trading is only uglier when you are a mere descendant of those who suffered but nevertheless prevailed.

I believe the greatest problem black America has had over the past thirty years has been precisely a faith in reparational uplift — the idea that all the injustice we endured would somehow translate into the means of uplift. We fought for welfare programs that only subsidized human inertia, for cultural approaches to education that stagnated skill development in our young and for affirmative action programs that removed the incentive to excellence in our best and brightest.

Today 70 percent of all black children are born out of wedlock. Sixty-eight percent of all violent crime is committed by blacks, most often against other blacks. Sixty percent of black fourth graders cannot read at grade level. And so on. When you fight for reparational uplift, you have to fit yourself into a victim-focused, protest identity that is at once angry and needy. You have to locate real transformative power in white society, and then manipulate white guilt by seducing it with neediness and threatening it with anger. And you must nurture in yourself, and pass on to your own children, a sense of aggrieved entitlement that sees black success as an impossibility without the intervention of white compassion.

> *When you trade on the past victimization of your own people, you trade honor for dollars.*

The above statistics come far more from this crippling sense of entitlement than from racism. And now the demand for reparations is yet another demand for white responsibility when today's problem is a failure of black responsibility.

When you don't know how to go forward, you find an excuse to go backward. You tell yourself that if you can just get a little justice for past suffering, you will feel better about the challenges you face. So you make justice a condition of your going forward. But of course, there is no justice for past suffering, and to believe there is only guarantees more suffering.

The worst enemy black America faces today is not white racism but white guilt. This is what encourages us to invent new pleas rather than busy ourselves with the hard work of development. So willing are whites to treat us with deference that they are a hard mark to pass up. The entire civil rights establishment strategizes to keep us the wards of white guilt. If these groups had to rely on black money rather than white corporate funding, they would all go under tomorrow.

An honest black leadership would portray our victimization as 10
only a condition we faced, and nurture a black identity around the
ingenuity by which we overcame it. It would see reparations as a
childish illusion of perfect justice. I can't be repaid for my grandfather. The point is that I owe him a great effort.

Web⁾ **Hear and Read It Now:** Reparations Overview and Debate, **bedford
stmartins.com/americanow**, Chapter 15. Listen to an overview of reparations for slavery aired on National Public Radio that includes African American perspectives on the issue, a debate on the issue, and links to other reparations articles and resources.

Web⁾ **Read It Now:** The Black Reparations Movement, **bedfordstmartins.com/
americanow**, Chapter 15. Read the mission statement of a leading organization in the reparations movement, The National Coalition of Blacks for
Reparations in America (NCOBRA). You will also find a brief history of
reparations payments and current articles on reparations.

Vocabulary/Using a Dictionary

1. Franklin says whites "were not only encouraged but authorized
    to exercise dominion over all slaves" (para. 2). What does it
    mean *to exercise* a power? How is this use like or unlike the kind
    of exercise we do at a gym?

2. "[W]e will suffer from the inability to confront the tragic legacies
    of slavery and deal with them in a *forthright* and constructive
    manner" (Franklin, para. 6). What does the word *forthright*
    mean? What is the opposite of *forthright*?

3. What would you call the person who takes care of a *ward* (Steele,
    para. 9)?

Responding to Words in Context

1. By using the phrase "physical *prowess*" to describe one of the
    stereotypical attributes ascribed to black people (para. 5), does
    Franklin subtly allude to another stereotype that has specifically
    plagued black men since slavery times?

2. Read the following sentence: "[The trading of honor for dollars]
    is only *uglier* when you are a mere descendant of those who suf-

fered but nevertheless prevailed" (Steele, para. 4). Why does Steele use the word *ugly* to describe a process that is somewhat invisible?

3. Steele refers to African Americans who want reparations as having a "*crippling* sense of entitlement" (para. 7). What does he mean by the word *crippling* here?

Discussing Main Point and Meaning

1. Franklin describes a "widespread opposition to affirmative action, as if [it] had not been enjoyed by whites for three centuries" (para. 5). What does he mean by this? Was there ever an official affirmative action policy for whites?

2. "And as long as there are pro-slavery protagonists among us, hiding behind such absurdities as 'we are all in this together' or 'it hurts me as much as it hurts you' or 'slavery benefited you as much as it benefited me,' will suffer from the inability to confront the tragic legacies of slavery and deal with them in a forthright and constructive manner" (Franklin, para. 6). What tone and point of view are the statements Franklin sets off in quotation marks meant to illustrate?

3. Why does Steele worry that he "may seem conceited" (para. 2) to some people?

4. When Steele says that rather than being owed a debt from white society for his grandfather's slavery, in fact it is he who owes his grandfather something (para. 10), what does he think he owes his grandfather? Why does he think this?

Examining Sentences, Paragraphs, and Organization

1. "*All* whites and *no* slaves benefited from American slavery. *All* blacks had *no* rights that they could claim as their own. *All* whites, including the vast majority who had *no* slaves, were not only encouraged but authorized to exercise dominion over *all* slaves" (Franklin, para. 2). Why does Franklin repeat the words *all* and *no* several times in this passage?

2. In paragraph 5, Franklin presents a list of the kinds of discrimination black Americans face today. Why does he present so many examples in one sentence?

3. In paragraph 2, Steele presents a list of the accomplishments of African Americans within the context of slavery and segregation. How would you characterize the tone in this sentence? What is its purpose?

4. Put the following sentences into your own words: "When you fight for reparational uplift, you have to fit yourself into a victim-focused, protest identity that is at once angry and needy. You have to locate real transformative power in white society, and then manipulate white guilt by seducing it with neediness and threatening it with anger" (Steele, para. 6).

5. In some paragraphs, Steele speaks of African Americans in the first-person plural (*we*), while in others he speaks of an individual second-person singular African American (*you*). Find examples of these two different cases and try to explain why he uses them both.

Thinking Critically

1. In paragraph 3 of his article, Franklin refers to a piece by James D. DeBow, "The Interest in Slavery of the Southern Non-slaveholder." Do you think this reference would be more effective if accompanied by a quote or at least a summary of the author's argument?

2. Steele makes the points that "a profound esteem...comes to [African Americans] from having overcome four centuries of oppression" (para. 3) and that this esteem is an "irreplaceable resource" (para. 4). One can also measure great damage to the esteem — perhaps the *self*-esteem — of African Americans as a result of the traditions of slavery, segregation, and persistent discrimination. Is it possible to feel both esteem and lack of it simultaneously? Which is the more powerful emotion: having a sense of profound esteem or feeling a severe lack of esteem?

3. Steele specifies the "last thirty years" (para. 5) as a period that is especially relevant to his argument. Why do you think he is so specific about this time period?

In-Class Writing Activities

1. What do you owe your ancestors? Write a short essay about the efforts made by your ancestors that may have benefited your life.

2. Do you agree or disagree with Steele? Are reparations an "ugly" trade of "honor for dollars," or do you think that reparations would show respect for the suffering that slaves endured? Write a short essay expressing your opinion, quoting from Steele's text as necessary.

III. STUDENT FORUM: A REPARATIONS DEBATE

Before You Read

Who should pay reparations? How should they be paid? Should they be paid at all?

Words to Learn [Luse]

incendiary (para. 3): provocative; inflammatory (adj.)

status quo (para. 3): from Latin, the existing state of affairs (at a particular time) (n.)

beleaguer (para. 5): to harass; to worry (v.)

Words to Learn [The Minnesota Daily]

xenophobia (para. 2): fear or dislike of foreigners (n.)

logistical (para. 4): of or related to the organizational and technical aspects of something (adj.)

Words to Learn [Wieben]

atone (para. 2): to make amends for a sin or a fault (v.)

liable (para. 3): legally responsible; accountable (adj.)

Words to Learn [Wakefield]

ambiguity (para. 2): vagueness; uncertainty (n.)

abomination (para. 5): disgrace; atrocity (n.)

Words to Learn [Khamisi]

antecedent (para. 1): precursor; predecessor (n.)

statute of limitations (para. 2): a time limit on the enforcement of a right (n.)

marginalization (para. 5): the act of pushing someone or something out of the center of attention (to the margins) (n.)

culpable (para. 6): blameworthy; responsible (adj.)

MONIQUE LUSE

Engaging Debate: Real Solutions to Racial Inequality

[THE MICHIGAN DAILY ONLINE, THE UNIVERSITY OF MICHIGAN–ANN ARBOR / April 12, 2001]

America is a nation that prides itself on being an exceptional melting pot with a particular brand of democracy. However, it is not, nor has it ever been, a true melting pot or a free democracy. In a nation plagued by racial profiling, a digital divide, disenfranchised national elections, and unjust, discriminatory drug laws, there is no democracy or melting pot (racial harmony). In one of the wealthiest and most industrialized nations there is a greater disparity in education, standard of living, and economics than in any other nation in the world. This disparity unequivocally exists along racial lines. To call us a free country is a lie. These are our nation's problems, created by our nation. If we are to call ourselves a democracy, a land of freedom, if we all are to aspire to the American dream, these problems must be addressed.

Affirmative action is often considered America's solution to these problems, and it has debatably done its job. Affirmative action has

1

2

Monique Luse was a sophomore at the University of Michigan when she wrote this piece for the Michigan Daily. *She is co-chair of the Michigan Student Assembly's Minority Student Affairs Commission and is vice-speaker for the Black Student Union.*

become a hot topic around the University of Michigan (as well as in the nation), and rightly so. The university is being sued to defend its admissions policy. However, an affirmative action admissions policy does not address the nation's problems in a comprehensive and multi-faceted manner. I contend that there are other solutions that must be engaged in order to address the roots of racism and inequality that affirmative action is said to correct. Reparations for slavery, apologies for slavery, and restitution have all been presented as other solutions to America's problems. It is time for those solutions to become part of our national discourse. This discourse can begin here at Michigan,

Disparity exists along racial lines. To call us a free country is a lie.

as we are already being pressed to examine present and past racial policies. These solutions are important to investigate because it forces us to look into history, into the causal effects of past policies, and into comprehensive solutions to today's problems.

David Horowitz is not out of order in attempting to bring the issue of reparations into the limelight on our campus[1]: I would prefer, however, that a real dialogue take place, in which investigations may be made beyond incendiary hearsay. There are many scholars, elected officials, and community leaders who are sparking debate and interest around this issue. U.S. Rep. John Conyers (D-Detroit) has put forth H.R. 40, a Commission to Study Reparation Proposals for African Americans Act during every Congress since January 1989. The bill now has forty cosponsors and gains increasing support each year. Renowned Harvard [now Princeton] University scholar Cornel West and activist/commentator Randall Robinson, along with countless others, have come together to begin work on a "Reparations Project." Resolutions have been passed by the city councils of Detroit, Chicago, Cleveland, and Atlanta to support H.R. 40. It has been introduced in Los Angeles. The Democratic Party placed a call for federal legislative discussion on reparations on last year's platform. The nation's leadership is moving toward a discussion on reparations, and we should take the lead. As university students we should be at the forefront of a challenge to the status quo and should be working towards creative solutions to today's problems.

Furthermore, it is important to note that the legislation proposed by John Conyers does not demand reparations, but rather demands

[1]David Horowitz spoke at the University of Michigan on March 19, 2002.

that we as a nation look at slavery and openly discuss how it has changed America, and how to remedy the problems it created. For our nation to heal its racial wounds, we have to address our past and its impact on our future. If our history is never discussed, then we will never have the option to decide if too much time has passed or if the impact of slavery has dissipated. All that these scholars, elected officials, community leaders, and citizens are asking for is a space to seek out those answers. The wounds of racial inequality and injustice will not heal until an open discussion about the origin of those inequalities and injustices is held.

To address reparations is to engage in real economic, social, philosophical, and political discourse. Many solutions have been presented throughout history to solve the gross inequalities that have and continue to beleaguer this country. It is time to address these issues and I see no reason why our generation cannot be the one to lead the discussion.   5

EDITORIAL BOARD

A Check Won't Fix the Problem

[THE MINNESOTA DAILY, THE UNIVERSITY OF MINNESOTA / September 5, 2001]

Slavery is a system based on exploitation and abuse, and it led to the racism and discrimination that still hinder blacks in America. Although slavery in the United States was a shameful violation of human rights and caused the incalculable suffering of millions, it was eradicated and after a long and painful civil rights movement, blacks achieved equal status to whites under law. Unfortunately, laws cannot influence social attitudes, and thus slavery is still close to the surface of black cultural identity. Recently the reparations movement gained increasing support in the United States as the debate gained global recognition. But reparations activists need to re-evaluate their platform and understand financial payback is not the most reasonable form of apology.   1

David Horowitz's ad, titled "Ten reasons why reparations for slavery is a bad idea — and racist too," Randall Robinson's book *The*   2

Debt: What America Owes to Blacks, and the United Nations conference on racism, racial discrimination, xenophobia, and related intolerance are all signs of the growing popularity of this civil rights issue.

Ultimately, American reparations advocates are responding to so-   3
cial problems such as poverty and unemployment, which they blame
on slavery and other historical wrongs. But reparations activists must
realize a one-time payment will not fix the current problem of inequality. Since discrimination cannot be signed away in a check,
blacks will be given what amounts to a bribe, allowing and, in fact,
fostering continued endurance of injustices. Angered at being forced
to pay reparations, the foolish and easily led will be pulled into the
inevitable conservative backlash and possibly even white supremacy
groups. In the end, reparations will furnish organizations like the Ku
Klux Klan with a flood of members and excuses.

Even if the private organizations or the federal government   4
agreed at some point to pay financial reparations, no feasible method
of compensation is foreseeable, especially if every black person in the
country expects to receive a check during his or her lifetime. Realisti-
cally, determining how the suffering of slaves re-
lates to a specific dollar amount presents a significant obstacle to financial compensation. Aside
from the ridiculous solution of devising a scale in-
tegrating levels of suffering with degrees of separation from the victim, it would be impossible to
tactfully devise a payment plan. In addition to the logistical issues, it
is degrading and insulting to try to quantify the pain and suffering by
telling someone that his grandfather didn't experience as much hardship as another person's.

> *Discrimination
> cannot be signed
> away in a check.*

Reparations advocates concerned with slavery's oppressive and   5
abusive methods should work to end the slavery that still thrives in
African countries like Sudan and Mauritania. And instead of seeking
financial compensation for individuals, advocates should lobby for
an international antislavery fund. Moving on from past wrongs will
help living slaves gain the independence they deserve.

KRISTIN WIEBEN

The U.S. Should Compensate for the Atrocities of Slavery

[THE BADGER HERALD, THE UNIVERSITY OF WISCONSIN–MADISON /
December 12, 2001]

When slavery was abolished in 1865, Congress passed a bill   1
promising freed slaves "forty acres and a mule." It was vetoed. Almost two centuries have passed since then, but the U.S. government has come no closer to making amends for the atrocities of slavery. It is time to fix this grievous wrong. It is time for the U.S. government to finally face its ugly past and try to make repairs.

Opponents of reparations often make the mistake of casting   2
reparations in a very individualized light. "I don't own slaves, and neither did my ancestors," they say. "So why should I have to pay?" They say the time to deal with the subject of slavery has already come and gone, and question the point of trying to atone for the sins of the dead by paying the living. Such logic fails to identify the real crux of the problem: the government's continued failure to uphold the rights of African Americans.

The government, unlike individuals, is timeless and contains a   3
built-in level of continuity. Individual slave owners may be long dead, but the government that supported and directly profited from slavery is very much alive and well. In other words, governments are immortal, and as such, they are liable for their actions even after the fact. And our government — whose very capitol was built with slave labor —

Kristin Wieben (b. 1982) is studying political science and French at the University of Wisconsin–Madison, where she was the opinion editor of the Badger Herald for 2001–2002. Wieben wrote this column as part of a point-counterpoint exchange when David Horowitz visited the Madison campus less than a year after his ad was printed. Wieben noticed the student response to Horowitz's visit was much less violent than the heated reaction that immediately followed the printing of the Horowitz advertisement in 2001.

has a lot to be liable for. From a Constitution that once classified African Americans as worth only three-fifths of a person, to racial profiling and discrimination in today's criminal justice system, our government has failed time and again to give African Americans their constitutional rights.

The relevance of slavery did not die when the last slave-holding plantation owners passed away. The wide gap in wealth between African Americans and whites is one of the most obvious vestiges of the problem. "African Americans couldn't even own property; they were property," writes reparations advocate and professor Thomas Shapiro. "There was just no way African Americans could accumulate assets that could be passed on from generation to generation." This economic gap, combined with both de facto and institutionalized segregation, is self-perpetuating and has left many African Americans disadvantaged from the outset.   4

Unfortunately, America has chosen to ignore and deny, for all practical purposes, slavery and its legacy. Some opponents of reparations even try to downplay the severity of the situation by pointing out that slavery has existed in almost every culture of the world. This argument is ridiculous. Two wrongs never make a right, and America's responsibility for its crimes is not lessened by the fact that its particular crime happens to be widespread.   5

These opponents advocate a continuation of the denial and say dwelling on past injustices is unhealthy and breeds a sense of helplessness and victimization. In the real world, however, problems don't go away just because you ignore them. This is no exception.   6

Reparations are necessary not because African Americans are incapable of succeeding without them, but because the government committed a terrible crime against humanity that has yet to be repaired, or even apologized for (lawmakers decided it would be too little, too late). Reparations are not handouts, they are the obligation of a government that has shirked its responsibility and refused to accept blame. African Americans can — and have — succeeded and thrived without reparations, but this does not negate the fact that the government has an outstanding debt to pay.   7

Our government supports reparations for other wronged nations, so why not for slavery? In fact, when speaking of a historic agreement to give $5 billion to Holocaust victims, then-Secretary of State Madeline Albright said it is was crucial to compensate "those whose labor was stolen or coerced during a time of outrage and shame. It is critical to completing the unfinished business of the old century be-   8 fore entering the new." Although she probably didn't even consider it, Albright's words explain perfectly why reparations are needed in America.

Obviously, a lot has changed since 1865; the idea of "forty acres and mule" is now obsolete. Just as it is impossible to lay all of the blame for slavery upon the shoulders of long dead slave owners, it is now unfeasible to settle the score by direct financial compensation for victims and their descendants. Rather, reparations should take the form of social programs, paid for by the government, such as aid for inner-city schools, scholarships, job-training programs, healthcare programs. Of course, such an initiative could never truly erase the scars of slavery; nothing could ever do that. But such a move would be an excellent first step toward facing a chapter of our country's past that has long been closed, and repairing the wrongs of slavery.

9

JOHN WAKEFIELD

Who Should Pay and Who Should Be Paid?

[THE PURDUE EXPONENT, PURDUE UNIVERSITY / September 6, 2001]

The proposal of Slave Reparations is that the U.S. Government has never claimed responsibility for the slavery that existed in early America and that the economic success of early America (and subsequently today) is largely attributable to slave labor. Never have slaves or any of their families been compensated for their toils. The proposal holds that African Americans deserve reparations for the injustice in the form of cash payments.

1

In my opinion, this proposal is counterproductive to the broader, more important goal of equality of all races, colors, and creeds. The first problem is the sheer size and ambiguity of the proposal. Who should pay and who should be paid?

2

JOHN WAKEFIELD *graduated from Purdue University in 2002. He wrote for the opinion column in the* Purdue Exponent *and was a senior when he published this piece.*

Of the 36.4 million African Americans living in the United States   3
today, which of them qualify for payments? Not all African Americans descended directly from slaves, and what is to be done with
African Americans with white ancestry as well, should they get nine-
sixteenths or some percentage of the payments based on their pedi-
gree of African American heritage? And what about successful
African Americans such as Michael Jordan and Oprah Winfrey?
Should they receive payments as well, or should it only be limited to
impoverished people?

The question of who is to be paid is actually the easy one. The   4
harder question is who should pay. Should the government pay or
simply the descendants of slave owners? I don't believe that the slave
owner descendants should pay because it is not their personal fault to
be born into a family whose wealth was earned by African American
slave labor. Besides, they are such a small minority of Americans; the
total monetary amount that they could supply would be rather insignificant and wouldn't really serve the purpose of Slave Reparations.

Therefore, should only the government and American tax dollars   5
pay for Slave Reparations? This too is flawed because most Americans' ancestors were in Europe long after the Civil War ended and
emigrated in the late 1800s and early 1900s. Why should people who
lived in Ireland or England until the twentieth century be forced to
pay for the sins of Mississippi planters in the early nineteenth century? On the topic of how much, the problem with calculating a fair
monetary amount for reparations is that no sum of money will ever
compensate for the torture and shameful conditions that slaves endured in America alone: 300 years of African American enslavement,
100 years of racial segregation, 3,000 mob lynchings, and decades of
discrimination. It is wrong to believe that simple cash payments and
an apology will make amends for the sheer monstrosity of injustice.
Some argue that it is better to get some money than no money. In this
case I feel that African Americans would be cheated. They deserve
something more honorable than a small payoff in return for the
abomination that early African Americans endured.

Another reason why I believe the Reparations proposal is wrong   6
is that it gives the government an excuse to wash its hands of its
wrongdoing. When asked to comment on issues concerning African
American enslavement, politicians could simply state, "Hey, it's already been settled, it's over and done with, get off it already!" In my
opinion, African American enslavement is an issue that should never

be forgotten, and the cries of anguish from those Americans should never fade away. I believe that these men and women deserve a more honorable memory and acknowledgment than petty cash payoffs. I think a perfect way to accomplish this would be the construction of a monument in Washington D.C. After all, the Capitol building and the White House themselves were built by slave labor, so why not erect a massive memorial to the hardships and toil of those African Americans who suffered through slavery? In this way, Americans could learn and never forget on whose backs the nation was built. As a symbol of the African American heroes to whom we all owe a debt that can never be resolved nor quantified into meaningless cash payoffs, this solution would honor the slaves and bring the nation closer together rather than split it further apart.

The goal of all of Americans, in my opinion, is to exist in the society that great men such as the founding fathers and Martin Luther King Jr. dreamed of: a place where all men and women are created equal, and where people are judged not by the color of their skin, but by the content of their character. Equality is the goal, not accountability. The reparations proposal only serves to redraw the line and accentuate the differences between races. Why are some people owed a debt for a crime that was not actually done to them to be paid by people who did not actually commit it? I believe that this proposal is founded on the "corruption of blood" doctrine specifically denounced in the Constitution of the United States — the notion that a criminal's blood kindred and descendants share in his guilt.

JOSEPHINE KHAMISI

Reparations: Concept and Context

[LOUISVILLE CARDINAL ONLINE, THE UNIVERSITY OF LOUISVILLE /
April 9, 2002]

There are several key principles that have to be understood be-   1
fore one can appreciate the concept of African Americans pressing for
reparations. The basis of recent claims against several corporations is
that those companies, or their antecedents, were "unjustly enriched"
by the economic system of slave labor and should return those profits. Furthermore, advocates believe that the approximately 246 years of
enslavement (and approximately 100 years of "Jim Crow") systematically deprived African Americans of the ability to accumulate and
pass on wealth during that time. Advocates for reparations believe
that there are causal connections between a history of economic dis-
enfranchisement and the economic conditions of the majority of
African Americans.

Unfortunately, I think that discussions of this topic get railroaded   2
into discussions of logistics. We first need to decide whether there
was economic injustice against slaves that led to undeserved profits.
While there are issues of statutes of limitations and the fact that those
who suffered directly have since passed away, anyone with even a superficial understanding of history can understand that for former
slaves getting the wrong redressed during their lifetime was hampered
by the still racist attitudes of those in all the branches of federal and
local government.

Despite what some opponents think, the reparations movement is   3
not some get-rich quick scheme. The movement for some form of compensation began as the Civil War was ending. It has its origins in General Sherman's Special Field Order No. 15 (1865) that mandated "each

JOSEPHINE KHAMISI *wrote this piece as a senior at the University of
Louisville, as a guest columnist for the* Louisville Cardinal. *She graduated
with a degree in sociology in 2002.*

family shall have a plot of no more than (40) forty acres of tillable ground." The order was eventually revoked by President Johnson. And while the Freedman's Bureau was given 800,000 acres of abandoned and confiscated Southern land to help resettle former slaves, by the end of the summer of 1865, African Americans who had been resettled there were forced out of their land. Between 1890 and 1903, there were at least nine bills introduced to congress by an Alabama Democrat William Vaughn calling for an exslave pension fund. Although nothing happened with those bills, some Southern slave owners were compensated for their property losses during the Civil War. As far as I can tell, there were no new cases during the era of Jim Crow, although since the passing of the Civil Rights Amendment, bills calling for reparations have been introduced in Congress at least thirteen times.

Many opponents of reparation payments also argue that since they were not individually responsible, they should not be liable. However, there often exists the need for the subordination of some values for fulfillment of justice and benefit of the greater society. I believe that many Native American nations deserve to be compensated for the additional hurdles they face as a result of being systematically destroyed. Even though I didn't do it, I recognize that I benefit from their suffering. And it is recognized that no money can possibly erase the suffering of those that lived through the slave system, and those who live under its shadow. The challenges of designing an equitable system to address this legacy should not be an excuse to do nothing.

One thing that wounds me daily is that, without living in my skin, others can tell me how I am and am not affected by both current and historical marginalization. Just because I, personally, and others have achieved a level of success within this country, does not negate the existence of discrimination nor white privilege. Reparations would be used for large-scale community development projects that would target inner-city neighborhoods to improve educational institutions, access to healthcare, and housing conditions. It is not merely individuals who benefit; in fact, the cycle of cash flow will distribute the money into the community and through various businesses and services throughout our economy.

While I agree with the present focus on corporations, I still think that the U.S. government is most culpable. It was our democracy that legalized and maintained the system of racial inequality and ultimately created a legal system that can defend the actions of certain corporations as well as countless individuals by claiming that they did nothing illegal, even though it was wrong.

Web Read It Now: *The Brown Daily Herald*, bedfordstmartins.com/americanow,
Chapter 15. Read an article — published with reader comments — in Brown
University's newspaper that reports on the scope of the controversy stirred
by David Horowitz's anti-reparations advertisement "Ten Reasons."

Vocabulary/Using a Dictionary

1. Luse calls David Horowitz's statements "*incendiary* hearsay"
   (para. 3), meaning they are casual statements (presented without
   evidence) that provoke controversy. How is this use of *incendiary*
   related to its more literal meaning, which is "flammable"?

2. The *Minnesota Daily* says that reparations would give black
   Americans "what amounts to a *bribe*" (para. 3). What does the
   editorial board mean by *bribe* in this case?

3. Wieben argues that "our government has failed time and again to
   give African Americans their constitutional rights" (para. 3).
   What does she mean by *give*? Don't African Americans now have
   (by law) the same constitutional rights as everyone else?

4. "[A]nyone with even a *superficial* understanding of history can
   understand that for former slaves getting the wrong redressed
   during their lifetime was hampered by the still racist attitudes of
   those in all the branches of federal and local government"
   (Khamisi, para. 2). What does it mean to have a *superficial* understanding of something? What would a *superficial* understanding of the history of African Americans involve?

Responding to Words in Context

1. "Unfortunately, laws cannot influence social attitudes, and thus
   slavery is still *close to the surface* of black cultural identity,"
   writes the Minnesota editorial board (para. 1). What do they
   mean by *close to the surface*? How is identity a *surface*?

2. Wieben writes that "*in the real world*, however, problems don't
   go away just because you ignore them" (para. 6). What does
   Wieben mean when she says *in the real world*? What is the opposite of the *real world*?

3. What does Khamisi mean by the word *railroaded* in paragraph 2?

4. "[T]here often exists the need for the *subordination* of some values for fulfillment of justice and benefit of the greater society" (Khamisi, para. 4). What does *subordination* mean in this context?

Discussing Main Point and Meaning

1. Why does Luse think that the students at her school should be especially aware of this debate?

2. "Angered at being forced to pay reparations, the foolish and easily led will be pulled into the inevitable conservative backlash and possibly even white supremacy groups. In the end, reparations will furnish organizations like the Ku Klux Klan with a flood of members and excuses" (*Minnesota Daily,* para. 3). Examine the reasoning in this passage. Is this a logical, ethical, or emotional argument, in your opinion?

3. What is so striking to Wieben about Madeline Albright's comments in paragraph 8 on reparations for Holocaust victims?

4. How do the years of Jim Crow laws (unofficial subjugation of African Americans between the Civil War period and the civil rights movement) factor into Khamisi's argument?

5. Why does Khamisi refer to the history of Native American suffering in her article (para. 4)?

Examining Sentences, Paragraphs, and Organization

1. Summarize Luse's introductory remarks about America as a melting pot. Why does she start her essay with this image?

2. Luse writes, "David Horowitz is not out of order in attempting to bring the issue of reparations into the limelight on our campus" right before she calls Horowitz's statement "incendiary hearsay" (para. 3). What effect does this combination of opinions have on the reader?

3. "Such logic fails to identify the real crux of the problem: the government's continued failure to uphold the rights of African Americans," writes Kristin Wieben in paragraph 2 of her essay. How does this paragraph serve as a major transition in Wieben's argument?

4. Wakefield ends his article with a reference to the Constitution. What is the substance of that reference, and why does Wakefield employ it as his conclusion?

5. "One thing that wounds me daily is that, without living in my skin, others can tell me how I am and am not affected by both current and historical marginalization," writes Khamisi in paragraph 5. How does this sentence stand out from the rest of her essay? How would you rate its effectiveness?

Thinking Critically

1. Today's college students are arguably the adult demographic group most removed from the history of slavery and civil rights. What qualifies these writers to express opinions on the topic of slavery reparations? Do some of these writers seem more informed than others about the historical context of the issue?

2. Wakefield writes, "I don't believe that the slave owner descendants should pay because it is not their personal fault to be born into a family whose wealth was earned by African American slave labor" (para. 4). Do you think Wakefield would have the same view if a person was born into a family whose wealth was earned by drug trafficking or organized crime activities? If one inherits money, does one inherit no responsibility with it?

3. Because slavery was legal until the end of the Civil War, opponents of reparations argue that slave descendants are not entitled to a monetary award for damages because they were not technically treated illegally. But because American society came to its senses and outlawed slavery, others argue that slaveholders can be effectively criminalized in retrospect. Which approach do you find most compelling?

4. Why does Khamisi describe all of the earlier failures to get compensation for slavery in the context of arguing in favor of reparations (para. 3)? Does including these failures weaken her argument?

In-Class Writing Activities

1. Wakefield suggests that a monument would be a "more honorable" response to slavery than "petty cash payoffs" (para. 6). How do you think reparations supporters would respond to this

suggestion? Write a short response to Wakefield as if from a reparations supporter.

2. Each of these articles is written by a college student at a different school, and thus to a slightly different audience in each case. How would you approach an article on this topic to the reading audience at your school? Write an article for your college newspaper stating your position on the issue of slavery reparations. Try to incorporate some references to how race is an issue (or not) on your campus — whether in its admissions policy, in terms of social discrimination, or with regards to the historical awareness of the student body.

3. Respond to the following passage by Wieben: "The government, unlike individuals, is timeless and contains a built-in level of continuity. Individual slave owners may be long dead, but the government that supported and directly profited from slavery is very much alive and well. In other words, governments are immortal, and as such, they are liable for their actions even after the fact" (para. 3). Do you agree that a government is responsible for all of the actions of its precursors? For example, should today's German government still be making amends for the horrors of the Holocaust? Compare the German example to the reparations debate.

Discussing the Unit

Suggested Topic for Discussion

Can we ever quantify exactly what present-day problems are a result of our nation's history of slavery? While it's easy to see that the institution of slavery helped build this nation into the prosperous world power that it is today while simultaneously creating an underclass that is still trying to recover, can we be much more specific than that? Do we need to be, or does the very fact of slavery legitimize some form of reparations?

Preparing for Class Discussion

1. A continuum of opinions is presented in this unit. On one end, David Horowitz is most offended by the idea of reparations for

slavery, perceiving it as a "racist" claim for special "victim" status; on the other end, Randall Robinson argues quite directly that the American government owes a debt to the African American community. But each of the many authors in this unit has an individual opinion that is distinct and different from the rest. For example, Kristin Wieben and Josephine Khamisi are in favor of general reparations to the community in the form of improved education, health care, and housing options. John Conyers and Monique Luse would prioritize debate and discussion on the issue more than outcome. John Wakefield thinks a national monument would help repair race relations, and the *Minnesota Daily* would like the focus redirected to present-day examples of slavery (for example, in Sudan and Mauritania). Shelby Steele is offended by the notion that honor might be traded for dollars. Given the range of positions on this issue, is it reasonable to expect we will ever come to a satisfactory resolution? Do you think the plurality of opinions represents a divided society or a healthy democracy?

2. None of the authors in this unit makes a claim for a specific amount of reparations, none refers to specific corporations that should be held responsible, and none presents any numbers if the burden were put to taxpayers. Would it matter to you if the sums were relatively large or small? Would your opinion be affected if you had some figures that establish who might pay whom and how much? For example, what if every taxpayer (including African Americans) had to contribute $5 to a reparations fund? Would the amount matter at all, or is this an issue of principle exclusively?

3. Why is this such a heated issue given that Rep. John Conyers's bill hasn't even come close to being passed in Congress yet? What motivates so many people to weigh in on this issue?

4. The debate here is both practical and philosophical. On the practical side, some authors debate the feasibility of making any reparations, given all of the logistics involved, while some are focused on the immediate problems in today's African American community. On the philosophical side, some wonder whether reparations can ever be made, given the magnitude of the wrongs of slavery; others argue that society cannot move on socially or culturally until some formal attempts to heal the wounds of slavery are made by the government. Which of these articles would you

say are more practical in nature? Which would you say are more philosophical? Which realm do most of your thoughts fall into?

From Discussion to Writing

1. Is this mainly a problem for the government, the ancestors of slave owners, or corporations that developed out of the profits of slavery? Write an essay that addresses the culpability of each of these groups in the reparations argument. Use the texts for support.

2. The American legal system allows citizens to sue the government, corporations, and individuals for damages related to just about any wrong or mishap imaginable — from manufacturers of faulty automobiles, to fast food chains that serve their coffee too hot, to property owners whose pools are not fenced in to protect children, to a city that doesn't fill its potholes frequently enough. How do the legacies of slavery compare to these examples of injury? Do you think that the larger context of the civil court system makes slavery reparations seem more feasible? Or has so much time passed that most can't see slavery's harm as easily as they can see the tragedy of a preventable car crash or a drowned toddler? Write a brief response to these comparisons. Can you think of any additional examples?

3. After the September 11 attacks in New York and Washington, D.C., the government set up family relief funds for those who lost loved ones in the attacks. By doing this, the government wasn't suggesting that it was directly responsible for the attacks, but it was saying that it felt the responsibility to take care of citizens who had suffered a catastrophic misfortune. Would a similar logic apply in the case of slavery reparations? Can the government offer to be responsible for unfortunate citizens while not being directly responsible or guilty? Write a short essay about the responsibility of government, as you see it, to care for those who have suffered great misfortunes.

4. How much did you know about the history of slavery and civil rights before reading the selections in this unit? Did you know, for instance, that there were black slaveholders, many of whom purchased their own family members to free them from slavery (Chrisman and Allen, para. 4)? Did you know that "some Southern slave owners were compensated [by the government] for their

property losses [slaves] during the Civil War" (Khamisi, para. 3)? How about that it took fifteen years to pass the Martin Luther King Jr. Holiday bill in Congress? Summarize the new things that you learned by reading the selections in this unit and explain whether such things have changed your perspective at all.

Topics for Cross-Cultural Discussion

1. Do you know of any countries that have paid reparations to small or large groups after a period of abuse or loss (for example, after a war, an economic crash, or a long period of subjugation of a group)?

2. How much financial responsibility do governments of other countries take for their individual citizens? How does that sense of responsibility compare to what's experienced in the United States?

3. Can you think of other countries in which there are longstanding racial or ethnic inequalities? Are the inequalities more or less accepted by society, or do they create a constant struggle?

4. What do you think this issue would (or does) look like from the outside the U.S.? Is this one of those "only in America" issues, or are the related problems recognizable to people from other cultures?

The Periodicals:
Information for Subscription

The Advocate: bimonthly. "America's award-winning gay and lesbian newsmagazine." Subscription address: The Advocate, Customer Service, P.O. Box 541, Mount Morris, IL 61054-0541; or call (815) 734-1157; Web site, *The Advocate Online:* advocate.com.

Africana.com: daily. Online "provider of African-American daily news and educational resources and home of Microsoft's Encarta Africana." Web site, *Africana.com:* africana.com.

The Arizona Daily Wildcat: daily weekdays. Student newspaper of the University of Arizona at Tucson. Subscription address: Arizona Daily Wildcat, Attn: Subscriptions, 1230 N. Park, Suite 201, Tucson, AZ 85721; or call (520) 621-3425; Web site, *The Arizona Daily Wildcat Online:* wildcat.arizona.edu.

The Atlantic Monthly: monthly. A magazine of public affairs and the arts, addressing contemporary issues through journalism, commentary, criticism, humor, fiction, and poetry. Subscription address: Atlantic Customer Care, Box 37585, Boone, IA 50037; or call (800) 234-2411; Web site, *The Atlantic Online:* theatlantic.com.

The Badger Herald: daily. The University of Wisconsin's independent student newspaper. Web site, *The Badger Herald Online:* badgerherald.com.

The Barnstable Patriot: weekly. Weekly newspaper covering community news, sports, opinions, events, letters to the editor, and village information for Cape Cod, Massachusetts. Subscription address: 4 Barnstable Road, P.O. Box 1208, Hyannis, MA 02601; or call (508) 771-1427; Web site, *The Barnstable Patriot On the Web:* barnstablepatriot.com.

The Black Scholar: quarterly. "The leading journal of black cultural and political thought in the United States." Subscription address: The Black Scholar, P.O. Box 22869, Oakland, CA 94618; or call (510) 547-6633; Web site, *The Black Scholar:* theblackscholar.org.

The Boston Globe: daily. General newspaper covering local, national, and international, Boston, MA, news; sections include metro/region, business, living arts, sports, and editorial. Subscription address: The Boston Globe, Subscription Department, P.O. Box 2378, Boston, MA 02107; or call (617) 929-2215 or (800) 622-6631; Web site, *The Boston Globe Online:* boston .com/globe.

Brain, Child: quarterly. "A brand-new, quarterly magazine full of essays, features, humor, reviews, fiction, art and cartoons that reflect modern motherhood — the way it really is." Subscription address: Brain, Child, P.O. Box 714, Lexington, VA 24450; or call (888) 30-4MOMS; Web site, brainchildmag.com.

The Brown Daily Herald: daily. Campus newspaper of Brown University. Subscription address: The Brown Daily Herald, P.O. Box 2538, Providence, RI 02906; or call (401) 351-3260; Web site, *Herald Sphere:* browndailyherald.com.

The Cavalier Daily: daily. Student newspaper serving the University of Virginia in Charlottesville, Virginia. Web site, *The Cavalier Daily online:* cavalierdaily.com.

The Chronicle: daily. Independent student daily of Duke University in Durham, North Carolina. Web site, *The Chronicle Online:* chronicle.duke.edu.

The Chronicle of Higher Education: weekly. A weekly news and job-information source for college and university faculty members, administrators, and students. Subscription address: Circulation Department, The Chronicle of Higher Education, 1255 Twenty-Third Street, NW, Washington, DC 20037; or call (800) 728-2803; Web site, chronicle.com.

Columbia Journalism Review: bimonthly. "The *Columbia Journalism Review* is recognized throughout the world as America's premiere media monitor — a watchdog of the press in all its forms, from newspapers and magazines to radio, television, and cable to the wire services and the Web." Subscription address: Columbia Journalism Review, Journalism Building, Columbia University, New York, NY 10027; or call (888) 425-7782; Web site, cjr.org.

The Daily Free Press: daily weekdays. The independent student newspaper at Boston University. Subscription address: The Daily Free Press, 842 Commonwealth Avenue, Boston, MA 02215; or call (617) 232-6841; Web site, *The Daily Free Press Online:* dailyfreepress.com.

The Daily Nebraskan: daily. Student-produced publication of the University of Nebraska at Lincoln. Web site, *The Daily Nebraskan Online Edition:* dailynebraskan.com.

The Daily Utah Chronicle: daily weekdays. Independent student newspaper of the University of Utah at Salt Lake City. Web site, *The Daily Utah Chronicle Online:* utahchronicle.com.

TheDePauw.com. The student newspaper for DePauw University. Web site, *The Depauw.com:* thedepauw.com.

Essence: monthly. "The preeminent magazine for African-American women, this monthly covers lifestyle, culture, media, and more." Subscription address: Essence Magazine Subscription Department, 1500 Broadway, 6th Floor, New York, NY 10036; or call (800) 274-9398; Web site, essence.com.

FSView & Florida Flambeau: biweekly. Twice-weekly student newspaper of Florida State University in Tallahassee. Web site, *FSView & Florida Flambeau:* fsunews.com.

Harper's Magazine: monthly. "*Harper's* explores the issues and ideas in politics, science, and the arts that drive our national conversation." Subscription address: Harper's Magazine, P.O. Box 7511, Red Oak, IA 51591; or call (800) 444-4653; Web site, harpers.org.

The Hoya: biweekly. Georgetown University's newspaper of record since 1920. Subscription information: subscriptions@thehoya.com; or call (202) 687-3947; Web site, *The Hoya Online:* thehoya.com.

Lexington Herald-Leader: daily. Kentucky news, sports, features, and classified advertising. Subscription address: Lexington Herald-Leader, Attn: Mail Subscription Services, 100 Midland Avenue, Lexington, KY 40508; or call (800) 999-8881; Web site, kentucky.com/mld/heraldleader/.

The Louisville Cardinal: The independent student newspaper of the University of Louisville. Web site, *The Louisville Cardinal Online:* louisvillecardinal.com.

The Lumberjack. Student newspaper for Northern Arizona University. Web site, *The Lumberjack Online:* lumberjackonline.com.

The Michigan Daily: daily weekdays. The only general daily newspaper at the University of Michigan in Ann Arbor. Web site, *The Michigan Daily Online:* michigandaily.com.

The Minnesota Daily: daily weekday. "*The Minnesota Daily* is an independent, student-produced newspaper on the Twin Cities campus of the University of Minnesota." Subscription information:

subscriptions@mndaily.com; Web site, *The Minnesota Daily Online:* mndaily.com.

Mother Jones: bimonthly. "An independent nonprofit whose roots lie in a commitment to social justice implemented through first rate investigative reporting." Subscription address: Mother Jones Subscription Department, P.O. Box 469024, Escondido, CA 92046; or call (800) 438-6656; Web site, *MOJO Wire:* motherjones.com.

Mustang Daily: daily weekdays. Newspaper of California Polytechnic State University in San Luis Obispo, CA. Web site, *Mustang Daily Online:* mustangdaily.calpoly.edu.

The Nation: weekly. "A liberal journal of critical opinion, committed to racial justice, anti-imperialism, civil liberties, and social equality," with commentary on politics, culture, books, and the arts. Subscription address: The Nation, P.O. Box 37072, Boone, IA 50037; or call (800) 333-8536; Web site, *The Nation Digital Edition:* thenation.com.

National Review: monthly. Conservative commentary on politics, news, and culture founded by William F. Buckley Jr. Subscription address: National Review, 215 Lexington Avenue, New York, NY 10016; or call (815) 734-1232; Web site, *National Review Online:* nationalreview.com.

Newsweek and *Newsweek International:* weekly. News and commentary on the week's events in national and international affairs. Subscription address: Newsweek Subscriptions, P.O. Box 59967, Boulder, CO 80322; or call (800) 631-1040; Web site, *Newsweek.com:* newsweek.com.

The New York Times: daily. with a large Sunday edition that contains *The New York Times Magazine* and *The New York Times Book Review,* as well as other supplements. Considered the definitive source for current events; daily, national, and international news; and business and arts reporting. Subscription address: The New York Times, 229 West 43rd Street, New York, NY 10036; or call (800) 631-2500; Web site, *The New York Times on the Web:* nytimes.com.

Oregon Daily Emerald: daily weekdays. Newspaper of the University of Oregon in Eugene. Web site, dailyemerald.com.

The Progressive: monthly. "A journal of cultural and political opinions from a left/progressive perspective." Subscription address: The Progressive Subscriptions, 409 E. Main Street, Madison, WI 53703; or call (800) 827-0555; Web site, *The Progressive:* progressive.org.

The Purdue Exponent: daily. "The *Exponent*, an independent college newspaper published by the Purdue Student Publishing Foundation, is Indiana's largest collegiate daily newspaper."

The Record: daily. Local newspaper, including stories and advertising information for Bergen County and Northern New Jersey. Subscription address: The Record, 150 River Street, Hackensack, NJ 07601; or call (888) 473-2673; Web site, *NorthJersey.com*: NorthJersey.com.

Ruminator Review: quarterly. "The independent book magazine published at Macalester College." Subscription address: Ruminator Review, 1648 Grand Avenue, St. Paul, MN 55105; or call (651) 699-2610; Web site, *The Ruminator Review*: ruminator .com/hmr/.

Salon.com: daily. Online Web zine that includes news, politics, technology and business, arts and entertainment, books, sex, life, people, comics, and Salon Audio, a digital audio hub that offers downloadable interviews and commentary from today's most compelling writers and performers. For information, write: Salon.com, 22 4th Street, 16th Floor, San Francisco, CA 94103; or call (415) 645-9200; Web site, *Salon.com*: salon.com.

San Francisco Chronicle: daily. Northern California's largest newspaper. Subscription address: San Francisco Chronicle Subscription Department, 901 Mission Street, San Francisco, CA 94103; or call (800) 281-2476; Web site, *SF Gate: San Francisco Chronicle*: sfgate.com/chronicle/.

The Spectator: weekly. "Seattle University's student newspaper since 1933." Web site, *The Spectator Online*: seattleu.edu/student/spec/.

Teen Newsweek: bimonthly. Provides hard-hitting world and national news, specially tailored for students in grades 6–9. Subscription address: Weekly Reader, 3001 Cindel Drive, Delran, NJ 08075; or call (800) 446-3355; Web site, *Teen Newsweek Online*: weeklyreader.com/teens/newsweek/.

Time: weekly. News and commentary on national and international affairs. Subscription address: Time Magazine, P.O. Box 60001, Tampa, FL 33660; or call (800) 843-8463; Web site, *Time.com*: time.com/time.

The Wall Street Journal: daily. Specializing in business and financial news, latest managerial trends and politics. Subscription address: The Wall Street Journal/Dow Jones, 84 2nd Avenue, Chicopee, MA 01020; or call (800) 975-8609; Web site, *The Wall Street Journal Online*: wsj.com.

Washington Post Magazine: weekly. The Sunday supplement of the *Washington Post.* Subscription address: The Washington Post Circulation Department, 1150 15th Street NW, Washington, DC 20071; or call (800) 477-4679; Web site, *The Washington Post Online:* washingtonpost.com.

Washington Report on Middle East Affairs: monthly. News, reports, opinion, editorials, information, and education on the Middle East and the American policy on the Middle East. Subscription address: American Educational Trust, The Washington Report, P.O. Box 53062, Washington, D.C. 20077; or call (800) 368-5788; Web site, *Washington Report on Middle East Affairs Online:* WRMEA.com.

The Western Herald: daily weekdays. The student newspaper of Western Michigan University. Web site, *The Western Herald Online:* westernherald.com.

The Yale Herald: weekly. "A not-for-profit, non-partisan, incorporated student publication run by Yale College students." Web site, *The Yale Herald:* yaleherald.com.

(Acknowledgments continued from p. iv)

American Civil Liberties Union (advertisement). "It Happens Every Day on America's Highways." Reprinted by permission of the ACLU.

Americans for Medical Progress (advertisement). "Primates in Research: A Record of Medical Progress." Appears by permission of Americans for Medical Progress Educational Foundation.

Anti-Defamation League (advertisement). "Religious freedom is only as strong as the wall separating church and state. . . ." © Anti-Defamation League. All rights reserved. Reprinted by permission.

Arizona Daily Wildcat Editorial Board. "In God We Trust—In Public Schools." *Arizona Daily Wildcat*, University of Arizona, March 6, 2002. Reprinted by permission of the *Arizona Daily Wildcat*.

Charles Atlas® (advertisement). "How Joe's Body Brought Him Fame Instead of Shame ©" 2002, "The Insult That Made a Man out of Mac®" Charles Atlas, Ltd. (www.CharlesAtlas.com).

Steve Baggs (cartoon). "New Organ Cloning Technology." The *Oregon Daily Emerald,* University of Oregon, February 5, 2002. Reprinted by permission of the author.

Jon Barrett. "This is Mark Bingham." *The Advocate*, January 22, 2002. Reprinted by permission of the author and Liberation Publications, Inc.

Dave Barry. "Punch and Judy." *The Washington Post Magazine*, July 9, 2000. Reprinted by permission of Tribune Media Services.

Yvonne Bynoe. "The N-Word: We're Talking Out of Both Sides of Our Mouths." Africana.com, December 14, 2001. © Yvonne Bynoe 2001. Reprinted by permission of the author.

Joan Jacobs Brumberg and Jacquelyn Jackson. "The Burka and the Bikini." *The Boston Globe*, November 23, 2001. © 2001 Joan Jacobs Brumberg and Jacquelyn Jackson. Reprinted by permission of Georges Borchadt, Inc.

Lamar Card (poster). "The Clones." (1973) Reprinted by permission of Lamar Card. The Clone's movie poster is distributed by Phoenix Fidelity, L.A.

Robert Chrisman and Ernest Allen Jr. "Ten Reasons: A Response to David Horowitz." *The Black Scholar*, April 2, 2001. Reprinted by permission of *The Black Scholar*.

Eric Cohen and William Kristol. "No, It's [Cloning is] a Moral Monstrosity." *The Wall Street Journal*, December 5, 2001. Reprinted from *The Wall Street Journal* with permission by the author. © 2001 Dow Jones & Company, Inc. All rights reserved.

Elizabeth Crane. "Do Toy Guns Teach Violence? No." *Brain, Child: the Magazine for Thinking Mothers*, Spring 2001. Reprinted by permission of the author.

Lloyd Dangle (comic strip). "Troubletown: Freeze or I'll Shoot." © 2002 Lloyd Dangle. Reprinted by permission of the author.

Daniel Cucher. "In Mottos I Trust." *Arizona Daily Wildcat*, University of Arizona, March 6, 2002. Reprinted by permission of the author and the *Arizona Daily Wildcat*.

Shane Dale. "What About the Money and the Pledge?" *Arizona Daily Wildcat*, University of Arizona, March 6, 2002. Reprinted by permission of the author and the *Arizona Daily Wildcat*.

Aka Lauenstein Denjongpa. "The Color of Aka." *Ruminator Review*, Fall 2001. Reprinted by permission of the author and the *Ruminator Review*.

Peter Denton. "What Can We Do to Curb Gun Violence?" *The Hoya*, Georgetown University, February 27, 2001. Reprinted by permission of the author and *The Hoya*.

Rachel Drevno. "Pop-Culture Is Destroying True Beauty." *The Spectator*, Seattle University, October 11, 2001. Reprinted by permission of the author and *The Spectator*.

Mariam Durrani. "No on Religion, Yes on Pride." *Arizona Daily Wildcat*, University of Arizona, March 6, 2002. Reprinted by permission of the author and the *Arizona Daily Wildcat*.

Wendy Dutton. "Do Toy Guns Teach Violence? Yes." *Brain, Child: the Magazine for Thinking Mothers*, Spring 2001. Reprinted by permission of the author.

Barbara Ehrenreich. "Libation as Liberation?" *Time*, April 1, 2002. © 2002 TIME, Inc. Reprinted by permission.

James Estrin (photograph). "In the Spirit of the Day." *New York Times*, November 1, 2001. Copyright © 2001. Reprinted by permission of James Estrin/*The New York Times*.

John Hope Franklin. "Horowitz's Hortatory Horror." Letter to the Editor, *The Chronicle*, Duke University, March 29, 2001. Reprinted by permission of the author and *The Chronicle*.

Thomas E. Franklin (photograph). "Three Firefighters Raising the Flag." © 2001 The Record (Bergen County, NJ), Thomas E. Franklin, Staff Photographer / Corbis.

Thomas E. Franklin. "The After-life of a Photo that Touched the Nation." *Columbia Journalism Review*, March/April 2002. © 2002 by the *Columbia Journalism Review*. Reprinted by permission of the *Columbia Journalism Review*.

Ian Frazier. "All-Consuming Patriotism." *Mother Jones*, March-April 2002. Reprinted by permission. © 2002 Foundation for National Progress.

Jason Gillikin. "Inclusive Language: A Problem That Isn't." *The Western Herald*, Western Michigan University, June 14, 2001. Reprinted by permission of the author and *The Western Herald*.

Jane Goodall. "A Question of Ethics." *Newsweek International*, May 7, 2001. © 2001 Newsweek, Inc. All rights reserved. Reprinted by permission.

Michael A. Goldman. "Is Our Fear of Cloning Unnecessary?" *The Wall Street Journal*, December 14, 2001. Reprinted from *The Wall Street Journal* with permission of the author.

Caitlin Hall. "What Do They Mean, 'We'?" *Arizona Daily Wildcat*, University of Arizona, March 6, 2002. Reprinted by permission of the author and the *Arizona Daily Wildcat*.

Elizabeth Hansen. "Defining 'Woman' Without The 'Man.'" *Daily Nebraskan*, University of Nebraska, March 1, 2002. Reprinted by permission of the author and the *Daily Nebraskan*.

David Horowitz (advertisement). "Ten Reasons Why Reparations for Slavery is a Bad Idea — and Racist Too." Reprinted by permission of the author.

Kay Hymowitz. "Thank Barbie for Britney." *National Review Online,* May 3, 2002. Reprinted by permission of United Features Syndicate, Inc.

Randall Kennedy. "Blind Spot." *The Atlantic Monthly*, April 2002. Reprinted by permission of the author.

Josephine Khamisi. "Reparations: Concept and Context." *Louisville Cardinal*, University of Louisville, April 9, 2002. Reprinted by permission of the *Louisville Cardinal*.

Annie Kiefhaber. "Criminal Profiling Not As Simple As Black and White." *The Lumberjack*, Northern Arizona University, January 16, 2002. Reprinted by permission of the author and *The Lumberjack*.

Jana Larsen. "The Draft: Debating War and Gender Equality." *The Mustang Daily*, California Polytechnic State University, October 16, 2001. Reprinted by permission of the author and *The Mustang Daily*.

Dan Levin. "Real Superheroes." *The Daily Free Press*, Boston University, January 15, 2002. Reprinted by permission of the author.

Monique Luse. "Engaging Debate: Real Solutions to Racial Inequality." *The Michigan Daily*, University of Michigan, April 22, 2001. Reprinted by permission of *The Michigan Daily*.

Kristien McDonald. "A SOARing Insult to Science." *The Daily Utah Chronicle*, University of Utah, April 19, 2001. Reprinted by permission of the author.

The *Minnesota Daily* Editorial Board. "A Check Won't Fix the Problem." *The Minnesota Daily*, University of Minnesota, September 5, 2001. Reprinted by permission of *The Minnesota Daily*.

Hadia Mubarak. "Blurring the Lines between Faith and Culture." *The Florida Flambeau*, Florida State University, March 4, 2002. Reprinted by permission of the author and *The FSView & Florida Flambeau*.

National Rifle Association (advertisement). "I'm the NRA." *National Review*, September 25, 2000. Reprinted by permission of the National Rifle Association.

Debbie Nevins. "The Colors of Courage." *Teen Newsweek*, February 4, 2000. Reprinted with permission from the author and Weekly Reader Corporation.

Evelyn Nieves. "Mark Bingham: Gay Hero or Hero Who Was Gay?" *The New York Times*, January 16, 2002. Copyright © 2002. Reprinted by permission of The *New York Times* Agency.

Emily Nussbaum. "The His and Hers Bible." *The New York Times Magazine*, February 10, 2002. Copyright © 2002 Emily Nussbaum. Distributed by The *New York Times* Special Features/Syndication Sales.

Pat Payne. "Factory 'Seconds' Could Save Lives." The *Oregon Daily Emerald*, University of Oregon, February 5, 2002. Reprinted by permission of the author.

Joel Pett (cartoon). "So Why Do They Wear Burkas If They Don't Have To?" *The Lexington Herald-Leader*, December 15, 2001. Joel Pett © Lexington Herald-Leader. Distributed by Universal Press Syndicate. Reprinted with permission. All rights reserved.

Virginia Postrel. "Yes, Don't Impede Medical Progress." *The Wall Street Journal*, December 5, 2001. Reprinted from *The Wall Street Journal*, by permission of the author and *The Wall Street Journal*. © 2001 Dow Jones & Company, Inc. All rights reserved.

Sunita Puri. "'Ethnic Fashion' Obscures Cultural Identity." *The Yale Herald*, Yale University, February 2, 2002. Reprinted by permission of the author.

Jacob Riis (photograph). "Homeless Boys." (titled "Street Arabs in their Sleeping Quarters, circa 1890") and excerpt from text. From Jacob A. Riis, *How the Other Half Lives* (Canada: Dover Publications, 1971) © Museum of the City of New York/Jacob A. Riis Collection (image 121).

Randall Robinson. "America's Debt to Blacks." *The Nation*, March, 13, 2000. Reprinted by permission of *The Nation*.

Richard Rodriguez. "Black and Tan Fantasy." *Salon.com,* May 30, 2001. Reprinted by permission of the Pacific News Service.

Joe Rosenthal (photograph). "Flag Raising at Iwo Jima, February 23, 1945." by Joe Rosenthal appears by permission of AP/Wide World Photos.

Laura Sahramaa. "When Patriotism Runs Amuck." *The Cavalier Daily,* University of Virginia, October 23, 2001. Reprinted by permission of the author and *The Cavalier Daily.*

The *San Francisco Chronicle* Editorial Board. "Allegiance to Absolutism." *San Francisco Chronicle,* June 27, 2002. Reprinted by permission of the *San Francisco Chronicle.*

Student Organization for Animal Rights (SOAR) at the University of Minnesota (advertisement). "Moral Monkeys." Reprinted by permission of the Student Organization for Animal Rights (SOAR), University of Minnesota, Twin Cities.

Brent Staples. "The Meaning of that Star-Spangled Hard Hat." *The New York Times,* November 9, 2001. Copyright © 2001. Reprinted by permission of The *New York Times* Agency.

Shelby Steele. "Reparations Enshrine Victimhood, Dishonoring Our Ancestors." (originally titled "Childish Illusion of Justice: Reparations Enshrine Victimhood, Dishonoring Our Ancestors.") *Newsweek,* August 27, 2001. Reprinted by permission of *Newsweek.*

Supporting Our Sons (advertisement). "Are Boys in Trouble?" and "Are Boys in Crisis?" *Brain, Child: the Magazine for Thinking Mothers,* Summer 2001. Reprinted courtesy of Supporting Our Sons (www.supportingoursons.org).

Steve Tefft. "A Monument to Multicultural Mush." *The Barnstable Patriot Newspaper,* January 25, 2002. Reprinted by permission of *The Barnstable Patriot Newspaper.*

Nicholas Thompson. "Hero Inflation." *The Boston Globe,* January 13, 2002. Copyright 2002 by Globe Newspaper Co. (MA). Reproduced with permission of Globe Newspaper Co. (MA) via Copyright Clearance Center.

Russell Thornton. "What the Census Doesn't Count." *The New York Times,* March 23, 2001. Copyright © 2001. Reprinted by permission of The *New York Times* Agency.

Eisa Nefertari Ulen. "Muslims in the Mosaic." *Essence,* January 2000. © 2000, Eisa Nefertari Ulen. Reprinted by permission of the author.

U.S. English (advertisement). "I Pledge Allegiance . . ." *National Review,* September 25, 2000. Reprinted by permission of the U.S. English Foundation, Inc.

John Wakefield. "Who Should Pay and Who Should Be Paid?" *Purdue Exponent,* September 6, 2001. Reprinted by permission of the author and the *Purdue Exponent.*

Scott Weaver. "The Power of Profanity." *The DePauw,* DePauw University, March 7, 2001. Reprinted by permission of the author and *The DePauw.*

John V. Whitbeck. "'Terrorism': The Word Itself is Dangerous." *Washington Report on Middle East Affairs,* March 2002. Reprinted by permission of the *Washington Report on Middle East Affairs.*

Kristin Wieben. "The U.S. Government Should Compensate for Atrocities of Slavery." *The Badger Herald,* University of Wisconsin at Madison, December 12, 2001. Reprinted by permission of the author and *The Badger Herald.*

Index of Authors and Titles

bedfordstmartins.com

Online Research and Reference Aids for Students

The English Research Room

bedfordstmartins.com/english_research

Mike Palmquist, *Colorado State University*
A good starting place for all researchers, this site offers advice on how to search and evaluate online sources. Interactive tutorials take you step-by-step through searches of databases, online catalogs, and the Web.

Research and Documentation Online

bedfordstmartins.com/resdoc

Diana Hacker, *Prince George's Community College*
This online version of Hacker's popular booklet provides clear guidelines on how to integrate outside material into a paper, how to cite sources correctly, and what the final format should be in MLA, APA, *Chicago,* or CBE style.

Exercise Central

bedfordstmartins.com/exercisecentral

The largest collection available online, Exercise Central includes diagnostic tests, tutorials, and thousands of editing exercises that help you improve your grammar and usage skills.

After September 11th: An Online Reader for Writers

bedfordstmartins.com/september11

Eric Crump, *Interversity.com*
This free online reader by Eric Crump, a nationally recognized online teacher and scholar, offers instructors and students up-to-date links to some of the best-written and most diverse articles, commentary, and news stories about the events and consequences of September 11, 2001.